TED BUNDY:
THE KILLER
NEXT DOOR

FOREWORD

Little should be said to preface an account of real events. Facts have their own weight, measured by the reader alone.

But the sources of those facts, too, have a place in a reader's understanding and interpretation. As much as possible in the text, we have attempted to make plain the ground of our information.

Police reports and files constitute a major resource for the story you are about to read. No matter how conscionable, the police are out to clear the cases on their books. The strength and significance of their findings must finally be tested in court. Personal letters and documents comprise a second major source of information. Again, the reader must judge context and intent. Finally, there were the hundreds of hours of personal interviews and contacts; here the limitations were those that any journalist must face.

In criminal cases of this magnitude, numerous innocent and unsuspecting individuals are drawn into the spotlight. The pain and discomfort they endure are considerable. We have supplied fictitious names and identifying details, in several selected instances, to minimize that circumstance.

But this is a true story. In the overwhelming majority of instances, the names, places, dates, and events are exactly as they occurred through the long years of suffering and suspense.

A book such as this is not written without incurring innumerable debts of gratitude—for time, patience, understanding, and much more. First, for those who found the strength to retell their painful stories, we offer a special thanks.

Only a few who helped can be mentioned by name. David Brewster and Paul Swenson provided the inspiration and support for the initial project. Oscar Lubow and Douglass Raff steered it along the way. Judy Rudow helped with the manuscript. Jane McGeehan and Katharine Weber provided criticism when needed, prodding when necessary, and unfailing support. And Chuck Dumas made a home for us when we needed it most.

S.W.
D.M.

Part I

DREAMS

1

Lynda glanced at the clock and let out her breath in a slow, even sigh. It was nearly 2:30, most of the session gone, and she and Darryl hadn't accomplished a thing. She squatted, one more time, in front of the desk.

"OK, Darryl, you ready? Here we go. Which one is like the big one over here?" Their fingers ran along a row of circles, triangles, and ovals in his workbook. He strained, stopped at one, went on. "Be sure," she said.

"This one," he announced at last, stubbing at a circle with an index finger just wet from his mouth. He looked up for approval.

"It's the next one," Lynda said a little unhappily, "but that's all right. We can try another."

Darryl got the next two right, matching rectangle to rectangle and star to star. They giggled, pleased with themselves and each other, and Lynda told him she couldn't wait to come back next week and see how much *more* progress he'd made. Nothing worked, she knew, like a little positive reinforcement.

Outside, pulling on her red backpack and dialing the numbers of her bicycle lock, Lynda wasn't quite so sunny toward herself. She'd done a few things passably, but she'd let the boy's attention wander, allowed his mood to control the hour. And she hadn't done a thing about his behavior—his squirming and his hands in his mouth. There was more to teaching than she ever imagined, more than her education and psychology classes at the university could ever prepare her for. And yet, even in her few hours of tutoring, she could feel what teachers of young children always feel: that precious weight of a life and mind in the making. Lynda Healy pedaled away from the school.

In Seattle, where the rains fall from October through May, January is a month to be endured, not enjoyed. The holidays are past, and little lies ahead but the soggy, predictable passage of the weeks toward spring, which somehow seems farther off each day. Overhead, unbroken ranks of

3

gray march in, masses of clouds that have gathered moisture from the Pacific Ocean, washed the western slopes of the Olympic Mountains, then restored themselves over Puget Sound. These are full, heavy, weary skies, and in the winter, when the rain is blown in slanting sheets, even the sturdy green face of the evergreen forests turns flat and recedes like a shadow. January is a month for waiting, for turning inward, for lighting up a bare wall at night with slides of a summer hiking trip to the Necklace Valley, where glacial lakes are strung like polished jewels and the sky is a flawless cap of blue.

But winter has its merciful moments too. Occasionally, in the late afternoon, the sky will lighten up along the horizon, backing the spiky skyline of the Olympic Mountains with a thin, gold light. It might last an hour, or only minutes; seen from a hill or a high window, it is an unexpected gift.

Lynda Healy turned a corner near the University of Washington and stopped, bracing her foot on the curb. Cars swerved around her, but she looked over them, looked over the houses and the humming freeway to a strip of sky in the distance with its startling, ragged edge of snowy mountains. She'd seen it ten thousand times before; she'd been out there, camping and exploring the Olympics since she was a child. But when the drab city sky opened up this way it was like a message to her, a promise of something new and mysterious and unknowable.

Lynda plopped back on the seat and hurried down the hill. It was her week in the kitchen, and she'd forgotten about the shopping until now. Noodles, an onion, hamburger—she made her way through the aisles at Safeway, picking what she needed for Company Casserole, a standby recipe she'd borrowed from her mother. Her parents were coming for dinner the next night—Friday—but she'd return and shop more thoughtfully for them. And then there was the party she and her roommates were throwing Saturday night. That would require some planning too. The checker helped Lynda wedge her purchases into her pack. She'd gotten through the line just in time. Students, woozy from an afternoon of reading and suddenly hungry at five, were streaming through the automatic doors. Lynda slipped into the traffic on Northeast 50th, then turned onto 12th and headed for home.

The house, five blocks north, was like hundreds of others in Seattle's University District, like thousands near college campuses across the country. Large, drafty, peeling paint,

4

and obstinate in its pipes, it had long since given over its proud single-family solidity for a more energetic second life. With two bedrooms made habitable in the basement, it was perfectly suited for five college women who had entered adulthood with a pact of mutual independence. Meals were eaten together, each member of the household taking a turn by weeks in the kitchen, and there was a common living room and bath. At night, everyone made for separate bedrooms—two upstairs, one on the main floor, Lynda and Elise in the basement.

Lynda had spent her first years at the University of Washington contentedly in the dorms. Since her freshman year at high school in nearby suburban Newport Hills, she had anticipated college life across Lake Washington at the big university. She imagined the bright and noisy halls of the dorms, waves of students across the lawns, music theory and voice classes. Hers was a clear, tremulous, uncommonly high soprano voice. She was unsure if she could—or if she wanted to—sing professionally, but in her way she was quietly proud of her talent. She was a ham, she'd happily admit to her friends. As a four-year-old ballet student in Portland, Oregon, she'd been a willing performer for any group. Years later, at a coffeehouse, she sang unrehearsed with a group of friends.

By the fall of 1972, however, the beginning of her junior year, she had ruled out a singing career. She enjoyed participating in the student choral group but still had trouble reading music and knew it wasn't for her. Instead, she was majoring in psychology, reinforcing the theoretical work with classes in early childhood education. Clearly her mission was to teach. And by the middle of that year, when she and her roommate Carolyn from Arizona had become close friends, Lynda Healy decided it was time for another change: a move off campus. Early that summer, in the university housing office, Lynda met a nursing student who told her there were two rooms available in a house on 12th Northeast. Bubbling with the news, she called Carolyn in Flagstaff and asked what she thought. The rent was good, the rooms were fine, the roommates seemed nice. They agreed to go ahead.

Carolyn stayed in Arizona until the fall, so Lynda, with a little time to spare, agreed to take the basement room, which needed some work. When her friend arrived, Lynda was paint-spattered and beaming. The room, cavelike before, was a glowing orange-gold, handsomely set off by a curving silver

5

section of furnace pipe in the ceiling. There was a desk and a bed, and stacks of wooden crates served as bookshelves. A curtain was still to be hung in place of a door. Lynda had a new haircut, too, a shoulder-length style that nicely framed her face. She and Carolyn hugged each other and pulled back, smiling. It was going to be a good year.

By January 1974 the house routine was well established. On Thursday the 31st, Lynda let herself in at the side door, parked her bike on the landing, and began unloading the groceries from her pack in the kitchen. The place was sparsely furnished and equipped, but at least it was clean and orderly—certainly more so than any male communal house they knew. Lynda's Company Casserole was on the table in just over an hour.

After dinner the women scattered—to the library, to a friend's house—and it wasn't until sometime after ten that Lynda came upstairs to say good night to Carolyn. They spoke briefly of their families (each was the oldest of three children), then turned to the party on Saturday. Lynda's ex-boyfriend was coming from Olympia, possibly with a date.

"You feel all right about that?" Carolyn asked.

"That's really over. It's fine," Lynda said. "I'm fine."

"Lord, I wish I didn't have to get up in the morning." Carolyn slapped a book shut and rolled over on the bed.

"Tell me about it."

(Both women had early morning jobs. Carolyn worked a shift at the hospital; Lynda broadcast a ski report for a local radio station.)

"G'night, Carolyn."

January's long haul was at an end.

" 'Night."

A half hour later Elise came in, went to the kitchen, then peeked into Carolyn's room. They were chatting, gossiping a little about their roommates upstairs, when suddenly Elise thought she saw something through the window at the side of the house. "A shadow," she said, her voice tightening; "it moved."

Carolyn followed Elise to the window without a word. Elise was easily the most security-conscious member of the house (conscious to the point of paranoia, the others sometimes thought), and it was best to play along with her. They peered out at a tree branch bobbing gently in the wind.

"All right, all right," Elise smiled. "So I'm seeing things. I'll see you tomorrow." With the two schooners of beer she'd

6

just drunk to celebrate her 21st birthday, Elise was sure to sleep soundly. She decided not to disturb Lynda on the way to her room.

Friday, February 1, was no different from any weekday morning in the house. Yanking on their jeans, combing out their hair, swinging open the refrigerator door for a glass of juice, the women were off to their various jobs or classes. Shortly after seven, however, one roommate who had a later class staggered out to answer the phone. It was Lynda's boss, wondering why his reliable employee hadn't showed up to read her ski report on the air. Checking downstairs, the roommate found Lynda gone, the bed made, and—oddly— the alarm buzzing away on the wooden crate nightstand. Sorry, she told Lynda's boss, no sign of her. She hung up and dressed for class.

That afternoon around three, when the women began drifting back to the house, Lynda still hadn't made an appearance. Carolyn sat slumped in a faded armchair, listening to her roommates' speculation. Maybe she'd gone to the gym. Or to Olympia to visit what's-his-name. Elise reported on the "shadow" she'd seen outside the window the night before. Saying nothing, Carolyn got up and pulled the phone around the corner. She'd make a few calls before jumping to a conclusion, but somehow, with Lynda's parents due for dinner in a few hours and Lynda unaccounted for all day, she knew that something was wrong. Just as Carolyn guessed, none of her friends, not even the ex-boyfriend, had seen her. Her next call was to Lynda's mother, and then to the police.

Missing-person reports, especially around a university campus, are almost as common as jaywalking. The police have learned to be businesslike and patient; such "cases" have a way of solving themselves when the missing woman shows up on the arm of a new boyfriend several days later. But everyone—Carolyn, her roommates, Lynda's parents who had driven across the bridge from Newport Hills—everyone knew Lynda Healy hadn't wandered off on her own. They were worried now—the sun had set—and they wanted a response.

A patrol car was dispatched at last, and two officers clomped up the wooden steps to record the minimal data. Lynda Ann Healy, white female, 21 years, five feet seven, 115 pounds, brown hair parted in the middle, blue eyes, pierced ears. They went downstairs, pulled back the curtain Lynda used as a door, noted nothing suspicious, and left. It wasn't until two hours later that an excited call from one roommate's mother (a friend of the police chief) brought a homicide detective to the scene. He moved quickly, as if he knew what he'd find. Carolyn was behind him, her breath short and shallow.

The detective tugged at the bedspread and peeled back the top sheet. And then they saw blood. It stained the pillowcase and a place on the sheets. Without a word he turned and opened the closet door. There, neatly hung on a peg, was Lynda's nightgown, with more blood smeared on the back of the neck. "Step back from the door," he said. "Don't touch a thing."

The next hours, Carolyn later recalled, were like a dream: slow-moving, repetitive, eerily deliberate. A careful search of the room, the yard, the slanting alley that ran behind the house turned up nothing. Steadying themselves, Carolyn and Lynda's mother inventoried the closet to see what was missing: a pair of jeans, a blue-trimmed white smock, waffle stomper boots, a belt, several turquoise rings, and Lynda's red backpack. The details were coolly sinister. Someone, it seemed, had made his way in, beaten Lynda Healy in her bed, then dressed her, carefully making the bed before he left, and carried her off without a trace. But the Seattle police department detective was not committed to this story. Upstairs in the living room he asked if Lynda ever had nosebleeds, if she ever went for late night walks. If, if . . . He closed his notebook and left.

Back in his cubicle, filling out a report, the detective recalled another University District incident less than a month old. Asleep around midnight in her basement apartment on 8th Northeast, 16 blocks from Lynda Healy's house, a young woman was beaten unconscious, apparently left for dead. The injuries were to the head, and a probe, or speculum, had been shoved in her vagina. She was recovering, miraculously, but she had no recall of the attack. There was no commanding reason to connect the two basement apartment assaults (Healy's, of course, was only a supposed assault), but speculation was about all anyone had.

Within a few days police had exhausted the neighborhood in hopes of a possible eyewitness, checked out the old boyfriend in Olympia, even paid a call on Lynda's new tennis partner, a regular at a neighborhood occult bookstore. There was nothing, absolutely nothing extraordinary about Lynda Healy's life or activities. If police wanted to fish for suspects, they might as well have started on the University of

8

Washington campus, a sea of 37,000, most of whom, with their backpacks and down jackets and busy ambitions, were as unlikely to be involved in crime as Lynda Healy was. The investigation was stalled before it got started.

Frightened and frustrated, Lynda Healy's roommates and friends initiated a search of their own that weekend. They fanned out through the neighborhood, then banded together for a walk through Ravenna Park, a steep, wooded ravine that twisted through the city nearby. At first they called Lynda's name, but slowly, one by one, they began looking timidly under bushes and nudging at piles of leaves. At night the four women left in the house pulled their sleeping bags together in the living room, their boyfriends taking turns keeping watch. That lasted a week before they abandoned the house.

The cryptic stories in the papers turned women in the University District wary and uneasy: more doors were locked; strangers got a second look. The Healys in Newport Hills and Lynda's roommates and friends faced a different, more agonizing uncertainty. It would be 13 months before they would know, finally, what had happened to Lynda.

But as February warmed into March, no one could have guessed that Lynda Ann Healy's disappearance on a blowy January night was only the beginning. The Northwest, emerging again from its winter rains, taking on the pale, transparent green of spring, was at the edge of a nightmare. The waking would take years, more improbable and terrible than the dream when it finally came.

In March, before the rains were done, the scene shifted to Olympia, 60 miles away.

2

Ever since high school, Donna Gail Manson had thought of herself as an unfettered spirit. Her poems and prose from an Auburn High creative writing class are filled with a boundless beneficence. "I'm just inside the door of that other world you can't explain later," she wrote, bent over a notebook in her room late one night. "You find so many treasures

9

inside this young world." Her grades in the class were low: Donna wrote only when the moment moved her. After graduation she took off for Europe with her boyfriend.

When she returned and enrolled at Green River Community College in the fall of 1973, she began taking photographs, lushly sentimental studies of sunsets and farm animals and tree boughs. Her taste in music was changing; she'd developed an interest in weaving; she attended an Indian rights demonstration in Tacoma. After a quarter at the community college, Donna decided that Evergreen State College in Olympia, with its greater freedom and innovation, was for her. She enrolled in January, and by March 1974 she had narrowed the field to alchemy as a topic for her special project.

On March 12 Donna set out a fresh pineapple she'd just bought, put a pot of soup on the stove, and began dressing for a jazz concert. She changed several times (her roommates assumed she was planning to meet someone) and took some pains with her long brown hair. She left the dorm wearing green slacks, a red-, orange-, and green-striped top, and a fuzzy maxicoat. On her wrist she wore a Bulova watch; on one finger, an oval-shaped agate ring.

Trees rise on the Evergreen campus like pillars in a cathedral. Donna set off between the rows of trees for the concert, 300 yards away. Footlights lit her way along the winding path. It was seven o'clock, and a heavy mist hung in the air. The concert started—and ended—without her. Donna Manson had disappeared.

Her friends in the dorm shared Donna's attitude and independent ways. Thinking she'd gone on a trip, respecting her rights, they didn't report her missing to campus security for five days. And it wasn't until Monday, March 18—six days after her disappearance—that a pair of Thurston County policemen appeared at the Manson home to inform Donna's parents that she was gone. If there had been a trail, it was probably cold by now.

Or damp. It had rained hard that week, and bloodhounds, trained to Donna's scent by a piece of her clothing, took detectives as far as a parking lot, where they stopped and snuffled and crossed each other's paths. There wasn't so much as a hint of a physical clue, and no indication of violence. Could Donna Manson be a runaway?

It was true, her mother told detectives, that Donna was

10

depressed by the rain and was anxious for a change. Then Marie Manson thought of the letter she had recently received from her daughter. "Anyway, I don't like to hang around here any more than I have to," Donna had written in her plain, looping script. "My roommate and her boyfriend are always bickering with each other. It drives me nuts." But no, she concluded, Donna never would have left her flute, her camera, her backpack and cosmetics behind. Besides, she was looking forward to spring vacation, a chance to visit the ocean (her mother had promised the trip in spite of the recent gasoline crunch), and an opportunity to shop for the yarn she wanted for a new project.

It was a virtually impossible chore for the police. Donna Manson, pretty, free-spirited, a now-and-then hitchhiker, probably had hundreds of acquaintances, and if any of them knew anything about her whereabouts, they weren't volunteering the information. There was little the detectives could do but file their missing-person reports and occasionally inform the Mansons of no progress. (A typical lead was a woman seen crying on the streets of Centralia; someone thought it might be Donna.) The Mansons could only wait, sending posters around the state, reading letters of sympathy (including one from Senator Henry Jackson), politely declining the services of a psychic. The wait lengthened.

"After two weeks I knew," Marie Manson later recalled. "Donna wasn't coming back." The mother was slowly flipping through her daughter's photo album, smoothing the plastic on each page. "You know, a mother and a daughter, there are all those agonizing conversations. We didn't see eye to eye, and I guess sometimes only showed the outer surface to each other." Marie looked up, a bright puzzle of pain and wonder in her eyes. "It may sound funny," she said, "but in a way I know what she meant now. I know Donna better than ever."

The Cascade Mountains form the dramatic, snow-topped wall between the two Washingtons: the rainy, temperate, populous cities of Seattle and Olympia and Tacoma to the west and the broad, bare desert to the east. Just off the eastern slopes of the mountains lies Ellensburg, an unremarkable college town that turns heartbreakingly beautiful in the spring. During the winter a dry, bright snow blows across the hills for miles. Then, as the sun comes closer, the earth

11

seems to unfold. Color, a brief, spectacular flare, lights up the wildflower-covered hills. Warm air, finely scented, rises. Time slows; evenings are longer than nights.

It had all inspired Central Washington State freshman Susan Rancourt. A cheerleader and homecoming queen in high school, the middle child in a large family, cheerful and conventional, she wanted to stretch herself now, to move off at a new pace. She'd started jogging with the campus police in the morning and working in an old folks' home in the afternoon. She'd thought of becoming a dorm counselor, and she'd made some new friends.

At eight o'clock on the evening of April 17, 1974, Susan dropped off a load of clothes at a dorm laundromat and hurried to an introductory meeting for would-be counselors. At five minutes of nine she left to meet a friend at Barto Hall for a German-language film. The film started; her clothes grew cold in the machine. Susan Rancourt was gone.

When her parents arrived from Anchorage, Alaska, her mother went straight to Susan's medicine cabinet to check for dental floss. If it was there, she knew, Susan hadn't run away. "She was such a creature of habit," her mother explained, "and so aware of her body. She always flossed after every meal, and she wouldn't go anywhere overnight without it." The dental floss, cap open from the last use, was right where Susan had left it.

The testimony to Susan's character struck a familiar chord: she was happy, a hard worker, troubled by nothing more than the choice between two boyfriends. Susan's family nickname, her parents added, was "Miss Prudence Pureheart." It was all the more frustrating for the Rancourts, then, when Susan was listed as a runaway for 48 *hours*. Regulations, her father was told. But Dale Rancourt *knew* his daughter hadn't walked off. He placed an ad about Susan in the Ellensburg paper, wondering to himself how hard the campus, city, and county police were willing to look for Susan.

The trouble was, once again, no one had an idea where to begin. The campus, the low, rolling hills, the dirt roads running out from town were all searched. April ended without a single live lead. The Rancourts went home to Alaska, pinning their fading hopes on a national letter-writing campaign. For months the posters went out in a steady stream. Susan Elaine Rancourt, blonde, blue-eyed, age 18, was last seen on the Ellensburg campus in a yellow coat and short-sleeved sweater, gray corduroys, and brown hush puppies. The national television networks delicately refused the family's request to have Susan's picture flashed on the air. With the number of missing women, you understand . . .

Back in Ellensburg, police routinely checked and cleared the dozens of "suspicious" people reported by students and others around the town. Two reports they *didn't* hear would later have a nagging, suggestive ring. On Sunday, April 14, a man with his arm in a sling and his finger in a metal brace dropped some books in front of the library. It was 10:00 p.m., a woman was passing by, and he asked her to help. Instead of the library, he led her to his car parked near a railroad trestle 300 yards off. He had hurt himself skiing at Crystal Mountain, he told her. They passed out from under the last streetlight. Three days later, same time, same place, it started again. This time a man with a sling dropped packages wrapped in butcher paper and tied with string. Another woman went to help, and again they started for the car. It was Wednesday night, April 17—an hour after Susan Rancourt was last seen.

The two stories differ from there. One woman figured the man about six feet tall; the other had him four or five inches shorter. One remembers a bright yellow Volkswagen with high-backed black seats; the other couldn't say. And one woman recalls an odd detail that made her uneasy: the front seat on the passenger's side was missing. She had quickly put down the books and walked off.

Neither woman reported her experience to the police for three months. "I don't know," said one, "it just didn't seem important."

Across the mountains in Seattle, detectives studied accounts of the Rancourt case with a professional calm and reserve. It was hasty and irresponsible to assume that Healy, Manson, and Rancourt were linked. Theorizing and panicky speculation could be left to the press. The newspapers were already noting the similarities of the vanished women in their stories: three college women who wore their long hair parted in the middle. (In fact, there were marked differences in appearance: Lynda Healy was five feet seven, Donna Manson just five feet tall.)

Besides, Seattle police had enough to worry about without fabricating a mass murder story. There were other cases, tough, exasperating ones. Like Heidi Peterson, the pixie-

13

faced four-year-old who had disappeared from Seattle's Capitol Hill neighborhood on a February afternoon. One minute playing in front of her house with her three-year-old brother, and the next vanished. "Heidi go," her brother told his parents. That had been two months ago.

Somehow 1974 had come up a bad year. In Seattle, in the Northwest, the crime rate was low; violent, motiveless crime was a real rarity. There were missing persons, of course, and some of the cases remained unsolved. (The investigation into Nancy Mae Winslow's 1970 disappearance from the college town of Bellingham, for one, was still an "active case.") And occasionally a missing person turned up dead. But this seemed different: four apparent abductions (including Heidi) paced with a steady, eerie tempo—one a month since the beginning of the year. Like the foul revelations of Nixon's unraveling presidency back in Washington, D.C., some awful expectation had caught hold in the Northwest. Everyone— even a professional skeptic like Phil Killien—felt it.

Killien is a senior deputy prosecutor for King County, a large, diverse swatch of the state that runs from the shores of Puget Sound up into the Cascade Mountains and includes the expanding suburbs of Seattle to the north and south. Seattle itself is the heart, and Killien's office in the County Courthouse offers a slender view of the downtown business district. On a cool spring afternoon he turned from the window and offered a visitor a seat: a television reporter who'd covered his cases for several years, managing, with a kind of diligent friendliness, to gain a share of his confidence. It was no small accomplishment. Killien could be moody, diffident, even explosive, and with reporters he was known to be courteous, civil—and unenlightening. The woman flopped down in a chair, dropping a stack of papers on the bare desk top. There was more in the morning edition about Susan Rancourt.

"Any wild ideas, Phil?" They smiled. Killien's prosecutorial style was anything but wild; he assembled his cases thoughtfully and logically, avoiding risky leaps that might not hold up in court. "Come on, let yourself go."

"I don't envy them," Killien said. "There's nothing to go on." With two of the disappearances taking place in other counties and the Seattle Police Department handling Lynda Healy, Killien was just a spectator, an interested spectator.

"Could Clausan—" the woman began.

"Maybe. Sure, maybe." It was a name they had mentioned many times, a prime suspect in the murder of a teen-age girl in north Seattle several years back. The case had not been prosecuted, but they both believed Kenneth Clausan was capable of homicide, repeated homicide.

The conversation turned to other things, mutual friends, a new restaurant in town. "Let me know when you crack the case," the woman said on her way out.

"It's not mine to crack," he answered. But for a moment after she left Phil Killien stared at the blunt end of a pencil in front of him. He had a feeling, nameless and unsubstantiated, that that was not to be his final word on the missing women of 1974.

Spring came to the western side of the Cascades, and with it, Nixon's incredible offer to the public of edited transcripts of his conversations in the oval office. Then the president arrived in person, climbing onto a platform in Spokane to officially open Expo '74 on May 5. Richard Nixon smiled and waved, but the cracks were widening: at one point in his speech he called Washington Governor Dan Evans "Governor Evidence."

The Northwest's own horror story resumed the next day, this time in the Oregon college town of Corvallis, 235 miles south of Seattle. The distance seemed not to matter: this was the same story all over again. Her name was Roberta Kathleen Parks, a freshman education major at Oregon State University, and she left her dorm room for a late night walk to the student union for an ice-cream sundae. She was alone, a lovely woman with fine, close features, walking head down and wearing navy blue cords, a light sweater top, platform sandals, and a cream-colored jacket. Once again no one saw a thing, there was no sign or sound of a struggle, and Kathy Parks was gone.

Investigators learned that Parks had been depressed on the night of May 6. She missed her boyfriend, who was in Louisiana, and she felt guilty about arguing with her sick father. But again the cosmetics, the personal items, everything that a runaway takes were left behind. She did have her purse, however, and $15. Certainly not enough to finance running away.

If police had named a thousand spots for the next abduction, the Flame Tavern in Burien wouldn't have been among them. Located in a featureless unincorporated south Seattle suburb near the airport, the Flame is well known for its local color: a fight is not uncommon; shootings and knifings are not unheard of. Hardly a re-creation of the mood and atmosphere of a college campus; rather, the sort of place where an unattached woman from one of the apartment complexes nearby might expect to meet someone who would entertain her through breakfast the next morning at least. Nearby roommates don't give it much thought when a bed at home stays empty a few nights. Brenda Ball's didn't.

Wearing blue jeans, a turtleneck with long sleeves, an overblouse jacket, and brown wedge-heel shoes, Brenda left the Flame at closing time, 2:00 a.m., on Saturday, June 1. Witnesses later said she was with a man. And that's all they said. The slim, bright-eyed woman in her early twenties with a dark cascade of hair might have drawn some attention if she'd left alone; no one batted an eye at her escort.

Despite Brenda Ball's superficial similarity to the other women, King County police investigating her disappearance assumed her case was not connected to the others. They couldn't be sure, of course, and again there were no strong clues, but the circumstances and location looked markedly different. By now, they had almost gotten used to the idea of people falling off the map.

Phil Killien read the papers with special interest that first week of June. The Brenda Ball case was the first in the King County jurisdiction, and like the detectives conducting the investigation, he had no business building bridges between it and any other case. But he couldn't help what he was feeling.

For students in June, time yawns just before the last final exam. Between the year's droning repetition of classes and homework and the first, free days of summer lies one long night, lit everywhere by the glare of desk lamps. Guilt, torpor, a sickening hollow in the stomach follow each other in turn. The weather is perfume. It is impossible to sit still.

On the night of June 11, 1974, Georgann Hawkins and two friends walked from their University of Washington sorority house, Kappa Alpha Theta, to a party a block and a half away in a University District house. There was beer and music; it was enough to put off the irritation of a Spanish exam the next day until almost midnight. But Georgann, responsible in a sort of junior miss way—a 3.6 student in

16

high school and now at the university, a Daffodil Princess in hometown Tacoma one year, a sorority girl—felt the tug of obligation. She and her friend Jennifer went home to study.

The two women ambled along, listening half to each other, half to the gentle, blurred sound of rock music coming from a dozen windows. It had been hot ever since early morning geography class. Now, after dark, it was pleasing to button the cuffs of a long-sleeved blouse at the wrist and trade shorts for light bell-bottoms. Georgann planned to roll up her sleeves and train the gooseneck lamp on her text when she got back to her room.

At the corner of 17th and 47th, Jennifer said good night, and Georgann climbed the stairs of the Beta Theta Phi fraternity. Her boyfriend Marvin had his books spread out across the bed. They talked a moment, kissed absently. She had to get back, she said. The stairs let her out in the alley behind the fraternity house. Duane, a fraternity brother of Marvin and a classmate of Georgann, leaned out an upstairs window and asked if she was ready for the test. She smiled, ready to linger again in the early summer air. A Spanish exam, really, it seemed such a tiny hurdle . . . "Adiós," she called up to Duane at last, and started down the alley for the back door of her sorority house.

Georgann Hawkins's eyesight was bad. She was just getting used to new contact lenses, so she kept to the middle of the alley where the light was good. She almost knew the look of this alley by heart: the wall of lighted windows to her left, the empty kitchens, a basketball net hanging limp from an orange rim. Two men drinking beer in a parked truck watched her go by. Any of a hundred students, glancing up from a book or a page of coffee-stained notes, might have seen her from a window. But once she was 40 feet from her door (Duane watched her down the alley that far), Georgann Hawkins was never seen again.

For the women streaming out of the University District as their exams ended that week, it had been a trying year. From Lynda Healy in January to Georgann Hawkins in June, the disappearances had swept through the Northwest in an ominously looped pattern: the alley behind fraternity row was 12 blocks from Lynda Healy's basement room. Stacking boxes and suitcases on a porch nearby, one woman, like thousands who wore their long hair parted in the middle, told a friend, "All the escort services, the business of staying

17

with friends, it doesn't seem to matter. Jesus, it could be *any*-
one. I just want the hell out of here. I don't know if I'm coming back."

Police may have wished they could look the other way
too. Exasperated, humiliated, they were feeling heat from
above. Seattle Mayor Wes Uhlman had told his police chief
he wanted action. The word was coming down in other jurisdictions as well. But even as they went about their work,
Seattle detectives began to feel a clammy, unmistakable air of
mistrust. A rumor leaked out that S.P.D. had "misplaced"
the bloodstained sheets from Lynda Healy's bed. What, the
implication seemed to be, would they foul up this time?
Nerves rasped. Wheeling on a questioner, one weary officer
snapped, "Whoever it was who took Hawkins didn't exactly
shout 'Banzai!' and run down the street."

Gamely, police did what they could with reports from
students of strange characters they'd seen in the neighborhood; but by now, they realized, women were seeing shadows in every corner and hearing things under the bed. What
could they tell a young woman, for example, who thought
her boyfriend was acting "odd"? Their spirits did pick up
when a pile of women's underwear was found not far from
the spot where Georgann Hawkins had last been seen,
but her roommate told them none of it looked familiar.
Square one again.

Slowly, since January, these abductions had grown braver
and riskier. First a woman vanished at night from a basement
apartment. Then three from college campuses. One from a
tavern parking lot. And now Georgann Hawkins from an alley in plain sight of students studying for their final exams.
But police hadn't seen anything yet. Next time the sun would
be straight overhead, warming 40,000 potential witnesses at
a state park. A Sunday in July at the edge of a lake. And at
last, something to grab hold of in the case.

3

Twenty years ago Lake Sammamish had the look of a
country retreat. Located near the foothill town of Issaquah

east of Seattle, the lake and its thickly grown banks of salal and Oregon grape were relatively untouched. A wooden-hulled sailboat might be seen drifting silently across the water, and a few city people came out to swim. That was about it.

By the 1970s, the rapid growth of Lake Washington's Eastside suburbs had ringed "Lake Sam," as it is known, with new homes, apartment complexes, and a steady pulse of traffic. Now it is close to people, not far away, and the natural appeal of the place is no secret. Its facilities, however —changing rooms, picnic tables, concession stand—are old and worn, and so on a hot weekend afternoon, Lake Sammamish State Park has a kind of timeless American feel. The scenes played out under the hot sun might be unfolding anywhere. Children, dazzled with self-pride, race back from the water shouting news of their latest accomplishments. Fathers press their spatulas down on meat. Powerboats buzz; a grandmother sits and squints in a chair; two girls, shooting identical looks over their shoulders, wear the same style of swimsuit.

On Sunday, July 14, 1974, the Lake Sammamish crowds peaked for a Rainier Beer promotion. The temperature was well up toward 90° before noon, and only the first to arrive could be assured of a parking space and a prime spot on the beach. More than 40,000 would come and go by sundown. A picnic table, Doris Grayling figured, would even be harder to get. The 22-year-old blonde nabbed one at 11:30, 45 minutes before her husband and her parents were due to meet her. She was staring out at the water, not thinking of anything much, when a man with his arm in a sling came toward her and said, "Hello."

She turned and lifted the sunglasses on top of her head. "Hello," she replied, instinctively sliding an inch away on the bench.

He needed help, he said, half lifting his injured arm. He wondered if she could lend a hand. Grayling looked him over: jeans, a white crew-neck T-shirt, sandy blond hair, about 25 years old. "Yeah," she said, "what do you want?"

It was his sailboat, he explained, walking her back to the parking lot between the bandstand and the shedlike restrooms; he couldn't load it onto his car by himself. They small-talked along the way. "This is out of sight," he said, stopping to hold his arm to his side and looking back at the crowd on the beach. "There are so many people here." She

19

agreed and glanced at his arm, hung in a beige sling with no cast. He told her he'd hurt it playing racquetball. Had she ever tried the sport, he wanted to know.

"Bellevue," she said when he asked where she lived. "I work at Boeing." He kept up a steady stream of talk.

In the parking lot the man approached what Grayling took to be his car, "a newish-looking Volkswagen Bug," she later recalled, "metallic brown." And no sailboat.

"Hey, where's the boat?"

"It's up at my folks' house. It's just up the hill," he said, motioning her to the passenger side.

"What time is it now?" she asked.

"Twelve twenty."

"Hey, forget it. I was supposed to meet my parents at twelve fifteen."

"Oh, that's OK. I should have told you the boat wasn't in the parking lot. Thanks for bothering to come up to the car." He walked her halfway back to her table and repeated his thanks. "I should have told you it wasn't here." He left her with a boyish grin.

Minutes later, when Grayling saw the man with a blonde woman wheeling a ten-speed bike, she smiled and thought to herself, "Boy, that guy sure works fast." The woman was Janice Ott.

Janice Ott's interest in correctional institutions and juvenile courts was no accident: her father, a Spokane doctor, was the former supervisor of the Washington State Board of Prison Terms and Parole. For the past six months she had worked as a probation officer for the King County Juvenile Court. But if her work had put her in contact with some raw young criminals, it never seemed to darken her spirits. Janice Ott, small, bouncy, relentlessly effervescent, was known as a "sunshine girl" at her office. True to her reputation, she had a habit of punctuating her letters and notes with a smiling, round-faced sketch of the sun. At noon on July 14 she left a note for her roommate signed with a happy face: "I'll be at Lake Sammamish sunning myself. See ya."

Ott rolled her yellow Tiger-brand bike to an empty spot in the grass at 12:30, threading her way through the families and couples. She stripped down to a black bikini, smeared her arms and legs with cocoa butter from a small orange jar, and lay down on a plain white towel. She turned herself once, and then again as a man approached and leaned over her towel.

"Excuse me. Could you help me put my sailboat onto my car? I can't do it myself because I broke my arm."

Ott never hesitated. "Sit down," she said. "Let's talk about it."

"It's up at my parents' house in Issaquah," he explained.

"Oh, really? I live up in Issaquah." He had made a friend.

Nearby, in various groups, two women and a man were eavesdropping on the conversation, taking in the scene. All three noticed the beige sling the stranger wore on his arm. And they remembered him wearing white: T-shirt, tennis shorts, socks, and tennis shoes. Two of them heard a slight English accent in his voice.

"Well, OK," Janice Ott agreed at last. "But what about my bike?"

"No problem," he said. "It will fit in the trunk."

She was interested in sailing, she told him; she'd never tried it.

"Oh, it'll be easy for me to teach you." He seemed encouraged by her friendliness.

"I get a ride in the sailboat?" she asked playfully, pulling on a pair of short Levi cutoffs and a midriff shirt. They started for the parking lot, introducing themselves to each other at last.

"I'm Jan. And you?"

"Ted."

No one saw Janice Ott alive again.

The idle day baked on. A child cut his foot; a motorcycle gang roared through—distant tremors in the slow pleasure taking of the afternoon. Cars left, and others poured in. Around 1:00 p.m., Denise Naslund, her boyfriend, and another couple felt fortunate to find a parking space for Denise's 1963 blue Chevy. They got out and unfurled their towels.

Denise went right to sleep, but not with an altogether easy mind. Dark-haired with wide, dreamy eyes, she was having problems with her boyfriend. She had talked with her mother about moving back home, ready for a change at age 18. But for the moment, the gritty, familiar feel of summer moisture under her rings and the tickle of grass on her cheek was soothing and made her forget.

By four o'clock on that Bastille Day, the sun felt hotter than it had at noon. People were up, wandering, looking for shade.

21

"Excuse me, young lady, could you help me launch my sailboat?"

The girl with long golden-brown hair was two years younger than Denise. She asked the man how he'd hurt his arm. It was sprained, he said, and he couldn't find anyone to help. But something bothered her. Was it his sharp nose and thin lips? Or the deeply set eyes with their tiny pupils? He seemed nervous, gestured with his bad elbow, tugged on her arm.

"No," she said. "I'm sorry. I've got people waiting." She watched him go. Perhaps it was that old, faded, light green sling that unnerved her.

4:15 p.m. A woman in a flowered halter top and long jeans was feeling ill, walking along a path to the concession stand. The man dressed in tennis clothes had his arm in a bleached white sling. "I need to ask a really big favor of you," he began, turning to follow her after they passed. His hair was parted in the middle and messy, but he was handsome, she thought. "I normally wouldn't ask this favor, but my brother is busy and can't help." He pointed to the parking lot, meaning his sailboat was there. She was in a hurry, she said. No.

"That's OK," he said politely. He stood a few seconds, then walked away.

5:15 p.m. A woman in cutoffs and a pink bikini top paused at the edge of the lake to watch the water-skiers skimming by. She didn't know how long he'd been there when she finally noticed him in the corner of her eye: a man with a sloppy beige sling on his arm. He approached her on the beach. "Hello. I was wondering if you could help me put my sailboat on my car?"

"I'm not very strong," she began uncertainly.

"It's better that I ask someone who was alone," he put in.

"Well, I'm waiting for someone."

"Oh," he said. His voice suddenly went flat. He turned back toward the changing rooms.

Individually, these encounters seemed like nothing. Compared to some of the brusque propositioning young women put up with all day at the park, worsening as one beer after another stacked up, a well-spoken request from an injured man was almost a relief. Only later would it form a maddening, meandering trail—with one more blank spot in it before the day was through.

Around 4:30, after a hot dog and a bag of potato chips,

22

Denise Naslund stood up and headed for the restroom, a wood-and-cinderblock structure nearby. Inside, a Seattle policewoman saw Denise (or someone fitting her description) chatting with another woman in a knit maroon bikini. The two strolled out together, and that was it—the last time Denise Naslund was seen alive.

When King County Police Captain Joseph "Nick" Mackie arrived for work at the County Courthouse on Monday morning, a promising puzzle was about to reveal itself in outline form. The reports of two more missing women came in early, followed by panicky, insistent reminders from Denise Naslund's mother, who knew, she said, that "something terrible" had happened to her daughter.

Mackie summoned his top detectives, including Kathy McChesney, a small, intense young woman, knowledgeable about rape and other sex offenses, and Robert Keppel, a serious, smooth-faced investigator who had a reputation for intelligence and hard work. Mackie told them what he knew —not much—and a low-voltage current of interest ran through the room. The captain felt it himself, his lower jaw working involuntarily. In broad daylight, they all thought to themselves, with all those potential witnesses, *someone* must have seen *something*. The story of the disappearances would be in the paper the next day, along with Mackie's appeal for assistance from anyone who had been at Lake Sam Sunday afternoon.

It paid off immediately. Doris Grayling volunteered her story about the man with his arm in a sling who had approached her, led her to a Volkswagen Bug, and then sought the help of Janice Ott. Ott's eavesdropping neighbors added what they knew: the English accent, the parents' house in Issaquah, the name "Ted." And then, once this long anticipated break was publicized, the other women who had been asked to help a disabled man eagerly told their stories to police. Before the week was out, the local media were routinely referring to "The Ted Case."

It was an inviting line of thought, the first in any of the missing-women cases to date. But there were problems and implausibilities about a "Ted" theory. The witnesses' descriptions, for one, were vague and inconsistent. One woman said he wore jeans; several others were sure of the tennis shorts. Accounts of his height and hair color differed. And his sling, they said, was beige, faded green, or bleached white.

23

This wasn't unusual, only frustrating. It is well known that most people are careless observers, especially when they have no reason to look closely for details.

The timing of the encounters posed another difficulty. Assuming that "Ted" was responsible for the disappearances of both Ott and Naslund, could he have abducted Naslund at 4:30 (the time she was seen leaving the restroom) and then returned by 5:15 to approach the woman at the edge of the lake? Perhaps there was more than one man with his arm in a sling that day, and only one (or none) of them had anything to do with either woman. One detective may have summed up the police skepticism: "Jesus Christ," he muttered to himself, "what the hell could one guy do with *two* of them in one day anyway?"

So while the unknown "Ted" was getting all the attention in the papers and on the news, police were quietly pursuing other leads as well. Frightened and fascinated, hundreds of people who had been at the park (and almost as many more who hadn't) phoned in their advice. More than a few remembered the motorcycle gang that had raced through the parking lot on and off through the afternoon. Others mentioned isolated incidents of harassment: a man following a woman to the changing rooms, a lewd remark near the lifeguard's stand. Police were particularly excited when they learned that a prisoner recently released from the state penitentiary, a man who wore his hair in a ponytail and cultivated marijuana in his backyard, was living in the Issaquah hills.

And then there were the automatic suspects: known sex offenders who had either been released or had escaped from prisons or institutions in the area. Laws barred police from a "fishing expedition" in the state's records of such persons, however, and the routine police work on them was laborious. "We just want to know who's on the loose," a homicide detective grumbled to a reporter.

By the end of July, none of the leads had developed. Nick Mackie made another appeal for help through the press, urging the abductor or abductors to "do some deep soul-searching" and turn themselves in. The *Seattle Post-Intelligencer* offered $5000 for information leading to a conviction. The theory that the disappearances were related to the position of the moon gained some ground, even among officers at work on the case. Anything, they figured, might help.

But it was "Ted," finally, who tantalized the detectives and drew their attention. Detective Bob Keppel carefully assembled the eyewitness visual data and fed it to a police artist for a composite sketch. The result was a roughly generalized drawing of a bushy-haired, high-cheeked man with straight, unremarkable features and curiously placid eyes that seemed to float up toward the lids.

The witnesses were interviewed and reinterviewed. Doris Grayling was hypnotized to see if she could remember anything more—a license plate on the VW, a dent, anything at all. The women's conversations with "Ted" were meticulously re-created. The English accent and Grayling's recollection of a reference to racquetball (a game popular with college students but not well known otherwise in America) led to speculation that "Ted" might be a Canadian and might, in fact, be connected to a string of homicides in nearby British Columbia.

But it was all guesswork. Without bodies, without evidence of sexual assault or homicide, a rape specialist like Kathy McChesney or a straight homicide detective was seriously hampered. Even the tedious chore of tracking down Volkswagen drivers named Ted seemed futile. The state motor vehicle registration computer spilled out nearly 3000 names (it couldn't select out for "metallic brown" Bugs), and even at that, police couldn't be sure that Ted was the man's real name.

But "Ted" was vividly real to the people of the Northwest, an image and a name for all those edgy months of waiting. Life changed for men named Ted, changed drastically if they happened to drive Volkswagens. One Northwesterner, far too young to fit the description of the Lake Sam "Ted" and the owner of a bright orange Bug, suddenly couldn't reach his new girlfriend on the phone. Another, a state employee in Olympia, was playfully, nervously teased by his co-workers. Hundreds were hauled in for questioning by the police.

And women were seeing "Ted," conjuring him up wherever they went. One ran screaming from a man who bumped his VW up on a curb in the University District. Another reported a man with his arm in a sling who tried to pick her up near a department store downtown; when she refused, he slipped his arm out of the sling and drove off. The two women from Ellensburg finally told their stories to police, struck by the coincidence of a disabled man and a VW Bug, untroubled by the different colors of the cars. And a barmaid at the Flame Tavern suddenly remembered a "Ted" look-alike buying beer the night Brenda Ball disappeared.

"We're checking everything," a detective curtly told a newspaperman. Privately they joked darkly that "Ted" seemed to be every goddamned place at once.

August came. Nixon resigned, admitting nothing. "I no longer have a strong enough political base in the Congress to justify continuing that effort," he told the country on August 8. "I leave with no bitterness toward those who have opposed me." The next day, waving madly to the cameras, he left the White House south lawn by helicopter. The long month passed slowly in the Northwest. School reopened in September.

On the first Saturday of the month, September 7, a Seattle construction worker named Elzie Hammons tromped out through the dry weeds grown up around the I-90 road work just east of Issaquah. Below him the cars whipped by, going east and west. His movements were painstaking, his eyes sharpened; he was hunting grouse. He stopped and looked down.

Two months before, on July 16, a state highway worker had stood ten yards from where Hammons stopped. Unwrapping his lunch in the cab of a truck, the man had suddenly smelled something odd. He had put his sandwich down and started back through the brush when he spotted a lump —a carcass—about 25 feet off. He stood and sniffed again and decided it was a deer. "Hunters," he thought as he walked back to the truck.

Now Elzie Hammons had stumbled right on top of the find. Where the highway worker missed a fresh kill, Hammons saw a streamer of hair and a skull with spinal column and several ribs attached. He turned and went for help.

Nick Mackie gathered the reporters in an empty room at the courthouse the next morning. The white television lights came on; microphones were jockeyed into place.

"The worst we feared," he began, "is true."

4

More than seven months after Lynda Healy's disappearance from her University District room, police and the public had some confirmation of what they had long believed. The missing women of 1974 weren't ever coming home. The last to go, Janice Ott and Denise Naslund, were the first found. For their families it was, at least, a resolution. "This may sound strange," Denise's mother said, dazed from two months of waiting, "but it's a relief to know. Her soul's in heaven."

Out in the dry September weeds, only a slight trace of the women remained. The sparse language of a police report rendered the scene:

The location where OTT and NASLUND were found is 4 miles east of Lake Sammamish State Park on Interstate 90. It is on the north side and access to the north side is by the old abandoned Sunset Highway; a median prevents a left turn when eastbound. The corridor along the highway expansion and all homes near the site were vacant. There is a small gravel road which leads north uphill from "old Sunset Highway" and across an abandoned railroad line.

When they were dumped, the stinging nettles and underbrush were very thick, but a vehicle could drive back into the brush to within 40′ of where the characteristic grease spots were found. There were two grease spots within driving distance with blond hair nearby. There was another grease spot a little farther uphill near NASLUND'S skull and mandible.

The skeletons were badly scattered by animals and no evidence of trauma, dismemberment, o̶ ~ult could be detected. There was no clothing, j other personal effects near the scene. In a of the site several articles of women's un were found but none belonged to any o

27

victims. No occult or witchcraft symbols were found near the scene.

The victims were probably killed elsewhere and dumped at this location shortly after their disappearance. They were found 55 days after their disappearance. An extensive search was made in the area but the skull of OTT is still missing as are the skull and mandible of the third person.

A large quantity of immature elk bones were found ¼ mile east of the scene on "Sunset Highway." These bones were bagged in burlap gunny sacks and bound with twine.

For Nick Mackie and his detectives, the discovery at the Issaquah site was disquieting in several respects. Cursing the bad luck that made them barely miss the bodies two days after Ott and Naslund vanished from Lake Sam, they now had only bones, which offered no clue to the cause of death. And then there was that third unidentifiable body. Could it be another of the missing women, or was it somebody else, somebody they didn't even know about yet? What did the bundles of elk bones signify? And perhaps most maddening of all, where was the jewelry, the clothing, Janice Ott's yellow bicycle? Like Gerald Ford's pardon of Nixon, also in the news at the time, this climax threw more shadow than light on the scene.

Police knew they needed help. A team of psychiatrists was consulted with the hopes that a projective psychiatric profile of "Ted" might focus and give direction to the investigation. One of the doctors began his work with a strong word of caution. "Profiling is a disastrously poor investigative technique," he said. "Without much information you're really flying by the seat of your pants." But everyone agreed it was worth a try. The psychiatrists drove out to the spot where the bodies had been dumped, then pored over the "Ted" file in Seattle. Afterward they spent hours reinterviewing the witnesses who had been at Lake Sammamish on July 14. Later a police report summarized some of the psychiatrists' judicious guesses: "There is no known cause of death or indication of mutilation on any of the victims which would give us insight into his personality. His actions and demeanor tend to categorize him as a sociopath and it is fair to say he is also sexual psychopath."

Such a "personality disorder" (the terms "sociopath" and "psychopath" are basically the same), the doctors explained, is characterized by certain typical traits, including a lack of emotion and an absence of remorse. Yet strangely, such people tend to be extraverts: likable, engaging, often deliciously hedonistic. High intelligence and motivation are common among psychopaths. In short, the experts said, such a person appears perfectly normal. But the secret to his personality lies at his hollow, conscienceless core. Untroubled by feelings of guilt, a psychopathic killer tends to repeat his act again and again and again.

Police thanked the doctors for their work and promised to call on them again if they turned up anything new. Unfortunately, the investigation was pretty well mired under the mountain of "Ted"s and brown VWs that needed to be checked. Occasionally, when a suspect looked promising detectives would drop his photo into a book of mug shots and run it past the witnesses. It was tedious, tiresome, and unrewarding. Nerves began to unravel as the weeks wore on.

One close observer later grumbled about some of the investigative techniques. Some of the officers involved, he said, just weren't prepared for this kind of case. "There was a lot of enthusiasm without much training. These people were doing the best they could, but they had never had a crime quite like this; they were *homicide* people, not sex-crime investigators. They were doing everything by the book when they should have thrown the book away. The result was that if there was a chance to look under the wrong rock, they did it.

"Take the underwear," he continued. "That should have been a red flag in this type of investigation. This was clearly a sex crime, and it's obvious to think of underwear and sex crimes having some possible connection. I don't think any effort was made to trace the origin or ownership of the articles of underwear or conduct any sort of laboratory analysis. Now, I have no idea what would have happened if they had analyzed the underwear or some of the other evidence in a different way. But something might have happened. It sure might have."

Years later, Phil Killien would still chafe at the criticism. Assigned by King County Prosecutor Chris Bayley to handle a case that might materialize from the crimes, Killien watched the investigation with a dogged interest. His faith in the police was absolute. At least once a day he was on the phone to Mackie or Keppel. "Nick, Bob, what've you got?"

"A hell of a lot of guys named Ted."

The King County police weren't the only ones investigating the "Ted" murders at the time. As the fall colors began to brighten the Issaquah hills, dozens of self-appointed sleuths combed the site where the bodies had been found. A square-jawed woman who lived in a house nearby marched her dog through the woods, whispering at him to keep his nose to the ground. Boys dumped their bicycles in the weeds and charged off to hunt for human bones. One amateur investigator, an off-duty security guard, went to the police with some "discoveries" he had made. Bad enough that they told him to "stay the hell out of it," he later said. But it took a gunshot whizzing past his ear one day near the site to convince him that "somebody didn't want him to find something."

There were, in fact, some curious additions to the possible evidence list, carefully kept private by police. Several days after the bones of Janice Ott and Denise Naslund had been found, a rough cross made of sticks and twine was stuck in the ground near the spot where the bodies had lain—a spot police assumed that few but the murderer would have known (the bodies had been dragged and scattered a good distance by animals). Later, a jeans-clad dummy was hung in effigy from a nearby tree. It was enough to get the occult theory percolating again. Ott and Naslund seemed to have no connection to witchcraft, but Lynda Healy's tennis partner was well acquainted with the literature of the occult, and Donna Manson was working on alchemy as her term project. Maybe that third body was one of them and . . .

The strangest discovery of all again wove "Ted" into the mysterious fabric of the Lake Sammamish murders. In October, after a drenching rain, a railroad worker picked up a pornographic book near the Issaquah site. The book was dry, suggesting it had been dropped there, by accident or design, just hours before. In one chapter a young woman narrates an experience with her boyfriend. The boyfriend's name is Ted.

"This happened when I was a junior in college, that would be about five years ago. I was going with this boy whose parents owned a ranch in Wyoming. I guess we had gotten pretty serious about each other—we'd done some pretty heavy petting. But we'd never gone all the way. I'd seen to

30

that. My upbringing had been rather strict and religious, and I'd been taught that premarital intercourse was sinful.

"But Ted invited me home to the ranch for spring vacation. He wanted to introduce me to his parents and I really did want to meet them. So we made the trip from Colorado, a day's drive. I must say I enjoyed being at the ranch and Ted's parents were wonderful." After a dance, Ted drove the woman to a remote place; the result was "a beautiful experience." The next morning, she says, "I tugged on the jeans Ted had lent me and was ashamed of the sexual thrill that went through me as the pants slipped up into place."

For police it was a final, taunting frustration, a weird reminder of that innocent afternoon when some "Ted" had invited a woman up the hill to his parents' house. It was October, and the skies lowered again with the fall rains.

On October 12, 1974, just after the opening of deer season, a hunter came down a path 17 miles from Vancouver, Washington, not far from the Oregon border. A hell of a place to find a wig, he thought, prodding a shank of hair with his gun. Then he saw a skull and went for help. The search of the hillside that followed was a virtual replay of the one a month before at Issaquah, 130 miles north. Hair, scattered bones, and teeth added up to two young women, dead for months. According to lab reports, which indicated the bones had not completely oxidized, the women's deaths were thought to have been sudden, possibly by suffocation. Again there was no clothing or jewelry found with the bodies; only one plastic Tampax case counted as a possible lead.

The Clark County sheriff's office immediately phoned Bob Keppel in Seattle. "You'll flip when you see this. It's just like yours." Keppel and another detective hurried to the scene and watched as the bodies were hauled off for identification.

The first ID came quickly: an 18-year-old woman named Carol Valenzuela, last seen at a welfare office in Vancouver on August 2. At 11:00 a.m. a case worker had told her to return at 1:00 p.m. for food stamps. She didn't show that afternoon and was never seen again. The other victim, whose time of death was fixed about six weeks prior to Valenzuela's disappearance, wasn't so easy to pin down. She was between 17 and 23; she had had a child; her long dark hair was thick with a natural wave. It didn't sound like any of the missing women from the Northwest, but the bones were packaged

31

and sent to Seattle for verification. In the meantime, the woman's dental chart was circulated to missing-person publications around the country. After a nibble from South Dakota and one from Everett, Washington, the line went cold. Just as at Issaquah, one of the victims—as well as the killer—was unknown.

The name of a man, however—Warren Leslie Forrest—did come to mind. Passing himself off as a Seattle University photography student, he had that same week struck up a conversation with a woman on the streets of Portland, Oregon, convincing her to pose for him in a park for a fee of $30 or $40. They went in his van to a spot overlooking the city, where he took out his camera. Next he took out some rope and bound his "subject" at the ankles and wrist. At a nearby department store he bought a roll of wide adhesive tape, then drove to a park across the state line in Camas, Washington, 30 miles to the north.

Forrest was a park employee, a quiet college type with a raft of loyal friends. With a key from his pocket he unlocked a park gate, shut it behind him, and drove down a rutted road. Finally the assault began. Stripped and still tied down, the woman watched as the man calmly sharpened a handful of darts. One by one, from a pellet gun, Forrest shot them into her breasts. Next he went at her with a dildo. Then he raped her. Hysterical, with a noose around her neck, she was dragged from the van, partly dressed, led to a log, and strangled. Finally, Forrest stabbed her five times with a pocket knife and covered the body with tree limbs.

Two hours later, miraculously, the victim flagged down a car on the main highway. She had crawled out on her own; remembered everything; was prepared to identify the man. Forrest eventually entered a plea of insanity and was committed to a state hospital. Although they couldn't place him in the area at the time of Carol Valenzuela's disappearance, detectives were intrigued by the recurring pattern of victims dumped in the woods. And they were struck by the testimony of most of Forrest's friends. To them it was a great surprise; he seemed so "normal," just as psychologists had predicted "Ted" would seem to his friends. It wasn't much, with no hard evidence, but it was a start. In December, police would get another boost, if the death of another woman could be counted as a boost.

At 11:00 p.m. on November 27, 1974, Vonnie Joyce Stuth was standing over a salad bowl in her south Seattle apartment. Her husband, who worked the night shift at a factory in Renton, was due home shortly, and as usual Vonnie had waited dinner for him. It was the night before Thanksgiving, and she was in a cheery mood when she ran to answer the phone.

It was her sister Alicia. They yammered a bit about the family dinner the next day before Vonnie interrupted to answer a knock at the door. Minutes later Vonnie returned and told Alicia she had to get off the phone. A neighbor from across the street was moving and couldn't take his boxer dog. He wanted to know if the Stuths would like to have the animal. Vonnie was touched; her own dog had been run over several months before. When Todd Stuth arrived at his apartment, tired and hungry, he found dinner half finished, a pack of cigarettes on the counter, and the television on. He didn't find Vonnie.

On December 5, the neighbor with the dog, Gary Addison Taylor, was located in Enumclaw and questioned for four hours. His van had been seen in his old neighborhood on the night of Vonnie's disappearance, and other neighbors recalled he owned a boxer. Taylor was unhelpful, refusing to take a polygraph test, but he did say he'd come back and talk to police later. With no evidence to charge him, they had to let him go.

There had been a respite in Seattle since the Lake Sammamish disappearances in July, but to police and the press it looked like the same sickening story all over again. Stuth was attractive; she wore her long hair parted in the middle; she had disappeared without a trace. As it turned out, she even knew Janice Ott (through work) and had been a classmate of Denise Naslund. "It's been nice knowing ya," Denise had written to Vonnie in an old yearbook. "Have fun this summer and stay away from the better things in life."

Shortly after the December 5 interview with Taylor, the police teletype punched out some alarming news about the man. Gary Addison Taylor, 38 years old, six feet even, 200 pounds, was an 11-year veteran of a Michigan prison for the criminally insane. His history included a variety of assaults on women with a distinctive M.O. (modus operandi) pattern. Sometimes Taylor used a .22-caliber rifle, other times a machete. He liked to operate in lovers'-lane-type settings. Gary Taylor did not return for a second interview with the King County police; and he was no longer to be found at his Enumclaw address.

33

Sergeant Randall relayed the news to Phil Killien, adding a relevant detail: Gary Taylor had walked away from the ward of an Ypsilanti hospital sometime in 1973—just before the women began to disappear in the Northwest. Killien tugged open the collar of his shirt. "At last," he thought, "they're looking for *somebody*."

At home, in a small house in Seattle's Wallingford district, Melanie Pattisen opened the paper each morning that fall with a queasy apprehensiveness. It had begun in the summer, then increased in October, when a friend returned from a trip to Salt Lake City. The paper in Utah had been full of news of a young woman's mysterious disappearance—a disappearance, the friend observed, that resembled the missing women cases in the Northwest. "That's exactly the same as the girls here," she said. Melanie gazed back at her friend.

It wasn't the first time the subject had come up. In July, when the Seattle papers first published the police artist's composite of the man with his arm in a sling, the friend had held a copy up to Melanie's face.

"You know who that looks like," she said. "Somebody that me and you know."

"Yes," Melanie said quietly, "I know, very much."

In September Melanie Pattisen stood up on her toes to kiss her fiancé goodbye. His truck was loaded down with books and furniture and clothes. A perfect Boston fern sat in the cab. He was leaving early, determined to make it halfway to Salt Lake City that night.

"Good luck, Ted," Melanie whispered through the window of the truck. He squeezed her hand and drove off.

Part II

FAMILY

5

Wendover, Nevada, is a kind of landmark in the contemporary West: remote, independent, and a weirdly accurate reflection of the contradictory impulses in the pioneer spirit. Situated squarely on the Utah-Nevada border in the porphyry foothills of the Desert Range, Wendover leads two lives. To the east, across the Bonneville Salt Flats and beyond, lies the Mormon legacy of Joseph Smith. In the cities and towns of Utah, a curiously resilient way of life thrives, a way of life predicated on home, family, service, and purity of personal habit. To the west, Nevada—gambling, alcohol, prostitution, profligacy—the West's wide, unbounded playground.

In the fall of 1974 the Tooele, Utah, Police Department, sponsors of the regular Intermountain Crime Conference, elected to move the meeting to Wendover's Stateline Motel. The gesture was surely based on geography: police representatives from Washington, Oregon, and California were joining the regulars from Utah, Wyoming, Idaho, and Nevada, and Wendover was centrally located. But there may have been a subconscious wish involved.

The December conference was unusual primarily because of one item on the agenda: the mysterious disappearances and deaths of young women. That wasn't enough to motivate police to think in terms of a traveling felon; dating back to 1969 there were almost 90 missing or murdered women cases on the books in western states, most of them unsolved. But recently a kind of pattern had seemed to evolve, similar victims and a similar M.O. One by one the representatives walked to the front of the Stateline Motel conference room and recited the particulars of their cases.

Detective Robert Keppel, who had flown to Salt Lake City and driven to the conference with two Utah investigators, sketched in the history of the Washington crimes, mentioning the names of a few suspects and referring to the Lake Sammamish "Ted," with his arm in a sling and the brown VW Bug. A spokesman from Rawlins, Wyoming, was next.

37

Between July 4 and August 23, he said, four young women had been abducted, all of them seen last near the Carbon County Fairgrounds. A string of San Francisco area homicides came up. And someone mentioned an unidentified body that a family of tourists had found near Grand Junction, Colorado, in early July. Her body was full of maggots, and she'd been beaten about the head, but the cause of death, according to the coroner, was suffocation.

The Utah detectives followed the proceedings with profound interest. Like Washington, Utah had experienced several evidence-free disappearances that fall. Nancy Wilcox, a pretty 16-year-old cheerleader, had vanished on October 2, and Debbie Kent, another high-school student, on November 8. The Salt Lake area had its confirmed homicides too: in October two young women disappeared from suburban streets. Both were later found, beaten about the head and strangled (like the unidentified Colorado victim, Utah police noted), and dumped in weedy, distant canyons.

Finally, the Murray, Utah, Police Department was working a case that had one crucial difference. On November 8 a young woman had driven to a local shopping mall. Inside, a man had approached her on a pretense and led her to his car. Moments later he was at her with a tire iron, raising it above her head, vowing to kill her. The difference was that the woman had escaped, and the car the man was driving, she told police, was a "light-colored" VW Bug. It was a coincidence, perhaps, that Keppel's "Ted" drove a VW. But perhaps not.

At the close of the meeting, the participants promised to remain in close touch, by phone and teletype. Several of the officers stopped to peer in at the Stateline gameroom on their way out, smiling, impressed in spite of themselves by the noisy clatter of ice and plastic chips and nervous voices, all lit by the reflected glow of the red velvet walls.

A California detective reached into his pocket and swaggered up to a silver-armed slot machine. Their colleagues from other states were serious enough about their cases, but somehow in Utah crimes against young women had a special torque. Yes, one of the victims was the daughter of the Midvale police chief. That mattered; that mattered a great deal. But even more, these abductions and murders of high-school-age girls in Utah, in the context of the Mormon faith, struck to the very heart of life in the state.

More than murders, these were crimes against the family, the community, the hard-won hope for the future.

"Joan." Louis Smith raised his voice as he stepped through the front door. "Joan!" His wife came from the kitchen, drying her hands on her apron front. "Look what I found on the bumper of the LTD." The Midvale police chief held up a hand-colored scene of flowers and trees, which had been stuck with bubble gum to his Utah Peace Officers Association insignia. The couple frowned seriously when their daughter Melissa rounded the corner just then. She saw her handiwork in her father's grip. "I didn't want the kids on State to think I was a narc," she began halfheartedly.

The Smiths, Louis and Joan, Melissa and Jolene, rolled back in good-natured laughter over the story that night. Eating together in their white frame rambler with a spruce tree out front, they were a typical model family in Midvale, tied to each other and their community by the Mormon Church. Six levels of priesthood (and dozens of offices) for men, Relief Society for women, Primary for children, and the Young Men's and Young Women's Mutual Improvement Association for teenagers: these are the cohesive elements of each "ward." Services, meetings, and get-togethers draw the families together most days of the week; on the weekends, social gatherings at the ward house, outings, dinners, bazaars, athletics, dramatics, choirs, scouting, dances, and holidays follow each other with seamless, confident regularity. "Home teachers" visit families in the evening, and the families reserve one night a week for each other. Self-enclosed and self-sufficient, the Mormon life of the Smiths was reflected and validated in a thousand ways by other lives like it. At the end of dinner Melissa asked to borrow the car.

Melissa Smith spent a lot of time in the car—her parents' gold LTD and a string of other family cars her friends could wangle on the weekends. Like hundreds of other teenagers celebrating their mobility, Melissa headed for State Street, where fast-food outlets, discount stores, and gas stations formed the ritual's familiar scene. "Cruisin' State," it's called in Midvale, Utah, a slow noisy migration of cars booming music and exhaust into the night air. At the open windows, along the way where a group of friends leans on a hood. No one misses a thing; everyone is seen.

On the evening of October 18, 1974, Melissa Smith perched herself on the edge of the bed, hair still wet from a shower, and pointed her toe into a pair of blue nylons. From the closet she grabbed out a pair of hip-hugger Levi's and a flowered navy blue shirt. Her brown loafers and two strands of wooden beads completed the outfit. She was dressing for a slumber party at her friend Greta's house. Melissa turned out the light and edged open her parents' bedroom door. Joan and Louis were getting ready for a dinner date with friends.

"Mom, I haven't got any money. Can I have part of my allowance?"

"I've only got a dollar," her mother answered, frowning a little at her husband.

"That's fine. I just don't want to be broke tonight." Mother and daughter agreed to meet at the beauty school the next morning at eight. As part of her vocational training, Melissa fixed her mother's hair at Continental Beauty each Saturday morning.

When Louis Smith backed the LTD down the driveway at six, Melissa was ready and waiting for her ride to the slumber party. By 7:30 no one had showed up. Annoyed, she phoned Greta's house and got no answer. Moments later her own phone rang. It was Sandy, a friend from the beauty school who worked nights at the Pepperoni Pizza Place. She was having trouble with her boyfriend and needed to talk right away. A few quick brush strokes through her long brown hair and Melissa was out the door. Her sister Jolene, busy with a church project in the basement, had declined Melissa's offer to come along.

The route to the Pepperoni was so familiar Melissa could have walked it with her eyes closed: down the dead-end street and the deeply rutted dirt road, over the guardrail and down the embankment to Wasatch Boulevard, under the highway and railroad overpass, and onto the junior-high playing fields, when she passed through a single circle of light. From there, out a driveway onto Center Street, it's a quarter mile to the restaurant.

Sandy was heartbroken. She'd been dumped by her boyfriend, and it took Melissa an hour just to calm her friend down. At last Melissa managed to break away and call Jolene. "I'll be home around ten," she told her sister. After another hour of support and consolation, Melissa left the Pepperoni shortly after 10:00 p.m. At 10:15 the wife of a police dispatcher raking leaves in her yard near the middle school heard a scream nearby. Those damn kids, she thought.

Home themselves that night by ten, Melissa's parents switched on the news and began undressing for bed. But Joan noticed something unusual: Melissa's dollar was still on the cupboard where she'd left it, and in her room the packed overnight case was still on the bed. "Greta stood her up," Jolene explained. "She went to the Pepperoni to talk to Sandy instead." A quick call to Sandy, and Joan learned Melissa had already left.

"Melissa's out walking this time of night," she called to her husband in the bathroom. "We better go get her, Louis."

The Smiths joined the throng on State Street, peering into the scattered groups of teenagers outside the Fashion Place Mall and sweeping through the restaurant parking lots. At J.B.'s, one of their daughter's favorite spots, no one had seen Melissa all night. Joan noticed Greta in a back booth, laughing with two boys she didn't know. Exhausted, the Smiths returned home at two and stepped inside to hear the phone begin to ring.

Joan grabbed it and heard only silence and some indistinguishable noise in the background. Was someone trying to call Melissa? Was she trying to reach them? Was it some terrible joke? Joan Smith raised her voice into the phone: "Melissa, Melissa!" An hour later she shot straight out of her troubled sleep and started to pace, shivering in the warm house. "Call it mother's intuition or whatever you want," she later said, "but I knew Melissa was dead."

The week passed slowly. Melissa didn't show up at the beauty school, at her friends' houses, at J.B.'s or the Pepperoni or anywhere. By Sunday, October 27, the Smiths were trying to reassemble themselves with one less member of the family. Church that morning had been comforting. In the evening Jolene sat with her parents in front of the television. All three went stiff when the news bulletin came on. The body of a red-haired woman had been found in Summit Park, one of the many twisting canyons in the Wasatch Mountains east of Salt Lake. Louis darted to the phone and dialed homicide at the Salt Lake sheriff's office.

Detective Jerry Thompson ticked off a description of the body: nude; badly beaten about the head; probable cause of death, strangulation. The hair was brown, not red as reported. A pair of dark blue nylons, he said, were tied around the neck, with a single strand of wooden beads caught in the noose. Louis was relaying the details to his wife, and at that moment Joan Smith stopped listening. Melissa had been wearing wooden beads the night she disappeared.

"It probably isn't Melissa, Jolene, but we're going up to the University of Utah Medical Center to make sure anyway," Joan bravely told her daughter downstairs.

A detective was waiting at the hospital morgue's door when the Smiths arrived. "You don't want to see her," he said to Joan. Louis Smith, over 20 years the chief of police in Midvale, went inside to perform the most difficult task of his life. But his daughter's body was so badly swollen he wasn't sure. It was the family orthodontist, finally, who had to certify that the woman stretched out behind the doors was Melissa Smith.

The autopsy began immediately. Melissa had been killed elsewhere and dumped at the site. Her head wounds, said the coroner, would have bled profusely, but little blood was found around the body at Summit Park. It was a toss-up whether the cause of death was the severe injuries to her head or strangulation with the blue nylons. The presence of acid phosphatase in her vagina suggested she had been raped. The coroner was certain that Melissa had been dead for 48 to 72 hours, meaning she had been alive as long as a week after her disappearance. His conclusion would later be hotly disputed. The body had been found on a shaded north slope, and even with temperatures in the sixties, normal decomposition might have been retarded.

Louis Smith is a professional cop. He knew that without a crime scene, a murder weapon, or an eyewitness report the chances of developing a strong suspect were very slim. His daughter's death, like the unexplained disappearance of Salt Lake cheerleader Nancy Wilcox on October 2, might very well go unsolved, unpunished.

Not long after Melissa's funeral a young man the Smiths had known peripherally for years appeared at their door with the gift of a hand-woven sofa pillow. Joan stood like a stone in the doorway. The man had a cabin in the woods, she suddenly remembered. Perhaps he had held Melissa there. His pushy manner now seemed monstrous. Jolene came around the corner and joined her mother, feeling the same dreadful chill. The man leaned forward with the pillow. After a few awkward thank-yous they shut the door in his face.

The pillow lay on the kitchen counter for a long moment.

Jolene and her mother were thinking the same unspeakable thing: Melissa's missing clothes were stuffed inside. It was Joan, finally, who composed herself. "No. It's not," she said. "Her clothes aren't in there. Let's just get rid of it. Jolene, you go next door and give it to the Morrisons."

Shirleen Aime glanced at her daughter Laura beside her on the couch. "The body of a 17-year-old woman found yesterday in Summit Park has been identified," the television newsman was saying across the room. "She is Melissa Smith, daughter of Police Chief Louis Smith of Midvale."

"You be careful, Laura, for God's sake. I don't want you hitchhiking anymore."

"Oh mom, I can take care of myself."

At six feet even and 140 pounds, Laura Aime looked like she could manage just fine. She wasn't muscle-bound—just a healthy farm girl—but even her father Jim shook his head whenever his daughter would heft a bale of hay onto her shoulder and trudge through the knee-deep snow of their Fairview farm to feed her horse, Arab. Animals had been an early love, and by her teens Laura was traveling all over southern Utah to ride Arab in 4-H competitions.

By high school Laura's size was causing problems. She pretended not to notice the nicknames and teasing, but by tenth grade the constricting life-style of rural Sanpete County had the best of her. She quit school, initially in favor of a job plucking feathers at the Moroni turkey plant. When her parents moved north to make Jim's commute to the Geneva steel mill less wearing, Laura moved in with her friend Judy Olsen's family in American Fork. Jim and Shirleen still saw their daughter when she came by their Salem house with a load of laundry, and mother and daughter talked by phone almost every day.

As if by instinct, Laura fell in with the latter-day counter-cultural life along Route 89, a kind of underground high-way in heavily Mormon Utah County. Later, many would remember the tall, long-haired girl sitting cross-legged on the grass in Robinson Park or parked in a booth with friends at Lehi's Naughty Pine Cafe or the Purple Turtle or any of a dozen others. To police, she already had the look of a "habitual runaway." But when, those who knew her would later ask, does a runaway become an adult with a life of her own?

On Halloween night, 1974, Laura dressed the same as always for a party at a mobile home in Orem: a sleeveless sweater with horizontal stripes, blue jeans, brown tie-shoes, and some silver cross earrings. Only her nails got special treatment, a black polish with silver flakes. Fred Strobbe picked up Laura and Judy and Mark Olsen at seven.

The party—cheap wine, music, and a roomful of empty stares—never got wound up, and around ten Laura left by herself. Thirty minutes later an acquaintance named George Roth picked her up in front of the Jack and Jill Bowling Alley, where, Laura complained, she had had who-knows-how-many Jeeps and pickups spray dust on her outstretched thumb. "Cowboys," she said to George, scowling. Laura got out at the Naughty Pine and went in for a Coke. But she got bored and restless again, heading for Robinson Park to check the action.

Laura Aime left the park shortly after midnight that Halloween. She never returned to the Olsens' house.

On Sunday, November 3, Mrs. Olsen was confused at first by Shirleen Aime's call.

"Isn't she with you?" she said. "We haven't seen her since Thursday when she and Judy and Mark left for the Halloween party."

Shirleen was bothered but not deeply concerned until Laura missed a date to go hunting with her father. That wasn't like her. She had stalked the hills with him since she was 11. One year they spotted a huge buck with a magnificent rack of horns. Jim leveled his gun and fired, wounding the animal, and Laura set off to track it for several miles, finally catching up in a stand of quaking aspen. Her father puffed up the hill behind her. "Don't shoot it in the head," she whispered urgently, thinking of the contest in a local sporting goods store. "This one's a prize for sure."

Finally, five days after Laura had last been seen, Shirleen Aime called the police.

"Look, lady," came the officer's tired response, "what are we supposed to do about it? Do you know how many runaway girls we have in Utah County? There's no way we could put out a report on every one of them. Why don't you put an ad in the paper?"

Shirleen didn't know how many runaways there were or how many girls were missing. She only knew about Laura. The sharp, clear days of Utah's fall grew shorter.

On Friday, a week before Thanksgiving, Shirleen was

home alone during the morning. She'd felt a vague, unnameable uneasiness since the other children had left for school. Wandering through the house, she climbed the stairs, to Laura's room. Strangely, among all these familiar things—Laura's clothes in the closet, the hairbrush and jewelry on the dresser, the fuzzy pink slippers near the bed—Shirleen felt hopelessly lost.

She returned to the room moments later with an armful of cardboard boxes. Slowly and methodically, Shirleen Aime folded everything from the closet, dresser, and shelves. On Monday, when her oldest son John arrived, en route back to Washington State from his army radar assignment in Nevada, Shirleen tried to give him the box with Laura's record albums.

"I'm not going to take them, mom. She'll be back."

"Please, John, I don't want them around the house."

John had to leave that night after dinner, turning the house hollow all over again. The Thanksgiving weekend coming up would be the saddest holiday the Aime family had ever spent.

By that time, the Aimes might have shared their misery and uncertainty with many others along the Wasatch Front. The events of a weekend night earlier that month finally joined the isolated disappearances and deaths in a full-blown terror with a name. FRIDAY NIGHT KILLER STALKS SALT LAKE, the headlines screamed.

But once again, as it had in the Northwest in July, a door miraculously opened for police. It began when a young woman turned the keys in her ignition, backed a Camaro down a driveway, and flipped on the lights. She was going shopping at a nearby mall.

6

Subdivisions jostle each other in a crazy-quilt pattern on Salt Lake City's west side. Rows of houses intersect at odd angles, as if the image of the orderly city had been shattered like glass. These are not the proud, ostentatious homes of Salt Lake's lawyers, doctors, and executives, but the split entries, bi-levels, and ramblers of miners and truckdrivers, warehousemen and factory workers.

Fred DaRonch, like his brother down the street, works for Kennecott Copper as a foreman at the Bingham Canyon mine. The families each own a rambler in one of Murray's older subdivisions, where, over the years, they've watched the nearby fields sprout tract homes in place of the meadow mushrooms that once popped up after a summer rain. But Carol DaRonch, Fred's daughter, was never troubled by her changing neighborhood. To her it seemed always about the same, the setting for a secure and sheltered upbringing.

From the start, hers could serve as the model for a sober Mormon childhood. Happy and unaggressive, Carol rarely forced her parents to be strict. She was "sweet" and "shy," everyone said, a contented girl for whom family, relatives, and a few friends seemed to suffice. Through high school she hardly dated, and by then about the hardest thing anyone had to say to Carol DaRonch was that she was a little naive.

The fall weather that first week of November 1974 was typical: cool enough to herald winter, yet occasionally sunny and warm. Salt Lake City still rested tenuously in the soft grasp of Indian summer. By Friday, however, huge wet storm clouds glided in from the northwest, and the city grew dark early under the hovering sky and misting rain.

Carol DaRonch left her parents' home on Seventh West and 5400 South about 6:30 p.m. on Friday, November 8. Rush-hour traffic was tapering off as she pulled her new maroon Camaro across State Street, past a strip of franchises, and into the Fashion Place Mall parking lot. The mall is a huge T-shaped building, the stem of the T running east and west. Anchoring the end of each corridor is a large department store—Auerbach's at the end of the stem, the Broadway on the north arm, and Sears on the south. She parked near the middle of the Sears lot and strode quickly through the violent glare of the arc lights reflecting in the rain.

The preceding June, Carol had graduated from high school, turned 18, and landed a job with Mountain Bell. After work that Friday, she headed for Fashion Place to shop and socialize. On a weekend evening like this one, she might expect to run into some old friends and exchange news in the wide arcades between stores.

Carol entered but did not linger in Sears and went straight

out onto the mall, a well-lit, colorful, cheerful interior. Orange and yellow tiles skirt the storefronts and direct the flow of pedestrians around a series of "park benches" and "focal points" with plants and commercial sculptures. Carol wandered past the small shops, stopping occasionally to peer in at the clothes. She turned left onto the main corridor where the smell of popcorn hung in the air, and headed toward Auerbach's.

Near the department store's entrance, under a chrome-tube tree with light-bulb leaves, Carol ran into her cousins. She chatted awhile, then turned and started back up the mall. Carol was ambling, willing to stop and look and buy, just as willing not to. A cat book in the Walden's Bookstore display caught her eye. Just as she was moving closer to the glass, a soft-spoken, articulate man in his late twenties approached her.

He was wearing a sports jacket, green dress pants, and reddish brown patent leather shoes. There was nothing to make her uneasy about this well-dressed, good-looking young man with wavy brown hair and a mustache cropped carefully over his lip.

"Excuse me," he said, "do you have a car parked in the Sears lot?"

"Yes," Carol replied.

"Would you tell me the license plate number?" he asked in an official, businesslike tone.

"KAD 032."

"A Sears customer reported spotting a prowler trying to break into your car with a piece of wire. Would you come with me to see if anything has been stolen?"

As they passed through the door between Auerbach's and Roper's, a mosaic of mirrors under the portico broke their image into a thousand reflections. It was some distance to the Sears parking lot from this door, and her companion explained the situation further.

"My partner has probably apprehended the suspect. Perhaps you can identify him."

As they approached her car Carol was growing suspicious. She asked to see the "officer's" ID. He gave her a patronizing laugh which made her feel, she later explained, "kind of dumb." Embarrassed, she didn't press the issue. Carol took the car keys out and opened the driver's side. Nothing was missing, and there were no signs of damage to the Camaro. The man crossed to the passenger side and asked her to open it.

"What for?" Carol said. "I know what's in my car and nothing's gone."

Her companion tried the door anyway, and Carol saw something shiny in his coat pocket. It was a pair of handcuffs, she realized. They walked quickly back to the mall. He opened the door for her, and they threaded their way through crowds of preoccupied shoppers to the parking lot on the other side. "My partner must have gone up toward Castleton's," he remarked briskly and started off in that direction with Carol in tow.

At Castleton's, the "officer" looked around once again. "My partner must have taken him to the substation on the other side of the mall. We'd better go there and identify him."

A little weary of the chase, Carol followed him back into the brightly lit mall and walked north toward the Broadway. They passed through the doors near Farrell's ice-cream store and out into the misty rain of the north parking lot. She was once again growing suspicious.

"What did you say your name was?" she inquired.

"Officer Roseland, Murray police department."

He led her past Skaggs Drugs, off the far end of the mall parking lot, and across 61st South to a combination dry cleaner/laundromat. Carol waited in a flood of light on the front sidewalk while he tried a door to the side marked "139." No one answered his knock.

"They must have taken him to headquarters," he said. "I really think you should sign a complaint against this individual. I'll drive you down there and you sign the complaint."

They walked about 100 feet down 61st South to "Roseland's" car—a beat-up, light-colored VW Bug covered with scratches, dents, and rust spots. A tear in the top of the rear seat was clearly visible.

"I'd like to see your ID, please," Carol finally demanded. "Roseland" took out his wallet and flashed a gold badge, too quickly for her to discern any writing or inscription. He smiled sympathetically and motioned toward the car, opening the door for her. "Roseland" went around the front, got in, and asked her to put the seat belt on.

"No, it makes me nervous," she said. "I don't want to put it on."

He made a U-turn and drove east on 61st, toward Third East. Carol began to wonder why he hadn't gone to State

Street and grew increasingly nervous. There was alcohol on his breath. "Roseland" made a left onto Third East, stopped at the four-way on 60th South, accelerated a little further, and pulled over into the bus lane near McMillan School, jumping the curb as he brought the car to a stop. He killed the engine.

"What are we doing?" Carol demanded.

In an instant she understood and threw open the door. She turned to yank herself out but could only get one foot on the ground before "Roseland" had reached across, grabbed her wrist, and slapped a handcuff on. Terrified, she began to struggle wildly, and the cramped space of the VW was filled with violent pushing and shoving. In the confusion of flailing arms and tense reflexes, her assailant missed her left wrist and latched both cuffs on the right arm. By this time, Carol's screaming and scratching was proving too much for him. He drew a pistol and threatened to shoot. "If you don't be quiet, I'm going to kill you," he said, pointing the pistol at her head.

A final lunge, however, and she was out of the car. "Roseland" dropped the pistol as he tried to hold onto her. In a moment he was on her again, this time with a crowbar. Carol grabbed it before he could use it. He pinned her against the car and jerked the crowbar wildly to free it from her grasp. With one frantic kick, she tore loose to run north up Third East, directly into the path of an oncoming car.

Wilbur and Mary Walsh had just finished dinner in their pleasant white frame house across the street from the Latter-Day Saints bishop's storehouse. It was shortly after seven, and Mary wanted to relax with a fresh cup of coffee. Wilbur wanted lunch meat for the next day. "Are you ready yet?" he asked impatiently. His wife gave up the coffee idea, and they left for the store, taking Third East toward the Fashion Place Mall. Wilbur drove while Mary gazed absently out the window toward the Cottonwood Hospital. Suddenly a young woman appeared in their headlights. Wilbur slammed the car to a screeching halt.

Carol jerked open the door and flung herself on Mary Walsh. The car crept along Third East, while the older woman tried to calm her. "You're safe, child, you're safe. It's all right." As she held Carol in her arms, Mary Walsh was nearly overcome by the trembling of the girl's slight frame. Carol's long brown hair covered her face in a sheet and muffled her hysterical sobs. Wilbur peered into the misting rain, but the street ahead was empty.

49

"On a night like that, because it was dark, very dark, we naturally got frightened," Mary Walsh said later. "But when I saw the state this child was in, I realized it couldn't be anything harmful to me. It was harmful to her. I have never seen a human being that frightened in my life. She was trembling and crying and weak like she was going to faint. She was just in a terrible state."

Mary was confused by the handcuffs swinging and clinking on Carol's wrist. Was this terrified young girl escaping from the police? Just then Carol mumbled her first words.

"I can't believe it. I can't believe it," she said and began tearing at the cuffs on her wrist.

"What happened, child?" Mary's soothing, motherly tone stirred Carol.

"He was going to kill me if I didn't stop screaming and be quiet or he would kill me." Sobs choked off the rest of Carol's explanation.

"Honey, you have got to quiet down, calm yourself. You are safe. Try to calm yourself, so when we get to the police station you can tell them what happened. Then they can go after this person immediately."

The car turned right onto 59th South and again onto State Street toward the Murray police station. Carol DaRonch uttered only stray bits of her experience—a battered VW, a long piece of iron or crowbar, a gun, a last-ditch struggle with her assailant. When they reached the Murray station, Wilbur got out of the car to help Carol, and she collapsed limp and disheveled in his arms to be carried in to the desk sergeant. "Hey honey, what happened to your shoe?" Mary Walsh called out.

The sergeant gave her a book of mug shots to help calm her down. Another policeman searched the area around McMillan School and found the shoe. They removed the Gerocal-brand handcuffs, dusted them for prints, but drew a blank. The rain had washed any fingerprints from her car door and the knob of door "139" at the laundromat. There wasn't a VW like the one Carol described in or around the Fashion Place Mall parking lot.

Murray Detective Joel Reit patiently prodded Carol for the facts, but his questioning ended in a frustrating muddle. Even as Reit wrestled with Carol DaRonch's memory, another young girl in Bountiful, only 20 minutes away, was about to have her own bad luck. Much worse, in fact: she would never get the chance to tell her story.

50

Dean Kent suffered a massive heart attack in the autumn of 1974 and was slowly recovering. By the first week in November, Kent had improved enough for him, his wife Belva, and their oldest daughter Debbie to take their first evening out in months—a Viewmont High School musical, *The Redhead*. Posters for the play had plastered the windows in Bountiful stores for two weeks, and the family felt a sharp sense of anticipation as they began resuming a more normal pattern of life.

H. Dean Kent is an executive with Triangle Oil. Belva has raised their five children and spends her spare time helping with activities in the local Latter-Day Saints ward. They own a comfortable home in Bountiful's suburban South Bench, from which they can view the town, the marshy shores of the Great Salt Lake, and the Promontory Mountains in the distance.

As they dropped their son Blair off at the Rustic Roller Rink on the way to *The Redhead*, Belva Kent arranged to meet him there at 10:00 p.m. after the play was over. The Kents drove north on Main Street, which ends at Fourth North, made a quick left, and then turned right onto Second West. They passed the Bountiful Recreation Center and four blocks later turned into Viewmont High's west parking lot. It was 7:45 p.m., Friday, November 8.

At that moment, Viewmont drama and French teacher Arla Jensen, who had just seated her husband in the auditorium, strode up the aisle headed for the dressing rooms. Arla was 24, with long brown hair parted in the middle—a "real knockout," police would later say. The hall outside was darkened, unevenly lit. Halfway to the dressing rooms stood a well-dressed, younger man in his late twenties. He looked about six feet tall, weighed 180 pounds, had medium-length wavy brown hair and a mustache which drooped slightly over his lips. Arla later said he was "very good-looking." He wore a dark-colored sports jacket with lighter dress slacks and patent leather shoes.

"Excuse me, but could you come out to the parking lot and try and identify a car for me?" he asked.

"I'm busy right now getting ready for the play. If you need help, I'll try and find somebody for you."

"It'll only take a few seconds," he insisted. "I just need to find out whose car this is."

Arla said she was sorry and brushed past him, intent on her dressing-room chores. His insistent attitude bothered her.

Thirty minutes passed. Arla finished preparing her students, and as the script did not call for another costume change until intermission, she returned to watch the play. The man was still waiting. She mustered a weak smile.

"Hi, did you find anybody yet?"

He didn't reply, but followed her with his eyes as she walked briskly past him and into the auditorium. When she returned just before the break for her third trip down the hallway, the man with the unidentified car was still there and walked toward her.

"Hey, you know you look really nice."

"Thanks."

"Are you sure you couldn't help me out with this car? It'd only take a few seconds." A note of friendly resignation had entered his voice.

"I'm in a hurry right now, but my husband might be able to help you." Her questioner moved closer, almost touching her, and blocked her passage down the hall. Arla moved resolutely to the side and out of reach. Not hesitating another moment, she hurried toward the dressing rooms.

Debbie Kent and her parents sat on the west side of the auditorium, near the back. The play had been late in starting, and Dean was worried about meeting Blair at the rink. "Deb got up and walked into the lobby during intermission to call our boy because the show was running late," Belva remembered later, "but they wouldn't accept a call at the rink. They said it was too big of a hassle to page kids or get a message to them." Debbie Kent chatted with friends during the intermission, went to the women's room, and in a few minutes returned to her seat.

An acquaintance of hers, Tina Hatch, went to the women's room also, then stood near the back of the hall during the play's second half. She saw the same man Arla had seen in the hallway near the theater's west door. He was pacing about 15 feet behind the Kents. Arla returned from backstage and also noticed him. He didn't stay long, exiting about halfway through the second act by the west door. "What a creep," Arla thought.

The play ran on. Debbie Kent volunteered to go for Blair at the rink. Arranging to meet her parents after the play, she left the darkened auditorium through the west door just as *The Redhead* was building to a finale. "Be careful and hurry back, Deb," Belva Kent whispered in her daughter's ear as she left.

As the final curtain drew near, Arla Jensen, exhausted and relieved, slumped into an aisle seat on the last row. Suddenly the man from the hall, breathing heavily, hair mussed, sat down across from her. The people in front of him turned around, Arla later recalled, annoyed by his labored breathing. Just as the curtain calls began about 10:30, the man with the mustache left by the auditorium's main doors.

The Redhead had lifted the Kents' spirits considerably. In the lobby, they waited patiently for their children: the Rustic Roller Rink is some distance from the school. But by the time almost everyone had left the school, they began to get nervous, and moved outside.

"We waited quite some time," Dean Kent later recalled, "and finally decided to walk to our friends' house nearby. That's when we noticed that our car was still in the west parking lot. It was midnight when we got to the police station."

"And they thought we were crazy," Belva interjected, "because we said our daughter's gone. She had only been gone from ten to twelve. They didn't see anything wrong with that. I said, 'Well, she's not that type of a girl, and she went to pick her brother up and has not returned. Dean has just had a heart attack. We went out tonight for the first time because she wanted to see the play so bad. She would not leave us stranded in the condition he's in.' And the police finally said 'OK,' but they didn't really get on it until the next morning."

Dean and Belva Kent hurried home. Belva called the doctor for some medication for her husband, then began checking with friends and acquaintances of Debbie. Dean used the other line—they had a separate number for their teenagers—but no one had seen her since intermission at the school. Several neighbors mounted an informal search of the Bountiful area in the early morning hours Saturday. Another neighbor woke Viewmont's principal, dragging him back to the high school to see if anybody had "played a joke and locked her in a room." Finally it took a call from Kent to his L.D.S. bishop (a friend of Bountiful Police Chief Anderson) to get things in high gear.

But it was daylight before investigators began a full-scale search of the high-school grounds. Their first real discovery, just outside the high school's south door, seemed curious indeed. What was a handcuff key doing there?

7

By late morning, Saturday, November 9, Bountiful Detective Ira Beal had seen the teletype on the attempted abduction of Carol DaRonch. A pair of handcuffs in one place and a handcuff key in another posed an obvious question. Beal raced to Murray. The key fit perfectly.

Gerocal brand handcuffs are slightly smaller than standard police issue, eliminating the possibility that the key had fallen out of an investigator's pocket during the Viewmont search; yet the key would also open most commercial brands of cuffs—a sad fact which reduced its value as evidence. It was an odd coincidence, even if it didn't prove anything.

After the search, investigators focused on several residents in the apartment house across from the school. Some had heard screams between 10:30 and 11:00 the night before. There's always a lot of yelling and noise around Viewmont, they said, but these screams had something serious and urgent about them. Several stepped outside to take a look, but saw nothing. Police also talked to Debbie's friends that morning, and everyone agreed: there was little possibility she was a runaway.

Police contacted Arla Jensen that afternoon, and her description of the man in the hallway was strikingly similar to Carol DaRonch's "Officer Roseland." The principal difference was the mustache: Carol remembered a neatly cropped growth; Arla said it was drooping and bushy. They asked her to write a more detailed account of her encounters in the hallway and give it to them the next day. That evening, Debbie's picture and a description of the suspect appeared on the six o'clock news on all three Salt Lake City channels and the following day in the newspapers.

On Sunday the tenth Tina Hatch talked to detectives. She assured officers that Debbie had been in good spirits during the intermission and corroborated Arla's description of the man in the auditorium. Police searched the Bountiful area with a helicopter, checking the roads, ditches, and drainage canals from the Great Salt Lake north to the Farmington marshes and into the eastern foothills. Nothing.

With all the media coverage, leads and information began pouring in to police. Every suspicious incident, every personal gripe, every unfounded piece of information was methodically checked. Police winnowed a staggering amount of data. Several dozen descriptions of young men in Viewmont that night turned up—they ranged in height from five feet four to six four, with every conceivable length and shade of hair and a virtual catalog of clothing styles. Investigators chose the best witnesses, evaluated conflicting and supporting evidence, and struggled to form an understanding of Friday's events.

Police checked a hundred "citings" of Debbie Kent. She was "seen" in Preston, Idaho; Cheyenne, Wyoming; Price, Centerville, Huntsville, Kaysville, and Salt Lake City, Utah. One informant said she "knew for a fact" that Debbie had gone to San Francisco and was "involved with drugs." A Jeep posse made a thorough search of every road in the area, scouting the underbrush on either side for 100 yards. Nothing turned up.

Not that there was any dearth of suspects. In the Wasatch Front area, several dozen young men loosely fitted Arla Jensen's and Carol DaRonch's description. Two Ogden men had bragged to relatives about raping and strangling a woman on November 8. Investigators searched the area where the body was supposedly left, but found nothing. The woman, it turned out, hadn't been murdered. The two men were caught and convicted of rape.

A Bountiful woman working in a Salt Lake City grocery told police that an "individual with long brown hair to the middle of his back and a monkey bite on the neck had been in the store and made her extremely nervous." The owner of a trucking company reported a driver who'd stolen one of his trucks as a possible suspect and suggested the police mount a massive search "right away." An Ogden man telephoned his guilt for Debbie's slaying to a Los Angeles talk show, but refused to give his name. One woman from Orem fingered her boyfriend as a possible suspect. "He's always saying Utahns are so narrow-minded and would condemn him for having sex with animals," she informed officers.

On November 15, a week after Debbie Kent's disappearance, Arla Jensen was drawn back into the dark whirlpool. A message in her box at Viewmont High said to phone a certain number in Salt Lake City. "Mrs. Jensen," said the voice at the other end, "tonight is your night. You're next." The line went dead in her hand.

One tip to the police stood out from the rest, a handwritten, badly spelled note whose author had apparently fed his fantasies on late night horror movies. "I just saw this little blond chicken, with short hair," the note read. "Little little love bumps did look so nice. Let's remove them with a dull rusted knife." At the center of the page, the writer offered his own self-analysis: "MENTAL ILLNIS STRIKS ME CONSTENLEY SICK, so very sick. Help me before this happens again to someone that's never hurt me or anyone. God what's rong with me. I don't want to but I just can't help it. It feels so good and I get off on just watching them squirm and jerk and twist." Dismemberment was mentioned in the last line. Police, already keen to the mood of paranoia, did not share this discovery with the press.

In Murray the last clue in the attempted abduction of Carol DaRonch had surfaced earlier that week: a drop of type O blood, (her own was A-positive) on her jacket. There was too little of it, however, to obtain an Rh factor, which would have significantly narrowed the pool of possible assailants. And another disquieting theme—Carol's wavering memory—had already emerged. On Sunday, two days after the attack, Carol was shown an artist's rendering of the man Arla Jensen had seen at Viewmont High. The mustache seemed wrong, she thought. She wasn't sure if "Officer Roseland" had had one at all.

On November 18, Bountiful police got what they thought was their first real break in the Debbie Kent case. The Summit County sheriff's office phoned and indicated they had a Park City man who not only fitted the description, but drove an older model Volkswagen. On the 20th Arla Jensen was shown a series of ten driver's license photos including the Park City suspect, William Madsen. By this time, however, she'd seen hundreds of police photos. Arla was hesitant in her identification. He looked somewhat like the man in the hallway that night, but she'd have to see him in person.

In Park City, at the restaurant where Madsen worked, Arla still seemed unsure. He looked very similar. His voice was a little higher and he seemed taller, but the mannerisms and walk fit perfectly. Not much of an ID, really, to build a case on. Looking to support this identification, police showed

56

Carol DaRonch the same series of driver's license photos, but she didn't respond to any of them.

Investigators continued to work on Madsen anyway. They discovered that his girlfriend owned the VW, that she'd sold it the previous summer. The new owner willingly showed police the car. The front fender and door were two different colors, and there was no tear in the back seat. To further complicate matters, Madsen's girlfriend had dated another man from California who was an incredible look-alike for Bill—so much so that he was mistaken for him by one of their close friends. Detectives decided, finally, to question Madsen directly.

The interrogation proved as inconclusive as the rest of their investigation. Madsen couldn't remember whether he'd been working or on a date. Police did discover he wasn't in a VW on November 8; his roommate had lent him a Jeep Wagoneer that night. Madsen's lawyer immediately volunteered his client for a lie detector test, and he passed easily. Police were back where they started.

Brigham Young University's Thanksgiving vacation began the next day, but the urge to take some time off had already hit Wendy Snow and Fred Anthony by Wednesday, November 27. Piling into Fred's old car, the young couple set out early that morning, climbing American Fork Canyon through the north slopes of Mount Timpanogos. Today, Fred told Wendy, he was going to show her a new trail he'd discovered earlier that month when falling leaves had made it visible from the road. It was uncommonly still when the car slid to a halt in the loose gravel. The air, the sound of a mountain stream rippling under a dense canopy of mountain ash and willow, a bottle of wine (strictly forbidden at BYU by a rigid Mormon code of behavior): it all heightened the pleasure of their day of freedom.

When the trail turned steep, Fred and Wendy sat down to talk, examine fossils, uncork the wine, and make out. But suddenly Fred felt uneasy. He started back to the car, wondering if he'd left the door unlocked, then worrying that they were being followed or watched from the ledge above the trail. Fred abandoned the wine bottle just as Wendy drew a quick, terrified breath.

"Oh, my God. There's a dead chick over there."

The corpse was lying just below a log they had skirted on their way up the trail, naked, covered with patches of mud,

57

and partly hidden by the dense, leafless tangle of the under-brush. A patina of dried blood spread from her head to her breasts. Fred saw her tongue protruding from between clenched teeth.

Detectives with unsolved disappearances in Salt Lake City, Bountiful, and Provo ran for their cars when they picked up the bulletin. By noon the lonely canyon site was full of in-vestigators and police photographers, and by that evening the unidentified-body story had made the news.

Shirleen Aime's first call to the sheriff's office met a flat rebuff. The victim was at least 25 years old and shorter by a couple of inches than Laura, a sergeant told her: "There's no way that body is your daughter." But next morning, the stories in the paper mentioned a ring with a green stone. Laura's birthstone, peridot, was green. Shirleen threw on her robe and ran to search her daughter's jewelry box. The ring was still there, but the coincidence was too close. She phoned the sheriff in Provo again.

Within an hour, Sheriff Mack Holley and the Aimes were on the way to the University of Utah morgue with Laura's dental charts. Detectives asked Shirleen to wait by the door while her husband faced the gruesome task alone.

Jim drew a deep breath as Holley gently lifted the morgue sheet, but he didn't recognize the face and turned to leave. The memory of Laura's riding accident caught him in mid-stride. Gingerly, he pulled out her left arm. The scars cut long ago by the barbed wire were unmistakable. "Even with those big heavy closed doors, Jim let out the most ungodly scream," Shirleen told friends afterward. "I couldn't believe it had come from a human being." Shirleen began preparing for the funeral, and a request Laura had made just before moving to the Olsens' came back to haunt her: "Mom, I don't want to be buried in a dress. Bury me in a nice warm night-gown and pink, fuzzy slippers."

Like the other Utah cases that fall, the trail was cold: no evidence, no leads, no suspects. The only thing detectives had were the startling similarities between the deaths of Melissa Smith and Laura Aime. Both were abducted without a trace, probably held somewhere before being killed, sexually as-saulted, bludgeoned on the head, strangled with nylons (which Laura rarely wore), stripped naked, and dumped with-in 20 miles of each other in the Wasatch canyons.

Gamely, Utah County detectives tracked down the sus-picious characters who frequented Route 89, developing no strong possibilities among them. A bundle of material went off to the FBI, but no hairs other than Laura's were found, no soil samples extensive enough for analysis, nothing in her scalp wounds to tell what the blunt instrument was made of, not enough semen for a blood type of her assailant.

After several weeks, the Aimes began to sense an unexpected stumbling block in the investigation of their daughter's death: competiton. Whoever cracked the case could write himself a ticket as Utah County's next sheriff. Soon one detective was showing up in the morning and another in the afternoon, asking the same questions. Jim Aime, fast losing faith, asked Utah County to call in experienced homicide detectives from Salt Lake City. "If we can't do it, nobody can," he was told. Jim Aime was hospitalized for depression.

Home alone, Shirleen grew angrier and angrier. When other police departments called and asked her to phone the local detectives, she realized that Utah County was refusing outright to cooperate with jurisdictions that had similar crimes. The last time Shirleen showed up for an interview, the detective kept her waiting for two hours before she learned he'd gone to lecture at BYU instead.

The Aimes had moved to American Fork, and Shirleen took some comfort in her new neighbors. Next door lived an aunt of a young woman attacked at a shopping mall earlier that month. One day, at the woman's kitchen table, a terrible sense of ominousness came over Shirleen. The other woman felt it too, leaning closer as her voice grew low and urgent: "Carol was very, very lucky. That man would have killed her if he'd gotten the handcuffs on." Shirleen nodded almost dreamily. "Oh, I'm sorry," her friend said, seeing the faraway look in her eyes. "It must be hard for you to listen to these stories."

By December, the once promisingly linked cases of Carol DaRonch and Debbie Kent were virtually stalled. Calls and contacts with police grew less frequent, less likely to enlarge the month-old store of information. On the 13th the police got the last hopeful word they were to hear before Christmas. A father coming to pick his daughter up from *The Redhead* had parked across the street to wait. About 10:30 p.m., he now remembered, he'd seen a "ratty-looking, light-colored Volkswagen" come from Viewmont's west parking lot and head toward Second West. That's all he'd seen, however—no license or driver, no identifying marks on the car.

The Kents, the Aimes, and the Smiths faced a difficult Christmas.

In Seattle, Melanie Pattisen wasn't any too sure about her Christmas either. She was taking her son to visit her family and her fiancé, Ted, in Salt Lake City. Free from her first, unhappy marriage, Melanie had high, nervous hopes that things would work out a second time. It bothered her that she and Ted were living in different cities now, but she knew that law school, his career, meant sacrifices along the way.

That wasn't Melanie Pattisen's only concern, however. Ever since her friend had returned from a trip to Salt Lake City in October with news of Melissa Smith's disappearance, Melanie's mind had been running, drawing in all her cloudy apprehensions and memories of the past year—the young women disappearing one by one from around the Northwest. And then—she couldn't help but see the pattern—it had started in Utah in the fall. "It's exactly the same," her friend had said, holding up a clipping from the Salt Lake paper, "and Ted is down there now."

Before she left for her vacation, Melanie phoned her father and asked him to phone the sheriff in Salt Lake and mention her fiancé as a possible suspect. No, he said; he wasn't going to get involved. It took some courage, but finally Melanie made the call herself. Detective Sergeant Ben Forbes thanked her for her concern and hung up the phone. He couldn't remember how many names had been called in since the craziness began in October.

Sheriff Pete Hayward's detectives would soon have yet another murder on their hands—dropped in their laps from another state. The word would come from Mesa County, Colorado, investigator Milo Vig, who had had an unidentified corpse on his hands for months. As it turned out, the young, brown-haired woman had been living near Salt Lake City when she disappeared the summer before.

For Milo Vig and his colleagues in Colorado, however, this match in early 1975 wouldn't mean the end of the mystery. If anything, it was only the beginning. The murders in Colorado were about to begin. And there was one person, at least, deeply relieved by the news that the killings in Utah had stopped: Melanie Pattisen. Her fiancé was still living in Salt Lake City.

8

The year 1974 had been a bad one for Milo Vig and the rest of Mesa County, Colorado. Since July, Vig and his colleagues in the county sheriff's office had been beating their heads against a wall trying to identify a corpse found by a family along Interstate 70 in De Beque Canyon, 40 miles from Vig's headquarters in Grand Junction. The body, caught in some tamarack bushes on the banks of the Colorado River, was that of a young woman wearing only a wooden cross on a chain around her neck and a single blue sapphire ring. Death, said the coroner, was the result of suffocation.

Reports of the discovery were circulated around the country, and hundreds of replies from agonized parents and exasperated police agencies poured in. "I never knew there were so many missing girls," one detective remarked. None of the photos or dental charts matched up with the victim.

It wasn't the only mystery for police on Colorado's sparsely populated western plateau. Still unsolved was the bizarre murder of a mother and her infant in a Grand Junction apartment. The killer had left a distinctive trace: seven slash wounds across the chest and a cross carved into the left breast of the mother. And then there was a quadruple homicide to sort through, with bodies dredged up from the Colorado River. The town of Gunnison to the east still had a missing-person report on a free-lance woman photographer. Police suspected foul play. One member of the force recalls the period: "Oh, yes, we have a homicide every now and then. But this was something different—you know, like the way airplane hijackings seemed to come and go for a spell. It was just happening to women then. That's all you can say."

On the morning of January 11, 1975, Milo Vig punched a button on his phone to take a long-distance call. Almost immediately his moon-shaped face brightened with a smile. "Mr. Vig," the caller said, "I think we've got a confirmation for you on that girl you found. The dental records and contact lenses are exactly right. She's Sandra Weaver from Arcadia, Wisconsin."

"Hot damn," Vig murmured to himself when he hung up the phone. It was his first break yet in the case, and he had a right to be pleased. But not too pleased: this Sandra Weaver had been dead for six months, and there wasn't a strong suspect in sight.

Vig, who had been in touch with Utah officials for several months, phoned Detective Jerry Thompson in Salt Lake City. Sandra Weaver, it turned out, had been living in Tooele, 40 miles west of Salt Lake, at the time of her disappearance. It appeared there might be a connection between the crimes in the two states. Vig flew the 300 miles to Salt Lake and began checking around. Sandra and two friends had worked as day laborers in the summer of 1974: an aimless, see-the-world diversion after the first year of college. On Monday, July 1, after a long weekend of drinking, Sandra told her supervisor that she was too ill to stay on the job and that she'd be back in the afternoon. She never returned to work.

Vig and his counterparts in Utah could develop no suspects (everyone at the weekend party passed a polygraph), but something nagged at them. Noting the presence of maggots in Weaver's body, the Colorado coroner had concluded she'd been dead at least five days—yet Vig knew she'd been alive in Utah on July 1, and dead in Colorado the next day. Jerry Thompson explained that the coroners in his state had set the time of death on both Melissa Smith and Laura Aime some days after their disappearances. Time of death could be crucial in a homicide investigation, and the two men had to wonder if they had the facts.

A hundred miles from Grand Junction that January 11, Raymond Gadowski snapped up his daughter's jacket and stepped out of the car. The air, cold and sharp, made his lungs ache, and the stinging in his eyes seemed to sharpen his perception of the view from the steps of the Wildwood Inn. Across the valley, as if across a room, the dark, snow-streaked face of a mountain stared back. Below, strung out like a wandering stream, the lights of Snowmass Village warmed the afternoon dusk. Nearby, skiers streamed back from a day on the slopes, their ski gear clomping and squeaking in the snow, voices ringing out with unnatural clarity in the cold air. Gadowski, a physician, was about to savor the institutionalized rewards of his career: a cardiology seminar at a Rocky Mountain ski resort. He turned and hurried his party inside.

This year's trip from Michigan had an additional air of celebration for the doctor: he had come with his two children and—in place of his recently divorced wife—his housemate and fiancée, Caryn Campbell. "Car" or "Cams," as he called her, was a nurse at a hospital where he practiced, and aside from some friction about just when she might expect to become the new Mrs. Gadowski, their relationship was on a smooth course. They'd even agreed to put the marriage question aside for the week; she and "Raymie" and the kids, Caryn decided, were going to concentrate on enjoying themselves.

An intestinal cramp and a touch of diarrhea slowed Caryn down at first. Raymond's medicine helped a little, and so, after unpacking their things in room 210, she followed Jennifer, Greg, and their father outside and down a flight of steps to the complex of restaurants and shops below. They picked up some ski clothing they needed after dinner and returned to the room early that night.

Gadowski was up by 7:00 a.m. on the 12th, determined to fulfill his obligation to the medical seminar quickly. By nine he had left to meet Caryn and the kids for a continental breakfast and a full morning on the slopes. After an hour or so, nine-year-old Jennifer began falling on the hard-packed snow too often. Caryn, still fighting cramps, took Jennifer back to the room for a nap. Things improved after lunch, and by the end of the day the children (buoyed by a swim in the Wildwood pool and a quick sauna) were whining happily about dinner.

Caryn and Raymond invited Paul Weinstein (another Michigan doctor, who'd dated Caryn before "Raymie" came along) and by 6:30 p.m. the five of them were headed for the Stew Pot, a small, crowded restaurant within easy walking distance of the hotel lobby. Caryn, still queasy, washed down her stew with milk.

Walking ranks next to skiing as the primary means of transportation around Snowmass Village. Carefully developed on the site of an old sheep farm, the village is close to the ultimate in planned resorts, a cunningly interlocked complex of condominiums, hotels, restaurants, and shops. Invitingly intimate pathways and steps honeycomb the place, and at the height of the winter season the jostling crowd of brightly

63

clothed skiers is everywhere. Gadowski, Weinstein, and Campbell wandered into the heart of it all after dinner, peeping into shop windows and shushing the kids' demands for knickknacks. Weinstein, attending the seminar alone, decided to console himself with a copy of *Playboy:* that drew some teasing from Caryn. Her own favorite, *Viva,* she said, was much the better magazine. They headed for the Wildwood Inn, keeping up the banter. Finally, on the steps, Caryn suggested they trade copies and compare. Agreed, said Paul.

Caryn wanted "Raymie" to fetch the magazine from the room, but he claimed weariness after the day's exertion and handed her the room key. After a brief argument, Caryn told Jenny and Greg to stay with their father, who'd planted himself in front of the stone fireplace in a corner of the lobby. She crossed the room and pushed the elevator button.

On the second floor, more doctors and their wives stood waiting in the cold for the elevator. The Wildwood Inn does not have inside hallways; instead, each floor is ringed with outdoor walkways leading to the rooms. Like mountain paths, stairways wind down from each floor to the village below. The elevator doors opened, and Caryn stepped off.

"Caryn, hi," said Dr. George Bond, an acquaintance of Raymond's, "how's it going?"

"Fine," she said, smiling and shivering. "And you?" Caryn Campbell turned and hurried down the dimly lit walkway.

"That's Ray Gadowski's new girlfriend," one of the doctors whispered to his wife.

"Oh, that's too bad," the woman said to herself. She had met Gadowski and his wife the year before and thought they were "a neat couple." Too bad it didn't work out.

Twenty minutes passed, and Ray Gadowski folded the Denver paper shut with a sigh. "Come on, kids," he said. "Let's go see what's keeping Caryn." On the way up in the elevator, Gadowski remembered he'd given her the key, so he had to knock on the door of room 210. There was no answer, and when he returned with a passkey from the desk, he saw no sign of Caryn. Her copy of *Viva* was still by the bed. Locking Greg and Jenny in the room, he began a quick sweep through the bars and lounges of the village. Twice he came back to the room to see if she'd returned. By the time he checked the cardiologists' wine and cheese party in the Opticon Theater a second time, Ray Gadowski was nervously searching the faces of the crowd in the village mall. Shortly after 10:00 p.m. he phoned the police.

Officers Carson and Wieditz drove from Aspen to the Wildwood Inn and took Gadowski's description of his fiancée: five feet four, 105 pounds, brown, shoulder-length hair cut in a slight shag. When last seen, she was wearing a black flowered blouse, flared jeans, brown boots, and a woolly beige jacket. The officers were calm and polite, suggesting that Caryn might turn up before morning. She had probably passed out on a couch somewhere, the officers thought. Gadowski stepped from his room later that night and stared over the wooden rail outside his door. The wind was moving up the valley, and a deep chill was settling in.

In the morning Sergeant Baldridge came to supervise the search of the hotel. Dispatching another officer to search the storage rooms, restrooms, elevator shafts, even the industrial-size trash bins behind the Wildwood Inn, Baldridge sat down with Gadowski in room 210 for a more thorough report. The doctor was badly frightened by now; he'd barely slept at all. But Baldridge had to do his job, wondering aloud if Ray and Caryn had quarreled, if she might have had any reason to run off. Gadowski was forthright, admitting the spat about the magazine and acknowledging their differences about their living arrangement. As for Caryn, he said, there's no way she would have taken off; she was afraid of the dark.

The next day, the area's top criminal investigator, Mike Fisher of the district attorney's office, joined the search. Like Ray Gadowski, Mike Fisher had reached his early thirties—ambitious, respected, sure without thinking about it of the legitimacy and efficacy of his social role. But to those who didn't know him, Fisher seemed nervous, standoffish, diffident; only his friends would have called Mike "sensitive." He was a short man; he moved quickly; he seemed to like working alone.

His first move at the Wildwood Inn was a methodical room-by-room interview of second-floor guests. It was slow work. Fisher had to catch people between skiing and the evening's entertainment. Anything unusual or violent? they asked, slowly repeating his question. *Here?* No one remembered a thing. In one room, a woman from California thought hard. She remembered the evening of the 12th clearly. Her husband and daughter, just returned from a trip to Mexico, needed some stomach medicine, and on her way to the drugstore in the mall she had passed through the lobby. Two men there had caught her eye. But now, Lisbeth Harter smiled, passed the incident off as unimportant, and said good night to the investigator.

By the end of the week, when the cardiologists and their families began floating away from Snowmass Village, Mike Fisher had nothing more promising in his file than an ex-junior-high-school teacher who "knew a lot of chicks in Aspen" and was fond of shouting "Howdy! Rowdy howdy! Welcome to Colorado!" in the bars.

By mid-February the Colorado winter had relented a bit. On the morning of the 17th, a ski area employee was driving along Owl Creek Road between Aspen and Snowmass Village with his window open a crack. The cawing of the magpies seemed particularly frantic and intense off the road, in an open field. Stopping his car, he got out and looked. A woman's nude body lay face down in the snow, toes shyly pointing together, one arm stretched to the side, the other gnawed down to the bone by animals. Two gold earrings—and nothing else—were found in the blood-soaked snow. Caryn Campbell's body was escorted to Denver by the Aspen sheriff.

The next day, before Dr. Donald Clark began his autopsy at the Howard Mortuary, a Denver dentist compared Caryn Campbell's records with the teeth in the body in front of him. There was no question, he said, that the missing woman had been found. Sergeant Baldridge phoned Caryn's brother, a Fort Lauderdale, Florida, police officer, with the news.

By 5:00 p.m. on the 18th, Caryn Campbell's body had thawed sufficiently for the autopsy to begin. Dr. Clark started with the head, slowly turning and prodding the badly gnawed skull. There had been blows to the back of the head, it appeared, and one fine, deep slit on the left ear might have been made by a sharp instrument. A broken tooth was consistent with the head injuries. But Clark, the experienced deputy coroner for Denver, wasn't about to make any hasty judgments. This was "blunt trauma," and that's about all he could say. With the extent of decomposition and the amount of flesh eaten away by animals, it would be impossible to pin down the exact nature of the injuries or the weapon used to inflict them.

The autopsy continued. An examination of the contents of the victim's stomach revealed bits of meat, red and green peppers, and curdled milk—consistent with Caryn's last meal at the Stew Pot and a reliable timepiece: she had died between two and five hours after eating. The acid phosphatase test on the vagina was positive, most likely indicating sexual intercourse. A few minor scratches and bruises on the legs completed Dr. Clark's findings. Sergeant Baldridge sealed several samples of head and pubic hair. Blood and the organs were reserved for toxicology tests. The deputy coroner's tentative opinion was that Caryn Campbell's death was caused by head injuries associated with exposure to cold.

Dreadfully final as it is for family and friends, the discovery of a body opens countless doors in an investigation. Here, at last, is evidence of a murder, offering suggestions about how it was committed, and an exact location where the killer has to have been. But with no strong suspects, Mike Fisher was still tossing out his line blindly. In one attempt he tracked down the rental car of Dr. George Bond (Gadowski's friend who had seen Caryn get off the elevator) and tried to match the dirt samples from under the bumper with those taken from the field where the victim was found. Negative.

The most promising news was dropped in Fisher's lap at the end of the month. A call from the Michigan state police turned up the name of Gary Addison Taylor, a former sex offender and mental patient in the state, who, someone recalled, "liked to talk about the ski slopes." For Fisher, steeped in the cases of other jurisdictions since the Intermountain Crime Conference in December 1974, the name clicked immediately. Taylor was the man with the boxer dog on Thanksgiving Eve in Seattle, the man who never showed up for his second conversation with police about Vonnie Stuth. Mike Fisher quickly arranged a flight to Michigan.

It was not a fruitful trip. There was nothing more to connect either man to his case than what Fisher had heard on the phone. Frustrated, he polygraphed Ray Gadowski and Paul Weinstein (with negative results) and talked to Caryn Campbell's parents. He couldn't have guessed how quickly things would unfold when he returned.

On March 7, 1975, a young Snowmass Village woman complained to police about a man who had been following her around. At first she'd pretended not to notice, but finally she wheeled on him and demanded, "Who are you?"

"I don't know," the man said. "Why don't you tell me?"

It wasn't the last she saw of the stocky, light-complexioned man with the strange blue eyes. The next time he was in a station wagon, coasting along beside her with the door open. "Here kitty, kitty, kitty," he sang. The woman ran off to tell her husband, recalling that she'd seen the man bothering other women, feeling their breasts and patting them on the rear.

The next day a condominium housekeeper offered more. The man was Jake Teppler, she said, a former employee who had distinguished himself on the job by sleeping in the laundry and "scaring the hell out of" another worker. The housekeeper, a former music therapist for the mentally ill, made no secret of how she thought Teppler richly deserved to be a patient himself. "He's very sick," she said, "the kind of person who would go in the corner and jack off." He was about 27, as she recalled, and very well built.

On March 10, Fisher interviewed another former employer of the man in Aspen. According to the job application, Teppler was a graduate of Tufts University in Boston and had worked a variety of odd jobs around the country. He'd only lasted three days on this one. That afternoon a woman reported having been chased to her car by a man fitting Teppler's description two weeks before.

A restaurant manager who had used Teppler's services as a dishwasher for three days in early January added his view: "He was living out of his car and sleeping on the floor. I got bad vibes from the guy. I don't think he's playing with a full deck." A woman employee remembered Teppler too. Scooping ice cream one day, she had suddenly sensed someone behind her. "What about a lay?" he had whispered in her ear.

Finally, on March 12, the sketchy picture came crackling to life. Oh, yes, said the manager of still another area hotel to Mike Fisher, he knew who Jake Teppler was—the one who slept in the sauna and called one of his maids a bitch, flinging her down a hallway. It was a familiar tale by now, but Fisher needed more. And he got it when the head of operations opened the book of employment records. Jake Teppler had worked January 4, 5, 6, 7, 8, 9, 10, 11, and 13, quitting after work on the 13th. Jake Teppler's one day off was January 12, the day Caryn Campbell disappeared.

Mike Fisher phoned Washington, D.C., immediately and requested the full criminal record on Jake Teppler. The FBI telexed back what it had, a spotty assortment of offenses in cluding possession of liquor under age 21, possession of marijuana and a stolen car, and offering to sell dangerous drugs. Two other charges caught Fisher's eye: indecent exposure in Florida in 1972 and again in Seattle on September 8, 1974. Teppler was acquitted in Florida, but sentenced to 180 days in Seattle. Mike Fisher picked up the phone again.

He reached a sergeant in the Seattle police department and quickly filled him in on Teppler. "Check it out," Fisher said, "and let me know." The sergeant called back the next day, heartily impressed with the suspect Mike Fisher seemed to have unearthed from Seattle's own files. Teppler, who'd had a University District address, exposed himself to a policeman's wife, the sergeant reported, and when they hauled him in he was violent and dangerous. The sentence of 180 days in jail was stiff for such an offense.

The sergeant paused. "And you know, we checked on this. All last year we're having one missing girl a month, right? But as soon as this guy's in jail it all stops."

Mike Fisher returned the receiver to its cradle with a soft click. A week ago, on his way back from Michigan, he'd hit a blank wall in a homicide investigation. Now it looked like he might have touched the first domino in a long line. One by one, he could almost hear them fall. His job looked easy now: find Jake Teppler.

The news was no less welcome in Seattle. As of March 1, the investigation of the disappearing women in the Northwest had started all over again. The scene was familiar and innocent: two community college forestry students plodding down a swampy mountain hill. The small, dome-shaped white rock in front of them was no rock. One of the students touched a woman's skull with his toe.

9

The news in Seattle in early March 1975 horrified everyone, yet surprised almost no one. The forestry students had been exploring a section of Taylor Mountain just off Route 18, five miles south of Interstate 90 and less than 12 miles from the site where a grouse hunter had stumbled upon the bones of Janice Ott and Denise Naslund six months before. A power transmission line hummed and sputtered overhead, and the shells from weekend skeet shooters littered the ground. Once they knew what they'd found, the students raced off to phone the police.

Within hours the location was sealed off; reporters and onlookers crowded the police barricades at the end of a dirt road. Phil Killien drove out from Seattle and conferred quietly with Robert Keppel, who was supervising the search. "We're going over every inch, Phil," the detective assured the deputy prosecutor. "Hands and knees and no tools so we don't damage a thing."

As it turned out, there was a maddening lack of anything to harm. Again, as at Issaquah, there was no clothing or jewelry or obvious weapon found, and the remains were even more cryptic: three skulls, three jawbones, and a few wispy strings of hair. It was enough, however, to match up with the dental charts of four women. Lynda Healy, Susan Rancourt, Roberta Parks, and Brenda Ball, strangers to each other, had lain together in the foothills of the Cascades.

Theories and questions multiplied. Did the absence of other bones indicate the activity of animals, or was decapitation a possibility? (Impossible to say, said police. On the one hand it seemed unlikely that animals, known to return to their lairs with the "treasure" of a head, would choose this relatively busy spot, where trail bikers and skeet shooters spend their weekends. But then the absence of any cervical vertebrae or distinctive markings on the skulls tended to discount decapitation.) Had the bodies been dumped at Taylor Mountain separately or all at once? (The four victims had vanished over a period of five months, from widely separated locations in two states.) Where were Donna Manson and Georgann Hawkins? And where was "Ted"?

Privately, some observers of the Washington police work were asking tougher questions about the investigation itself. One who was involved in the case complained about the way the Taylor Mountain skulls were handled. Instead of shipping the bones to the FBI or a similar crime lab, police turned them over to a university anthropology professor for identification and study. If there had been any particular impressions or irregularities on the skulls, he explained, police had just jeopardized them as evidence. "The FBI won't touch anything once somebody else has had his hands on it

70

Unhappily, it's a very common error in a jurisdiction of this size: the need to know quickly overcomes prudence." There were grumblings, too, that the various Washington police agencies involved were bickering with one another instead of cooperating. Inexperience, oversights, bumbling—the charges increased.

It all exasperated Phil Killien. Several months before, the missing-woman cases had seemed like a spiderweb: tenuous and trembling, yet bound to unravel if they could only touch the right thread. Gradually, however, the silver promise was turning to dust. Kenneth Clausan, the man Killien and his friend from the television station had mused about so often, was out of state, disassociated from the Washington crimes. Another suspected killer who had been placed in Seattle during the disappearances was in Georgia now, with no solid links to the Northwest. James Edward Ruzicka, the frail, studious-looking sex offender charged with the deaths of two West Seattle girls—one hanged, the other strangled and buried—couldn't be tied in, either. It was a year for blank walls. In January, Heidi Peterson, the four-year-old who had vanished from her front sidewalk, was found buried in an empty lot several blocks from her house. There were no arrests.

But Killien and the police had not given up on the missing-woman cases. Warren Leslie Forrest, the former park employee charged with torturing the Portland, Oregon, woman in his van and now the suspect in a string of Vancouver area homicides, remained a possibility in the other cases. One of the Lake Sammamish witnesses, while stopping short of identifying Forrest as "Ted," bit her lip and stared hard at his picture. "He does look good," she said tentatively. Finally, Killien had heard about the crimes in Utah and Colorado, and was struck by their similarity, struck even more by what he knew of Jake Teppler.

But until police could turn up some solid evidence on any-one, Phil Killien the prosecutor had to remain in the audience. It was King County's show now; all the bodies had been found within county lines. The first move was a brassy flourish: the formation of a "Ted" task force, an unprecedented union of the criminal investigative teams of King County and Seattle. King County's Captain Nick Mackie, the de facto leader of the police work on "Ted" to date, was named to head the task force.

It was not to be a happy enterprise. With crimes committed as long as 13 months before and virtually no evidence developed at the time, it was unlikely that such a task force could break new ground. A more obvious purpose was to improve a ratty public image: this way, it would look like something was being done. Mackie, tall, blocky through the shoulders, strikingly molded in the face, hosted the regular press conferences.

Behind closed doors, however, some observers saw him as the stumbling block. He was "difficult," said one, "single-minded"; even his gaze across a room—a steady, immobile fixation of the eyes—seemed to exclude possibilities. More likely, the task force was a doomed alliance by virtue of the different approaches of the two agencies. Where King County was generally looser, less bureaucratic, more open, Seattle was conservative, rigid, strictly hierarchical.

Meetings were often edgy and unproductive—which is not to say they weren't intriguing. Along with Warren Forrest, Jake Teppler, and a few promising "Ted"s who drove VW Bugs, a hazily sinister occult theory continued to draw some attention. Its chief proponent was from out of state, a California police sergeant. Officers from the Bay Area had been stumped by a series of homicides dating back to 1969; many of the victims, young women, had been dumped nude in wooded areas. Recently the California detective had been following the murders in Washington, Utah, Colorado, and some in New Mexico, and he had his explanation for what was going on: a single man, possessed by witchcraft, was killing them all.

His evidence to connect the cases was pretty slim. All the Washington victims, he pointed out, had disappeared during the waning, or sacrificial, phase of the moon. And like the women in California, they had all been dumped on the east side of a road. Finally, the officer added importantly, investigators had found an unmistakable occult symbol on the road above a bank where one of the California victims had been found: a pattern of sticks laid out in two connected squares which meant "carrier of the spirits."

In Seattle several members of the task force listened without comment. The unconvincing shadow of witchcraft had passed over them before, when the Lake Sammamish victims were found. Such speculation was eerie and entrancing, they felt, but nothing more. One afternoon in March, however, even the doubters felt a jolt around the room. Midway through a task force meeting, a deputy was called into the

72

hall. When he returned, he was holding what looked like a top-heavy doll on a stick. "They just found this," the deputy muttered, "out by Taylor Mountain." The room went silent; it was no doll.

Perched on the end of a long stick tightly wrapped with twine was a shrunken monkey's head, hair and tiny square teeth intact. In place of eyes were turquoise orbs, and halfway down the stick the monkey's stubby, slender-fingered hands were tied into place. The thing was as heavy as a softball, swaying on its stick as one man passed it to the next. Finally, after it had made a circuit of the room, it was carried off. Still no one had spoken. The detectives and officers, many of them career term men, stared at the edge of the table or at their laps. Papers shuffled. The next item of business came up.

Later that week the friends and family of Lynda Healy drove through a fine rain to the Eastgate Congregational Church in Newport Hills. Inside the shallow wooden dome of the church the Reverend Jim Fairbrook looked up from his notes during the eulogy. There is, he said, "a terrible and unbelievable mystery hanging like a dark and gruesome shadow over our area and the lives of us all."

Julie Cunningham felt defeated when she returned to Vail, Colorado, in the middle of March 1975. She was pleased enough with her job in a sports equipment shop and her part-time duties as a ski instructor, but her vacation had been a bust. The two weeks in Sun Valley with a new friend, anticipated with a nervous optimism, had gone from bad to worse when he happened upon a former flame at the resort. He was not, Julie quickly saw, what she had hoped for. Her voice sounded weary and flat when she phoned her mother long-distance on the night of March 15. It was weird, she thought, but at age 26 she felt older than her mom.

Julie hung up just before nine and ran a brush through her long dark hair. She pulled the door to her tiny room shut and started off toward a covered bridge that leads to the town mall. Between 9:00 and 9:30 p.m., her roommate had said, let's meet for a drink. Julie Cunningham never made it to the bar.

Investigator David Bustos of the Vail police department responded to the roommate's panicky call. Cunningham's well-kept apartment offered no clue, and the roommate had

73

only upbeat things to say about the missing woman: she was well liked, outgoing, conscientious. Bustos began asking around town and got the same picture from some of the men Julie had dated. A second check of her room tended to confirm the belief she had not run away, even granting her post-vacation depression. Her wallet, car keys, and a special face soap for her skin problem were all in her bedroom drawer. Together with the roommate, Bustos prepared a description and bulletin to be broadcast by the Colorado Bureau of Investigation. Five feet five, 110 pounds, long hair, pierced ears, Julie Cunningham had last been seen in a brown suede jacket with sheepskin lining, jeans, leather boots, and a ski hat.

The next step was routine and unproductive: to polygraph any men they knew she had dated. A stronger intuition made Vail police think of their skiing village to the southwest, Aspen. For the most part Vail and Aspen had little to do with each other: the former was a solid, family sort of place, just right for Jerry and Betty Ford and the kids; the latter was loose-jointed, chic, self-consciously hedonistic. But now, reading each other's reports, police in the two towns felt a kinship. The disappearances of Caryn Campbell and Julie Cunningham were dead ringers.

Mike Fisher took the call from the Vail investigator. "No word yet," he said. "We haven't found Teppler."

By April, on Colorado's high-skied western plateau, it's easy to forget. Easy to forget the stinking clank of the coal mines in the energy-rich desert and the smoggy snarl of traffic through Grand Junction and the long, gassy-smelling winter in a sagging wood frame house; for everywhere the mesas seem to rise and swell larger and softer with the fragrant bloom of sagebrush, blue-green like an ocean wave. Denise Oliverson stepped hard on the pedal of her bike, and felt the breeze.

It was three o'clock on a Sunday afternoon, finally warm enough so that Denise could wear just an India print blouse tucked into her levis. She turned off LaVeta Street, whirring past the pickup trucks and tiny houses in the south end of Grand Junction. She was going to Lincoln Park, she'd told her boyfriend at the end of their spat. The park was across the Colorado River, near her parents' house on the other side of town. He figured she'd go there later to cool off. Normally her route would have taken her over a metal bridge across the river and then over an arched bridge across the railroad tracks. But apparently Denise Oliverson never made it over the gentle bow of the Fifth Street Bridge. The last sign of her was on the tracks underneath.

Mildly concerned, Denise's boyfriend phoned her parents on Monday afternoon to confirm that she was still there. He learned she'd never arrived. Grand Junction police immediately searched Denise's presumed route. It was several hours before anyone thought to look under the bridge, and there, flung across the tracks near an auto salvage yard, was her yellow bicycle; her red exercise sandals were nearby. The boyfriend volunteered for a polygraph (and passed) and again it seemed unlikely this was a runaway. No, said her parents, Denise wasn't that discouraged by the layoff from the electronics firm.

Days, then weeks passed. In Grand Junction, as it had in towns across the West for several years now, a heavy weight seemed to hang in this investigation. It was two things, really: first, a sense of importance in stopping someone or something that was quick and skillful and deadly. But second, dragging against that, wearing it down, was a leaden cynicism, a low, dreadful feeling that everyone was powerless—the police and the law as much as a trusting young woman.

Like an echo from a deep canyon, the Denise Oliverson case had its one last, delayed reverberation: disheartening in a way but seemingly inevitable. Her bicycle, corralled by the police from under the bridge, disappeared.

Later there was no reasonable excuse. "Kids had access to those racks," one officer began, and no, he said, the bicycle was never dusted for fingerprints. "Denise Oliverson is still a disappearance, not a homicide," he said.

"It was the only goddamned piece of evidence," her father snapped, "and they lost it." His daughter has never been found.

Speaking before the City Council later that spring, Police Chief Ben Meyers pleaded for an increased budget for detectives. As Meyers's Mesa County colleague Milo Vig knew only too well, Denise Oliverson made it eight known or probable homicides in that area that year, all unsolved.

The Grand Junction police department underwent a change over the next few years. One officer, complaining he "spent too much time writing reports," went to work for a building supply firm; several others followed. It wasn't a big move:

Building Mart is across the street from the headquarters of the Mesa County and Grand Junction police.

In Aspen, Mike Fisher skimmed the Colorado Bureau of Investigation report on Denise Oliverson. He smiled and hit his knuckles on the desk. Ben Meyers, he thought out loud, would be happy to hear what he'd learned from Oregon that morning. The call was from Roseburg, Oregon, about 100 miles north of the California border. "Got a fella here name of Teppler, Jake Teppler," the caller said. "Understand you want to talk to him."

10

Jake Teppler jerked and twisted free of the grip on his arm. "Yeah, all right," he agreed at last; he'd take their polygraph test.

The test approach is slow and orderly: lots of nonstressful "control" questions at first and then, suddenly, something the police badly want to know. He ticked off his initial answers as expected. Yes, he'd been in Aspen in January. Yes, he drove a beat-up brown station wagon. And yes, he even remembered swinging the door open one day and calling "Here kitty, kitty, kitty" to a woman. Teppler glared at the Oregon officer administering the test.

But then this hottest suspect yet in the disappearing-woman cases began to slip away. He'd left Aspen the day after he quit his last hotel job, he said, and slowly driven to Los Angeles, picking up odd jobs along the way. After that he was in San Diego and then in Oregon, planting trees. According to the polygraph equipment, Teppler was telling the truth. If he was, he was off the hook for Julie Cunningham and Denise Oliverson.

Finally he was asked point-blank what he knew about the woman who had vanished from Snowmass on January 12, Caryn Campbell. Not a thing, Teppler said; he hadn't even known she'd turned up dead.

Mike Fisher supervised the double-checking process on

Teppler's alibis. The word from California only strengthened Teppler's claims. Fisher wasn't about to junk him as a suspect for good, but the long anticipated interview with the Seattle flasher and Colorado creep was a severe disappointment. And back in Colorado, more bad news continued through the spring.

Melanie Suzanne Cooley, an 18-year-old Nederland High School student, was next. On April 15 she never made it home from school. On the 23rd, county workers found her body on a Coal Creek Canyon road, 15 miles away. Unlike the previous victims, Cooley was clothed, although her blouse was torn and her jeans yanked down from her waist. She'd been struck once at the base of the skull and then again with a rock police said must have weighed 35 to 45 pounds. Blood stained the sleeve of her jean jacket. Green nylon cord knotted her hands together in front of her. A dirty pillowcase, apparently used as a blindfold, loosely looped her neck.

Investigators from Boulder developed a few suspects, including one who was supposedly sleeping with Melanie and a girlfriend of hers as well. But something about the pillowcase made them guess a "hippie type" was involved. That was it: a guess.

July 1, 1975, was bright and clear in Golden, Colorado— the beginning of a new fiscal year for the Silver State Printers. But by noon Elmer Robertson was annoyed. His daughter Shelley, notoriously unreliable, hadn't showed up to put in her time as a bookkeeper and binder. Her brother Gary was working at Shelley's Denver apartment that day. No, he told his father, he hadn't seen Shelley since Friday, the day her boyfriend Ron had left for California. They were getting into Ron's red Karman Ghia, he remembered, and Shelley was crying. Gary hung up, thinking to himself that if she could really get into transactional analysis, his sister would be a little happier.

But Gary was worried too, and he began checking around. A mutual friend reported seeing Shelley on Monday morning near Tony's Bar. She was with a bushy-haired man in a faded, older model pickup truck. Another acquaintance said she'd talked to Shelley on the phone that night. Finally her boyfriend's brother, a rental car manager, told Gary he too had

had a call from Shelley on Monday night. They had talked about Ron, and Shelley had been giggling. Shelley Robertson was reported missing on July 1.

It was a long wait. Everyone remembered Shelley as a veteran hitchhiker. She could be anywhere, police explained. On August 23, they found her. Two students from the Colorado School of Mines were exploring an abandoned mine shaft near Berthoud Pass when they sniffed something odd—not a chemical fume they recognized. Their hand-held lamp shot a beam down the narrow tunnel. "I see something, something white," one of them said. And then she saw a foot and bare buttocks. "We've got a body. Let's get out of here."

Shelley's nude body, bound with duct tape and badly molded, offered little clue of how she'd died. A beer can and a cellophane wrapper from a package of ham were all that police found in the mine shaft with her. A routine list of suspects included a chronic sex offender in the area, a man in Shelley's transactional analysis group who claimed he'd been alive during the Civil War, a quiet friend of hers who drove a VW Bug, and, almost automatically, Jake Teppler.

The Clear Creek County sheriff's office would have another name to add by the end of the month.

The Fourth of July. A fine late afternoon sun still shone strong against the distant horizon. Nancy Baird squinted out through the plate-glass window at the waves of heat rising slowly from the blacktop of Utah 84. The money from her Fina gas station paycheck, cashed that afternoon, was in her purse. About this time, 5:30 p.m., moisture from the sun-baked Farmington marshes would always catch the sun's rays and cast a hazy glow over Bountiful. Moments later Nancy's boss came around the corner and called her name. It was odd, he thought after checking around the station for her: her car, both doors locked, was parked where it had been all day. Nancy Baird was never seen again.

Everywhere across the West, police investigations had run as dry as the creek beds in the summer of 1975. There had been bodies in Colorado and Utah, bones in Washington, and always the pages of reports, sightings, suppositions, superstitions. After the excitement of tracking Jake Teppler to Oregon, Mike Fisher had nothing new. The Grand Junction police had one victim's name, and they'd lost another's bike. In Vail there was no body at all.

The clues in Salt Lake City had grown progressively more unreal, impossible to read. One woman, who claimed she'd been selling dope to Melissa Smith, Laura Aime, and Debbie Kent, failed a lie detector test miserably. In May a man was found dead in City Creek Canyon with a strip of four-for-50-cents photos in his hand. On the back was written "Debbie Kent." But Dean and Belva didn't know the man or any of the girls in the photos.

Finally frustration turned to despair. Everything had been tried. The Kents, besieged by offers from mediums, half-heartedly encouraged Bountiful police to hire a psychic to locate Debbie's body. It was a merry chase—over the Viewmont grounds and out to a garbage dump near the Great Salt Lake in the Farmington marshes three miles northwest of Bountiful. Again and again the woman returned with police to the dump, saying she could see a body in the water. A dry summer wind beat down the weeds where they stood.

The Aimes, too, were drawn into the world of psychics, mediums, and clairvoyants. Shirleen's grandmother had been a spiritualist. An acquaintance from American Fork brought them to a séance conducted by the woman who had stalked the marshes for Debbie Kent. The first words out of her mouth sent the skin on Shirleen's neck crawling: "Buy Arab some nibs." There was no way the psychic could have known that Laura had ridden Arab to town every year on its birthday for a package of cherry nibs. No way she could have known how to mimic Laura's pronunciation, "A-rab."

Shirleen began scouting the countryside with her sister, looking for the "crime scene" the police so desperately wanted. At an abandoned smelter two blocks away from Melissa Smith's home, she began to shake so violently that the car nearly left the road. A second visit produced the same effect, but the company guard at the smelter wouldn't hear of it. "You must be crazy, lady," he said. "I'm not going to let you in there. That place's dangerous."

In Seattle, where the killings had begun more than a year and a half before, Nick Mackie called a press conference at the end of May. Since July of the previous year, he explained, he and his officers had investigated 2877 possible "Ted"s. A few were still being watched, but a task force was no longer practicable. Its work was concluded. Another group, spearheaded by the mother of Vonnie Stuth, was just gathering steam. Through letters and other public appeals, the parents of victims of violent crime began lobbying for reform of the criminal justice system, specifically, the reinstatement of the death penalty. "At the present time," Vonnie's mother wrote to Washington Governor Dan Evans, "my daughter is a statistic."

On May 29, the grieving mother had an answer of a kind: Gary Addison Taylor was arrested in Houston, Texas, and charged with the murder of Vonnie Stuth. Her body had been found earlier that year in a shallow grave in Enumclaw, Washington, near Taylor's new home. Phil Killien had flown to Texas to negotiate arrangements with authorities there who had Taylor under $340,000 bail for another assault. The long search for the man with the boxer dog was at an end.

But Taylor had been cleared of the other Washington crimes. Around those six homicides and two unaccountable disappearances, strange, conflicting innuendos prospered. The occult theory took a blow when a family of tourists came forward with an explanation for the strange pattern of sticks found on a California roadside. Their son had been left by himself while the others explored the hillside, and he'd represented the family car pulling the trailer with little sticks, one square connected to another—a perfect likeness for "carrier of the spirits."

Yet in June a man named Bill Atkins told police in Idaho he had witnessed a series of cult killings in south King County in 1974. The gang rode motorcycles, he said, and they beheaded their victims. A King County officer flew to Idaho to hear the story himself. Nick Mackie, 65 pounds lighter than he was in January of the previous year, stared straight at a reporter several days after. "There's no evidence," he said, "but I'm not saying we're discounting it either."

Nothing counted more or less than anything else. A cult group picking off victims in Seattle, the city named "most livable" by the national magazines, was plausible, even a welcome explanation in a way: at least everyone would know.

But one officer close to the case suggested a more troubling possibility. "Let's just say we had a straight set of identifications across the board on 'Ted.' What would you have then?" he asked. "Nothing," he said, poking the air with his finger. "We'd know some guy was at Lake Sammamish State Park on a Sunday afternoon, asking girls to help him with his boat. And there's no crime in that."

It was a disturbing truth. Not nearly so disturbing, however, as the man who appeared at the top of the deck before the summer of 1975 was through. A man who appeared so wrong for the part of mass murderer that only wishful malice or incompetent design or the airy web of circumstance could explain the mistake police had made. A man parked in his Volkswagen Bug on a Salt Lake City street. A man whose name was Ted.

No crime in that.

11

Utah Highway Patrol Sergeant Bob Hayward pulled off the I-215 belt route in Salt Lake City and drove the familiar mile up 35th South to his home. Only two months before, he'd been moved from the highway patrol's drug and alcohol enforcement unit to special investigations. As SI's new cop on the block, he was drawing more than his share of weekend and late night duty.

Bob Hayward turned into the older Westside subdivision, where the houses run in neat, short rows—tiny brick and wood rectangles the size of mobile homes. Weary after a busy night, Hayward eased the unmarked patrol car to a quiet stop in front of his home. He'd use the last 20 minutes of tonight's shift to fill out reports. In the background his radio squawked and crackled as a typical Friday night—now the early morning of August 16, 1975—began to wind down.

It must be comforting for Hayward's neighbors to have him in their subdivision—a friend to keep a paternal watch over their safety. Twenty-three years on the force have given him the habit of memorizing license plate numbers, and he knows almost every plate in the neighborhood.

Hayward glanced at his watch: nearly 2:30 a.m. Three cars drove by. The first two he recognized, but the last, a grayish white Volkswagen Bug, bore an unfamiliar plate. A rash of recent robberies had made him more than usually suspicious. Hayward followed the Volkswagen with his eyes as it turned toward Brock Street and headed south out of the subdivision.

Ten minutes later, a Salt Lake County patrol car called for assistance. They'd surprised a group of teenagers sitting in a parking lot with the better part of four cases of beer littering the ground around their cars. Caught with the illegal booze, the group had decided to make a run for it and were scattering in all directions. Hayward pulled around the corner, pointed his car north on Brock Street, and hit the high beams as he picked up speed. Suddenly, 200 yards off, the Volkswagen he'd seen earlier bolted from the curb with its lights out.

Hayward instantly forgot the drunken teenagers and fixed his attention on the VW in the darkened streets. Ahead, its tires squealed through a fast left onto Lehi Drive. As Hayward followed through the turn, the VW was already making another left onto Lemay. The smaller car, much more adept at cornering than the patrol car, managed to stay ahead of Hayward in the subdivision's tiny streets. The chase ran one full circuit around the block until the lead car jolted across the storm drain on Brock Street and headed out toward 35th.

The VW's headlights finally flipped on as the car hit the main road, the bright beams reflecting in store windows as it roared away down 35th.

Hayward grabbed his microphone and called for a backup. He knew that burglars case a neighborhood before picking a target. The VW's return trip down Brock Street had fueled his suspicions. Had his unmarked car been spotted? Why had the Volkswagen rabbited when he hit his high beams?

No match for the overpowered patrol car, the Bug retreated to an abandoned gas station a half mile later. The two cars were alone in the lot, and the first door to open was the VW's. The suspect walked straight for the officer's car. A lifetime of police work made Hayward cautious as he carefully opened the door and swung out, his hand firmly on the grip of his .38. Out of habit he noted the other man's clothes and appearance: dark blue turtleneck, blue jeans, tennis shoes. He looked about six feet tall, medium build, with long wavy brown hair.

"May I see your license?"

Hayward tensed as the man reached around for his wallet —but he only slapped his back pocket; he'd left it in his car.

When the suspect returned, Hayward clicked on his flashlight and read aloud.

"Theodore Robert Bundy, 565 First Avenue, Salt Lake. You ran a couple of stops back there, Mr. Bundy."

"I guess I got a little confused. I was lost in the subdivision," Ted replied sheepishly.

"What are you doing out in Granger this time of night?"

"There's really no reason for me to be here. I was just out driving around," Ted offered, a pleasant smile broadening his face.

Hayward's suspect was the model of casual cooperation. He seemed relaxed, almost too relaxed. It didn't jibe with the high-speed chase around the block.

"Wait here, Mr. Bundy."

The flashlight made a slow arc over the VW's interior. The front passenger seat lay on its side in the back. Up front, where it belonged, a ski mask, brown canvas bag, ice pick, crowbar, and some other tools were piled in a heap on the floor. It looked as if Hayward had found his burglar.

A county patrol car arrived with Sergeant Fife and Deputy Twitchell. Ted continued his amiable chatter with Fife, explaining that he had been to see *The Towering Inferno* at the nearby Valley-Vu Drive-in earlier that night. Twitchell radioed the dispatcher for a confirmation, but *The Towering Inferno* wasn't playing at the Valley-Vu. Ted barely blinked at the contradiction.

"I might have that confused," he said, looking puzzled. "I guess being lost has got me confused."

A third county car pulled into the gas station. Deputy Daryl Ondrak and Sergeant Fife began a meticulous search of the car while Ted leaned against the front fender, one foot cocked behind the other. Fife produced the brown gym bag and began rummaging through it, placing each object in a line on the car's roof—rope, two gloves of different makes, a pair of panty hose with eye, nose, and mouth holes, strips of torn sheet, a pair of handcuffs, a flashlight, and a box of black plastic garbage bags. Hayward turned to Bundy.

"I'm going to arrest you tonight for evading an officer, Mr. Bundy, but I intend to ask the county attorney for a complaint against you for possession of burglary tools."

Grabbing Ted's arms, Hayward yanked the police handcuffs from his belt and locked them into place. Ted was secured in the patrol car's back seat with a seat belt and the

83

doors were locked on either side. Ondrak would call a wrecker for the VW.

Ted Bundy sat straight and silent during the ride to the

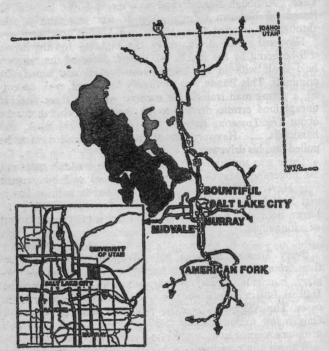

City-County complex in downtown Salt Lake City. The wide streets were almost empty in the early morning hours as they slid past the Metropolitan Hall of Justice. While the rest of Salt Lake lay dark and still, lights from the sheriff's office cast a bright, busy glare onto the street. For the first time Ted really looked at it, at the rows of squad cars, the thicket of antennas on the roof, the men in blue uniforms only half visible through the windows.

Hayward let his prisoner in, and a desk sergeant dispatched the routine requirements of booking—fingerprints, mug shots, arrest forms. The "junk" from the canvas bag was locked safely in the evidence room. Ted kept his Seiko watch and $32 in cash.

"You're charged tonight with evading an officer," Hayward repeated, "but I'm going to request a complaint for possession of burglary tools. I advise you not to leave Salt Lake." Although Bundy's bail was set at $500, he was released on his own recognizance. It was less than a mile through the deserted streets to his First Avenue apartment.

Hayward rolled slowly down the highway toward home, still bothered by the night's odd arrest. Most of the burglars he'd dealt with in his long career looked and acted like criminals. This Bundy was obviously intelligent, well educated, a young man trained for success. And yet there was his unexplained erratic drive through the neighborhood, his lie about *The Towering Inferno,* the panty hose, ski mask, and handcuffs. . . . Hayward's troubled thoughts trailed off as he pulled into his driveway.

There was something else, something he couldn't quite put his finger on. Maybe tomorrow he would call his brother Pete Hayward, head of the county detective unit, and suggest he take a look at this guy. But for now, pulling the screen door shut behind him, it was just a hunch at the end of a long night.

Every Tuesday morning Pete Hayward summons detectives from the sheriff's department's various divisions—burglary, homicide, special investigations—to the Metropolitan Hall of Justice's ninth floor to trade information on current cases. The August 20 meeting promised to be a short one. Only a few minor cases dotted the agenda. Even the city's criminals seemed to have gone on a late summer vacation.

Without the pressure of a big case hanging over the conference, the conversation was relaxed and informal. Detectives traded plans for family outings on Labor Day or news of the latest minor-league baseball scores. Only Daryl Ondrak's account of Bob Hayward's traffic stop managed to hold everyone's attention.

"We have enough evidence to get a complaint for possession of burglary tools," Ondrak began in a montone. "But there's something more here. I thought for a while that Bundy was an armed robber, but we didn't find a weapon. He's not just your ordinary prowler. Some of the stuff we found in his car is obviously for tying someone up. I don't know. Bundy is the strangest man I've ever met."

Homicide Detective Jerry Thompson leaned across the

table. He'd heard the name Bundy before, but couldn't quite place it.

"What do you mean 'strange'?" Thompson inquired. "How is he different?"

"I used to be in the Marine Corps," Ondrak replied slowly, searching for the right words. "You meet a lot of strange people in the corps. I don't know. It's just a gut reaction. This man's into something big."

The meeting ended to the sound of shuffling chairs and voices drifting off down the hall. Thompson stayed in his seat long after everyone had left. Bundy. The name teased his memory. He pushed back his chair and headed slowly for his office.

Thompson flipped open his "suspects" drawer and began leafing through the B's. Sure enough, he thumbed a thin file marked "Theodore Robert Bundy." The file brought back a conversation with Detective Bob Keppel from Seattle almost a year before. Keppel had said: "We had women disappearing all over the place up here this summer and almost nothing to go on. Just a composite I had made, the name 'Ted,' and the fact that this guy drove a Volkswagen. We checked every goddamned Volkswagen in the state owned by someone named Ted—3000 registrations—but nothing came of it.

"We had several anonymous tips on a guy named Ted Bundy and worked a little on him, but he seems clean—a degree in psych from the University of Washington, a good family, even worked for the governor's campaign committee. So, for whatever good it is, I thought I'd let you know that he's moving down to Salt Lake to go to law school. I'll send along a little picture and most of the material we have. It's not much."

So Thompson hadn't paid much attention to his city's new resident. At one point in early 1975, he remembered, when Butch Carlstedt of the Sonoma County sheriff's office called about the missing-woman cases in California, he had sent Bundy's picture and a copy of the file along. Maybe they could use it, he had thought. And he vaguely recalled a conversation Detective Sergeant Ben Forbes had had with Bundy's girlfriend almost a year ago. But since last October, when he had drawn in his breath to read the description of Melissa Smith's body to her father over the phone, Jerry Thompson had been preoccupied with his own cases and his own suspects. Now he leaned back and began mulling over Ondrak's story: VW Bug . . . crowbar . . . handcuffs . . .

86

handcuffs . . . Carol DaRonch! He grabbed the phone and dialed the records division. "Get me a mug shot and anything else you've got on Bundy," he snapped, "Theodore Robert Bundy." A moment later he burst through Ondrak's door.

"I'd really like to talk to this guy Bundy, Daryl. We had a call last year from Seattle where they had that bunch of girls murdered." The urgency in Thompson's voice was unmistakable.

"Sure. I think that can be arranged," Ondrak said, his own voice picking up the excitement. "We told him we were going to get a complaint for burglary tools. I'll go down to the county attorney and see what I can do."

Two days later, on Thursday afternoon, Ondrak and Sergeant Ben Forbes hauled Ted Bundy down to the Hall of Justice and booked him. Their suspect, relaxed and cooperative, stood joking with the officers in the interrogation room while they waited for Jerry Thompson to show. Forbes grilled Bundy a little on the "junk" found in his car; Ted had an explanation for everything. He claimed to have found the handcuffs in a bag of garbage near his apartment. The landlord had given him a discount on the rent for mowing the lawn and carrying garbage out to the dump in his truck.

"I once wrestled with a thief in Seattle who was stealing a ten-speed bike," Ted remarked righteously. "When I saw the handcuffs, I thought they'd come in handy next time. Not that I make a habit of wrestling with criminals, but it would have been nice to have handcuffs."

"What about the panty hose?" Forbes shot back.

"You know, I saw a ski movie once (I enjoy skiing), and it suggested that nylons are an excellent insulation against the cold. I wear them under my ski mask to keep warm." A benign expression illuminated Ted's face. He was winningly handsome, with his straight nose and searching blue eyes. The detectives frowned back at him.

Bundy continued to tick off explanations for the items in his car. The rope and torn pieces of sheet served to secure his raft to the VW. The ice pick and crowbar were "common pieces of household equipment." Jerry Thompson stood by, listening, waiting for a break in the questioning, gauging the right moment to hit Bundy with the key request.

"Ted, would you allow us to search your apartment? We have a consent search warrant here."

"Sure. I have nothing to hide."

While Forbes filled out the form, Thompson leaned against the wall, troubled by Bundy's overly cooperative manner. Usually a suspect will deny detectives a search, or at least ask what the cops are after. Thompson was as suspicious of someone too willing to help as he was of someone totally unwilling.

Ted Bundy's First Avenue place was in the heart of Salt Lake City's "Avenues" district—a melting pot of student apartments and young family homes, graceful old Victorian structures rubbing elbows with cement block apartment houses. The patrol car pulled over to the curb in front of the barn-roofed house where Ted rented a small second-floor apartment. Sergeant John Bernardo and Thompson followed him upstairs.

Thompson paused in the doorway, struck by the apartment's immaculate orderliness. In front of the windows, a collection of ferns and other houseplants stood in a lush tangle. The kitchen was clean, the dishes put away, the sink white—and there was no dust anywhere. Ted's clothes hung trimly in the bedroom closet, just a few feet from the neatly made bed. The search began.

Thompson had reread his material on the Seattle killings and had sketchily researched other crimes in neighboring states. He looked for anything to do with women—names, addresses, clothing—while maintaining the pretense of hunting for stolen goods. He casually copied down the serial number on Ted's white ten-speed Peugeot leaning near the front door.

In an alcove off the living room, a desk and some brick-and-board bookshelves, lined with law books and papers, formed a tiny study space. Thompson busily combed the makeshift office, sorting out several letters regarding Bundy's work on Dan Evans's Washington State gubernatorial campaign, some phone bills, a Bountiful Recreation Center brochure, a Colorado ski country pamphlet. In a drawer full of bills he spotted several Chevron credit card receipts. Thompson had used credit card numbers in an investigation before, and almost as an afterthought he decided to take a receipt.

On the bookshelves, Thompson noted with interest, was a copy of *The Joy of Sex*. And in the kitchen, they observed, Bundy's knives hung from an old bicycle wheel mounted on the ceiling.

During the search Thompson and Bernardo kept up a steady conversation with Ted.

"How long you been in school here?" Thompson said.

"I'm in my second year studying law at the U. I moved to Salt Lake in September '74 from Seattle, to this apartment, and started school. I moved with that old truck parked in back. It doesn't run now."

"Have any other cars?"

"Just the Volkswagen."

"You ever been in Colorado, have any friends there?" Thompson looked up after finding the ski country brochure.

"No, never been there. I don't know anyone there either." Jerry flashed the road map and brochure at Ted.

"Oh. Those were left here by a friend of mine who was talking about how good the skiing was over there," Ted replied, unconcerned.

Thompson began digging around in the closet and found several dark sport coats and some patent leather shoes. Bernardo grabbed the Bountiful recreation brochure.

"You ever been in Bountiful?"

"The city just north of Salt Lake? I've heard about it and have probably driven through it, but I've never been there to speak of." Bernardo held up the brochure.

"Oh. Another friend of mine left that here. Some kid of his or something went up there to some kind of deal."

The search was nearly over when Thompson asked to photograph Ted's VW, parked beside his truck in the back. Bundy shrugged. "No problem." The detective retrieved a Polaroid from the patrol car and snapped the dents, scratches, rust spots, and the large tear in the back seat of the light brown Bug. Bundy accompanied the detectives back to the county jail, assuring them he'd be "happy" to talk with them again the next day.

Early on the morning of Friday, August 22, however, Ted's attorney John O'Connell phoned Sergeant Forbes.

"I've advised my client not to talk further with you concerning the burglary charge. I also understand he signed a consent search warrant and I'm going to rescind that right now," said O'Connell with businesslike authority.

"We served that warrant last night and searched Mr. Bundy's apartment," Forbes replied. "Detectives Thompson and Bernardo got him out of jail here, and he went with them during the search." There was a moment of silence on the other end of the line. O'Connell knew that Jerry Thompson was a homicide detective. Why would Thompson be involved in a burglary tools charge?

"What are you looking at?" O'Connell demanded. "You're certainly not looking at him in regards to the murder of all these girls?"

"No. We just wanted to talk to him this morning," Forbes said.

For Jerry Thompson, denied access for the moment to his first real suspect after months of waiting, the path of the investigation was clear, the next steps obvious.

The telephone index sprang open to the K's. Keppel in King County was the first stop. Thompson had barely said hello before Keppel's voice broke excitedly in his ear.

"We got your mug shots and rap sheets yesterday on Bundy. You'll never believe this, but his old girlfriend was in here not two hours later. She knew Ted had been arrested and broke off their relationship."

Last year, Melanie Pattisen's nervous phone calls had just been a few among the thousands. Now, said Keppel, she had a richly detailed story to tell. And now, after what began a week before as a routine traffic arrest, she would have a very attentive audience.

"Can she give us any dates on his whereabouts?" Thompson pressed, hoping for a tie-in to the Utah murders.

"Only that he went hunting with her father last October 20 in some place called Blacksmith Fork Canyon." Thompson knew it, a favorite deer-hunting spot 80 miles north of Salt Lake City.

"Since this guy's out of Seattle, can you do some background on him for us?" Keppel promised an immediate check and hung up.

Colorado was obviously next. The ski country brochure brought Mike Fisher's name to mind. Jerry had only spoken to him once, but knew the Aspen investigator's reputation as a thorough, meticulous detective.

"Mike Fisher? This is Jerry Thompson in Salt Lake. I remember that you had a young woman murdered over there earlier this year. Have you got anybody you're looking at?"

"We had a couple of suspects." Fisher sounded curious. "But they didn't pan out. Why? Have you got someone?"

Thompson briefly related the sketchy evidence on Ted Bundy—VW, handcuffs, the call from Keppel. "We searched his apartment last night and came up with a bunch of things —a Colorado map and a ski country booklet—but I don't see nothing in it. This guy bought gas on a credit card a lot. I have the number."

Fisher had been this route before. It sounded too good to be true. "Why don't you go through the Colorado stuff again while we're on the phone," Fisher pressed, rolling his chair closer to the desk and shifting the phone to his other hand.

The map, said Thompson, was clean—no marks, traced routes, or circled destinations. The ski pamphlet, too, with its pages of accommodation and resort descriptions, seemed unremarkable. But the Utah detective did notice two little ink marks in the margin at one point.

"I've got something here, an *x* next to a hotel called the Wildwood Inn in Snowmass." Thompson flipped the page.

"Jesus Christ," Fisher shouted in his ear. "Jesus Christ! You're kidding me. We have Caryn Campbell murdered there in January."

Mike Fisher hurriedly concluded business with Jerry Thompson, almost forgetting to thank him for the call, and hung up. For a moment he sat at his desk and ran a fingernail along one edge. He'd had his hopes up twice before: first with Gary Addison Taylor, the ex-Michigan inmate who turned up in Seattle, and then, more strongly, with Jake Teppler, the blue-eyed dishwasher who had a habit of turning up when young women were killed.

Ted Bundy looked like a third chance. Fisher was going to take it nice and slow.

12

Early Monday morning, August 25, 1975, Jerry Thompson leaned over his desk, concentrating on a growing list of evidence he would need to subpoena that week: phone bills, law-school records, bank statements, Ted Bundy's gasoline credit card records. (Colorado law only granted Mike Fisher direct access to one year's receipts of a suspect; Thompson would have to go after Ted's 1974 credit card charges through Utah channels.) The list Thompson faced ran on to a second page. He would walk each subpoena through the complicated legal and bureaucratic process. And as if the red tape wasn't enough, there were the frantic calls from a dozen jurisdictions for Bundy's mug shots and rap sheet. Word had gotten around in a hurry.

On Thursday, Thompson collected Assistant County Attorney Gerald Kinghorn and headed for the University of Utah College of Law for Ted's academic records. At one time Kinghorn had been John O'Connell's law partner, but he had switched jobs, wanting to see what the criminal process looks like from the other side. Kinghorn, known as a "defense-minded D.A.," occasionally butted heads with zealous detectives.

They left the unmarked patrol car behind the law building and threaded their way through the lounge, where several dozen students were pinned to their chairs under the weight of lawbooks. The registrar's office lay ahead and down a side hallway. Thompson heard someone calling his name as they reached the hall. It was Ted Bundy, running lightly across the lounge area to shake his hand energetically.

"I saw your car parked around back, Jerry." How had Bundy spotted the unmarked car? Was Ted, as he now suspected, watching *him?* Kinghorn disappeared into the hallway. An opportunity had clearly presented itself. Jerry fell in with Ted's comradery.

"I always park in my reserved stall."

"I'm sorry to make you work so hard," Ted said, grinning, "but you get paid for it. I guess you're here for my records. Don't look at the grades." Thompson waited for a break in Ted's friendly chatter to try to point the conversation in a new direction. Ted added, "I understand you've been talking to my professors. Hey, I sure am causing you a lot of trouble."

Kinghorn returned. "You shouldn't be talking to Detective Thompson, Ted," he said firmly. "You've retained John O'Connell and he wouldn't want you saying anything to Jerry without him present."

"Look, Kinghorn, I'm a law student. I know my rights. There's no harm in passing the time of day with Jerry."

"I'm not going to allow you to talk with Thompson," Kinghorn repeated emphatically and turned away: that was that. Jerry nodded goodbye and followed him down the hall, fighting back the urge to punch Kinghorn in the nose.

On Friday morning the chair seemed harder, Thompson's weariness deeper, and the pile of pink memo slips littering the desk more hopeless. Inquiries about Bundy were multiplying every day—from Oregon; Sonoma County, California; Rock Springs, Wyoming; Utah County; Vail and Grand Junction, Colorado; Santa Fe, New Mexico—many of the names and places familiar from the Intermountain Crime Conference of 1974.

Jerry balked at the paperwork. A nagging urgency made the tedium unbearable. He was ready to take the next pivotal step. The only survivor of the murderous fall of 1974 had to positively identify Ted. Without Carol DaRonch's ID, the little pieces of the puzzle that had fit so easily together in the last week would never form a picture convincing enough for a jury or judge.

He finally rebelled, grabbed his coat, and pocketed the brown envelope with a photo lineup of mug shots and the Polaroids of the VW. The paperwork could wait. Police protocol dictated that he contact the Murray police department first. The station looked sleepy when Thompson pushed open the door.

"Paul Forbes, the officer who handled Carol's case, is on vacation. Maybe I can help you." Joel Reit had been on duty last November 8.

"I've got a pretty good suspect for DaRonch and I want to show her a photo lineup." Thompson began a lengthy recounting of his investigation and watched as Reit's face grew more skeptical.

"I don't mind if you show her the pictures. I'm sure Paul wouldn't either. Frankly, I don't think you'll get anything out of her. We had a hell of a time trying to get her story straight. She's young and very shy. I don't think that girl has ever said anything straight out in her life."

If Ted ever came to trial, Thompson knew, Carol DaRonch's testimony would have to be solid enough to withstand the battering of some sharp defense lawyer. He had to try.

"Well, I think I'll go ahead anyway," he said, friendly but insistent.

"Sure. Go ahead. Why don't you try her at work on Monday. She's here in Murray at Mountain Bell."

Monday began a new week and a new month. Even with temperatures in the eighties, September somehow always marks the beginning of autumn. At 10:00 a.m. Thompson sat across the table from Carol DaRonch. Pushing a strand of hair from her face, she looked half bored, half frazzled at the prospect of yet another pile of suspect photos. Jerry handed her the Volkswagen pictures first.

"I believe that could be the Volkswagen, but I cannot make a positive identification from those pictures. The tear looks like the one I remember seeing." Carol seemed diffident, ready to retreat at any moment. She looked up uncertainly at the detective.

The pile of mug shots took somewhat longer. Carol had developed the habit of running through them all at once and removing those that sparked her memory for a second look. Thompson knew he was not allowed to prompt her in any way, but it was hard to keep calm when she pulled Bundy from the pile, placed the photo on her knee, and went on. She handed the stack of photos across the table.

"I don't see anyone in there who resembles him," Carol said, apparently unaware of the photo in her lap.

"What about that one there?" Thompson asked, pointing to it.

"Oh. Here," she replied absentmindedly and handed Ted's likeness over.

"Why did you pull that one out?" Carol held it up for another look.

"I don't know, ah, I guess it looks something like him."

"Are you afraid to identify him?" Thompson asked, dangerously close to the edge of proper conduct.

"No. That looks maybe something like him, but I just don't know. If I saw him in person, maybe I could tell."

Gerald Kinghorn leaned back and clasped his hands behind his head. Thompson had just related the story of Carol's identification.

"She said if she saw him in person, she could give us a better ID," Thompson offered hopefully. "Why don't we go for a lineup?"

Kinghorn's many years behind a defense table had made him skeptical of lineups. It was a tense, unnatural situation, not conducive to accurate identification.

"What might work better than a lineup, Jerry, is if we could have her ID him in person. Why don't we get DaRonch and take her up to the law school? If she can pick him out of several hundred students in his natural environment, I'd feel

94

a lot better about it. Why don't you arrange that for to-morrow?"

Carol's trip to campus proved fruitless. Ted was nowhere in sight. She and Thompson stood in the lounge for half an hour before admitting defeat. The police, it turned out, weren't the only ones mapping strategy: at that moment Theodore Bundy was in conference at his attorney's office.

It was up to Thompson and the other detectives to try to firm up Carol's hesitant identification of Ted and the VW. Maybe the August 16 mug shot, taken almost a year after Carol's attack, had kept her from being certain. On Wednesday, September 3, Ira Beal and Ron Ballantyne from Bountiful (investigating Ted in connection with Debbie Kent's disappearance) proposed a photo lineup of driver's license pictures. Ted's license was dated December 1974, a photograph more likely to approximate his appearance on November 8. Bountiful was pursuing its own hectic investigation with some success. Only the day before, Arla Jensen, the French and drama teacher harassed in the Viewmont hallway, had said, "If you put a mustache on him, he's the one."

For the third time in three days police appeared at the door to Carol's office. This time there was no hesitation. Carol leafed quickly through the license photos, returned to Bundy's, and said, "I'm sure this is the man, except he had a mustache."

She was, as even Jerry Thompson would admit on one police report, a "poor witness." But he had what he needed now: a positive identification. With it, the investigation of Theodore Bundy took on a new, self-generated, almost alarming momentum.

Thursday, September 4. Thompson spent the day scrutinizing Ted's telephone records, checking each call with the details of the Smith, Aime, DaRonch, and Kent crimes. Ron Ballantyne marched into the Murray police station at 8:00 a.m. and rescued Carol DaRonch's handcuffs from the evidence room. They would be shipped—along with the key found at Viewmont and the pair of cuffs seized by Bob Hayward—off to the FBI for analysis.

Carol had barely returned from lunch when Ira Beal hauled her out to the car again. Would she come identify a suspect Volkswagen? The two drove by Ted's apartment, then the law school, downtown, back to the apartment, and finally combed the Avenues, but no luck.

95

Friday. Another futile attempt to locate the VW.

Monday. Thompson himself got free of his paperwork and drove out to Ted's apartment. There at last was the Volkswagen, but it looked different: a new paint job, different hubcaps, and a fresh back seat with no tear. An ID from a Polaroid wouldn't stand up in court. Beal, Ballantyne, and Captain Pete Hayward got the bad news on the radio on the way to First Avenue with Carol. DaRonch was indecisive enough without having this thrown at her.

The little group gathered on First Avenue must have made an odd sight: four unfashionably dressed middle-aged men and a waifish teenager carefully examining an old Volkswagen. All Carol had said the night of her kidnapping was that the car had numerous "chips and dents." Now, her gaze was riveted on a long, creased dent in the passenger side.

"I remember this scratch," she said, thrusting an index finger with a long red nail at the dent. "Where that paint is on the front, there was a lot of rust. Also, there's no front bumper and no license plate, so this must be right. I don't remember seeing a front bumper or license plate on the car that night."

"This is the car we took the pictures of, Carol," Thompson said, trying to prod her memory. "So you can see that the back seat has been fixed. Are you sure you remember those dents?" Now that she was sure, Thompson said to himself, she was sure about the wrong things.

"Yes. When I walked around this side of the car, he opened the door for me. I remember looking down and seeing that long scratch there." Carol pointed again. "It looks like the car—except that the back seat is not torn—that I got into the night I was kidnapped."

It was a frantic week in Salt Lake City—and not so easy to make sense of, either. One afternoon Jerry Thompson heard a loopy story in the jail about a killing Melissa Smith supposedly knew about several months before her death. Maybe, the informant suggested, she'd been rubbed out.

But it was no match for the drama of Mike Fisher's discovery in Colorado. He'd heard from Chevron on Bundy's credit card receipts for 1975. One strike would have been something—but three was almost too much to believe.

Yes indeed, Fisher told Thompson, his boy Bundy had been to Colorado. Forget what Ted had said in his apartment. According to the records, Theodore Bundy bought gas on January 12 in Glenwood Springs, some 30 miles from the Wildwood Inn, where Caryn Campbell had disappeared that night. And, said Fisher, that wasn't all. On March 15 he was in Silverthorne and on the 16th in Dillon, each town about 20 miles from Vail. Julie Cunningham, Fisher reminded Thompson, vanished from Vail on the night of March 15. And finally, they had Bundy buying gas on April 6 in the western Colorado town of Grand Junction, where Denise Oliverson had pedaled off on her bicycle the day before, never to be seen again.

Word spread like a summer storm across the West. First Mike Fisher contacted his colleagues in the appropriate Colorado towns, where Ted Bundy was suddenly, unexpectedly suspect number one. And there were investigators in Nederland to inform (they were still looking for Melanie Cooley's killer) and others in Golden (the Shelley Robertson case remained unsolved). And then, of course, the Washington cops would want to hear this news. It was going to be difficult for Mike Fisher to take it nice and slow after all.

Several days later Jerry Thompson received a copy of the credit card records in the mail. Bolstered by the records of 1974 that Thompson had obtained, the detective traced an intricate pattern of Bundy's movements over the past year. Three different license plates were involved—one from Washington and two from Utah—and there were trips around Utah and through Wyoming on the way to the Colorado jaunts. For Thompson's immediate purposes, however, there were still frustrating blanks. On November 8, 1974, he could now conclude, Ted had bought gas near his apartment sometime in the afternoon, cashed a check for $2.50 at a Texaco station near the Cottonwood Mall, and called Melanie Pattisen in Seattle around midnight. In those long intervening hours Carol DaRonch just barely escaped and Debbie Kent disappeared. Where, the question remained, had Ted been?

Shaky as it was, Carol DaRonch's positive ID was in the bag. The next step now was to focus attention directly on the suspect. On September 10, Pete Hayward ordered a 24-hour surveillance of Ted. The results, to say the least, were not rewarding. "September 10, 1750 hours: Subject came out, sat on the porch for a minute, conversation between him and girl continued, he went over and took something from her, went back to the front porch, went back into the house, got a yellow box, small one, came back out, sat on the porch, still conversing with this girl, and started to repair an object which I could not determine what it was."

It wasn't long before Ted spotted the officers' big, plain sedan (the car was a dead giveaway in the bohemian Avenues), and one evening, after they'd set up, Ted circled the block and came up behind the car to copy the license number on a scrap of paper. The two detectives, fuming but helpless, radioed word to headquarters they'd been "made." On the next shift two new detectives set up on the second floor of an insurance building across the street, but by now, Ted had enlisted his neighbors in the cat-and-mouse game. One of them camped under the surveillance window, staring up at the cops, then wheeled and got their license number from the car in the lot.

By Monday, after a weekend trip with his Mormon church group to Bear Lake, Ted had had enough. Camera in hand, he marched straight up First Avenue and began shooting pictures of the unmarked police car, then hopped in his VW and led the officers erratically through the Salt Lake streets and onto the U. of U. campus. They lost sight of him momentarily and turned back to search the area around the administration building. There, standing in the middle of a busy intersection, was Ted, camera clicking furiously as the detectives drove by.

Their final reports were almost comically sober: Ted was "nervous," "extremely nervous," "frustrated," and his purpose on campus that last day of the chase "was not one of study or attending any classes." Hayward called off the surveillance teams.

Four days later, through an ad in the newspaper, Ted sold his refurbished Volkswagen Bug to a Sandy, Utah, teenager. The following week he moved to a new apartment on Douglas Street, with a shorter walk to campus. It was a time for belt tightening: Ted also canceled his Chevron credit card.

From the start, Bob Hayward had echoed one of the basic assumptions of all police work: criminals look and act like criminals. Somewhere, beneath the smooth, appealing polish of Ted Bundy's personality, there had to be another, more violent human being. And, if that existed, someone

98

somehow had seen it. Bundy's phone records, Jerry Thompson had observed, included a number of calls to an executive named Borden in another Utah city. When he called to arrange an interview, Jerry was surprised to learn the man was Melanie Pattisen's father (Melanie had retained her husband's last name following a divorce some years before). The man was guarded and uneasy when Thompson and Ron Ballantyne arrived. There was, he said, an on-again-off-again relationship between Ted and his daughter. He remembered, too, her growing fears that Ted "had some weird hang-ups."

"I don't think Ted's violent, though," Borden quickly put in. "When we went hunting that day at Blacksmith Fork, he didn't even carry a gun. He never seemed to enjoy hunting, although we did go fishing together quite often. I own a mobile home near Flaming Gorge National Recreation Area. I will say this, however: he is extremely moody on occasion. He can be very nice, pleasant, helpful, and then all of a sudden he'll go sour on you. It'll look like he's really thinking hard about something."

"Did you ever hear that Mr. Bundy was arrested for anything?" Thompson suddenly escalated the conversation.

"No."

"We apprehended him recently and are investigating him in connection with some very serious crimes. On the night of his arrest, these items were in his possession." Thompson dropped a photograph of the "burglary tools" on Borden's desk.

"You know, Detective Thompson, my daughter called me a year ago, extremely upset. She had called off their wedding. She mentioned his weird hang-ups and seemed convinced that he was involved in killing some girls up in Seattle. She wanted me to call the Salt Lake City police, but I thought it was a waste of time. Melanie didn't mention anything specific to me, but I'm sure she'll be glad to talk to you."

Clearly, it was time to pay a visit to Melanie Pattisen in Seattle.

On the flight west, Jerry Thompson and Ira Beal thought about the paradoxical woman they were about to meet. Suspicious of her boyfriend more than a year ago, she had called police and asked them to investigate—called repeatedly, in fact. And yet she'd gone on visiting Ted, writing and exchanging frequent phone calls. Was it possible to stay engaged to a man you thought might be a murderer? Her own father couldn't figure it out, the detectives told each other. How were they supposed to?

Melanie Pattisen met Jerry Thompson at Seattle police headquarters on the afternoon of September 17. She was visibly nervous, a thin hand trembling as she held onto her purse, and her smile was weak. Thompson tried to be reassuring, but she looked stunned, this fair-skinned, oval-faced woman who could hardly believe where she was and what she was about to do. They found an empty polygraph room and sat down to talk. Melanie had laid the ground rules: no tape recorder, Thompson only in the room with her, strict confidentiality. She had a cigarette out before they began. Thompson had only one question he really wanted to ask: "What made you suspicious of Ted?"

Melanie launched nervously into her story: the composite in the papers after the Lake Sammamish incident, her friend's hints after a trip to Salt Lake City last fall, a lot of soul-searching when she couldn't place her boyfriend on the days of the disappearances. Gently Thompson probed, wondering if there was anything else, anything specific, about Ted.

Oh, yes, she said, it went back to the fall of 1973 when she'd seen a paper sack of women's clothes in his apartment. On top was a bra, but she was too embarrassed to look any farther down; later, she said, he told her the clothes belonged to his landlady. And there were other things she'd noticed: a pair of crutches and some plaster of paris (stolen, he admitted to her, from the medical supply firm where he worked); an oriental knife in a wooden sheath (a gift from a friend, Ted said); a lug wrench taped at one end and stored in her car (in case she ever needed to defend herself during a student riot, he explained); a meat cleaver. Melanie lit another cigarette. And, she went on, that wasn't even to mention his petty thievery (a bicycle, perhaps a television) or his lies or his infantile habit of jumping out from behind bushes to scare her.

What about his sexual habits, Thompson wanted to know.

Melanie drew in a long breath. He had started experimenting a little, she said, after buying a copy of *The Joy of Sex*. She'd gone along with some of the unorthodoxy for a while, then called a halt. The story was intriguing to Thompson—

100

especially the part about Ted wanting to tie Melanie to the bed—but she quickly steered the discussion to an area that mattered much more to her. Other women. Again and again she returned to the subject of Ted's possible or presumed liaisons until finally Thompson flashed a picture of a woman friend of Ted in Salt Lake.

"Well," Melanie said, "that even puts more icing on the cake." Plainly, Melanie Pattisen was a deeply jealous woman.

"The more I think of it now," Melanie said as the interview stretched to a second hour, "the more I think he's two kinds of people. I couldn't see it before, but he has been using me. He wants seven hundred dollars for his attorney and he needs five hundred dollars for school." Through all her rambling, Thompson was able to pick up just two hints directly relevant to his own investigation. Melanie remembered Ted wearing a fake mustache on occasion, but she'd never seen him in a pair of patent leather shoes.

But Thompson had already decided Melanie, with her waffling and jealousy and ambiguous feelings, was hopeless as a witness—for either side. "I keep praying about it and I keep praying that you'll find out," she said, "and I guess I keep hoping that you'll find out that it's not Ted, that it's someone else. But deep down I'm just not sure. I like him one minute, but the next I keep telling myself I don't want to, that he is involved."

The next day, in a second interview with Melanie, Thompson was far less guarded, keen to find out what Ted knew of the investigation. Not much, he gathered. An acquaintance, who wrote for a crime magazine, had tipped him off he was a suspect in the Washington cases, and Bundy himself had joked darkly with Melanie, remarking, "It's not a good thing to be named Ted in Seattle." Melanie then elaborated on her character analysis of Ted: she could see now that *he* was insanely jealous of *her* activities.

Finally, toward the end of the session, Thompson took control, as he had with Melanie's father, by laying the photo of the items confiscated from the VW in front of her. "And the handcuffs, the rope binding," he said soberly, "what would you surmise they might be in a person's possession for? To tie somebody up, I would assume." It all felt so terribly inevitable to Jerry Thompson, but it wasn't Melanie Pattisen he had to convince. She asked her last question: "I read in the paper long ago that there was a girl in Salt

Lake City that had gotten away, that she'd been abducted and the guy tried to handcuff her to him . . . and I wondered if you had shown his picture to her."

"Yes." Thompson answered.

"And?"

"You put me on a spot, don't you? I can't tell you, Melanie."

"Oh, God."

She wouldn't be in the dark for long.

October 1, 1975. Jerry Thompson and David Yocom of the county attorney's office kept their appointment with Judge Leary to present the evidence for an order to appear. The deposition was concise: a summary of the DaRonch kidnapping for "probable cause that a crime was committed," then just enough facts to connect Ted Bundy to the crime. Any more than absolutely necessary might have telegraphed the prosecution strategy to John O'Connell.

That Wednesday morning's lecture dragged on unbearably, and Ted crept from his seat before the class was over. He had been home barely ten minutes when the knock came. Jerry Thompson stood in the doorway, the flush of congeniality drained from his face.

"Theodore Bundy, I have an order here from the Third District Court." For the first time since Thompson had met him, Ted looked afraid. "You are ordered to appear tomorrow morning at nine thirty at the Metropolitan Hall of Justice for a lineup."

"Oh. Is that all?" Ted relaxed and smiled. "Sure, Jerry, I'll be there."

Dave Yocom arrived early Thursday morning. A 45-minute search of the jail for men with a build and look similar to Ted's produced one inmate. The only other ready pool of bodies was the sheriff's deputies. They would have to do.

Just after nine, Lieutenant Ron Ballantyne arrived with Tina Hatch (the Viewmont High student who had watched the second half of *The Redhead* from behind the last row) and Arla Jensen. Thompson and Carol DaRonch, forcing a relaxed look, followed a minute later. The lineup room filled quickly—Pete Hayward, Ira Beal, John O'Connell and his partner Bruce Lubeck, a court reporter. A bad joke, nervous shuffling, coughing, the squeaking of shifted seats, the barely audible intensity of whispered conversations betrayed the underlying tension in the room.

102

Yocom marched in, and as if a switch had been flipped, the proceedings began. O'Connell offered a pro forma objection to Ted's presence, the ritual first skirmish between prosecution and defense.

"Each individual will have a number," Yocom explained to the three women seated several spaces apart in the first row. "If you recognize anyone, write that number on your slip of paper. If you don't, leave it blank. Put your name on top."

Between suspects and witnesses there is only a thick sheet of glass. The runway, unreal as a stage under the spotlights, shows eight places with lines for marking height. "Can they see us?" Carol was trembling. "The glare from the light prevents that." Yocom's voice was low and reassuring. He nodded to the jailer, and eight casually dressed men walked stiffly to their assigned spots.

As number seven turned, Jerry Thompson shot Captain Hayward an unhappy glance. Ted Bundy's wavy brown hair was clipped short, his part moved to the other side. He looked like a different person.

After a minute Yocom ordered each man to repeat the same phrase, and the lineup moved to its final segment. "Number one. Step forward please. Turn to the left. Now to the right. Walk to the end of the platform and return."

The runway emptied and only the soft scratching of pencils disturbed the silence. Finally Yocom collected the three slips of paper as Carol, Tina, and Arla filed out of the room. All three women had scrawled a "7" on their slips.

Downstairs, the county attorney's modest office was crowded. Six weeks of investigation had to be debated and distilled. Should they bring a charge? Carol DaRonch's lineup ID had almost tipped the scales. But she'd seen photos of Ted twice before, and O'Connell was sure to contest her identification at any trial. Dave Yocom wanted to hear her reason for choosing Bundy. Carol looked around at the crowd of lawyers and police. "I picked number seven," she said, "because that was the man who tried to kidnap me."

Judge Cowans signed the complaint. Theodore Robert Bundy was charged with aggravated kidnap and attempted criminal homicide. Bail, thanks to the county attorney's chilling arguments, was set at $100,000. The story that police investigators across the West had been sharing since August suddenly went public. Ted Bundy was overnight headline news.

Earlier that week, on the afternoon of Sunday, September 28, a pretty, brown-haired, green-eyed woman named Katherine Kelley started on a hike up the Bear Creek Canyon Road near the town of Telluride in southwestern Colorado. Several days later, when she had not returned, a familiar scenario was played out again: search teams, a proffered reward, tedious interviews with the woman's friends and acquaintances. Shortly after, without a speck of evidence to link him to the crime (and a high probability he had not slipped out of state without Salt Lake City police noticing), Ted Bundy was added to the list of suspects.

Ted, in fact, was on everyone's list by mid-October. Frustrations in dozens of western police departments boiled over, and the name of Theodore Robert Bundy was automatically linked to the murder of young women everywhere. One phase of Ted Bundy's life has come to an unalterable end.

He himself would put it in a letter one day: "In short, when I first came under attack by the legal system, I was twenty-eight, a bachelor, a law student, engaged to be married, and enjoying the brightest period of my life. I had come to terms with many things," he went on, "and one thing I had come to terms with long ago was the circumstances of my birth."

13

In September 1946 a young Philadelphia woman out of high school, seven months pregnant and unmarried, registered at the Elizabeth Lund Home for Unwed Mothers in Burlington, Vermont. Sixty-three days later she gave birth to a blue-eyed boy, naming him Cowell, her maiden name—Theodore Robert Cowell. The boy's father, a sailor in his early thirties, was not around to help choose the name.

Louise Cowell brought the baby back to her parents' comfortable home in the Roxborough section of northwest Philadelphia. There, with the warmth and support of her parents and two sisters, she resolved to apply herself to the joys and obligations of motherhood. It was no overwhelming chore, she later said: "He was a good baby."

But a working-class Philadelphia neighborhood in the late 1940's didn't offer the most tolerant and understanding atmosphere for an unwed mother. "It was terribly difficult at times," a relative living at the time on the West Coast recalled. "We didn't know Louise very well then, but we sure thought she deserved a fresh start, a new beginning." Late in 1950 Louise accepted the invitation. In October, just before Ted's fourth birthday, she changed her son's name to Theodore Robert Nelson in a Philadelphia court, packed her things, and moved across the country to Tacoma, Washington. Nelson was a neutral name chosen at random: no one would know her as a Cowell; no one would guess her past.

Louise and Ted moved in with the sympathetic relatives, and shortly after, Louise found work as a secretary. She'd found a church she liked too: the First United Methodist. It was there, at an evening social, that she met John C. Bundy —"Johnnie," everyone called him, a short, bashful man with a winning smile. Johnnie worked hard as a cook at the Madigan Army Hospital. Within six months Louise found the solid second start she was hoping for. On May 19, 1951, Louise and Johnnie were married at the Methodist church. Ted, 4½ years old, stood up in his pew surrounded by new faces. After the ceremony, Johnnie officially adopted the boy and changed his name for the third and final time. He was Theodore Robert Bundy now, his mother said.

The Bundys moved several times in the first years of their marriage, a difficult and sometimes lonely period of readjustment for Ted. "Life was not as sweet," he would later recall, "but not a nightmare." By Ted's third year in the public schools, the family had settled in a house on Skyline Drive in Tacoma's West End, not far from a graceful suspension bridge that stretches across the waters of Puget Sound. The air was clean, washed by the rains from October through May, and in the spring, a dense tangle of Scotch broom bloomed a brilliant yellow near the house. It was a boy's jungle, full of paths and secrets, and Ted had his friends to explore it with: Bert, whose birthday was the same as Ted's, across the street; Michael down the block. True, Ted suffered the worries and oppressions of most elementary-school kids—a father who sometimes made his point with an open hand across the rear, a second-grade teacher who "put the fear of God in you"—but already he had struck friends and relatives as bright, physically active, a promising and thoroughly likable boy. Louise and Johnnie Bundy couldn't have been prouder.

Brothers and sisters came along to enlarge the household: Linda (next oldest after Ted), then Glenn, Sandra, and finally Richard, the little brother for whom Ted developed a strong and protective attachment. To outsiders the family presented a low profile: quiet, noncombative, unremarkable.

By junior high Ted was just like his peers: in and out of the house, preoccupied (without thinking about it) with growing up. He had not grown especially close to his stepfather; nor, for that matter, did he have much time for searching conversations with his mother. He played football in fifth and sixth grade, then joined the track team at Hunt Junior High, placing third in the hurdles once. He was too short for basketball, however, and his first foray into politics—a bid for student body vice-president—was unsuccessful.

"I began," Ted later explained, "to restrict myself to the friends in my neighborhood" instead of the "broader social schemes." To those friends Ted was one of the gang, a follower, a believer—a portrait deepened here and there by flaws and humanizing touches: a habit of carrying dry dog food in his pocket to snack on, a mock sword fight suddenly turning serious, a "wild look" in Ted's eyes during a footrace. In 1961 he enrolled at Wilson High.

A quiet and undemonstrative student, Ted had developed a strongly selective kind of motivation and enthusiasm. "He wasn't an egghead," his mother would remember, "but if he had a mind to do it, he'd stay up all night to get a special notebook done." Overall, his high-school record was good but unremarkable (a 3.02 average out of 4.0). When it was something that mattered to Ted, however, he left an indelible mark. "Ted was highly motivated, personable, curious, a student you liked to have," said the teacher of an honors political science class at Wilson. "But more than that he had the air of a concerned scholar, most unusual for a high-school kid."

Ted made no secret of his mounting ambitions at home. He would go to college and then to law school. He would enter politics. He would be elected to office. He had his heroes, like Senator J. William Fulbright, and his early political ideology, though conventionally Republican and conservative, had a visionary personal cast to it. Ted Bundy wanted to do something about America.

His participation in the less exalted life and society of Wilson High was minimal. Since junior high he had tried most activities once, then moved on: little-league baseball and football, scouts, student council, the high-school cross-country team. His entrepreneurial activities were brief but resourceful and successful: from baby-sitting to a lawn "company" to a scheme with friends for forging lift tickets at a nearby ski slope.

Comfortable and secure with old friends, he spent his evenings studying, idly cruising Sixth Avenue, drinking a little. He dated sporadically, hardly at all by his senior year. He'd had some "social deficits," he later explained, but by graduation Ted felt perfectly comfortable with girls, even if he couldn't count a steady girlfriend among them.

The 1965 Wilson High yearbook was dedicated to Winston Churchill and Herbert Hoover and carried a large portrait photograph of the state's newly elected, idealistic Governor Daniel Evans. With his eye on college in the fall, Ted took a well-paying summer job as a forklift operator, bought a 1933 Plymouth coupe with some of his savings, and enrolled at the University of Puget Sound, a private university in Tacoma, that fall.

Living at home and attending classes at UPS grew confining. Convinced that a coming rapprochement between the U.S. and Red China would open important political and diplomatic opportunities in the next decade, Ted turned his attention to the Asian studies courses at the University of Washington, 50 miles to the north in Seattle. He was accepted for transfer in September 1966, and after another summer on the forklift, Ted moved to McMahon Hall, a dormitory in Seattle, and enrolled for a full slate of Chinese language and history classes.

Years later Ted would tell a psychiatrist that his first year at college was marked by a "longing for the beautiful coed," but, as he said, "I didn't have the skill or social acumen to cope with it." At the university, that all changed. Ted met a pretty, older student named Linda, from a well-to-do Los Angeles family. His first serious relationship with a woman was under way. Theirs was a stormy courtship, "very intense," as Ted put it, occasionally marked unhappily by the disparity in their backgrounds and resources. Her money was a source of intimidation to him at times.

107

Ted's grades in intensive Chinese were good enough to get him accepted for summer study at Stanford's prestigious Chinese Institute, but that was an end rather than a beginning. He had soured on Chinese, and when he returned to the University of Washington in the fall of 1967, Ted was untracked academically. Following a disastrous bout with urban planning and sociology courses, he withdrew during the winter 1968 quarter. Ted dropped out, a relative later said, "because he needed to get his head together."

He began by traveling: to California, to Colorado for some skiing, back to Philadelphia (at one point, he later said, he had it in mind to locate his real father). On his way west again Ted visited relatives in the South, delighted and impressed by their stories of European travel. Law school, Ted told his uncle one night; he thought he wanted to attend law school. In the meantime Ted had to support himself with a string of odd jobs back in Seattle—parking cars at a yacht club, stacking boxes at a Safeway, busing dishes at a hotel, selling shoes. It was a dark, futureless time for him; as Ted later put it, "It became evident that I would have to thoroughly realign my priorities before I could continue my education."

And, just as he had planned it, Ted had slipped his foot onto the bottom rung of the political ladder, serving as Seattle chairman and assistant state chairman of the New Majority for Rockefeller. At the Miami Republican convention, Ted was an unhappy witness as Dan Evans went down with the sinking Rockefeller ship. That fall Ted worked as a driver for Arthur Fletcher (an unsuccessful black candidate for lieutenant governor), then took off again for Philadelphia, determined to spend some time in the urban core. In January 1969 he enrolled in classes at Temple University and arranged to assist in an inner-city high-school social studies class. Ted Bundy's politics were more modest and reserved than many of his peers', but like his contemporaries in the late sixties he saw America's dilemma in terms of personal mission.

It lasted five months. By September, after another swing through California (to visit Linda) and a tough summer job in a lumber mill, Ted had returned to Seattle's University District, where he found a reasonably priced room in a well-kept house on 12th Northeast. It felt like home, this broad, green campus thronged with fair-haired students.

Years later he would rhapsodize about the area, recalling the pleasures of window-shopping, of browsing the rows of a well-stocked drugstore at the corner of 45th and University Way. "I love the district. I fancy myself a connoisseur, along with several million other people who grew up away from home amid the temptations of the district. I have never become so attached to any other place that I lived. I never felt so totally a part of the ecosystem."

Once again Ted's sure touch for finding jobs paid off, first at a legal messenger service and then at a medical supply firm. But neither job, nothing that happened that fall, would matter as much to Ted Bundy as a conversation he struck up in a bar one night. She was small, soft-spoken, rather plain-featured with a prominent nose; but her long hair framed an earnest, open expression, and they liked each other right away. She worked in an office downtown, she said, and had gone to school in Utah, majoring in home economics. Later Ted would learn that she was divorced and had custody of a child and that her last name was Pattisen, Melanie Pattisen. He asked for her phone number.

"We began to see a lot of Ted and Melanie right away," Louise remembered. "I liked her. We all did. She had a child, and you could see she was ready to get married again." Ted spent Christmas 1969 at her parents' house, and they made another trip together the following summer, after Ted re-enrolled at the University of Washington.

This time he seemed to know what he was after, switching his major to psychology and doing well in his course work from the start. He impressed his professors and startled old friends. "I hadn't seen him since high school," said a former classmate, "and I was really struck. He walked with a confident air; he had a new hairstyle. I remember thinking to myself, 'Jesus, this guy really knows where he's going.'" Another acquaintance, then a UW law student, saw more than a swagger: "Both of us were part of a breed: eager, young, fairly aggressive politicos. But there was something aristocratic, a note of character in Ted. In his very civility there was something there you couldn't anticipate. He was an individual operating within a system—no way he'd be suckered in."

Successful as he was in the classroom, Ted had his misgivings about the study of psychology. "It was an interesting, interesting study," he later said, "but it just didn't offer

109

enough. Really the state of the art is so low. What can you know from your fellow human being, aside from what he does overtly? You try to get inside his head, and it's a difficult task." There's a built-in bias in professional psychiatric work, he once said: "You'd rather label a guy sick than not because if he ever goes and does anything, then if you said he's well the burden's on you."

Ted Bundy's views would have an eerie irony one day. In 1972, when he graduated from the University of Washington—bright, handsome, articulate, swelling with promise—no one would have dreamed of calling him sick or thinking him a potential burden on society. If anything, he symbolized society's hope. That spring he prepared his applications to law schools around the country.

His overall academic record and test scores were not outstanding, but the testimony of his professors was striking. "He conducts himself more like a young professional than a student," wrote one associate professor of psychology. "I would place him in the top one percent of the undergraduates with whom I have interacted." Said a colleague, "It is clear that other students use him as a standard to emulate. . . . His personal characteristics are all of the highest standards. Ted is a mature young man who is very responsible and emotionally stable (but *not* emotionally flat as many students appear—he does get excited or upset appropriately in various situations) . . . I am at a loss to delineate any real weakness he has."

And Bundy lobbied on his own behalf, enclosing a lengthy personal statement with his application. "To counsel a client; to arbitrate questions between individuals and institutions; to search for the facts; and ultimately, to provide for the orderly resolution of conflict and the avoidance of 'violence'—these activities have attracted me to a program of legal study," he wrote. "I see the legal profession engaged in a quest for order." For now, however, the glowing words weren't enough: Ted was rejected by the law schools.

With his experience as a telephone counselor for a Seattle crisis hot line, he landed a summer internship at Harborview Hospital's psychiatric counseling center. It was discouraging work; he had trouble with some of the clients. One afternoon a fellow counselor named Joan observed Ted with an older woman patient. After 15 minutes of watching him correct the patient's grammar and use words she didn't understand,

Joan confronted Ted about his cold, callous style of counseling. They quarreled hotly in the hallway, but Joan was impressed as well as irritated with Ted. A modest summer romance began—trips to Chinatown, the waterfront, late night visits to her apartment on his bicycle.

It was his smile she liked—quick and warm—and his tireless flow of altruistic political ideologies. "He was charming, witty, suave, and very much the I've-got-it-all-together type." He was often low on cash too: Joan recalled paying for most of their dates and lending him her car on occasion. Their relationship ended abruptly one night in his apartment. The phone rang, and after several minutes of murmuring in the next room, Ted stood up in front of Joan and asked her to leave. "That was Melanie," he said. "She's threatening to jump off a bridge."

Despite the law-school disappointment and the pressures of a jealous girlfriend, Ted's star was steadily rising. In September 1972 he signed on with the Committee to Reelect Dan Evans; it was to be a brief, notorious episode. Bundy's assignment was to "monitor and analyze the public statements" of Evans's opponent, Albert Rosellini. According to campaign associates, Ted was a diligent worker, traveling around the state to pass himself off as a college student or newspaper reporter, rising from the crowd (occasionally with a fake mustache) to ask Rosellini embarrassing questions. More than once, some recall, Bundy managed to slip into his questions names of women that might prove especially uncomfortable for Rosellini to handle in public. "You know," said one who remembers him, "I don't think anyone knew exactly what Ted was doing but Ted."

Whatever his activities, Ted's assignment was in character with the election of 1972, marked by a poorly documented (but perfectly timed) story about Rosellini's supposed connections to some dubious characters in Honolulu. Ted's introduction to serious politics was of the "hardball" variety. He may have been "coarsened and diminished" by the experience, as some friends said, but Theodore Bundy's migration from the dewy idealism of the late sixties to the cynical pragmatism of the seventies only mirrored the country at large.

In October, on the strength of a recommendation from a friend and professor at the University of Washington, Seattle's Crime Prevention Advisory Commission hired Ted. His duties included a review of the state hitchhiking law and some work on a white-collar crime project. He became familiar with police reports on violent assaults in connection with another commission project. His associates were impressed enough with Ted to make him a finalist for the directorship, but when he lost in January 1973, he moved on.

Another reference landed him an immediate job with the King County Law and Justice Planning Office. There, from January through April, he worked on a report on recidivism and the effectiveness of correctional institutions. The depressing conclusion—that the prisons had virtually no effect on the recidivism rates—may have gotten to Ted. After filing several intermediate reports, he failed to hand in the final one, which cost him a substantial portion of his grant.

In February 1973, when he reapplied to the University of Utah College of Law, Ted Bundy already had more practical legal know-how under his belt than most first- or second-year law students and more direct familiarity with police procedures than many graduates. (Ted, himself, in fact, apprehended a purse snatcher at a shopping mall one day.) This time he appended a brief statement of purpose to his list of credentials. "My life-style requires that I obtain knowledge of the law and the ability to practice legal skills," he wrote. "I intend to be my own man. It's that simple.

"I could go on at length to explain that the practice of law is a lifelong goal, or that I do not have great expectations that a law degree is a guarantee of wealth and prestige. The important factor, however, is that law fulfills a functional need which my daily routine has forced me to recognize.

"I apply to law school because this institution will give me the tools to become a more effective actor in the social role I have defined for myself."

In a stack of vague and timid applications, this one must have stood out—confident, direct, almost arrogantly self-assured. But it was coming from an unusual applicant, a young man blessed with intelligence, good looks, experience, and most striking of all, an unwavering sense of personal direction. With his application bolstered by more strong letters of recommendation (including one from Governor Evans), Ted's acceptance came within two months.

It was puzzling, then, when Ted wrote back to the admissions office at the end of the summer. He was sorry, he said, but he wouldn't be able to attend classes that fall. An invented automobile accident was his excuse, but Ted Bundy was staying in Seattle for another year.

The following spring, 1974, Ted Bundy made up his mind a third time to apply for admission to the University of Utah College of Law. His record was stronger than ever. Since September 1973 he had held an impressive, well-paid job as assistant to the Washington State Republican chairman. "A believer in the system," his boss said of Ted, "a believer in starting at the bottom and working up, a believer in the importance of elected officials." The admissions office promptly informed Ted he was welcome to begin classes at the U. of U. in the fall.

But Ted Bundy also had his worries and aggravations that spring. Not the least of them were his night classes at the University of Puget Sound Law School, which he'd attended fitfully since winter quarter. The school was in its first year of operation, and Ted didn't especially like or respect what he saw of it; several classmates would remember him grousing over a beer more than once at the Creekwater Dispensary. Finally, quarreling with a professor over credit on a paper and justifiably uneasy about upcoming exams, Ted withdrew from UPS before the year was out, neglecting to mention this phase of his education on his Utah application.

In May 1974 Ted began a summer job with the State Department of Emergency Services in Olympia, a 60-mile drive in his tan VW from the rooming house in Seattle. He quickly impressed his colleagues with a marathon work session to re-create some files that had been discarded. But it was just a summer job; Ted was thinking of the future. "He felt politics and the law were the proper way to handle things," a co-worker said. "Most of his attention was on law school. He was very much looking forward to it. He wanted to be out of the area and experience something else."

In the meantime Ted's social life began to trouble him more than ever. He had known Melanie Pattisen now for more than five years, and for some time they'd been talking about marriage. Melanie was anxious to move back to Utah, but for the time being she would be in Seattle while Ted moved to Salt Lake City. Meanwhile, Ted hadn't exactly put Linda, his wealthy first love, out of mind. She and Ted skied together in late 1973, and at one point, Ted later admitted, he was engaged to both women at once.

113

The news was bad in 1974—Watergate and the missing women in the Northwest. In a way, it all seemed to parallel Melanie Pattisen's gnawing uneasiness. She was unsure about her future, unsure if she and Ted could make a go of it. And ever since learning about his fling with Joan from the hospital in 1972, she was increasingly unsure about Ted. Having other girlfriends was one thing—a big thing to Melanie, who, said those who knew her, was driven by jealousy and possessiveness. But there were other things about Ted that made her wonder: his stealing and lying and that irksome habit he had of jumping out from behind bushes to scare her. One time, she remembered now, she had caught him with a pair of surgical gloves in his pocket. And that wasn't all . . .

Finally, in the summer of 1974, he seemed to lose interest in her sexually. Was there something wrong with her? Or him? What?

For Ted, compared to Melanie's crabbing and depression, the irritation of his co-workers in Olympia teasing him lightly about driving a Volkswagen when your name was Ted in that fearful summer in the Northwest seemed minor. Absolutely forgettable.

And the summer itself in Seattle has a way of clearing out worries, sweeping them away like so many cobwebs. Things seem clear and precise in the steady sunlight.

Ted and Melanie got out in the good weather for his last weeks in the Northwest, bicycling around Green Lake, riding the rivers in a bright yellow raft she had given him as a graduation present. On July 7, Ted went alone to the beach at Lake Sammamish State Park, where, a week later, Janice Ott would unroll her towel and Denise Naslund would wander to a rest room a final time. In September Ted packed his truck full and drove off, then returned for his VW Bug.

His new life in Utah was about to begin, and Melanie said goodbye a second time. Before she saw him again, she would have placed her calls to the police.

Half-empty boxes and piles of books still littered the floor of Ted Bundy's apartment when law classes at the University of Utah began in September 1974. But his neighbors at 565 First Avenue, the usual heterogeneous collection of college students, misfits, and young working people still on the fringes of university life, didn't mind. The Avenues was much like Seattle's University District, and Ted Bundy felt right at home. It wasn't long before he could count several neighbors as friends.

The landlord gave Ted a discount on the rent for mowing the lawn, collecting the rent checks, and carrying garbage out to the dump in his truck. One day, as he was cutting the lawn in neat rows, Fred Burk jogged over to say hello and pump Ted's hand. Fred needed help moving furniture into his new apartment next door. Thanks in part to some of Fred's girlfriend Carol's home cooking, the trio became close friends. One thing puzzled Ted's new neighbor: for a law student, his friend didn't study much; in fact, Fred couldn't recall ever seeing Ted crack a book during the fall of 1974. Fred chalked it up to the erratic hours Ted kept—home during the day and out at night. For someone as compulsively neat and orderly as Ted, Fred thought, he sure had an irregular schedule.

Fred and Carol had lived together long enough that marriage didn't seem so daunting. When the young couple decided to make it permanent early in 1975, Ted stood up as best man. He looked genuinely proud as he handed the ring to Fred during the simple ceremony.

Ted's charming ways and good looks gave him a steady social life when he wanted it. Wanda Hancock from the apartment just below quickly became a good friend and an occasional date. After graduating from the University of Utah, she had taught high-school English for one frustrating year. Following a stint in the Peace Corps, Wanda moved back to Salt Lake City, back to her old friends living on First Avenue. Like Ted, most of them had been through

115

college in the sixties, picking up the counterculture's visceral distrust of cops, its idealism, and its open-minded attitude toward drugs.

Ted became a regular with Wanda's little group of friends, trading stories with them in the evening as they passed a joint around her apartment. Sometimes the whole crew would pile into her red Toyota and go for a long drive, swigging crème de cacao straight from the bottle. (Ted's VW wasn't as convenient. More than once Wanda complained about the way the front passenger seat slid back and forth freely.) Melanie began to worry when Ted described his new friends. She disliked the fact that Ted was smoking more pot, and worried about the new women he was meeting.

Wanda came from a prominent Mormon family, but felt ill at ease in the narrow world of Mormon culture. Ted appeared to be the perfect compromise: conventional enough to be acceptable, intelligent, handsome, and not wrapped up in any one religion. They sometimes talked about their families and the pressures of growing up, Wanda wrestling with her parents' expectations of success and Ted describing, with forced casualness, the problems his illegitimacy had caused with some of his siblings. There had been a coolness with his stepfather, too. The epithet "bastard" had left its mark.

Wanda was terrified when a rapist began victimizing the Avenues that summer and fall. She carried a hammer in her purse and decorated her apartment with objects heavy enough to use in an emergency. When bodies began turning up in the nearby canyons, Wanda followed the stories with morbid fascination. She and Ted were watching television one night when the bulletin on Debbie Kent's disappearance led off the six o'clock news.

"It worries me to have a guy like that running around loose. Why would a woman let something like that happen to her? I would kill him first," she said forcefully, thinking perhaps of the hammer in her purse. When she turned to Ted, his eyes had grown very wide.

"You would kill him?"

"Yes, I would kill him."

"Well, you don't have to worry about that," Ted remarked amiably, as if to allay her fears. Wanda let the matter drop.

She was accustomed to his habit of dropping an odd remark or pulling some practical joke—all in the spirit of good fun. Sometimes he would sneak along the side of her first-floor apartment and stare through the window without saying a thing until she noticed him. It never failed to frighten her, especially with the Avenues' rapist in the back of her mind. On occasion, too, he would dart out from behind bushes, grab her, and hold her until her rigid body relaxed.

At one point Ted convinced Wanda that he knew who the rapist was. In a decrepit apartment building down the street lived a group of men, transients in their younger days, now marking time on welfare in Salt Lake City. He cajoled Wanda into walking over one day. Just as the two arrived, the man Ted told her about stepped out on the front porch and sat down.

"Go on, walk by, see what he'll do."

"Ted." She turned on him, a note of tension in her voice. "I'm too nervous. I don't want to."

"Go on, go on, walk by. Nothing's going to happen." A playful smile lit Ted's face. She refused.

Although Ted was never a regular all-night guest at Wanda's, the two enjoyed an easy sexual comradery. He teased her occasionally, claiming a great predilection for virgins.

"Well, you know, Wanda, I really prefer virgins. In fact, I can have one anytime I want." He wore a mischievous grin. Wanda joined in the playful spirit of the conversation.

"Oh, really, Ted? Aren't they kind of hard to find nowadays?" Wanda got up and shot a sidelong glance as she poured herself another Scotch.

In January Ted put the hiatus of the fall behind him and began attending classes regularly. He worked hard, and helped by his practical legal experience managed to complete two semesters' work during the spring. (Mostly B's and C's dotted his grade sheet.) His classmates and professors were impressed with how quickly he grasped the essentials of jurisprudence. Although he was seeing law students more regularly in 1975, Ted never immersed himself in their social circles. He did make more contacts in the legal community and became well acquainted with some of his professors.

Ted's comings and goings became more regular. Generally he stayed close to his apartment during the week, wading through a thick pile of law books on his desk each night. If he planned a weekend out of town—to visit his parents in Seattle—Fred Burk watered his plants.

Ted occasionally disappeared for two or three days

without letting Fred know. "I would be happy to take care of your plants. There's no point in letting them die," he said, mildly reproving Ted.

"Oh, it was just a spur-of-the-moment thing." Ted shrugged. "I didn't really know I was going."

Just as unexpected to those who knew Ted around the apartment building was his new interest in Mormon ward parties. It began when he met Sue Monsen, who worked as a legal secretary for John O'Connell. While most Mormon wards are predominantly made up of married couples and families with children, the university had "singles" wards with a hectic round of dances, outings, and parties geared toward marrying their members off.

In the spring Ted met Roger Kirkham and Mark Swenson, two missionaries for Sue's ward. Gradually they became friends, and Ted soon was socializing as much with his Mormon friends as with Wanda's group. The evenings and weekends with Roger and Mark had a very different flavor from the get-togethers on First Avenue. Ted often discussed his plans for the future with the two missionaries and re-examined his life.

Roger quietly prodded his new friend to think about religious matters, to ask himself if there wasn't more to life than the pleasures of the here and now. At first Ted seemed merely curious about Mormon culture, but gradually the always open arms of ward members and their sincere commitment to a moral life appeared to win him over. He began attending the Sunday meetings and immersing himself in the Mormon world view. One day he confided to Kirkham:

"It's interesting, Roger, since living here in Utah I have had quite a change in what I want from a date. It used to be I would go out, in my college days, and it was a race to see how long it would take to get into bed. I found that to be completely repulsive since moving here to Utah, where the atmosphere is so different."

Kirkham seized the opportunity and suggested Ted talk to their ward bishop, Melvin Thayne. Thayne realized that this was only an exploratory interview, so he didn't press Bundy on his belief in Mormon theology's divine origin. Instead the talk turned to the church's attitude toward the family.

"You know, what I'm most impressed with about the church, Bishop Thayne," Ted blurted out when their cordial conversation had slowed. "That the family is so important,

118

that family closeness is so meaningful. I really wanted to talk to someone who was married about the church's attitude toward the marriage relationship." Ted related the story of his upbringing and family life.

"I've always felt somehow lost in my life. That's why I appreciate so much the comradery of people like Roger and Mark. They've really made me feel like I have an attachment to the people of this ward, people who care about what happens to me."

Ted did not immediately join the church. When classes ended in the spring he began his travels again, and Kirkham and Swenson lost track of the prospective convert.

Things were stabilizing for Ted in other areas too. For several months that spring he worked as a night manager at a University of Utah dormitory, earning $2.10 per hour. Bundy wasn't very responsible in his duties (he lost the job for showing up drunk or late or both too often), but in July he found another position with the university as a security guard, with more pay, $2.50 per hour.

A new woman entered Ted's life that summer. At a party thrown by Salt Lake County Attorney Paul VanDam he met Linda Brown, whom he courted through July and August. Linda and her husband had been amicably divorced the year before, and Linda had custody of their son Peter. When Linda's ex came by to visit, Ted would gather up Peter and some of the other neighborhood kids for swimming or a movie. Sometimes he would drive over to spend the day. And, often enough to make Linda notice, he cleaned his old VW within an inch of its life.

During the summer new neighbors, Bill and Brenda Edwards, moved into the apartment across the hall. Often unemployed, Bill Edwards seemed an unlikely friend for Ted. Perhaps it was their lack of education——Bill and Brenda had barely graduated from high school——but they didn't mix well with the college crowd downstairs. Wanda regarded Bill as something of a misfit, and was not surprised when he was arrested some months later for armed robbery.

Bill saw Ted as something of a hypocrite. On Saturday night Ted would drop by, smoke dope, and joust with Bill about homosexuals. "They really are fun people, Bill," he said one night, "happy people who know how to have a good time." Then on Sunday morning, Ted would walk coolly by them on his way to pick up Sue for Sunday school. Their peculiar friendship ended when Ted slipped unannounced into

119

the Edwards's bedroom and woke a friend of Brenda's by pinching her crotch.

By the middle of that month Ted Bundy's life had taken its irreversible turn. A Utah highway patrolman had caught up with him on a darkened subdivision street. The group at Wanda's place were confirmed in their hatred for the police. No one could believe that he'd been arrested for possession of a ski mask and a crowbar. It was obviously a prime example of some cop out to make a name for himself. Ted had neglected to mention the panty hose with the face holes, or the handcuffs.

Kirkham and Swenson knew nothing of the August arrest. Mark Swenson telephoned the third week of August to find out what had happened to the prospective convert, and was surprised to find Ted ready to be baptized. He joined the church on August 30 and was ordained to the lower priesthood on September 6. In keeping with Mormon tradition, Ted immediately had two jobs: teaching Sunday school and visiting ward members as a "home teacher." An outing to Bear Lake in mid-September was a kind of celebration for the group. Many of them felt that their efforts to bring Ted Bundy into the fold had paid off handsomely. His new role in the religious world was something else Ted didn't discuss with Wanda and her friends.

Linda Brown saw Ted regularly in September, but she was disturbed by his depression. He was drinking more, a lot more, and she watched him trying to stay busy in an effort to keep from dwelling on whatever was bothering him. Maybe it was money problems. He explained that he would have to sell the VW, and spent a weekend at her house fixing it up. First he sanded rust spots, put on a new front bumper, and spray-painted primer on the front hood and over the dents in the side. New chrome wheel rings and a wax job finished his exterior work.

Ted pulled the hose from underneath Linda's front porch and began washing the interior. He pitched the old floor mats in the garbage and washed everything with strong detergent and a strong spraying from the hose. He sanded the VW's floor to remove all the rust spots and painted it blue. A new back seat and new floor mats made it ready to sell. A week later Ted pocketed $700 from a Sandy, Utah, teenager and bid goodbye to his car.

When Ted moved from First Avenue he left good friends behind. They were bitter at the police for the surveillance

120

and interrogation and protested to Ted that they didn't mind the inconvenience. But Ted said he had to move closer to law school. He didn't want to depend on them for rides.

On October 1, 1975, when a poker-faced Jerry Thompson showed up at Ted's door with an order to appear for a police lineup the next day, Ted smiled and maintained his unflappable veneer. That afternoon, however, he sat before the ward bishop, visibly shaken. Ted told the story of his arrest and offered an explanation for the crowbar and the handcuffs, again not mentioning the panty hose. He was afraid, he said, that the criminal proceedings would ruin his standing in the ward.

The bishop tried to comfort him. They all knew Ted, knew that he was a decent, upright, moral person. Whatever his involvement with the courts, they would stand behind him. Ted thanked the bishop and stood up. Ted had betrayed his nervousness to the bishop for the last time.

The next morning, three women behind a sheet of glass picked number seven, the man in the light turtleneck with the new haircut. Theodore Bundy was instant news.

"Could my son do these things?" Louise Bundy's jaw quivered as she held it out and snapped back at a reporter on her doorstep in Tacoma. "Of course not. What a stupid thing to ask a mother. In no way could he do these things."

Indeed, in Ted Bundy's home state of Washington, it was hard to find anyone who disagreed, from old schoolmates and friends to political cronies to the governor himself. They had all expected to read about Ted in the papers someday, about his high-minded legal pursuits, his campaign promises, his acceptance speeches. But this? A man calling himself a police officer, grabbing a girl and trying to handcuff her and beat her with a tire iron? Ted Bundy doing *this?* Management at the *Tacoma News Tribune* agreed to run a cautious first story about the case. Anything else, they agreed, might mean a libel suit when Ted was released, as he surely would be.

But in Seattle, the obvious question flew across the front page of the *Post-Intelligencer:* IS UTAH TED SEATTLE TED? The story offered a fairly guarded response. Said Nick Mackie, King County police captain and former head of the defunct "Ted" task force: "We looked at Ted Bundy as a suspect and pretty well eliminated him." That didn't mean they had stopped looking, however. Detective Bob Keppel phoned

Jerry Thompson and immediately arranged a trip to Salt Lake City to compare notes and plan strategy for the now revitalized Washington investigation.

But the media were even quicker. Robin Groth, a bright-eyed television reporter for a local station, had followed the "Ted" murders and the futile police work for more than a year. She hadn't forgotten the name or misplaced the address of Doris Grayling, the one witness at Lake Sammamish who had seen the VW in the parking lot. Grabbing a friend from one of the papers who had access to a 1972 photograph of Bundy, she drove east across the Evergreen Point Bridge. The dogs were barking madly in the Graylings' front yard when the car pulled up.

Doris Grayling looked drawn and tense when she answered the door. It had been an agonizing year for her—session after session with the police, repeated and unsuccessful attempts to improve her memory under hypnosis. Groth thrust the photograph into her hands. "Is that the man?"

The woman studied the grainy photograph for a long minute, then handed it back. "No," she said, "that's not the one." Grayling's husband reached over her shoulder and shut the door in the reporters' faces.

For Nick Mackie it was an inglorious end of the line. Fuming and sputtering about the "flagrant irresponsibility" of a reporter showing a suspect photo to a witness, he was soon admitting privately that the Bundy trail in Washington was colder than it was in Utah or Colorado. With crimes more than a year and a half old, Ted Bundy became the leading suspect with little more than meager circumstance and supposition to connect him to the killings. In his long career, Nick Mackie had never suffered like this with a case.

But no one in Washington, least of all Mackie's prize detective Bob Keppel, was willing to give up. Curious and intelligent, a man who "read everything he could get his hands on" and was well educated in the sociology and psychology of crime, Keppel set out to learn anything he could about this "favorite son" of Washington State. Little by little the chronology fell into place, from Ted's illegitimate birth to his departure for Salt Lake City. The clues that Keppel picked up were slim indeed: a Bundy relative who *might* have known one of Lynda Healy's roommates in the University District; several recollections that Ted liked to go driving in the Issaquah hills not far from where the victims' remains had been found; a surplus store that carried Gerocal handcuffs and remembered taking several checks from Ted. Employment records in Olympia showed Bundy had been absent from work several days around the time of the Lake Sammamish disappearances.

Detectives got a dramatic break in Tacoma when a young woman wrote out a sworn statement that Ted Bundy was the man who raped her there in 1973. She'd seen his picture in the paper, and, she said, she could never forget that "jawline." But Ted Bundy had had a beard in 1973, police learned. Another wishful case disintegrated.

Late one windy October afternoon, the woman from the television station caught up with her friend Phil Killien on his way out of the King County prosecutor's office. They chatted a minute, and then, as it had for more than a year, their conversation turned to "Ted." Killien's mouth was set in a frown. His friend was a colleague of Robin Groth.

"You know if Groth hadn't pulled that stunt," he began, but Killien didn't finish his thought. He knew too much to be genuinely angry. Of the eight witnesses who had seen or talked to a man with his arm in a sling at Lake Sammamish, only two picked Bundy as the man. Even more discouraging, neither made a definite identification until Bundy's picture and name, suggestively linked with the Washington crimes, had appeared in every newspaper in sight.

Phil Killien was never going to face Ted Bundy across a courtroom.

Mike Fisher and his colleagues in Colorado had only slightly better luck the first month after Bundy's arrest. In Dillon, 32 miles from Vail (where Julie Cunningham disappeared), a Chevron station attendant claimed to remember the battered old VW Ted drove. Nearby, in Silverthorne, the station manager picked Bundy out of a photo lineup as the man who had bought 89 cents' worth of gas on March 15. And according to the Silverthorne police chief, Ted Bundy was definitely the man who had strolled into the local Holiday Inn that day, then turned to go as soon as he saw the chief. The skittish behavior of the man in the yellow turtleneck and blue parka stuck in his mind—enough, he said, to make the identification seven months later.

In Golden, Colorado, investigators uncovered a small coincidence: Bundy had once bought gas from a pump operator who knew Shelley Robertson, the young woman who turned up bound with duct tape in a mine shaft. There was a shred in Nederland, too: one of Bundy's relatives had a boyfriend who attended the University of Colorado in Boulder, near the site where Melanie Cooley had been found.

It was sketchy, but detectives were in touch with one another constantly, sharing what they knew. The California authorities joined in when a traffic citation and a hotel receipt bearing Ted's name placed him in the state approximately at the time of two of *their* homicides. To some zealous detectives, these coincidences looked too good to be true. By the end of the month, word of the Colorado credit card links had leaked to the press. Ted Bundy's reputation was growing fast.

Things went forward at a steady, busy pace in Salt Lake City that month. First there was a search warrant for Ted's new apartment on Douglas Street. But when the manager of the building let Jerry Thompson in to retrieve the patent leather shoes, they, along with a substantial quantity of the clothing Thompson had seen in his search of the First Avenue apartment, were gone. The haul this time: one blue coat, 19 cassette tapes, and a can containing some "suspected marijuana seeds." That day, too, Thompson appeared on the doorstep of the teenager who had bought the VW just three weeks before. The young man watched unhappily as his first car disappeared up the street behind a county tow truck.

Ted's past became a major preoccupation. A list of law-school friends was compiled and proved surprisingly short. Summoned to police headquarters, his classmates told Pete Hayward almost identical stories: a few shared beers, good conversation, an occasional party. One woman remembered that Ted had come to class in January with scratches on his face. His usual charm evaporated when she tried to tease him about his "love life." No one, including his professors, remembered seeing Ted more than two days during the fall 1974 quarter. A series of special exams had rescued his course work the following spring.

Like the law students, Ted's other friends showed unstinting support for him. His arrest was an example of overzealous police harassment. Bundy, evidently secure in his friends' attitudes, had even asked a fellow law student for a ride to the lineup.

Former neighbors in the First Avenue apartment could barely conceal their hostility when Jerry Thompson began asking about Ted. Wanda Hancock, downstairs, refused to "remember" Ted's new address. Fred Burk, next door, had chosen Ted as the best man at his wedding. The idea that his

124

friend kidnapped or murdered young women was preposterous. The less Ted looked like the criminal that detectives believed him to be, the harder they worked to knit the sporadic threads of damaging information into a criminal profile.

The hard physical evidence remained slight. The FBI lab in Washington, D.C., reported back on the two sets of handcuffs and the key found at Viewmont High: no toolmarks or other peculiarities indicated a connection among the three. A sample of Ted's blood tested as O-positive, the most common type; although it matched the speck found on Carol DaRonch's coat, the sample hadn't been sufficient to provide an Rh factor.

Finally it dawned on investigators that maybe they had their crime scene after all. On October 15, Paul Forbes from the Murray police department and Jerry Thompson removed everything not bolted down in the VW, vacuumed the interior, and took a scraping from a dark red stain on the front seat. The hope was that in all the bags of dirt or somewhere on a floor mat a hair or speck of blood might match up with one of the victims.

On October 30 Judge Gibson granted Ted Bundy's request for a reduction in bail from $100,000 to $15,000. Pete Hayward and his detectives believed Ted and his family couldn't raise even that amount right away, but they didn't want to take any chances. If Ted walked out on bail, an important opportunity to interrogate him directly would be lost.

It was November 3, 1975, a clear autumn afternoon in Salt Lake City. Ted Bundy gazed from the ninth-floor window at the expanse of orange and yellow leaves. "It's almost blinding to look out a window and be able to see things without bars," Ted murmured. "It sure is beautiful."

"How are they treating you in the jail, Ted?" It was the most innocuous topic Jerry Thompson could think of.

"Well, the food's fairly good, and the jailers are good people. I've learned a great deal from my fellow inmates—not all of it good. I hate to say it, but some of these guys are good teachers."

Pete Hayward joined the discussion, which turned from psychologists ("No more insight than a lot of people," said Ted) to marriage ("I didn't want to drag my wife and children through the times of hard work and sacrifice") to politics. Hayward's attention picked up: he had run for Salt Lake County sheriff several years before.

"It's a very commendable rat race," Ted said. "I don't attach to it all the corruption and influence peddling that many people do. I just think people are too critical of politicians—mayors, senators, congressmen, assemblymen, state representatives, even sheriffs."

"Right, all the way down." Hayward smiled.

"You should have gone into politics, Ted," Thompson broke in, "instead of going into the lawyer field."

Just then the phone buzzed, and John O'Connell joined his client. Thompson shut off the bright banter immediately. "We brought Ted up here to talk to him in regards to numerous homicides in Utah and the Intermountain area. We do not wish to question him on the present case, whatsoever."

"The way I see it," O'Connell said, quickly defending his flank, "I don't think we're going to convince you of anything. I don't see any point in talking to you."

Hayward broke in. "John, we have an outline and questions that we would like to ask Ted. Of course, at any particular point when the questions are asked, you have the right to tell Ted not to answer. We are conducting an investigation into these various homicides, and we feel it's imperative we talk to Ted."

"We have not been given access to information about these offenses," O'Connell shot back. "For some reason the newspaper people have been given information in some detail, but we've been shut off. I object to being here at all." The debate went on several minutes until O'Connell ended it, instructing Ted not to answer any questions.

"Where are you originally from, Ted?" A moment's silence followed Thompson's first query.

"He's refusing to answer that," O'Connell replied firmly.

"After leaving Seattle, did you ever go into the Portland, Oregon, area?"

"Refuse to answer that."

"Are you married, Ted?"

"Refuse to answer that."

"Have you ever been in the northern California area?"

"Refuse to answer that."

"Did you ever attend the University of Washington at Seattle?"

"Refuse to answer that."

"Were you in the state of Utah attending the University of Utah law school during the period of September through December 1974?"

126

"Refuse to answer that."

"Have you ever been in Colorado during 1974, '75?"

"Refuse to answer that."

It was like a litany, a mock interrogation perfectly matched between accuser and accused.

"Have you ever traveled extensively through California, Oregon, Washington, Colorado, and Utah through the period of 1973 to the present?"

"Refuse to answer that." O'Connell's frustrations boiled over. "You asked us whether or not we wanted to talk, which you're required to do by law, and our answer was 'No.' I think that means you stop trying to interrogate Ted. I mean, you've got a gun and I don't, so you win."

"You know me better than that, John," Hayward snapped. "Ted, have you ever committed murder?"

"Refuse to answer that."

15

By November police in Washington, Utah, Colorado, and California agreed that they wanted to meet and talk over their newest and hottest suspect—Theodore Robert Bundy—in detail. Salt Lake City was an obvious, centrally located choice, but Dave Yocom, touchy already about the press coverage of the case, vetoed the idea of a "Bundy summit conference" in town. He suggested Reno or Boise instead. Over in Colorado, Mike Fisher and his Pitkin County colleagues were increasingly excited about their possible case against Ted in the Caryn Campbell murder and quickly offered to host the meeting in the ski resort town of Aspen. Detectives from the four states convened on November 13, 1975.

It was an incongruous sight, these crumpled-looking, self-conscious cops filing into the Aspen Holiday Inn, styled, with its exposed wooden slats, like a Swiss chalet. Skiers with bright, reddened complexions and bulky layers of sweaters hurried through the lobby, curious and amused by the crowd of middle-aged men. An orthodontist on vacation from Milwaukee was puzzled when he saw one of them brush aside a reporter's question and disappear into the conference room. "What was that all about?" he wondered to himself.

Behind the closed doors, the high seriousness of the meeting was lost on no one. A stenographer assigned to transcribe the proceedings was moved to poetic expression as she watched the detectives find their seats after lunch:

> What strange quirk of fate or combination of genes separates the heroes from the monsters?
> At what point in time is conscience created or on the other hand forgotten, dismissed, destroyed?
> These are the questions that have nagged at me all day today,
> Watching dedicated men striving to put together the pieces of a puzzle that boggles the mind at its sheer, unbelievably terrifying magnitude.
> What type of twisted mind could spend endless time plotting the demise of young women who have barely tasted life?
> Cruelly and calculatingly, this perpetrator of evil ticks off the minutes and seconds until he can rob another human being of her right to witness another sunrise.
> I pray for endurance for the dedicated men.

Bob Keppel from Seattle was first, offering a long and richly detailed account of Ted Bundy's past. Keppel couldn't concoct the demoniac monster the stenographer imagined, but his portrait of Bundy was unflattering: a self-serving manipulator who lied at will, pinched goods from his employers, and stole his girlfriends' cars. It was in many ways a textbook picture of a psychopath, but as far as explaining any motivation or deep aberration in Bundy's personality, Keppel came up short. He knew almost nothing of the circumstances surrounding Bundy's birth and early years in Philadelphia, and the rest was flimsy speculation: Ted was naive about sex in junior high; he *may* have had a homosexual contact at one point; he strayed from the missionary position now and then.

In linking Bundy to the 1974 disappearances and murders in Washington State, Keppel could spin only the barest web. Ted and Lynda Healy were enrolled in some of the same psychology classes at the University of Washington. A friend of Donna Manson at Evergreen was Bundy's occasional racquetball partner. Ted, like Brenda Ball, had been seen at the Flame Tavern in Burien. Keppel concluded his talk with the disappointing news that only two of the Lake Sammamish witnesses picked Bundy as the man with his arm in a sling—neither one before his picture was in the papers.

One by one the investigators from various states followed Keppel to the podium. There were eight murders in California dating from 1972 through the disappearances of Katherine Kelley in southwestern Colorado less than two months before. Jerry Thompson recounted Ted's August arrest for burglary tools, the lineup ID, and the Utah investigation. Colorado's evidence was somewhat stronger than Seattle's: the gasoline credit card links between Ted and three homicides plus some solid identifications. It was a tantalizing pattern, one that the 27 detectives and prosecutors were anxious to accept, but it was unconvincing in many ways. Virtually no evidence, even circumstantial, connected Ted to most of the cases—Nancy Wilcox, Melissa Smith, Laura Aime, and Nancy Baird in Utah; Sandra Weaver, Melanie Cooley, Shelley Robertson, and Katherine Kelley in Colorado; or any of the California victims. And there were problems with the supposed similarity of the crimes. If, for example Melissa Smith and Laura Aime had been held for a period of days before their strangulation deaths, that suggested a different sort of killer, a different sort of crime from grabbing a woman (like Caryn Campbell) and immediately beating her about the head. Also, for all the publicity that the women looked alike, with their long brown hair parted in the middle, there were marked differences in ages and weights.

Circumstance, after all, had a way of attaching itself to more than one man. There was Jake Teppler, Mike Fisher reminded the seminar participants; polygraph or no polygraph, he couldn't be discounted as a suspect in the Caryn Campbell case or the Washington cases. And Warren Forrest, added Chuck Brink from the Clark County, Washington, sheriff's office. One of the Lake Sam witnesses thought this known sex offender looked awfully much like the man with his arm in a sling. And there were others: a man on death row in New Mexico; another who had reportedly had sex with Melanie Cooley and one of her friends. Most vexing of all, perhaps, was the Pacos, Texas, inmate who confessed to killing a sheriff's daughter (Melissa Smith was the only one on the books) and then hanged himself in his cell.

From all the jurisdictions there was a boggling weight of investigative work to assimilate and understand. By the end of the second day patience had worn thin. Jerry Thompson had to stand up at one point and enlighten a colleague who had the names and facts of a Utah case badly confused. The meeting ended before noon on November 14, with investigators cautioning each other to clam up with the press. One participant assessed the outcome: "It was a beneficial meeting; however, there was nothing that came out of it that gave anyone else enough to make a charge against Mr. Bundy."

No one was daunted by the failure of this law student and good Republican to emerge as a provable mass murderer at Aspen. Police returned home to keep the phones and teletypes busy with an ongoing exchange of inquiries and information. Bundy's fingerprints, rap sheet, and credit card records went out to Spokane, Philadelphia, several Oregon towns—almost anywhere, it seemed, where detectives had an unsolved female homicide on the books. In Aspen, a young woman identified Bundy as the man who had followed her on crutches the previous April. In Salt Lake City, a 72-year-old woman said Ted had raped her.

In jail, stoutly proclaiming his innocence, Bundy couldn't have guessed the scope of things police across the West had hopes of. Already more than the accused suspect in a crime at a shopping mall one November night, he was fast becoming, in many minds, the most fearful embodiment of evil: familiar, trusted, reassuring—on the surface, just like everyone else.

On November 20, Louise and Johnnie Bundy fronted the money for their son's bail. It had been raised in their name by a Seattle attorney, a friend of Ted. On the 21st, five days of preliminary hearings began, with one bit of good news for Bundy at the end; the attempted homicide charge was dropped. On November 26 Theodore Bundy was bound over to Stewart Hanson's Third District Court, charged with aggravated kidnapping of Carol DaRonch. Hanson, Ted knew, had a reputation as one of the state's most liberal judges. Ted was free on bail, and chattily hopeful of the outcome. At the end of the proceedings he left the courtroom by a rear door and disappeared.

Ted returned to the Northwest, like a migratory bird, for his several months of freedom before the trial began. Friends on Seattle's Queen Anne Hill put him up for a while; he did some Christmas shopping; life proceeded in its altered way. Ted gazed out at the ferries steadily inching their way across Puget Sound in the distance and tried to visit old friends a little. But it was difficult. One woman, the wife of a high-school friend, wouldn't let him in her house. Even the solitary chore of working on his upcoming defense had its hazards. When Ted showed up at the University of Washington Law School library to look up some Utah statutes, mild pandemonium set in among the students and staff who knew his face. The law-school dean suggested to Ted in a letter that it might be more "comfortable" if he used the county law library instead.

But Ted still had devoted followers. Each morning when he stepped outside they were waiting—two, four, sometimes six or seven cars parked at the curb. The cars weren't marked, of course, but Ted knew exactly what was up: not one jurisdiction investigating a murdered woman case in western Washington was going to let him out of sight. They followed wherever he went.

It was a poky, pointless game, with unwritten rules. After a day or two Ted began to play along. At first he toyed with the police, ambling out in the morning, offering coffee, wanting to chat. Some did; others drove off nonplussed. After a while Ted readjusted the rules, losing his escorts on the city streets, whipping down an alley, ditching his car, vaulting a fence. Once he went out a bathroom window to shake them off.

It was a comedy of sorts, a Keystone Kops chase scene without a point. Oh, but there was a point, said Ted's friends. Just as bumbling and reckless as their silent film counterparts, these real-life cops were after the wrong man.

But for now, for these few short weeks, it was only a practice run.

By January 1976, when Ted returned to Salt Lake City to help his attorneys John O'Connell and Bruce Lubeck prepare his defense, legal maneuvering was already under way. O'Connell's motion to suppress DaRonch's photograph and lineup identification of the defendant had been taken under advisement by Judge Hanson. O'Connell cited the "impermissibly suggestive manner" of the photo IDs and the stacking of the lineup with policemen (tending to make Bundy the "focus of attention"). But Ted lost the first round: Hanson denied the motion.

Meanwhile, police weren't about to settle for a single

charge. On January 28 at 2:45 p.m. Jerry Thompson picked up the phone. It was Special Agent Robert Neill from the FBI who had news, he said, based on his study of the vacuumed debris from Bundy's car. Two months before, when Neill had called to inform Thompson there were human hairs found in the bags of dust, word had gone out to various jurisdictions: send in any known hair samples from your victims. Neill had two matches now: two head hairs found in Bundy's care were "microscopically identical" to those of Caryn Campbell, the Michigan nurse murdered at Snowmass. A pubic hair matched up with Utah victim Melissa Smith.

But, Neill advised, "microscopic hair comparisons are not as good as fingerprint identifications. They're just circumstantial. If you've got some other things for him that look good also, you know, that always helps in building up a circumstantial case. We can't eliminate the possibility that there would be other Caucasian women who had pubic hairs which would be similar. It could happen."

Thompson could barely contain himself. "Thank you," he said breathlessly. "I really appreciate this phone call, and if there's anything else, please don't hesitate to get ahold of me. I appreciate this." He was up and out of his office almost before Neill signed off.

Circumstantial or not, this shred of evidence renewed police hopes. Clear Creek County, Colorado, undersheriff Robert Denning bundled off the duct tape, earrings, burned clothing, and hair of Shelley Robertson to the FBI the next day. Elsewhere, investigators called on parents and boyfriends in search of samples of their victims' hair. On February 2, Detective Ron Ballantyne from Bountiful joined Thompson in the Salt Lake County garage, and the two went at the now notorious Volkswagen Bug with knives, ripping off front and rear seat covers, and revacuuming the whole interior. Off went more bags of debris to Washington, D.C.

Mike Fisher had had a second strike in his Aspen investigation. It was winter again, just over a year after Caryn Campbell's death, and the cardiologists were back in town. On an off chance Fisher had returned to the Wildwood Inn to see if anyone remembered anything suspicious happening on or around the night of January 12, 1975. Lisbeth Harter, the California woman who had been out to buy stomach medicine for her husband and daughter that night, had thought long and hard the past year. Now, Fisher said, she could pick Ted Bundy out from a pack of photos as one of the men lurking around the hotel elevator that night. Fisher was excited, and he wanted to come to Salt Lake City.

The meeting was set for February 10—and the news to be discussed was intriguing enough to draw investigators from around the state of Utah and from Seattle as well. Fisher methodically outlined his case: the Colorado ski country brochure with the *x* by the Wildwood Inn found in Ted's apartment, the credit card receipts placing him in the area in January 1975, the match of the hairs, and now Harter's identification. It was powerfully suggestive, everyone agreed, but circumstantial all the same. The next day an Aspen judge agreed. Not enough, he said, to warrant a murder charge. Fisher was discouraged but not beaten.

In Salt Lake City, with the DaRonch trial just weeks away, prosecutor Dave Yocom was still trying to bolster his case against Bundy. A career man, well acquainted with the habits and testimony of habitual criminals, Yocom had paid more attention than his colleagues to a story he'd heard in November. It came from Bill Edwards, the floater who had lived in the apartment across the hall from Ted in the summer of '75. In his cloud of recollections, Edwards had recalled a morning when Bundy was drunk, staring into space, mumbling to himself. As Edwards told it to Jerry Thompson:

"He goes, 'Well, I abducted three girls and they're trying to get me for it,' and he slurred as he said it.

"So I said, 'What did you say, Ted?'

"And he says, 'Nothin', nothin'.'

"He was just like in a daze; he was just like staring at the wall when he said it, and I asked him to repeat himself. Right after, I ran over to Brenda [Edwards's wife, who was standing just outside the door] and I says, 'Did you hear what he told me?'

"And she goes, 'Yeah.'

"And I go, 'Man, he must be drunk, you know.'

"I didn't think nothin' of it then, and then he got arrested . . ."

But on February 19—four days before the trial was to begin—Yocom heard a significantly different version of the incident from Bill Edwards. Pulling the story from Edwards's disjointed memory was no easy matter. Finally Yocom worked around to the point:

"He never came out and said that he had tried to abduct three girls?"

"I'm pretty sure he didn't," Edwards admitted now. "I

probably got mixed up—but I'm pretty sure he told me he got pulled over because the cops *said* that he tried to abduct three girls and they identified the rip in his backseat. That's exactly what he told me. I'm positive."

Yocom ran a hand through his hair and left. What Bill Edwards was sure of, Yocom knew, would be no help in court. He'd have to go to trial with what he had.

16

"Judge Hanson?" Dave Yocom had slipped through the door with only a light knock. "Can we talk to you about this case for a moment?" Hanson looked up from the papers on his desk as John O'Connell followed Yocom into the room. Theodore Bundy's kidnapping trial was to begin Monday. Yocom and O'Connell, prosecution and defense, had been maneuvering for weeks.

"Sure," said Hanson. "Are we going to need a court reporter, or is this informal?"

"No reporter," said O'Connell. He looked tired and troubled, lines set deeply around his eyes. "I just wanted to let you know we are going to waive the jury."

There was a long moment of silence, and then the two lawyers turned to go. Hanson had no choice but silent assent. The right to a trial by jury is absolute, and can be waived absolutely by the defendant. The principle was simple, but the implications for the judge were complex.

Hanson gazed out the window, shaken by this unexpected event. One of the reasons the jury system works so well is that jurors can make a decision together that each might not be sure or strong enough to make alone. The full weight of O'Connell's announcement finally sunk in. "Oh, God," Hanson thought. "Am I really brave enough to do whatever the evidence tells me must be done in this case?" Hanson was still pondering his new responsibility as he left the old City Hall that Friday afternoon and crossed the frozen lawn to his car.

In October, when Ted's arrest had hit the papers, Stewart Hanson was out of town, attending judicial college seminars in Reno, Nevada. He'd missed the initial furor, and he understood now why Judge Leary had passed the case on to him. Rumors about Ted had circulated in Salt Lake City's legal community that winter; perhaps Leary had felt his objectivity was impaired. Through the pretrial motions, Hanson himself had learned the facts (like Arla Jensen's and Tina Hatch's identifications) and suppositions that tended to connect Ted Bundy to far more than the crime against Carol DaRonch. It was a delicate, complicated case—no way around that.

But O'Connell's eleventh-hour move was still a puzzle. "Yocom's case rests primarily on Carol's identification, which is sure to look dubious to at least some members of a jury," Hanson thought. And that, he realized at last, was just the point. O'Connell had said he was going to call an expert witness on the degree of reliability in an eyewitness identification. But even the Supreme Court was skeptical of so-called experts in this fledgling field. It would be difficult to admit the "expert" testimony before a jury.

But not before a judge. Who would be better qualified, any appellate court would hold, than a trial judge to evaluate the legal implications of such testimony? Yocom, O'Connell, and Hanson had debated the question a week before, with Yocom vowing to challenge the "expert's" qualifications.

Even so, by resting his case on the judgment of one man— Stewart Hanson—John O'Connell was taking a gamble.

Monday, February 23, 1976. Members of the local press had been waiting in the courtroom for two hours when Judge Hanson mounted the steps to the bench at 10:00 a.m. Spectators had long since filled the small courtroom's rows of seats and more were camped in the aisles. Outside, a half-dozen cameramen blocked the hallways. John O'Connell, Bruce Lubeck, and Ted Bundy leaned back comfortably at the defense table, all three dressed in the legal profession's uniform—a three-piece suit. O'Connell's incongruous black felt ten-gallon Stetson with the braided band sat on the table before them.

The proceedings began with a reading of the charges and Ted's plea of not guilty. Judge Hanson looked out, scanning the faces in the crowded, tense courtroom. The only one who appeared relaxed was the defendant.

"The record will show that this matter was originally set for trial by jury, and it is my understanding that the defen-

135

dant desires to waive a jury in this matter. Is that correct, Mr. O'Connell?" Heads turned in the gallery, and a dozen reporters began scribbling.

O'Connell questioned Ted extensively on his understanding of his right to a trial by jury, eliciting his experience with and education in the law to support the decision, until Hanson seemed satisfied.

Ted had chosen well in O'Connell, whose reputation as a brilliant trial tactician was well deserved. "I don't know anyone," Hanson said after the trial, "who is better suited—intellectually and and emotionally—to the practice of criminal law." O'Connell had kept the pressure on Yocom's case from the beginning. Through a series of pretrial motions he'd sought to suppress virtually every key piece of evidence the state had, particularly the conduct of the lineup and the August search of Ted's car. Now he opened fire. The state's charge listed four separate criminal acts which it intended to prove. If the defense could limit that to one charge, the task of poking holes in Yocom's case would be considerably easier. Hanson denied the motion, but granted O'Connell's request to exclude witnesses from the courtroom while they were not testifying. At least a wavering memory would not be reinforced by the testimony of others.

Yocom launched into his opening round, a methodical recounting of Carol's walk through the Fashion Place Mall with "Officer Roseland," the Walshes' rescue, and the Murray police department's subsequent investigation. He'd reached the story of Hayward's arrest and the description of the "junk" in the VW when O'Connell jumped to his feet.

"Excuse me. I don't want to interrupt your opening statement, but may it be understood that I am not waiving any objections I may have to the evidence that he's discussed at this time."

For a trial barely under way, the tension of the courtroom was already overpowering. Scarcely an hour had passed before Hanson decided on a short recess. During the break, Ted leaned over to John O'Connell. He had seen the cops frisk a man sitting in the back before they let him into the courtroom.

"Who is that man in the last row? He's been staring at me the whole time."

"That's Louis Smith from Midvale," O'Connell whispered. Ted took a longer look at Smith's sullen face. "I requested that he be searched," O'Connell continued. Smith came to the trial every day.

"All rise." The judge seated himself and nodded to the defense. O'Connell concentrated on the personality of Carol DaRonch. She was "immature," "relatively unsophisticated," "sheltered," "unobservant"; she had a "malleable memory," was "submissive to authority," and "spends a lot of time looking down." Carol had remembered only "Roseland's" shoes and pants distinctly, he claimed. She had caught the police feeling that they had a "hot suspect," and changed her description ultimately to suit her purposes.

The investigation came under sharp attack. Carol had seen Ted's picture twice before the lineup, and remembered different things at different times about the Volkswagen. O'Connell accused Ben Forbes of having shown her Bob Keppel's photograph of Ted in the fall of 1974, which she refused to identify. Again and again, the defense lawyer returned to his charge that detectives had communicated their sense of excitement to Carol.

"When I criticize," O'Connell explained, "I want to make it clear that I don't believe they are trying to frame him, but I do believe that it's impossible for them to prevent their conveying to the witness their sense of closing in on this individual, and how strongly they felt. The atmosphere at that lineup was so tense because those officers were so afraid that she was not going to make this identification. I think she picked up on that; the evidence will show that they had a hot suspect, that he was the man, and if she failed to identify him at that lineup it would have, indeed, from the officers' viewpoint, been a damn tragedy. She did identify him, and it turned out to be a damn tragedy—for the defendant."

Dave Yocom lacked O'Connell's flair and drama. As a prosecutor he was known for his logical, thorough, meticulous cases. Hanson had tried cases by other county attorneys before where the preparation had been so sloppy that the state would fail to make a prima facie case. Yocom had had an occasional witness fall apart on him on the stand, but it was a rare case where a loose end lost him the trial.

Detective Paul Forbes from Murray took the stand first for the prosecution. He moonlighted as a security guard for the Fashion Place Mall and had been primarily responsible for Murray's investigation of the kidnapping. O'Connell didn't bother challenging Forbes's description of the Mall, but picked up on the "malleable memory" theme.

"Hadn't Carol identified another VW in 1974?"

"No. She'd indicated that some of the rust spots and dents were similar, but there was no tear in the backseat."

"Hadn't Murray uncovered another suspect with handcuffs?"

"Yes, but he was much heavier than the defendant," Forbes countered, motioning toward Ted.

Hanson called a recess for lunch, but few spectators left the courtroom. No one wanted to lose a seat. The press corps waited for Ted in the hallway. It wasn't often that the media had a defendant as articulate and witty as Bundy, and they took full advantage of it. After he made statements for the television crews, he joked and traded stories with reporters. This is all very unfortunate, he said, but the truth will be uncovered in the end. Ted turned to leave, still grinning after a last remark, when he realized that a woman standing nearby was staring at him. He thought to nod a friendly hello, but something stopped him. Belva Kent's unwavering gaze followed him into the elevator.

The bailiff's voice rang out as the afternoon session began. "The state calls Carol Ann DaRonch." Yocom eased Carol into her story. Their exchange had an even, slow pace that echoed a dozen rehearsals in the county attorney's office. Yocom elicited detail after detail until her narrative had a smooth, irresistible logic, nothing incongruous or out of place.

"Now, as you were walking to the car, was there any conversation between yourself and Mr. Bundy?" Yocom asked.

O'Connell leaped to his feet before Carol could open her mouth. "I object to Mr. Yocom referring to this man as 'Mr. Bundy.' I realize she has identified him, and I suppose if she wants to do it, that's all right. All the way through these proceedings he, whenever he is talking to this lady, refers to the person that night as 'Mr. Bundy' and is reinforcing in her mind the identification."

"Objection sustained."

Yocom argued briefly, but to no avail. From then on he'd keep everything safely in the third person.

During Carol's testimony Hanson turned to look at her. If he believed what she had to say, then Yocom's circumstantial case would send Theodore Robert Bundy to jail, possibly opening the door to further, even more serious charges. She seemed so frail and thin to have fought off an attack of this kind. And he couldn't help noticing how much more nervous she was now than she had been in the pretrial hearings. But the mood in the crowded court was remarkable. O'Connell would later say, "The atmosphere in this case got to me, and I've never let it do that. *I* usually control the atmosphere in the damn courtroom. There was just this feeling that everybody knew [Bundy was guilty]—everybody except the people I had to deal with, family and friends. They knew just the opposite, that he didn't do it."

While Stewart Hanson listened to Carol's description of the lineup, he watched her hands make involuntary movements in her lap. When she recalled something that she was more sure of, the skin over her knuckles whitened. Hanson weighed Carol's testimony against his own experience with eyewitness identification. Hadn't O'Connell said she typically looked down? Carol seemed most sure when she claimed to have recognized his walk at the lineup. Her memory of his face was obviously sketchy, but she spoke up with a forceful voice when Yocom asked, "Did you notice anything about his appearance that was identical to the way you observed him on November 8?"

"The way he walked."

During Carol's testimony, Ted slouched behind the defense table, tapping a pencil quietly against the table. He looked irritated during the lineup testimony, but oddly sympathetic at other times. Here was a poor, naive young girl who had obviously been misled by police, his expression seemed to say. She wasn't responsible.

O'Connell got to his feet slowly, and watched as Carol hunched forward to meet the onslaught she knew was coming. An hour on the stand had already sapped her energy, and the tension in the courtroom was becoming unbearable. She started to cry, quietly, big tears rolling slowly down from the corners of her eyes.

"Now, you have testified in court about this incident on two different occasions before this, haven't you?" Carol's tears were having an obvious effect on the spectators.

"Yes."

"And those times Mr. Bundy was present, wasn't he?"

"Yes."

"Mr. Yocom?"

"Yes."

"And you described this incident both times, didn't you?"

"Yes."

"Did you cry during those times?"

"No."

"Is it the crowd here that is making you nervous?"

"Yes."

That was the best he could do to soften the heartrending spectacle. O'Connell's plan of attack was simple, and just the reverse of Yocom's handling of Carol—fast, illogical, and occasionally brutal. Instead of following her story line from the night of November 8, he darted in and out of the conflicting, erratic statements she had given to police and to the court in pretrial hearings. Carol had waffled on her description of the badge, her assailant's mustache, and the multiple descriptions of the VW. He pointed out one inconsistency in her identification of Ted, moved on to the VW, and then back to the lineup. The shakiest portion of her testimony, the VW, came under the heaviest fire. She had said several times the way she identified Ted's car from the Polaroids was that the car didn't have a license plate. But none of Thompson's photos showed the front end.

"There were a couple of unsuccessful attempts. Then, on September 8, Sergeant Collard took you up and showed you a car on the Avenues, didn't he?"

"Yes."

"Did that car have a license plate on it?"

"No."

"And that's what you remembered, isn't it, when you were talking about how you identified the photograph?"

"No."

"What were you thinking of when you said that you identified the car in the photograph because it didn't have a license plate?"

"I was thinking of the car that night."

"Well, obviously you were thinking of the car that night, because the car and the picture didn't have the license plate on it. Now, my question was: were you just confusing the car that you saw in the pictures with the car you saw on the street? You were just wrong. Is that it?"

"I don't know."

"Did you tell Officer Collard that the car you saw up on the Avenues was the car you were kidnapped in?"

"I might have, because it didn't have a license plate. But it looked completely different."

"Well at the preliminary hearing you said you didn't identify it, right?"

140

Carol was badly disoriented by this point. She could no more remember the details of what she'd said at the preliminary hearing than what she'd told officers six months before. O'Connell waited a few moments to let the effect of her confusion sink in.

"What else about it made you think it was the car, other than it didn't have a license plate? It looked completely different, but you identified it anyway. Isn't that true?"

"Because it was supposed to be the car in the pictures," Carol replied with as much firmness as she could muster, thinking of Thompson's assurances about the backseat tear.

"That's right, and that's why you identified it, because it was supposed to be the car?"

"Because it didn't have a license plate, and I knew it had been changed." O'Connell had her. He pressed on with his point, hardly noticing the reply.

"That was your testimony also at the preliminary hearing. The reason that you identified it was because it was supposed to be the car that was in the picture, and you knew the officers weren't taking you up to see the wrong car, right?"

"Right."

"You pretty well identify what you think the law enforcement officers want you to identify, don't you?"

"No."

"You did at that time, didn't you?"

"No."

"Let's go on to another item . . ."

Hanson watched the exchange intently, trying to get inside this young woman's mind. As the afternoon wore on, Carol began replying "I don't know" to questions she had answered only a few minutes before. It was obvious that she was trying to cut her losses on the poor memory she had of her experience, but whenever O'Connell hit something she was certain about, her answer never wavered. Hanson grew more convinced that, in her own mind, Carol was adamant about remembering Ted Bundy from November 8. The question that remained, however, was how much that certainty reflected the events of November 8, and how much was embroidered later, as O'Connell was charging.

Judge Hanson had never liked the custom of everyone standing when he entered the courtroom. At the opening of trial on Tuesday he offered an explanation that was his trademark as a judge. "You will notice that the bailiff, when he calls the court to order, asks everyone to stand. And, you will notice that I am standing as well. It used to be in the old days—our traditions, of course, come from England—they stood because the judge was a lord. But that is no longer the case. We stand now symbolically because we are representing justice, and we stand in the hope that justice will be done."

Mary Walsh took the stand first and retold the events of November 8 in a clear, simple style. "He was going to kill me," she remembered Carol saying. Yocom was trying to bolster his case for "aggravated kidnapping" by showing that, although Carol's assailant hadn't used the gun, his intention was obviously to hurt her.

Ted's mood the second day remained buoyant. He continued joking with reporters and his First Avenue friends during each recess. But the tension began to show in the afternoon. A woman was following him in the hallways. Whenever he turned around, there she was. Finally, her stare drove Ted back into the courtroom. "Who is that woman that's been following me all day?" he demanded of Bruce Lubeck. "That's Shirleen Aime. Her daughter was found last November in American Fork."

The prosecution had only one major witness remaining: Jerry Thompson. O'Connell was sure to criticize the detective's second Bundy photo lineup, but the rest of his testimony was ironclad. For nearly an hour he sat on the stand, and when he stepped down, the conduct of his investigation emerged unscathed. By Wednesday morning Yocom was through. The informal poll he'd taken the first day with reporters in the hallway had become a daily ritual, and the vote was still a toss-up.

On Tuesday Johnnie and Louise Bundy flew to Salt Lake City to join the other parents in the courtroom. Their son would be on the stand Thursday morning. The new bishop of Ted's ward had invited the couple to stay at his house. Over dinner that evening, they explored Ted's new religion and their son's new interest in marriage and family.

Ted's bishop watched sadly as Johnnie and Louise entered the waiting taxi Wednesday morning, Johnnie in a tidy older suit, Louise in a print dress with an inexpensive quilted overcoat. They had been so earnest the night before. There was nothing in Ted's background, Louise declared, to show him capable of such a thing.

Judge Hanson provided extra chairs for the Bundys at the

defense table. Melanie Pattisen had flown in for the trial's conclusion too. She sat with Louise, sometimes holding the older woman's hand. As Yocom's prosecution closed that morning, Hanson had time to survey the courtroom. For the third day in a row Ted wore a completely different style of clothing. He's parted his hair on the other side and added a pair of wire rims, Hanson noted to himself.

It was a good tactic for an eyewitness case, but something else disturbed the judge, something that only today was noticeable enough to draw his attention. Ted could look so very different—not just the clothes and hairstyle. His mood had an astounding effect on his face, altering his features as easily as changing a mask.

The tension had finally gotten to Ted as he, Johnnie, and Louise sat down to lunch on Wednesday. Ted couldn't have missed Belva Kent's implacable stare. A minute later he jumped up from the table. "I'm too nervous to eat today. You go on without me. I'm going to go jump over a building." Belva caught Ted's parents exchanging a worried glance as he dashed out of the cafeteria.

John O'Connell had hired Dr. Elizabeth Loftus, an associate professor of psychology at the University of Washington, as an expert witness on eyewitness identification. She was here to impeach Carol's memory. As he'd threatened earlier, Yocom challenged the admissibility of her testimony. Was Loftus testifying to general theories of memory and perception, or testifying that Carol DaRonch's identification of Ted had been faulty? The Supreme Court had traditionally ruled that an expert may not testify to anything a layman can be reasonably expected to know. Surely that was true in the case of Judge Hanson, who dealt with eyewitness identification on a daily basis, Yocom said. Hanson overruled the objection, contending that his solid knowledge of eyewitness identification only made him better able to evaluate the testimony.

"What does the term 'unconscious transference' mean?" O'Connell's question opened Wednesday afternoon's session.

"That's a term used to refer to the mistaken recollection or the confusion of a person seen in one situation as the person who has been seen in a different situation. The classic example is the case in which a clerk in the train station was held up, I believe at gunpoint. Later on, the clerk identified a sailor in a lineup. The clerk said that the sailor had committed armed robbery. It turns out that the sailor had an

143

ironclad alibi, but had purchased tickets from the clerk on three prior occasions. So when the clerk went to the lineup, the face did, indeed, look familiar, but the clerk confused that familiarity and recalled the face as being the face of the robber rather than properly recalling it as the person who purchased the tickets."

"Could you describe your own experiment for us?"

"I showed thirty subjects in my experiment six photographs, one at a time, while they heard the story of a crime being committed. All of the people involved in this incident were innocent except the fourth person, who committed an assault. My subjects learned, then, that this person was essentially a criminal.

"Three days later, the subjects came back. They didn't even know that they were going to be asked any questions. They thought they were coming back for their checks. We presented four photographs of people they had never seen before and one innocent bystander from the previous story and asked them to select the criminal. Their correct answer would have been: 'The criminal is not here.'

"What my subjects did is as follows: 60 percent chose the innocent bystander, 16 percent chose another incorrect person—meaning that 76 percent were incorrect. Only 24 percent refused to make a choice. This experiment indicates that the phenomenon of unconscious transference can be demonstrated in the laboratory and is a very real phenomenon."

O'Connell then asked Dr. Loftus if she had seen an example of this phenomenon in Carol's testimony at the preliminary hearing. Loftus pointed to DaRonch's confusion over "Officer Roseland's" badge, which she initially said was simply gold until she had seen Murray police badges, which are gold, silver, and blue. She then began to add these colors to her account of the badge. O'Connell had Loftus emphasize throughout her testimony that, contrary to popular belief, people remember less well in a stress situation such as kidnapping than when they are calm.

"Nothing I haven't thought or felt before," Hanson said to himself. But he wanted to clear something up. What did O'Connell's expert feel about how Carol's experience might affect her memory of it?

"Dr. Loftus, do you have any data to form a conclusion about how a victim in an actual situation might be affected?"

"If I assume that the victim of a crime is experiencing

144

extreme stress, arousal, and fear, my best guess as an experimental psychologist is that the performance of memory is going to be less good. So, if you assume that a crime victim is experiencing extreme arousal, that memory is not going to be as good as if the arousal were more moderate."

Hanson focused on this point. Moderate arousal apparently produced a better memory of the event. He outlined to Dr. Loftus in an abstract form Carol's 15-minute encounter on November 8. Elizabeth Loftus didn't hesitate.

"Performance when the person was moderately stressed prior to extreme stress? In that case, you would expect fairly optimal memory performance."

The defense called a number of Ted's friends that afternoon. No one had ever seen him in patent leather shoes or wearing a mustache without a beard. The owner of a Volkswagen shop testified that a tear in the backseat was a common VW defect. By adjournment Wednesday afternoon, nerves were frayed. Even Yocom had begun to feel the pressure. Someone had phoned late the night before and accused him of railroading Ted Bundy. He decided to avoid the press that day.

Even for the seasoned prosecutor, the prospect of facing Ted on the stand the next day was a little intimidating. Dave Yocom's specialty was career criminals, and Bundy was obviously a lot more challenging than most of them. Sure, Yocom had said at the Aspen conference that if Bundy took the stand, the prosecution would win. But the words seemed like bravado now. O'Connell had hit pretty hard on the patent leather shoes evidence. Maybe he should call Bill Edwards. True, he thought, Edwards's story about Ted's "confession" had been a little confused, but he was certain about having seen him in patent leather shoes.

Ted spent the evening at Roger Kirkham's. The missionaries had rescued his plants after the arrest, and he wanted to thank them. The mood of the visit was surprisingly happy. Ted seemed to feel that Elizabeth Loftus had sunk Carol's identification. As they shook hands that night on Kirkham's doorstep, Mark Swenson teased Ted. "It's been nice knowing you."

On Thursday morning John O'Connell eased Ted slowly through the events of November 8. There was a canceled check from a Texaco station showing some repair work on the VW that afternoon, and a telephone call to Melanie just before midnight. But only Ted's memory supported his alibi for the period when Carol DaRonch was assaulted.

Yocom had leaned heavily on Ted's guilty reaction to Bob Hayward's patrol car. Why, he had asked rhetorically, did Ted Bundy try to evade Officer Hayward, even after the patrol car's spotlight was on? O'Connell needed a convincing explanation. The story he was now about to offer was a calculated risk. What had Ted done after finishing work on the night of August 16? he began.

"I was feeling hot and dirty from work that night, so I took a bath. I was wide awake, not ready to go to bed."

"So what did you do?"

"I went into my closet and I rolled some marijuana—a cigarette."

"Did you smoke?"

"Yes."

Bored with watching television, Ted claimed, he had decided to drive by his girlfriend's house in Salt Lake's south end. But the lights were out, so he just "went for a drive."

"Then what did you do?" O'Connell had only heard this story the week before, and the expression on Dave Yocom's face promised trouble.

"I decided to explore an area of the city I hadn't been in before. I just started west, went through some residential areas, and I was feeling pretty good, sort of watching the lights and enjoying myself. It's kind of embarrassing, but I was feeling pretty good. Then I decided to smoke another cigarette."

"Marijuana cigarette?"

"Some more dope. Yes. It didn't seem wise to do that on a main street, so I looked for the first dark side street. I consumed most of it, and as I started to pull away from the curb I wasn't really very attentive. I happened to see a car in my rearview mirror."

Ted explained he had become paranoid "because I was a law student," and fled, trying to throw his "paraphernalia" out the window as he raced through the suburban streets. He let Hayward chase him to air out the car.

The next part was going to be tricky. Ted had obviously lied to everyone—including O'Connell—about what had happened that night. It would be best just to bring it out here and now and blunt the prosecution's obvious attack.

"When you first consulted with me in August, did you tel

146

me the truth about the incident on the early morning of August 16, 1975?"

"No, I didn't. The whole thing at the time seemed rather absurd to me. I was embarrassed about it. It's not something you care to admit."

"Are your friends and family in Seattle aware that you smoke marijuana?"

"No, I don't think it's generally known." Ted looked over John O'Connell's shoulder to his parents and Melanie Pattisen at the defense table. Melanie's face looked slack and sour. She had been unhappy about Ted's friendship with Wanda, and now, here was proof.

If Yocom had seriously been afraid of cross-examining Ted Bundy, it didn't show in court the next day. He realized that much of the account O'Connell had laid was unsupported. If he could confuse Bundy about the details, the whole edifice would crumble. But Ted refused to be rushed. He had carefully solidified the story in his mind. The more Yocom pushed, the more determined Bundy became to repeat his version precisely.

"Do you remember making this statement, that when you were in Seattle you had occasion to arraign a subject who was stealing a ten-speed bicycle and you had a scuffle with the party until the police arrived? When you found the handcuffs in this dump by your apartment, you thought they would be a good idea for a similar situation?"

"If I could correct the officer's recollection, I apprehended someone who had stolen a woman's purse."

"You didn't tell us when Mr. O'Connell was questioning you that you kept the handcuffs for that purpose. Is that right?"

"I didn't have the occasion to, no."

"Asked why you kept them, you said you didn't know?"

"Well I couldn't—"

"They were interesting, right?"

"They were indeed."

"Then you told Forbes you were going to use them at a future date, if necessary, to apprehend criminal suspects?"

"I don't go looking around for them. I think that was the impression I had at the time, but something that I think was not plausible under the circumstances." Ted had anticipated Yocom's next question.

"Did you even have a key to those handcuffs?"

"I don't believe so."

147

"Wouldn't be of much value in apprehending people without a key, would they?"

"Well, again, if that was my purpose, as I say, the absence of a key was one of the primary factors in saying they were more of a curiosity than saying they were something one could use that would have any utility. So that's why—I mean, I had forgotten all about them. I didn't know where they were, what they were doing in my trunk."

It was growing clear that Ted was losing his grasp on the situation. He had struggled to make every detail of his testimony plausible, to leave nothing unexplained, and so far had succeeded. But now, it appeared, he was not recalling an experience, but telling a well-honed story.

"But you told Forbes you were going to use them to restrain people. Is that right?"

"Detective Forbes had informed me that his game was homicide. I must tell you that he wanted—"

"Answer my question rather than editorializing." Ted jerked his head in Yocom's direction. He looked startled.

"Oh. Sure. Would you re-ask the question."

"You don't remember it?"

"No, I don't."

"You just want to answer the way you want to answer, right?"

"That's right."

O'Connell had let this go on long enough. "Objection."

"Sustained. That's argumentative, Mr. Yocom." Hanson, watching Ted Bundy as closely as he had Carol DaRonch, should have put a stop to Yocom's questioning earlier, but like everyone else in the courtroom he was entranced by the drama.

Yocom called Hayward, Ondrak, and Twitchell to testify that they hadn't smelled marijuana on Ted that night, but Hanson was already convinced that Ted's story was a fabrication. He listened patiently to Friday's closing arguments. It was going to be a rough weekend.

Hanson's longtime court reporter Ruth Price was startled Monday morning when the judge climbed to the bench. "My God," she thought, "he has never looked worse. Look at the bags under his eyes." Stewart Hanson had passed an exhausting weekend over his notes: Yocom's airtight prima facie case, Carol DaRonch's believable testimony; Elizabeth Loftus, too, he thought, had been an excellent witness, an excellent

148

witness. And then there was Bundy. He finally admitted to himself late Sunday night that he simply hadn't believed the defendant's story.

"At the conclusion of the last session," Hanson began to a hushed courtroom, "the court retired to deliberate and has now reached a verdict. I find the defendant, Theodore Robert Bundy, guilty of aggravated kidnapping, a first-degree felony.

"Under the laws of the state of Utah, it is the duty of the court to impose sentence in not less than two nor more than ten days. I would like a presentence investigation report. Would the defendant consider waiving the ten-day period?"

"Yes, Your Honor, he'd waive." O'Connell's voice was faint. He didn't seem the match, now, for his jaunty, outrageous hat.

"I would just like to say in closing that this decision was a very difficult one. I cannot say that there weren't any doubts, but I can say there weren't any reasonable doubts."

17

For several seconds after the verdict, in a silence no one seemed willing to break, Stewart Hanson observed the effect of his decision in the spectators' faces. It was the moment he had feared since O'Connell's surprise announcement waiving jury trial two weeks before.

He thought, later in his chambers, about how dark the courtroom had looked that day. How far away the audience had seemed. Even with a bright wet snow slowly erasing the gray winter landscape outside, he thought, the courtroom had looked darker.

Ted Bundy rose to his feet and spoke softly. He seemed shaky and pale. "I wonder if I could have a couple of minutes with my parents, Judge Hanson?"

"Go ahead, Mr. Bundy. Officer, would you escort him to the jury room?"

Pete Hayward and Jerry Thompson sprang forward. This was their case and a moment they had known would come since early that morning, when Hanson had called them in to discuss security. The judge had asked for two guards at every door and officers placed strategically around the courtroom. Such heavy security could mean only one thing, and the detectives had left elated.

In the jury room they searched Ted and snapped a pair of handcuffs on him, more out of habit than out of any real fear he would escape.

"You don't need these handcuffs." Ted stared bitterly into Thompson's eyes. "I'm not going anywhere."

Johnnie Bundy helped a still tearful Louise through the doorway with Melanie Pattisen and John O'Connell close behind. Hayward and Thompson stepped back from the little group to plan a route back to the jail.

"There's a mob of reporters by the side door," Hayward whispered. "Why don't we take him out the front and down the main elevator? My car's in front."

They waited several minutes longer while the Bundys clung to Ted, then moved to take him away. As Jerry Thompson reached past Melanie for Ted's arm, she hissed vehemently under her breath: "Revenge is sweet, isn't it?" Thompson had been through similar situations before, but never like this. Melanie's line seemed double-edged—she blamed herself as well as him—and it stung.

Outside, in the heavy snow that had been falling all day, a television crew near Hayward's car rushed up.

"Would you make a comment at this time on Judge Hanson's verdict?"

"I have nothing to say," Ted replied, looking straight into the camera, jaw muscles rippling under his cheek.

Thompson tried repeatedly to draw Ted out on the ride back to the jail, but his offers of assistance were met with a cold, furious silence.

Judge Hanson's decision raised some intriguing questions, along with a feeling of relief, among the media and the public. But the conviction brought pure bitterness and outrage to Ted's family and friends. Ted had been railroaded by "the system," by "vindictive cops" out to clear the books of unsolved crimes. Someone had to take the heat and they figured it might as well be Ted Bundy.

Roger Kirkham and the other members of Ted's Mormon church group, shocked by the verdict, resolved to visit their friend often. Generally they stopped by on weekends, bringing church books, news of the ward, and a religious message to keep his spirits up. They all had faith in Ted's victory on appeal.

It was a saddened and confused Fred Burk who pushed open the door to Jerry Thompson's office on the Wednesday after Hanson's verdict. Only that morning the newspaper had run an article that pointed out a new, dark direction for Ted: MURDER CASE TO INVOLVE BUNDY? OFFICIALS QUIET. Pete Hayward was quoted, coyly suggesting that he had "turned over physical evidence to authorities from Pitkin County, Colorado, concerning the murder of a Michigan nurse," but he would neither "confirm nor deny" that Ted Bundy was connected. The echo of the DaRonch conviction was loud and strong in the Rockies.

"I want to apologize. I was a little hard on you the first time I talked to you," said Burk as he eased into a chair opposite Thompson. "I hope you understand my point of view. I have known Ted since September 1974, and he was my closest and best friend, I thought. I guess you don't really know who your friends are."

Jerry remembered Burk's hostile reception during the investigation, and a sense of vindication made him angrier and angrier as Burk continued.

"Do you truly believe without a shadow of a doubt, Detective Thompson, that Ted is guilty?"

"That's a hell of a question," Thompson replied sharply. "Do you think I investigate and sign complaints on individuals who are not guilty?"

"I didn't mean it that way. I'm sorry."

"There is no doubt in my mind," Jerry continued, almost without hearing Burk, "that Ted is definitely guilty of this case."

The two spoke for several minutes more about Burk's relationship to Ted, then arranged a meeting at Fred's apartment. Thompson probed a little to check if Burk knew anything about Ted's Colorado trips, but with no luck.

Later that same afternoon, Donald M. Hull, an investigator for the adult probation and parole board, began a meticulous inquiry into Ted's life and personality for Judge Hanson's report. Its purpose would be to aid the judge in deciding Ted's sentence.

It was an odd first meeting between Bundy and Hull. What could an investigator say about this calm, rational kidnapper who insisted he was innocent? Ted calmly recounted O'Connell's defense, charging that Carol had been under "extreme pressure" to identify someone; that he and his lawyers had walked the route through Fashion Place Mall, demonstrating that Carol had had only three to five minutes with her abductor "and could not make a positive identification on the basis of that paucity of time."

"I was not convicted on the basis of physical evidence alone," Ted said over and over to Hull. "I don't harbor any paranoid feeling about a personal vendetta having been launched against me by the judge or police or any other officials. But Carol DaRonch was placed under considerable pressure, and the police used their several tactics on her, which resulted in her misidentification of me."

Ted answered Hull's questions easily and articulately, only once losing his calm. It was during the exchange on his "family constellation" and background. Ted had just finished describing his close relationship to various members of the family, and his somewhat strained relations with Johnnie Bundy ("I later learned to love him") when Hull asked, "Do you know your real father's whereabouts?"

Across the small table, Ted's face reddened at the obvious implications. It was a hurdle he would face over and over as the summer progressed.

"You might say," Ted said, leaning back and regaining his composure when he realized the futility of protest, "that he left my mother and me and never rejoined the family."

The presentence investigation continued throughout the next two weeks, with interviews of Thompson, DaRonch, and Bundy's family and friends. The search was an extensive one, leading to people in Seattle who hadn't seen Ted Bundy in years. Most could provide nothing to explain a violent side to their old acquaintance.

For one woman, who had dated Ted briefly, the call from a Utah prison psychologist brought back a curious memory. She didn't mention it over the phone and really hadn't thought of it in years, but there was one thing about Ted that had always bothered her. Under all that easygoing, confident talk, there was a powerful insecurity. Not once, she would later recall, did Ted Bundy agree to come home and meet her family.

"He didn't think he was good enough," she said. "It was strange. On the one hand he didn't seem to respect his mother, and he dragged down his family name, and on the other he complained how unfair that kind of attitude was."

Jerry Thompson didn't have much to add to his court testimony and the thick pile of "follow-up reports" he turned over to Hull. He was busy, anyway, with the murder of a young woman found in a canyon east of Salt Lake City. "I have been tied up with another female homicide in our area," he wrote to another police agency, "which does not appear to be connected with the ones we are working on with Mr. Bundy." It was the first such case in months, it seemed, where Ted was not automatically a prime suspect.

When Hull slipped his report on Hanson's desk, the judge turned to it right away. Was there some deep psychological explanation for the kidnapping? All the report showed was a man with a few flaws, but nothing to indicate a desire to kidnap or threaten a young woman with a crowbar. In fact, the report contained numerous letters of praise for Ted, the result of a campaign organized by Louise Bundy in Washington.

"Dear Mr. Hull," one neighbor from Tacoma wrote, "until Ted graduated from Wilson High School, he lived one block from us. As a classmate and friend of our son, he spent many hours at our house and beach place. . . . We looked forward to his visits and have enjoyed them very much. . . . We are proud of the way he applied himself to his chosen career, and we even looked forward to voting for him some day. In 1970, our three-and-a-half-year-old granddaughter strayed from her parents at Green Lake in Seattle. I only wish I could impress you with our double surprise when a young man pulled a child from the water and it was our granddaughter. And her savior, good old Ted Bundy!"

The record of a telephone call to Melanie Pattisen caught Hanson's interest. It was a disjointed, nervous, evasive conversation between Hull and the young woman who had sat weeping in his courtroom. Yes, Stewart Hanson read with disbelief, she had contacted the Seattle police in late October 1974 and suggested Ted might be involved in the murders of young women. And yes, she had in fact found some plaster of paris in his apartment, surgical gloves, crutches, an ax, a meat cleaver, and some knives. But now there were plausible explanations for all these items. Ted was a gourmet cook and needed the cleaver. He'd part-timed at a medical supply house.

Even her suspicions of Ted's infidelity and lack of sexual interest now had a basis. He frequently took night classes at

153

the University of Washington and came home late, claiming he was too exhausted for sex. Melanie now claimed she was "rattled" during her talk with Thompson and Ira Beal the previous September, and not thinking too clearly. Terror of a murderer on the loose had unsettled her, and that's why she went to the police. "I do not suspect Ted Bundy of having murdered the girls or of being guilty of the present charge."

A week after the first call Hull grabbed the phone and heard Melanie's voice again. The hesitant, evasive tone was gone now. "I just want to make sure you understand that I do not feel that Ted Bundy is linked to any murders in Seattle, or in any other area for that matter. I wish I had never talked to Keppel or given an interview to Jerry Thompson."

Hull's report, in the end, was scarcely different from the psychological evaluation Bundy's lawyer, John O'Connell, had had done of Ted before the trial. In December University of Utah clinical psychologist Gary Q. Jorgenson had ticked off Bundy's attributes: "good social presence," "ego strength and good self-concept," "positive self-identity," "highly intellectual, independent, tolerant, responsible." Ted seemed to have "a normal psychosexual development," according to Jorgenson, and a healthy curiosity about his real father. Like Hull, about the worst thing Jorgenson could say was that Ted exhibited some hostility on the tests, but that may well have reflected his reaction to the charge and the fact that he had to put up with the tests in the first place. The two conclusions were virtually interchangeable: "Mr. Bundy is an extremely intelligent young man who is intact psychologically," Jorgenson had written. "In many regards he is the typical young Republican that he has been in the past."

Both before and after the trial Ted Bundy had come up with high marks from psychological experts. But now, just ten days after the verdict in his kidnapping trial, Ted wasn't thinking much about that shiny, official image in the files. There was another expert who wanted his time—investigator Mike Fisher from Aspen—and that meant the stakes had suddenly gone up. It was murder this time, a charge that could mean the death penalty in Colorado.

The date was March 11, 1976. John O'Connell was at Bundy's side in the Salt Lake County jail, and for the record, he wanted the first word: "I want to start by saying that for the last five or six months we have been attempting through local law enforcement agencies and through the county attorney's office to get information on the Colorado cases. We have been constantly informed that the authorities from Colorado refuse to allow them to release any information. . . . Also, Mr. Bundy does not have his gas records and things like that. That makes it very difficult. Now if you have those records and can show them to him, I suppose that might help."

Mike Fisher and Sergeant Bill Baldridge hadn't made the trip from Aspen to beat around the bush. "OK," said Fisher into the tape recorder set up between them, "what we're here for specifically is a murder which involved a young lady by the name of Caryn Campbell. It occurred near Aspen, January 12, 1975. All right. Now that's specifically what we're going to be talking to Mr. Bundy about now."

"All right," O'Connell shot back gamely. "Now on the gas records, can you give the dates that he was in Colorado? There were three days, I understand, that he was in Colorado. Is this the first of them?" But O'Connell could only spar a few minutes more. Ted would have to answer Fisher's questions—or not answer—as he could.

"I'll give you whatever I can," Ted said. Fisher went to the task.

"During January 1975, Ted, were you ever in the state of Colorado?"

"Possibly."

"It's possible?"

"I can't say for sure."

"OK. If you were in the state of Colorado, do you know where you would have been at that time?"

"Ah, the general Rocky Mountain area. You know, I don't recall the names of the routes or cities—ah, I don't know the area that well to say for sure."

"Ted, I'm going to show you a gas record here, dated January 12, 1975, and have you look at that. It's from a gas station in Glenwood Springs, Colorado. Do you recall being in that town, Ted?"

"Well, not specifically. It appears to be my signature, and you know, I certainly wouldn't deny that it's my signature on my gas receipt, but I don't remember making that purchase. I've made many purchases of gasoline. I don't remember that particular purchase—no."

"Do you remember ever going to Glenwood Springs, Colorado, before or in January 1975?"

155

"As a name—I mean if I was to see it, I could probably say whether or not I'd been there before. As a name, it's not something that stands out in my mind."

"Have you ever been to Aspen, Ted?"

"I recall clearly one time years ago, ah, I think it was '69. I was there, and ah, I'm trying to remember if for sure I was there any other time, in January or last year . . . I'm not denying it," he said a few moments later, "but I can't really recall."

Fisher fixed his eyes on Bundy, intent on every pause and stammer. Ted was measuring each question before he answered, testing it as he would a Chinese box for a false panel somewhere. Suddenly Fisher veered off.

"Have you ever had any problems with lapses of memory, amnesia, or blackout spells—anything like that?"

"No," Ted said. This time he didn't hesitate, and it made Fisher begin to peel.

"The reason I ask," the investigator started in, "is because Aspen is rather a unique place. It's well known all over the country. It seems that a person, even going from Salt Lake City—if you'd ever traveled you'd remember."

Ted didn't waver. It was his mind, his memory, his answer. "Well, I can't remember traveling there for any specific reason."

But Fisher was far from through. He produced a second Chevron gas receipt, also from Glenwood Springs, dated January 11. Ted couldn't remember that one "specifically" either. Then Fisher asked if Ted remembered skiing in Colorado, if he remembered any hotels or bars he might have visited. Finally he worked Bundy around to tacitly agreeing he had traveled in Colorado the previous winter. But as for details, Ted's recollection was just as vague.

"Um, I remember I slept in my car on a couple of occasions, simply because I didn't have much money. But I don't recall the name of any motel I might have stayed in. I think I stayed in one at some time during that period. It was along the road, and I couldn't give you the name on it, even the general location of it, aside from the fact that it was somewhere, you know sometime during my trip." Restaurant names, unique signs, highway numbers—none of them came to mind. "I think mainly I just drove—drove off on the side roads somewhere, came to a point where I didn't want to go any farther or the road got too steep or something—and I turned around and went back to the main road."

"Which main road would that have been?"

"Well, the highway, whatever the highway would be that I was on."

Fisher steadied himself and tried to reset the pace. He asked Ted what his favorite beer was, questioned him about his remarks to Jerry Thompson during the first search of his apartment, and mentioned several other Colorado cities and dates. But Mike Fisher had one thing on his mind. Finally, almost an hour into this exasperating interview, he could contain himself no longer.

"I'm going to ask you real specifically: did you meet a young lady at Snowmass in Aspen, Colorado, on January 12—that's a Sunday, and it's in the evening. Did you meet a woman anywhere near that area on January 12, 1975?"

"No, I didn't. If I met a young woman I would have remembered it. I would remember it now, but as I say, my purpose in being there was to get away and be by myself and think."

"Were you by yourself for quite a bit of the period of that time on that trip?"

"In all probability I was, yes."

"Do you remember being alone or with someone on the trip?"

"Alone."

"Alone." Fisher repeated Ted's answer and paused. "OK. I'm going to come right to the point and I want a truthful answer to this. On January 12, 1975, did you kill that young lady up there near Snowmass at Aspen, Colorado?"

"I certainly didn't kill anyone anywhere, and I, wherever it was I didn't kill anyone."

Fisher and Baldridge ground on for another hour, but Bundy had met them squarely. Ted lectured them a little about police tactics of harassment and the attempt to build public sentiment against him, sticking to his story that he just couldn't recall the towns or the places or the dates they were asking about. To Ted Bundy, it seemed, his own movements through Colorado the year before were as evanescent as a dream.

The Colorado investigators returned home, undaunted by their failure to elicit a confession from Ted, to continue work on the Caryn Campbell murder. The Utah kidnapping conviction had emboldened Fisher, but he wanted more: another eyewitness, perhaps, who had seen Bundy in the Wildwood Inn on January 12, 1975. Through the spring and summer Mike Fisher hunted down Aspen ski area employees, a search that extended as far as Europe, where cooperating police hauled tourists from Colorado off the trains and asked if they remembered Bundy.

Fisher also requested a "psychological stress evaluation" of Bundy's voice, based on the tape of his unrewarding interview in the Salt Lake County jail. Pointing up the limitations and unreliability of the relatively new PSE technique, University of Utah psychologist Gordon Barland offered little support for police suspicions: "The level of stress generally present in Bundy's voice was less than had been anticipated, in view of the investigator's comments about his highly nervous appearance." Barland suggested that the cassette recorder used had not been up to the task.

It was not going to be as easy for Mike Fisher as it once had seemed.

18

Aspen investigator Mike Fisher wasn't the only one with problems. In the spring of 1976 police in Utah and Colorado were having trouble with a Bundy-the-one-man-murder-machine theory. The Debbie Kent case, which had looked so promising at first with its handcuff key and double identification of Ted as the suspicious character at Viewmont High, was stalled in its tracks: with no body, no evidence of a homicide, there was no charge of murder. Police had only a flimsy one-hair match from Bundy's car for Melissa Smith, and the squabbling Utah County detectives had only an informant who failed a lie detector test to tie Ted to the Laura Aime case. The files were wide open for Nancy Wilcox and Nancy Baird.

In Colorado credit card receipts made Ted a suspect in three cases—and nothing at all connected him to four others.

For several years, especially since the Intermountain crime conference of 1974, police across the West had held high hopes that one man, one case might emerge to sweep clean their unfinished files. Such is the perennial, some say dangerous optimism of the police. Theodore Bundy, caught racing through a Salt Lake City suburb, had fired those hopes as no one before had. But now, a year later . . .

Undaunted, several dozen jurisdictions in the West were keeping Bob Neill at the FBI lab busy with hair and blood samples. Jerry Thompson had not shipped anything since he and Paul Forbes had ripped the interior out of the VW in December, but each day he returned to his desk to face a chaotic stack of requests for information on Theodore Robert Bundy. This was quickly getting to be the case that wouldn't go away.

On Monday, March 22, Thompson and another deputy picked Ted up from the county jail at 9:00 a.m. and escorted him to Judge Hanson's court for sentencing. Police weren't the only ones puzzled over what to make of Ted Bundy. Stewart Hanson was quite unsatisfied with Hull's presentence report. Not that Hull had done a bad job, but here, seemingly, was a model citizen—a few foibles, maybe, perhaps some intimations of a darker side—but nothing that provided a psychological explanation for the crime Hanson believed Ted had committed.

Looking beaten and tired in his jail clothes, Ted Bundy slouched next to John O'Connell and Bruce Lubeck. O'Connell, having regained his equilibrium, was prepared with a series of motions to lessen Ted's sentence. But the judge had a surprise.

"I am going to delay sentencing of Mr. Bundy," Hanson began, "because I need more information before a decision can be made. Subsequently, I am ordering a ninety-day diagnostic evaluation at the Utah State Prison and will set the date for sentencing as June 30. I understand you have some motions, Mr. O'Connell."

Ted looked wearily at his mother, who'd flown from Seattle with a friend of his.

"I am going to ask the court to acquit my client," said O'Connell, a note of self-righteousness in his voice, "by handing down a judgment notwithstanding the verdict and by reducing the charge from aggravated kidnapping to simple kidnapping." O'Connell cited the "rumors," "the weird feeling of mass hysteria," even his own "subconscious feelings" as factors in the trial. Shortly he was at a rhetorical peak: "Years from now people will look back on this case and compare it to the Sacco-Vanzetti trial."

Yocom argued briefly against the motion to reduce the

charge. Then Judge Hanson offered his final remarks: "I would like to say in closing that I wish this case had been tried by a jury. Spectacular trials put a great burden on a lone judge. It would have been easier to find Mr. Bundy innocent. I made the harder of the two decisions."

Bundy was allowed time with his mother and his friend before Thompson arrived. Irritation hardened Ted's usually controlled features, and his only comment to the detective was a vow: "I'm going to appeal it as far as I can." Bundy would be running a maze in the next three months whose logic he knew only too well. Run ragged by tests and techniques for only one purpose, he would emerge afterward to be put on display, like some psychological sideshow, for the media and public.

An unusual request arrived for Detective Thompson that Friday. Four psychologists who'd worked on the Seattle task force wanted to hear the tape of Fisher's interview. It was a tired Jerry Thompson who left work that day. All the real police work had ended months ago, and he was beginning to feel like a clerk instead of a detective.

But when he fumbled the phone from its cradle Monday morning, the familiar voice of FBI lab man Bob Neill caught his attention immediately: "I have found another hair from the original batch that you sent from Mr. Bundy's car. It matches a known sample of Carol DaRonch."

Thompson grabbed a pen to make some notes. "One hair's definitely the same," Neill went on, "and just between you and me, there are several other hairs that I will say are hers, and some more which are close, but the lab won't let me state positively on those."

Over the last few months the Salt Lake City detective had come to know Neill fairly well. For the last 14 years this expert had peered at thousands of hairs under a microscope and testified in dozens of trials. Neill carried a well-earned reputation.

"Bob, how does this hair stuff work exactly?"

"I tell juries all the time that hair examination is like comparing faces. You look under a microscope at a known sample for its physical characteristics, mostly the arrangement of the pigmentation particles. Sometimes they come in long streaks, or clumped up in discrete packets, or in swirls. There's about fifteen to twenty-five characteristics you can see under 300X magnification. After a few years of experience it becomes very similar to identifying faces. Sometimes you get look-alikes, but not often."

"You ever had two hairs from different people match up?"

"Yeah, maybe twenty or thirty times. I've had a number of situations where two individuals are so close I can barely distinguish them, but for the vast majority it's pretty easy. I'm sorry we're so slow on this, Jerry, but unless you put an 'expedite' on a shipment we put it in the hopper with everything else."

"That's fine, Bob. Mr. Bundy was convicted and he's down at the prison diagnostic evaluation unit right now."

When Thompson relayed Neill's report to Judge Hanson the next day, the judge made a few deprecating remarks about the circumstantial nature of hair evidence, but he could barely suppress his smile. Hanson never would have said what he was thinking, but prosecutor Dave Yocom beamed for him over the news. "I'm not too worried about appeal," he said. "The county won its case without its best piece of evidence."

Ted settled into a cell on the top tier (called the "fish tier") in the medium security building at the Utah State Prison and rapidly became well liked by his fellow prisoners and his tier counselor, Fred Hornick. The tiny cells were crammed with boxes, books, and anything else a convict could get friends or relatives to provide for entertainment. Between exercise and meal periods, Ted Bundy read—mostly lawbooks in preparation for his appeal and the Colorado investigation looming on the horizon.

To almost everyone on the fish tier, the new inmate was a disarming, gentlemanly, intelligent addition, but they saw little of him during those three months. Almost every day Ted faced some new psychological test or an interview with a member of the diagnostic staff. Here was a real challenge for the prison's psychiatrists, psychologists, and social workers, and they spent more time testing, analyzing, and discussing Ted Bundy than anyone in the program's history.

First, there were psychiatrist Van Austin's skull X rays, electroencephalograms, and thermographic brain scans, plus a series of interviews. Then A. L. Carlisle, staff psychologist, administered a series of "objective tests"—the Minnesota Multiphasic Personality Inventory (MMPI) and the California Life Goals Evaluation Schedules—and a series of "projective tests" using inkblots and other devices. Most of them were familiar to Ted, as an ex-psychology major, and the intent behind the questions was as plain as the bars on his cell.

When Austin and Carlisle began repeating some tests, Ted grew indignant at the obvious bias displayed. He vented his anger in a steady stream of letters to Judge Hanson. The verdict was influencing the staff's attitude toward him, he charged. So was the Colorado investigation. The "burden" to discover a "psychological basis" for Bundy's "violent crime" permeated their interviews. His letters began as a pressure valve to let off steam at the diagnostic staff, but soon took on a different tone as Ted grew more frustrated.

"This is really a conflict between two people, yourself and me," he wrote Hanson. "You believed that I was guilty, and I knew I wasn't."

Refusing to write "his version" of the November 8, 1974, kidnapping was one weapon Bundy used in the growing conflict. But he finally relented under pressure and issued a long, sarcastic, tightly written diatribe against Yocom's case, brusquely sweeping aside its arguments like so many cobwebs. Calling his account the "most reliable statement pertaining to the occasion," Ted reviewed Carol DaRonch's many hesitations and waverings, and for the first time the diagnostic unit's star patient began to formulate arguments that he would repeat over and over in the future.

On his lack of an alibi: "My memory does not improve with time, but it is safe to say what I was not doing. I was not having heart surgery nor was I taking ballet lessons, nor was I in Mexico, nor was I abducting a complete stranger at gunpoint. There are just some things a person does not forget and just some things a person is not inclined to do under any circumstances. The point is that my version of my whereabouts and activities on November 8, although understandably vague, has not been refuted by any testimony or physical evidence other than the testimony of Carol DaRonch. The fact is that evidence tending to exculpate me was not successfully challenged or refuted. The reality is that the entirety of the defense's case was disbelieved."

Bob Hayward's traffic stop, too, came under fire—not for the physical evidence it produced, but for the "imaginative insinuations" Dave Yocom had drawn from the fact that Ted had "ostensibly" failed to stop in the subdivision. Calling the lie about seeing *The Towering Inferno* a "regrettable subterfuge," and his subsequent admission of having smoked marijuana "immaterial and itself potentially prejudicial," Ted contended that one lie in his life did not discredit him as a witness for all time.

"Judge Hanson, when administering 'jury instructions' to himself, openly assured those present that only testimony and evidence probative to November 8, 1974, would guide his determination in the kidnapping trial. The conclusion, I believe, was that he would ignore the 'bad man' inferences offered by the prosecution based on August 16, 1975. In the final analysis, the only remotely probative force arising out of August 16 was my possession of handcuffs nine months after a kidnapping in which a different pair of handcuffs was used. The prosecutors' preoccupation with a motor vehicle violation unrelated in time and circumstance to the offense in question belied their desperation and the weakness of their case. Hopefully, the judge was able to dismiss the immaterial allegations associated with August 16, 1975.

"Such are my opinions and observations regarding November 8, 1974 and August 16, 1975. My testimony stands as my definitive statement about these occasions."

The diagnostic report Hanson received on June 22 reflected growing hostility. The staff's conclusions and observations were drawn up into a "negatives" and a "positives" list. On the plus side, as before, were "high intelligence," "no severely traumatizing influences in childhood or adolescence," "few distortions in relationship with mother and stepfather," "no serious defects in physical development, habits, school adjustment, emotional maturation, or sexual development," "adequate interest in hobbies and recreational pursuits," "average environmental pressures and responsibilities," and "no previous attacks of emotional illness."

First on the list of negatives was Judge Hanson's verdict. The "bad man" inferences would shadow Ted from now on.

One theme ran constantly through the report's negatives. "According to the psychological and psychiatric evaluations, when one attempts to understand Mr. Bundy he becomes evasive." Put another way, "The defendant is somewhat threatened by people unless he feels he can structure the outcome of the relationship. . . . Passive-aggressive features were also evident. There was hostility observed on the subject's part directed toward the diagnostic personnel, even though Mr. Bundy would carefully point out that it was not aimed directly at those responsible for his evaluation."

The report's most telling information came from Bundy's MMPI scores. Originally this test consisted of a series of questions that people with certain psychological disorders could be predicted to answer in a particular way. Early critics contended that the decision about who was sane and insane was essentially the opinion of one man. Subsequent versions were based on the diagnoses of many professionals, and with the advent of the computer, a company in California began compiling a bank of test scores and diagnoses in an attempt to statistically eliminate the human factor. More complex mathematical calculations with the scores also became possible.

When Bundy's scores came back from California, what had first appeared as a "relatively sane profile" had some disturbing surprises.

"A fairly strong conflict was evidenced in the testing profile, that being the subject's fairly strong dependency on women, yet his need to be independent. Mr. Bundy would like a close relationship with females, but is fearful of being hurt by them. In addition, there were indications of general anger, and more particularly, well-masked anger toward women."

On the morning of June 30 Stewart Hanson leaned back in his chair to review the report. Once again he found the results frustratingly inconclusive. The testing profile was troubling but not damning. Where was the evidence to support a violent crime? In the absence of a solid indictment of Bundy, he would have to give him the benefit of the doubt. After all, Carol DaRonch had walked away unhurt.

Theodore Bundy faced Hanson for sentencing that morning in a prison T-shirt with the word "DIAGNOSTIC" stenciled across it. He had filed his own motion to "show cause why Utah State Prison Warden Sam Smith should not be held in contempt for failing to . . . provide an evaluation to Your Honor and a recommendation based on that evaluation."

Hanson named O'Connell and Lubeck as cocounsel for the motion, but it was clearly going to be Ted Bundy's day in court. Over the next 90 minutes he would hold the lawyers and the judge silent and move spectators to tears.

Under the guise of summoning witnesses for the motion Ted had compelled Van Austin, A. L. Carlisle, and Don Morgan to attend the hearing. In an oddly appropriate gesture, the judge seated the diagnosticians in the jury box. Hanson issued a warning that he would allow Ted to rebut some of the report's conclusions, but would not permit a wholesale review of the procedures.

Striding to his place in front of Hanson, Ted Bundy laid down his notes and grasped the sides of the lectern in a self-consciously dramatic gesture. The report, he began, applied labels to him without offering an example or a reason why they should be applied.

"Passive-aggressive, for instance. I was told yesterday by Dr. Austin"—Ted nodded in the direction of the impassive psychiatrist—"that was not a diagnosis he made of me, but there are features. I will be darned if I know what 'passive-aggressive' means. Sounds pretty terrible." He broke into hollow, forced laughter. "But when I read Dr. Carlisle's illustrations of passive-aggressive as he witnessed it, I sit back and say, if that's passive-aggressive, that's fine with me. If passive-aggressive is being hostile toward a man who's given you the same test four times, three times, who questions your basic credibility and goes into very private areas of your life, then I admit to being hostile, but not angry."

Words began tumbling out of Ted's mouth, his voice gradually fading as the tempo picked up. He had to make an effort to control himself.

"As Your Honor has read, Dr. Austin made a conclusion that 'Mr. Bundy has no mental illness.' Now, he did qualify himself, and noted here on page two some 'features of an antisocial personality.' "

Ted held Austin's three-page letter up and gestured angrily toward the psychiatrist.

"He made that statement on the basis of lack of guilt feelings, and to this date I'm not exactly sure what he is referring to here, but I suppose he made this observation to support it: 'Callousness, and a very pronounced tendency to compartmentalize and rationalize.' My problem in dealing with Dr. Austin's observations is that there's no substance, no illustrations of these characteristic traits he saw in me."

Ted let his objection sink in, then added offhandedly, "He did tell me that these might be good traits for a lawyer, but he wasn't sure."

The halfhearted attempt at humor passed unnoticed, and Ted rushed on to his next arguments, stressing the positive points and denying Austin's criticisms.

"I think the basic misunderstanding of these three gentlemen, Mr. Morgan, Dr. Carlisle, and Dr. Austin, was my at-

165

titude about my innocence in the case." He drew a deep breath. "Here is where we really reach a parting of the ways between an evaluation and a basic human motivation, possessed by even professional people: a fear of being wrong, a fear of bucking the system, a fear, perhaps, of even insulting Your Honor."

Ted dabbed at his eyes before he continued. "Dr. Austin's a very experienced man, practiced years at the state hospital at the prison. But in conclusion he states: 'I feel that Mr. Bundy is either a man who has no problems or is smart enough and clever enough to appear close to the edge of normal.'

"That's a hell of a choice, Your Honor. I think it revealed the basic lack of security, maybe even the pressure that is on these men that a man with a great deal of experience and education is going to make a preposterous—but perhaps honest—statement like that. I remember Dr. Van Austin saying to me during one session we had that he was good—frightfully good, in fact—at detecting violence in people. I'm trying to paraphrase, but he said he wouldn't make any such prediction in my case. Being an optimist, I took that as a compliment."

Ted's sniffling and labored breathing were clearly audible in the courtroom. He shuffled Austin's letter to the bottom of his notes. A. L. Carlisle's psychological report came under fire next, specifically the section about hostility toward the interviews and a charge that Ted had deep feelings of insecurity.

"One thing which I probably neglected to bring up in open court because members of the media are so apt to jump to conclusions in this case . . . but I'm not sure I care about them anymore. It involves my relationship . . . Excuse me." Tears were rolling steadily down Ted Bundy's face, and he took a few minutes to compose himself before he began again by reading from Carlisle's report. " 'The constant theme running throughout the testing was a view of women being more competent than men.' " Ted shot a glance toward the jury box. " 'There were also indications of a fairly strong dependency on women, and yet he also has a strong need to be independent.'

"Now draw from that what you will. I admit to being dependent on women, for whatever that means. I don't know that there's a man in the courtroom who isn't, and if he isn't, maybe there's something wrong with him. Our mother

166

is a woman. Our teachers in grade school are women. There's no reason why women shouldn't appear as competent as men."

In focusing on the dependency remarks, Ted was obviously skirting the much more damaging results of the MMPI. But Ted continued his attack, zeroing in on social worker Don Morgan's findings. How could you possibly get to know someone intimately in 90 days? he demanded. They wanted a lifetime's knowledge in only a few short weeks.

After an hour and 15 minutes, Ted finally came to the incident that angered him the most. Generally, diagnostic prisoners are transferred to a minimum security prison farm. But Deputy Warden Leon Hatch had refused the staff's suggestion about Ted, who fired off angry letters to Hatch, then Warden Smith, and finally Hanson, but never received a reply. This was just one more example of the "bad faith" that governed the whole diagnostic study. The memory of this "injustice" revived him, and when Ted raised his voice again it was clear and strong.

"Summarizing my bad points again: I was defensive, a private person, insecure because I wanted freedom from want, didn't want to be bored, wanted to live my life my own way. I was dependent on women. Good grief! I couldn't handle stress, but sure did well in prison, bullying these people—at least that's what they thought. If anyone wants to go through stress, let me advise that they go through the process that I have just been through.

"Uh oh," Ted interrupted himself, the sarcasm heavy in his voice. "There were signs of incongruity and dishonesty in the assessment of Dr. Carlisle. I apologize to Roger Kirkham in advance for this, but Dr. Carlisle discovered that I continued smoking after I joined the L.D.S. church. Don't mind me saying so, Dr. Carlisle, the L.D.S. church is a hell of a lot more than not smoking and drinking. I feel sufficiently bad about that, and I think we have a misunderstanding about my behavior after I joined the church. But if that's an illustration of my incongruity and dishonesty, so be it. I'm sufficiently reprimanded.

"But here's the kicker: If you thought I was bad before, because I was dependent on women, and a private person, insecure, passive-aggressive, now what we have to tackle is the biggest—the biggest line of them all: that the above personality profile is consistent with the nature of the crime for which he is convicted. I think you ought to write a paper on

167

this, Dr. Carlisle. It's probably the first time it can ever be substantiated that a person with that kind of profile was prone to commit kidnapping, or anything else, for that matter.

"There are probably tens of thousands of people in the city walking around, especially on the university campus here, more or less like me. And as you told me, those characteristics are not predicted by anyone necessarily, because many people have them and are never violent, and there are many people who are violent who never have those characteristics." Ted Bundy had just laid bare what was for many observers the fascinating focus of the case. Here was a "criminal" just like anyone they knew—just like them. His defense, his indignation were the best they might have managed in his shoes.

"Let me summarize, then, my basic objection to the evaluation as it applies to me and, I think, as it operates in general. The evaluation was written, designed, and conformed to your verdict, subconsciously, I think, as valiantly as those who evaluated me tried."

Ted lost control once again, and the tears poured down his cheeks. It was unclear whether he had finished or not, but no one moved to close the proceeding.

"As I said, this was written to conform to the verdict."

Ted stopped again.

"Two critical, independent variables which inhibit my case are my conviction for the offense of kidnapping and my continued insistence that I did not commit the crime. One or the other of these propositions is invalid. Since I do not, will not, and cannot accept responsibility for the act, and since there is no objective, verifiable psychological data to support my committing such an act, the evaluators are unwilling to venture an opinion on the matter in fear of changing the judge's verdict."

Hanson called a ten-minute recess before hearing further statements from O'Connell and Yocom. There was some minor bickering before Ted was allowed to make his final plea before sentencing. O'Connell pointed out that, although the psychologists had not been able to get close to Theodore Bundy, "There are a half-dozen people in this courtroom right now, and I know dozens of others who call me constantly, who feel very close to Mr. Bundy." Despite Ted's eloquent plea, however, the contempt motion was swiftly denied.

"Is there any reason that sentence should not be imposed at this time?" Hanson's question seemed almost rhetorical. "Mr. Bundy, do you have anything you desire to say at this time?"

Ted rose from the chair, like a prizefighter rising for the last round.

"Yes, Your Honor. I think I tried in numerous letters to somewhat vehemently express my feelings about incarceration as an alternative, as a punishment, as a tool for rehabilitation. I can only hope that you have read those letters for whatever value they had. I don't know what you are going to do, Your Honor, until you do it. But I have a feeling since I didn't agree with the first decision that I won't agree with the second. It is neither a rational nor a humane alternative under the circumstances to commit me to prison. I can assure you this: don't send anybody down to the prison who shouldn't be there, because he will be down there . . ."

By this point Ted had broken into uncontrollable sobbing. Only a disjointed mumbling came out, incoherent to the court and audience. Ted looked up slowly and began again.

"Some day, who knows when—five, ten, or more years in the future . . ."

The words choked in his throat again, and Ted hit the sheaf of papers in his hand down on the lectern.

". . . when the time comes for my release, I suggest you ask yourself where we are, what's been accomplished? Was the sacrifice of my life worth it all? An eye for an eye, measure for measure is child's play . . ."

The papers came slamming down on the lectern again.

". . . in comparison to what you are about to do today. Yes, doctor . . ." Austin came under Ted's bitter stare. "I will be a candidate for treatment—not for anything I have done, but for what the system has done to me."

On June 30, 1976, the Honorable Stewart M. Hanson sentenced Theodore Robert Bundy to 1 to 15 years in jail.

19

"Prison," wrote Ted Bundy to an old friend from political campaigns in Washington State, "is a most powerful experience, an entirely alien way of relating to people. I have learned much about people, and myself, but I wonder to what practical purpose all this delightful knowledge can be put. . . . The whole incredible ordeal remains both nightmarish and startlingly real. All we can do is hope and pray. My love to you and all my other friends."

In July, when he returned to the Utah State Prison at Point of the Mountain to begin serving his sentence for kidnapping, Ted settled into an unspectacular routine in his medium security cell: exercising, sleeping, reading law, staring emptily at reruns of "The Brady Bunch" on television. His work assignment was in the prison's print shop, and his dealings with other inmates, not surprisingly, were peaceful and positive. As a former law student Ted provided valuable, inexpensive legal advice for his new neighbors.

Ted Bundy followed news of the upcoming Ford-Carter presidential election with only half his attention. His own concerns—the Colorado investigation and work on an appeal of the DaRonch conviction—were more than enough to occupy him.

From the beginning John O'Connell had raised the loudest voice of indignation about the trial. "Police framed Bundy on the DaRonch case because of these other crimes," Ted's lawyer said. "It just bothered the hell out of me. I said to the police, 'If you guys are so sure that he's killing all these girls, you're *absolutely* sure he did it, why don't you just kill him?' And they said, 'Oh, God, no, that's radical.'

"If I were absolutely sure he were guilty, I would. I would do that before I began screwing up the judicial system. Because if you get in the habit of doing that, one of these days you're going to nail somebody who's innocent." O'Connell, never one to deny a subject its grandest implications, immediately began preparing an appeal.

Another sentiment about the case, a darker one, was running through the Salt Lake City legal community. Ted Bundy, the thinking went, may have been the only man in Utah history framed for something he actually did.

On August 16 Jerry Thompson received an anonymous letter from an inmate at the Utah State Prison. He didn't want to be killed as a snitch, the letter writer said, but he hated to see a killer get away. Ted Bundy, the letter claimed, had talked about killing one girl in Utah and one in Colorado. Thompson was on the phone to Fisher that afternoon, and within hours the Aspen investigator and Assistant District Attorney Ashley Anderson caught a flight to Salt Lake City to hear the story in person.

"No dice," their informant said, "I've changed my mind."

Fisher was having similar luck back home: no one—in Colorado or Europe or anywhere—remembered a man lurking around the Wildwood Inn on a January night more than a year and a half before.

It just wasn't going to be as easy as it had seemed.

The same day, August 16, 1976, marked an unhappy anniversary for Ted Bundy. It was one year ago to the day that he'd lost a chase to Bob Hayward's Utah highway patrol car, one year ago that Hayward had peered down the beam from his flashlight into a pile of junk on the VW floor. This August 16 was doubly unhappy for Ted when he learned that Judge Hanson had turned down his appeal bond, and the appellate court his appeal. Now he would have to ask the Utah State Supreme Court for a reversal of the kidnapping conviction. It looked like Ted Bundy would be in jail for quite some time.

Ted didn't know yet about some still unhappier news. A rejected appeal was just what Mike Fisher and the Pitkin County D.A.'s office needed to firm up their decision to seek a warrant for Ted's arrest for the murder of Caryn Campbell, even if their case wasn't any stronger than it had been months before.

Mark Swenson, Roger Kirkham, and other friends from Ted's church group had been regular visitors at the prison. With the denial of his appeal, his bishop, Mike Preece, dreaded having to add one more straw to Ted Bundy's burden. But church policy was church policy, and convicted felons had to be excommunicated. As he sat in the barren,

171

ugly visitors' room waiting for Ted, he recalled a remark his new convert had made the previous fall: "I didn't ride my bicycle past the zoo. I couldn't stand the thought. All those caged animals."

Despite it all, Ted seemed to be in a good mood as he shook the bishop's hand. He acted like an old friend, somewhat embarrassed, and apologized that his bishop had to visit him in this "stark place." When Ted heard the news, his happy facade vanished. "Do what you need to."

Bundy had continued to study his new religion at the Point of the Mountain prison. He made a friend in a neighboring cell, a Mormon sentenced to prison for filing a blank income-tax return. They discussed religion together, and Ted gave him a copy of the Book of Mormon fittingly inscribed: "Like the brothers of Amulek, we are being persecuted for our beliefs." Amulek was freed from jail by an angel.

When he tired of lawbooks, Ted's staple diet included a volume of radio talks and quotations by Mormon church authority Richard L. Evans, a book which Ted called the "best he'd ever read." Whatever lay in store for Ted Bundy, he staunchly maintained to his new friend that his two greatest goals in life were to return to law school and "get active in the church once I get out."

In Bundy's primary contact with his Seattle family and friends, through the mail, he maintained a brave, witty, sometimes touching face. He talked about his diet and his new interest in Adelle Davis, reminisced about holidays past, and joked darkly about prison life. He was lifting weights, but admitted, "The strongest muscles will always be between my ears."

"What century is it?" he jested in one letter. "Last I heard I was in the ninth century and falling. . . . As I recall, we last saw each other in the twentieth century, on or about the seventy-fifth year. Planet Earth, wasn't it? And superb spring weather. Since that time I've been captured by Wogs and sold to Klingons, who are presently imprisoning me on an asteroid against my will."

He was writing to a tall, regal-looking, articulate woman whom he had met at one of his jobs in Seattle. Nancy Hobson wrote back immediately. She was to become his most important friend in the world. Two weeks later, when he wrote again, his mood was tenderly self-aware: "I am far from being immune to pain, but I am handling the situation. So in the next few weeks, as things grow more steamy and hostile, understand that I am still fond of and finding small pleasures in living."

In the printshop he made another friend, George Metropolis, who was serving a life sentence for murder and parole violations. Metropolis knew the prison routine far better than Ted, and was considered an escape risk by authorities. The warden had enough experience to know that the printshop was an open invitation for inmates to fashion any printed odds and ends they might need should they leave the facility unexpectedly. So occasionally he would conduct a surprise shakedown.

Ted Bundy was more than a little surprised when Sam Smith walked in that September morning. What, Smith wanted to know, was Ted doing with a forged Social Security card with another man's name on it? The warden suspected Metropolis immediately. Both men would be moved to maximum security. Well versed in the ways of prison escapes, Sam Smith searched Ted's cell before he was allowed back in. Tucked carefully away were a sketch of an Illinois driver's license, airline schedules, and a road map. When the prison reclassification committee met three weeks later, Ted got 15 days in isolation.

As the stiff autumn winds bent down the prison yard's tall grass and sagebrush, Ted's foreboding of his upcoming difficulties in Colorado deepened. "The threat I face is considerable for numerous nonevidentiary reasons," he wrote to a Seattle lawyer. "First and foremost is the publicity. Next comes my conviction for kidnapping in Utah. The third strike against me involves the significant potential for official misconduct (i.e., falsification of evidence) on the part of those who 'believe' in my guilt and feel it is their duty to bring about my conviction."

Bundy rued his own depleted resources and the prosecutor's abundance of money and time. "Without more assistance," he concluded, "the consequences to my life could be fatal." The fight in Colorado, he knew, could be a fight for his life.

But another famous inmate of the Utah State Prison was fighting to die that fall. Gary Gilmore, sentenced to death October 7, 1976, for the murder of a gas station attendant, demanded that the state of Utah carry out his execution.

"You sentence me to die," Gilmore told the judge. "Unless it's a joke, I want to go ahead and do it. I don't want to spend the rest of my life in jail."

173

After two suicide attempts and several involuntary appeals forced on him by his court-appointed lawyers, Gary Gilmore was shot to death in January 1977—the first man executed in the United States in over a decade. Antideath penalty forces feared the floodgates would now open.

Ted spent the final months of 1976 gearing up for his Colorado defense. Convinced at first that he could better prepare himself where he was, in Utah, than on the unfamiliar turf of Colorado, Bundy fought extradition. He was aware, of course, that fighting extradition could have a harmful effect on his public image, making him look uncooperative, stalling guiltily for time. But the alternative, working with a strange attorney in a strange state, was "literally suicidal." By late November, after turning 30 almost without noticing it, Ted didn't feel much better about his prospects. The Colorado public defender assigned to represent him— Chuck Leidner—hadn't impressed Bundy in their one meeting, several phone conversations, and exchange of letters. And Bundy still wasn't sure whether to keep up his fight against extradition or cut his potential losses by giving in.

But the challenge Ted faced in Colorado was far more treacherous than mere unfamiliarity or a tarnished public image. Through routine "discovery" procedures, he had learned that the prosecution in Aspen planned to call (along with such expected witnesses as Mike Fisher, the California eyewitness Lisbeth Harter, and the doctor who performed the Caryn Campbell autopsy) Carol DaRonch, Jerry Thompson, Dave Yocom, even Bob Keppel from Seattle. What it meant, Ted knew, was that he would have to combat a prosecution strategy based on the doctrine of "similar transactions," whereby other crimes exhibiting a "common scheme or plan" are introduced to bolster the charge at hand. It is a dangerous and murky legal concept, an invitation for abuse by the prosecution and nothing less than a nightmare for the defense. Ted Bundy's long-held claim—that police were trying to railroad him for a string of their unsolved homicides—was about to become an ominous legal reality.

"It is like they have formed a kind of road show to play in any courtroom where Theodore Bundy is a defendant," he told his lawyer in Seattle. "Your fear that a conviction in Colorado could inspire the King County authorities gathers more credibility." For Ted Bundy, it felt like a stone was poised at the top of a hill. Once it began to roll, there would be no stopping it.

"My Christmas gift to you," Ted wrote to a friend in late December, "cannot be tangible or material. Instead I want to give you the satisfaction of knowing that your kindness and friendship have eased the suffering and given me happiness. You help take away the loneliness. My Christmas gift to you is my peace of mind, which you help preserve."

By January 1977 Ted had decided to drop his extradition battle. "Yes, Virginia," as he put it, "Theodore Bundy will have his day in court."

The decision spread ripples of apprehension and anger among his friends. "I don't know what's going to happen up there," said one. "All along Ted believed he was going to be vindicated. When he was convicted, he began to lose faith in the system. And now this." Roger Kirkham, too, was wrestling with his faith in the system. A person he trusted, even admired, was accused of crimes he could barely imagine. He had to see Ted one last time, had to ask him himself, had to hear that the feelings he bore for Ted were justified.

Kirkham caught a look of understanding—even, strangely, of sympathy—in his friend's face. "I've stolen some stuff in my life, but I have never assaulted anybody, kidnapped anybody, or murdered anybody. That is beyond my comprehension," Ted Bundy replied to Kirkham's halting question. "What is happening to me is a dream. It seems so unreal."

On January 28, closely guarded, Ted Bundy stepped into a car for his ride 500 miles up into the Colorado Rockies. A fine white snow, bright as diamonds, blew across the road he had driven on, a long, long year and a half ago. How surprised he would have been if only he could have peered into the future during those long hours on the road.

If only he could do so now.

BUNDY
& WOMEN

Ted Bundy in his high school
political science class.

THE NORTHWEST WOMEN

Lynda Ann Healy disappeared in Seattle, January 1974. Her body and those of Susan Rancourt and Roberta Parks were found in March 1975, 20 miles southeast of Seattle.
WIDE WORLD PHOTOS

Donna Gail Manson disappeared in Olympia, March 1974 and was never seen again.
WIDE WORLD PHOTOS

Susan Rancourt
disappeared in Ellens-
berg, Wash., April 1974.
WIDE WORLD PHOTOS

Roberta Kathleen Parks
disappeared in Corvallis,
Oreg., May 1974.
WIDE WORLD PHOTOS

Georgann Hawkins
disappeared in Seattle
in June 1974. Her body
has not been found.
WIDE WORLD PHOTOS

Janis Ott (top) and
Denise Naslund disappeared
from Lake Sammamish
State Park on the afternoon
of July 14, 1974. Their
bodies were found on
Sept. 7, 1974, four miles
northeast of the park.
Ted Bundy, who was
known to be in the area at
the time, is considered
by police the prime suspect
in these seven murders
and disappearances.
WIDE WORLD PHOTOS

UTAH

Above: Bundy's home in Salt Lake City.

Opposite: Melissa Smith's body
was found Oct. 27, 1974.

Missing Person

Melissa Smith
Age 17

daughter of Midvale Police Chief
White, Female American
5'3", 105 lbs., hazel eyes, light brown hair
Wearing blue jeans, blue flowered blouse,
heavy Navy blue shirt
Last seen in Midvale-Murray Area
10:30 P. M. October 18, 1974

Any Information Call Midvale Police

or Salt Lake County Sheriff's Office

801-255-4291   801-328-7441

Left: Debbie Kent disappeared in Salt Lake City, Nov. 8, 1974, the same day as the DaRonch kidnaping. Bundy is thought by police to be the prime suspect in Smith's murder and Kent's disappearance. COURTESY OF FAMILY OF DEBBIE KENT

Below: Walden Bookstore in shopping mall where Bundy, posing as "Officer Roseland," stopped Carol DaRonch.

Opposite, top: Laundromat that "Officer Roseland" told DaRonch was a police substation.

Opposite, bottom: Bundy kidnap victim Carol DaRonch testifying in 1979 at Bundy's Miami presentence hearing. WIDE WORLD PHOTOS

Far left: Mug shot of Bundy
at his first arrest for burglary.

Left: Mug shot of Bundy two
months later. He had cut his hair
for the police lineup.

Below: Police lineup for the
DaRonch kidnaping, Oct. 2, 1975.

Above, left: John O'Connell,
Bundy's Utah lawyer.

Above, right: Caryn Campbell,
an alleged victim of Bundy's,
disappeared from a ski lodge
near Aspen on Jan. 12, 1975.
Her body was found Feb. 17.
WIDE WORLD PHOTOS

Opposite, top: Bundy being led
into Pitkin County courthouse.
WIDE WORLD PHOTOS

Opposite, bottom: Pitkin County
courthouse in Aspen. Bundy made
his first escape by jumping from
the second story (second window
from left) on June 7, 1977.

FLORIDA

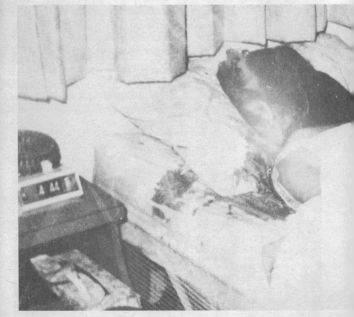

Opposite: Lisa Levy (left) and Margaret Bowman, clubbed to death at the Chi Omega sorority house in Tallahassee, Jan. 15, 1978. WIDE WORLD PHOTOS

Left: Kimberly Leach who disappeared from Lake City, Fla. on Feb. 9, 1978, and whose body was found April 7, 1978. WIDE WORLD PHOTOS

Below: The body of Margaret Bowman as she was found in her bed. WIDE WORLD PHOTOS

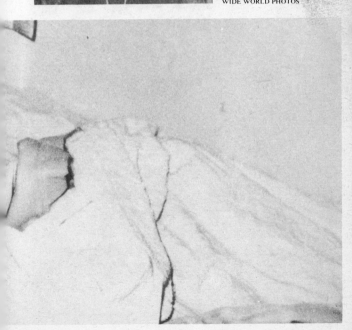

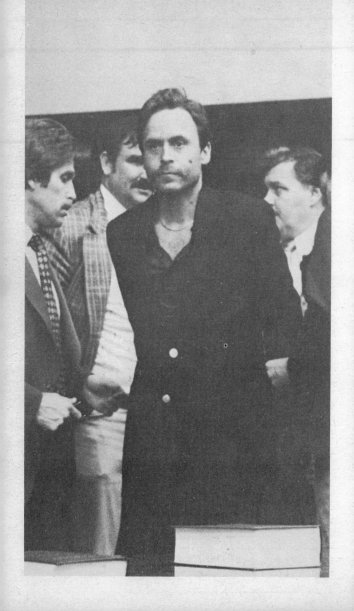

Opposite: Bundy after his Feb. 15, 1978
arrest in Pensacola. Behind him in
plaid jacket is Norman Chapman. Mark on
Bundy's left cheek is the result of his scuffle
with patrolman David Lee. JIM RIFENBERG

Above: Bundy awaiting arraignment in Pensacola
circuit court Feb. 16, 1978. WIDE WORLD PHOTOS

Opposite: Bundy in Tallahassee court,
April 1978, where he was charged with
burglary and car theft. UPI

Above: Bundy listening as Tallahassee
sheriff Ken Katsaris reads murder
indictment, July 27, 1978. WIDE WORLD PHOTOS

Bundy confers with his
defense attorney on opening day
of trial, June 25, 1979. UPI

Bundy, acting as his own attorney,
presents a motion in court. WIDE WORLD PHOTOS

Top, left: Karen Chandler, who survived a beating in the Chi Omega attack, testifies at Bundy's murder trial. WIDE WORLD PHOTOS

Top, right: Kathy Kleiner DeShields, another survivor from the Chi Omega house. WIDE WORLD PHOTOS

Left: Cheryl Thomas testifies about her beating. WIDE WORLD PHOTOS

Above: Police sergeant Howard Winkler
shows Bundy jury a photograph of Lisa Levy.
At center is Defense Attorney Lynn Thompson.

Opposite, top: police technician shows jury
a pair of pantyhose made into a mask,
which was found in Cheryl Thomas's house.

Opposite, bottom: Judge Cowart ruled
that *this* pair of pantyhose, found in
Bundy's car in 1975, was inadmissable
as evidence in his murder trial.

JUDGE
EDWARD D. COWART

Top: Patricia Lasko, Florida state microanalyst, discussing hairs found in pantyhose mask. WIDE WORLD PHOTOS

Bottom: Forensic odontologist, Dr. Richard Souviron, gives crucial evidence at Bundy's trial. WIDE WORLD PHOTOS

Opposite: Eyewitness Nita Jane Neary testifying at Bundy trial. Holding picture at left is prosecution Attorney Larry Simpson. WIDE WORLD PHOTOS

Below: Bundy, seated between his defense attorneys, Margaret Good and Lynn Thompson, as he hears the jury's verdict of guilty, July 24, 1979. UPI

Right: Bundy listens as Judge Cowart reads jury recommendation of death in the electric chair. UPI

Left: Louise Bundy after hearing jury's recommendation.
WIDE WORLD PHOTOS

Below: Bundy and his lawyer, Margaret Good, stand as Judge Edward Cowart reads death sentence.
WIDE WORLD PHOTOS

Right: John and Louise Bundy as they hear death sentence.
WIDE WORLD PHOTOS

The many faces of Ted Bundy.
WIDE WORLD PHOTOS

Part III
FREEDOM

Under other circumstances, the arrival of Theodore Bundy in Aspen, Colorado, would have been a natural, almost predictable event. Thirty, bright, savvy, well-traveled, trimly handsome, and possessed of an ever drier cynicism, Ted was cut perfectly for the self-satisfied chic of this ski town in the high Rockies. The fact that he'd called himself a Republican once—and then a Mormon—could only have added to his appeal over a glass of cabernet after a day on the slopes: a real specimen of Americana, this Ted.

But things were different in Aspen in January 1977. First it was the weather, a strange, snowless season that left raw patches of rock where skiers usually followed each other down Aspen and Buttermilk mountains in long crisscrossing lines. It was a shock, the worst in memory, for the lift operators, hotels, and restaurants. And then a spectacle, an odd, distorted image of Aspen's jet-set style of living, had come along as if to replace the dismal skiing. Ten months before, singer Claudine Longet, ex-wife of Andy Williams, had shot and killed her lover, onetime ski champion Spider Sabich, in the bathroom of his $250,000 Aspen home. Now she was on trial in a high-powered melodrama that had brought Williams, Jack Nicholson, and gossip columnists from around the world to watch. Judge George Lohr's courtroom was packed every day. It was the source of some amused whispering that Longet was free to walk the streets of Aspen on Williams's arm during the course of the trial. "I never called her a crazy chick," Williams said righteously under oath. The verdict: guilty of criminal negligence.

Bundy made an impression the moment he arrived at his new quarters, two floors below Lohr's courtroom in the basement of the Pitkin County courthouse. Gee, thought Sheriff Dick Kienast's secretary as Ted was led through the open office and locked in his cell, he sure is a good-looking guy. I've danced with lots worse at the Paragon. Ted flashed a smile and nodded hello. He did look like someone whose mother had cared for him, another woman in the outer office said to herself. Louise Bundy had called the sheriff's office the week before to find out what sort of accomodations were in store for Ted.

Sheriff Kienast, a chubby, benign ex-theology student, conferred with his deputy Don Davis about their new prisoner several days later.

"He's smart," said Davis, "and very observant. He's making himself just as personable as can be to everyone around here. He's fine," Davis paused, "until he wants something." Davis recounted the fuss Ted had mounted when he was told he couldn't keep shaving implements in his cell.

Kienast agreed and made it a point to remind everyone to watch the new tenant closely. But it was hard not to be charmed by Bundy's ways. One afternoon, while Kienast and his secretary were lunching on a pizza, Bundy called out through the bars, "Hey, how about a little in here? After all, I am your star prisoner." Kienast grinned and handed over the last piece. Law enforcement could be tough, the thinking in Aspen went, but still civilized.

Adjustment to life in Colorado was not too taxing for Ted. He complained about the food and the lack of windows and the thin mountain air that tired him out, but his companions—mostly drunk drivers and car thieves—offered more pleasant company than the "goons and amazons" back in Utah. And it seemed to please him to learn that this 19th-century jail had once held Butch Cassidy, Doc Holliday, and other outlaw-heroes of the old West. Aspen's code of justice today entertained him too: "A local resident, busted with a pound of pot, was given a thirty-day suspended sentence," he wrote to his friend Nancy Hobson, "whereupon he went to the police evidence room and secured the return of his smoke. It's a wonder Aspen doesn't float away."

Ted Bundy's first appearance in a Colorado courtroom was edged with an unmistakable irony. Just the day before, District Judge George Lohr had sentenced Claudine Longet for the criminally negligent homicide of Spider Sabich, and it had inspired a rousing joke in the local bars. What's the difference, the line went, between stepping on an ant and killing a spider? Thirty days: that was the sentence Lohr had imposed on the woman, who many felt had been more than just "negligent." Even if Ted Bundy was found guilty of the brutal, willful murder of Caryn Campbell, the barflies at the

Hotel Jerome reasoned, he wouldn't get a day over two years.

But Bundy's attorney Chuck Leidner wasn't smiling when he stood up to argue that Ted should be permitted to appear in court without handcuffs. "Others in this town charged with murder are allowed to walk unfettered," he said. A giggle ran through the crowd. Dick Kienast disagreed, citing the bogus driver's license and airline schedule found in Bundy's Utah cell as evidence that he was an escape risk. Lohr ruled in favor of the defendant: Ted could appear in court in street clothes without handcuffs.

It was a small but positive first step for Leidner and his client. George Lohr, who had only been appointed to the district judgeship the year before, already had a reputation as a fair and cautious jurist—one who was as likely as any judge to recognize the important and potentially prejudicial implications of pretrial maneuvering.

Leidner's next request—to close the preliminary hearing to the press—was unorthodox but possibly crucial. The details of the just-completed Longet trial had been smeared for months across the papers, and that's just what Leidner didn't want to happen to Bundy. Could Ted get a fair trial if all the hearsay (permitted under the relaxed rules for a preliminary hearing) became daily grist for the press mill? If, as a result, a change of venue became necessary, Leidner felt, one of the defense's strongest cards would be snatched from their hands: a pool of the most tolerant and potentially sympathetic jurors in the state. Right from the start, Chuck Leidner had told Ted, he was committed to coming to trial in Aspen, where the "quality of life" was just right. Attorneys for the *Denver Post* immediately challenged the move to exclude the press. Theodore Bundy was just too big a story to let pass.

Even as Chuck Leidner was steering the various motions and countermotions through their legal channels, Ted Bundy was one step ahead. On March 9 he composed a letter to Judge Lohr, writing in longhand on a yellow legal pad. "I filed with your clerk today a motion through which I hope to be allowed to conduct my own defense," he began, and went on to cite his irreconcilable differences with the public defender and the Supreme Court–established precedents for "pro se" defense. "Believe me," Ted told Lohr, "I am taking the initiative after considerable review and introspection. I

181

am convinced that my new course of action is intelligently charted in my own best interests, and my interests demand that I secure the best defense possible and a fair trial as well."

The preliminary hearing was less than a month away, and Bundy agreed, after a short consultation with Lohr, to postpone such an important move until after the hearing. Frankly, Lohr told Ted, he was dubious about this whole idea of a defendant acting as his own counsel. His skepticism, it would soon turn out, was well placed.

The April 4 preliminary hearing began in Judge Lohr's airy second-floor courtroom with the defense moving once again to exclude the press and disallow any testimony related to other crimes (the purported similar transactions). Leidner and Jim Dumas (another attorney working on Ted's behalf) sought to prevent Carol DaRonch from testifying, claiming they hadn't had proper notice of her appearance. Lohr denied the motions and signaled for prosecutor Milton Blakey to begin.

Blakey, along with Bob Russell, had been imported by Pitkin County District Attorney Frank Tucker from Colorado Springs to handle the Bundy case. Both were tough and experienced—qualities that Tucker himself had hardly exhibited in his recent, much-criticized handling of the Claudine Longet case. The local press had pounced on the revelation that Tucker had taken Longet's diary (a potentially damaging piece of evidence) home with him and lost it. Those weren't the only murmurings about Tucker. The move to extradite Bundy, Aspen opinion makers pointed out, had been timed most conveniently in the fall of 1976: just weeks before the November election. But with Tucker and his staff too overworked to handle the Bundy prosecution, it was Blakey's and Russell's show now.

Raymond Gadowski, the Michigan doctor, was first on the stand, and his recall of the hours at the Wildwood Inn before Caryn Campbell's disappearance on January 12, 1975, brought nothing new to light. Leidner's cross-examination did elicit that Gadowski and Campbell had had sexual intercourse the night before her abduction—which would be consistent with the presence of acid phosphatase in her vagina when she was found, showing that she might not have been raped. The more questions the defense could raise about the

182

exact circumstances of Campbell's death, the more difficult it would be to prove its "similarity" to any other.

After a short recess Blakey called Lisbeth Harter, the California woman who had told Mike Fisher, a year after the fact, that she remembered several suspicious-looking men lurking around the elevator at the Wildwood Inn on January 12, 1975. Harter's identification was an important element in the circumstantial case against Bundy, and Blakey gently coaxed the story from his witness. First he had her set the stage: who she was with, when she left her room to go for the stomach medicine for her husband and daughter, just what she had seen near the elevator.

There were two men, Harter remembered, one standing right beside the elevator and the other leaning on a refrigeration unit some 25 feet away. Neither was wearing ski clothes, and that had struck her as odd. Finally Blakey had her at the point of a dramatic reenactment of her identification.

"All right, Mrs. Harter," he said evenly, "I would like you to look around the courtroom right now. Tell us if today, in this courtroom, you see either of the men that you have testified about seeing near the elevator." Blakey encouraged her to step down from the witness stand for a better look.

"I can't be sure," Harter said, craning her neck to take in the crowd stacked up into the tiny law library at the back of the room.

"Do you see anyone in the courtroom that looks like either of these men?" Blakey coached.

"Could I have one of them stand up?"

"Certainly."

"The man in the first row, stand up, on the outside."

Blakey's heart skipped a beat. Did she mean the man in the blue pants and blue jacket? he asked. And he looked like which man, the man by the elevator?

"OK," said Blakey, and turned to the crowd. "I would ask the gentleman to identify himself for the record."

"I'm Ben Meyers, the undersheriff for Pitkin County."

The lunch spots around Aspen were soon buzzing with the news. Legal handicappers had rated the murder case against Ted as weak to begin with, and now the only eyewitness had crumbled on the stand. True, Blakey had tried to restore her credibility, suggesting that perhaps the man Harter identified from Fisher's photo packet was the other suspicious

183

fellow, the one back by the refrigeration unit. (Later he would attempt to invoke a Colorado statute as a means of legitimizing the prior identification.) But the damage—and Blakey and Russell knew it—was considerable. Harter had passed over Ted Bundy and pointed at somebody else.

The remaining day and a half of testimony was fairly routine, a straightforward recitation of the details and circumstances of the prosecution's case. Both sides scored a few minor points. Donald Clark, the Denver doctor who had performed the autopsy on Caryn Campbell, granted that an injury to the woman's head was consistent with a blow with a crowbar: the prosecution was intent on tying in the Carol DaRonch assault. But Clark also said she could have suffered such an injury in a fall if her head had struck a sharp rock. FBI Special Agent Robert Neill told the court that the three "microscopically indistinguishable" hair matches linking three known victims (Campbell, DaRonch, and Melissa Smith) with one defendant (Bundy) was unique in his 14 years of experience. But he also confirmed, under cross-examination, that such comparisons do not constitute a conclusive basis for personal identification. Mike Fisher, Carol DaRonch, and Jerry Thompson told their stories to complete the prosecution's case—a case with no fingerprints, no murder weapons, and a badly damaged eyewitness.

On April 6, Judge George Lohr delivered his opinion. The prosecution had demonstrated "probable cause" to believe the crime was committed by the defendant, he said. "It is not the function of the court at a preliminary hearing," he added, "to determine the probability of conviction at an ensuing trial." Lohr went on to acknowledge the "highly circumstantial nature of the evidence." But Ted Bundy would stand trial for murder all the same.

The following week, Ted changed his address to Glenwood Springs, 40 miles away. The Colorado Health Department had ruled that no prisoner could stay longer than 30 days in the Aspen jail, now classified a "short-term facility." As Bundy packed his things, a Pitkin County undersheriff stood by and watched. Either Ted Bundy's guilty, he said to himself, or he's the unluckiest son of a bitch in the world.

As much as Ted Bundy may have felt at home in Aspen, he was an anomaly in the provincial valley town of Glenwood Springs. Here, in place of the easygoing, open-necked plaid-shirt style of the Aspen authorities, the sheriff and his deputies wore their narrow ties cinched up tight against their throats, and the jail they manned was a trim, anonymous-looking one-story brick building near the Colorado River in the center of town. Ted's new quarters here were even smaller than before: a shoe-box-shaped cell 12½ × 6½ feet with two metal bunks, torn plastic mattress, shower, sink, and stained toilet seat. The window in the door was a foot square. He shared one wall with the kitchen, and the fumes and clatter seeped through all day.

It wasn't long, however, before Ted made his unusual status known. Judge Lohr had grudgingly granted Bundy's motion to act as his own attorney, and Ted's first priority was improving his living and working conditions. He rained down requests on the court: for a haircut and dental care, sheets, pillowcases, vitamins, 2600 calories and three meals a day instead of two; a typewriter and typing table, file folders with metal clips, free long-distance phone privileges and the use of the law library, the services of his own experts in hair and handwriting analysis, a private investigator, even the right to talk with the other prisoners.

Lohr was careful (he allowed the file folders but not the metal clips), but within a matter of weeks Ted Bundy seemed to be spending as much time camped on the pay phone in the prison common room or across the street in the Garfield County law library as he was in his cell. Even there he was in a near-incessant fever of activity, sometimes pecking away at his typewriter and reading for 16 hours a day, then jumping up to walk his three miles—1300 trips the length of his cell. Again and again, formally and informally, he pleaded with Lohr for the Glenwood jailers to relax their grip: "What justification is there for being treated like a dangerous animal with a big sign over my door saying 'Caution'?"

By phone and by mail Ted carried his story to newspeople and friends across the West. Explaining his reasons for acting as his own attorney, he told a Salt Lake City television reporter, "I wanted to get involved because I'm such a part of the defense. After all, I'm going to bear the consequences. Why not bear the responsibility of seeking my own acquittal and sustaining my own innocence?" The sound of his story was always the same: "It is no secret that I have expressed my innocence of this very tragic charge."

Sheriff Ed Hogue and his undersheriffs and deputies couldn't help but overhear Ted Bundy's long, often high-flown

185

conversations on the phone. It was more than a little unorthodox for a prisoner to engage top legal and investigative experts from around the country in detailed conversations, and the cops didn't like it. "He's smart and he's clever," said Undersheriff Jack McNeel darkly. "Ted Bundy's always thinking." A second undersheriff added, "Every time he doesn't get his own way he gets on the phone to Judge Lohr and gets what he wants." By the end of April, Ted was free to spend three hours most weekdays in the law library.

Protest as they would (Hogue even showed Lohr a diagram of the prison's exits and ventilation system, intercepted by his deputies), the men who guarded him were just going to have to live with Ted Bundy. Slowly but steadily, Ted's unflappable charm began to wear away the irritation. He was unfailingly friendly, polite to the women secretaries and dispatchers, and good company for the deputies assigned to the inglorious routine of walking Ted back and forth to the library or along the railroad tracks for his daily exercise. One deputy especially, fair-skinned and bright-faced, fell into a comfortable pattern with his charge.

"Hey, Ted," he called on their way out the door one morning. "A Coke or something?"

"Sure."

It became a kind of ritual between the two. Sometimes the deputy paid, sometimes Ted. Their conversation touched on family, friends, sports, almost anything. "If I was maybe having a little trouble with a case of my own," the deputy later recalled, "I enjoyed sounding him out. He really was very interesting." There were limits to the friendship, however. One afternoon, when Ted was having his hair cut at the local barbershop, several of the police began teasing a woman in the shop. Ted, spinning around in the chair, never cracked a smile.

After a month Ted Bundy was on agreeable terms with almost everyone around the jail—the ones who didn't trust him as well as those who did. Even the iron-eyed Bob Hart had to admit: "Just to talk to him he's a right likable fellow. He sure can win your confidence."

But for the moment Ted had more pressing concerns than making new friends. His trips to Aspen were frequent through April and May as he moved forward on his defense. The court heard Ted's motions for discovery; for suppression of Carol DaRonch's testimony and Lisbeth Harter's original photo identification; for exclusion of the public from the suppression hearings; and for disclosure of any notes or transcripts from the notorious Aspen summit conference of November 1975, when law enforcement officials from across the West had met to discuss Bundy as a mass murder suspect.

Much of the pretrial procedure was routine, but the hearing scheduled for June 7 was not. At that time Jim Dumas (acting now as a "legal adviser" to Ted) would argue his case to Lohr for striking the death penalty. Since 1974, when Colorado voters had enacted a capital punishment statute at the polls, public defenders like Dumas had been crusading in courtrooms across the state to disallow the death sentence in individual cases. It had been a difficult, uphill fight. For Ted Bundy it might be the crucial fight.

The night before, Ted tried to unwind and forget his troubles for a while. His mother had sent him a transistor radio in the mail, and there was a pleasant surprise on the air that night: a rock-and-news format station, KGLS, was making its first broadcast ever—and from a studio not three blocks from Ted's cell. News director Nick Isenberg's big story was the hearing in Aspen the next day.

21

Almost before his eyes opened on the morning of June 7, Ted Bundy was wide-awake. He listened for a few moments. Jail noises could mark the hours of the day as well as any clock, and the stillness of the early hour reassured him. Even the kitchen next door was quiet. "Still, no time to lose," Ted thought, lifting himself lithely off the bunk.

In a wooden crate a neat stack of clothing waited. A pair of cutoff jeans, some thermal underwear, two pairs of woolen socks—already he was beginning to sweat. Even after he'd donned another two turtlenecks, a pair of corduroy pants, and a bulky sweater, the effect was not too obvious. All this exercise is doing some good after all, he smiled to himself in the mirror. Instead of the usual brown loafers, Bundy laced up his Utah State Prison boots. Into the pocket of his cutoffs he stuffed a small plastic bag containing some matches, a bandana, and an aerial photograph of the Aspen area he had acquired while preparing his defense.

There was a tense moment when Aspen deputies Rick Kralicek and Pete Murphy arrived for the drive to Lohr's courtroom, but neither noticed a thing. It took all his willpower to calmly walk through the familiar procedures—first handcuffs, then his place in the front seat, then one deputy behind the wheel with the other in the back. Perhaps the police figured that Ted Bundy would never jump from a moving patrol car. Or perhaps his unfailing cooperativeness and the task's boredom made them lax—but they never used leg chains. What would be the point anyway? they thought.

After the mild winter the Colorado Rockies were dressed in their most stunning finery for spring. Lacelike, the pale green aspen tree branches ran on and on across the distant ridges. For Theodore Bundy the familiar ride passed like a dream, the whirring tires a soothing background for his controlled joy, the wide valleys opening like a promise of things to come. For the first time in months he allowed himself to experience, to really feel the beauty of the mountains around him, and he ached for the gorgeous colors and smells of spring.

Even the courthouse pleased him today, a graceful Victorian relic of a more romantic era, before the condominiums, the celebrities, and the high-priced resorts. Up on the second floor, in the courtroom, the cuffs came off, and Ted was free to roam while the reporters and lawyers geared up for another day over coffee in the clerk's office. Ted wandered toward a jury room that connected to the law library in the back and also opened onto the main stairway. To trip lightly down these stairs . . .

Just then he heard the hollow sounds of Judge Lohr's footsteps mounting the bench. A lawbook sprang open in Ted's hand. He was deep in study a second later.

Boredom soured the faces of those in court that Tuesday morning. Jim Dumas waded slowly through the 12th reading of his brief opposing Colorado's death penalty statute. Lohr leaned back and did not interrupt. The clock's hands crept toward midmorning recess. When the courtroom emptied, only Deputy Dave Westerlund, putting in his second day on the Bundy job, stayed to guard Ted.

Over the months familiarity had gradually loosened the

security around Ted, who now began to pace across the back of the courtroom. He had already timed the deputy's every movement. Six seconds to light a cigarette. Sixty seconds to get a cup of coffee from the clerk's office. Bundy turned abruptly down the narrow aisle between the spectators' benches and walked straight for Westerlund, who was forced to back up and allow him to pass. Ted only looked more preoccupied, almost unaware of the deputy's existence. He wheeled around, repeated the maneuver, and the deputy gave him a little more distance this time. Then once more, and again, and finally Westerlund walked irritably into the hallway and lit a cigarette.

Noiselessly Ted negotiated the stacks of lawbooks in the library and grabbed the window. Outside, traffic on Aspen's main street was thin at ski season's end, and the spring air touched his face like a reassuring hand. No one was coming. The nearest car rolled along leisurely several blocks away. With a springing motion Bundy was free, hitting the ground firmly behind an old fir tree in front of the courthouse.

"Nothing broken," he thought, and sprinted around from behind the tree, across the courthouse front lawn, and toward the Roaring Fork River two blocks away. Rocks shot from under his boots as he scrabbled down the embankment. Now, hidden from view, he stopped to listen. Only the rush of icy water at his feet broke the silence.

Two events happened simultaneously in the courthouse soon after. A woman, inquiring about a parking ticket, finished her business and asked offhandedly, "Oh, by the way, is it usual for people to jump out of the courtroom window?" Two secretaries looked at each other, mouthed "Bundy," and one ran to get the sheriff.

Upstairs, an *Aspen Times* reporter thought he'd take advantage of the recess to get the quote of the day. He glanced into the courtroom and Westerlund, noticing his confusion, pointed to the clerk's office in front: "I think he's in there."

"I hope so," replied the reporter.

A quick search ended just as the secretary hit the top stair. "Bundy has escaped" came screaming out of police radios all over Pitkin County.

The word was soon on everyone's lips and traveling fast. At KGLS, Ted's newfound radio station, one employee ran to the microphone, and over the frantic waving of the DJ cut

189

into a song to shout the news over the airwaves. It was almost too much to be true: go on the air one day, and the next day this.

Escapes from Aspen date back to the early 20th-century mining days, when inmates from the work crews would walk away undetected from their duties. Recapture in the rugged terrain, however, was usually no great problem. Hopping into the town garbage truck, Sheriff Loren Herwick would beat a quick path out to Henry Stein's ranch, which overlooked the one sure route through the mountains to freedom: the railroad tracks. It wasn't long before the unsuspecting walkaway would stroll right into the sheriff's trap.

But years of development—new roads and logging trails—had made their mark by 1977. Immediately, almost desperately, Undersheriff Don Davis erected roadblocks covering every route out of the valley. Newspapers and radio put out the word. Searchers went on 12-hour shifts. Within an hour a helicopter equipped with an infrared heat sensor began combing the outskirts of town. Theoretically the sensor should have been able to detect the heat of a human body in the dense underbrush. "We were trying to look organized," Davis's secretary later recalled, "but really all hell broke loose."

The organization got tangled in a hurry. Thanks to a mix-up at the Denver Airport a team of tracking dogs was held off the flight: it seems they didn't have the proper kennel facilities. When the dogs finally arrived, police cut apart the sweater Ted had left in the courtroom and trained the dogs on the pieces. The pack took off, tracing Ted's path around the courthouse and down the riverbank. Several hundred yards farther, the trail climbed back up the embankment near the Herron Park Bridge on the town's east end. But nothing will foul a sensitive canine nose faster than the petroleum distillates spewing from an automobile tailpipe. As soon as the hounds reached the highway they began to circle helplessly. Several attempts to restart them failed. Only one dog seemed sure where he was going, following the sheriff's secretary's perfume to her home on the other side of town.

Hundreds of volunteers and law officers from surrounding areas poured into Aspen. A house-to-house search began, and Ted Bundy's face soon decorated walls and windows. Local officials closed the gun stores and suggested that women going out at night use the buddy system.

The atmosphere in the sheriff's department may have been tense, with guns and reputations on the line, but for the rest of Aspen it was just more fuel for an evening at the tavern. One merchant put a "Bundy burger" on his menu: a bun only, he explained; the meat had fled. Another resident, who'd named his dog Bundy, tried to turn it in to the police the following day. A professor at the bogus Aspen University nominated Ted as teacher of a course on Escape. "Aspen isn't exactly anticop," a town lawyer explained. "The people here just get a kick out of seeing anyone in authority outwitted."

Every lead, no matter how remote, was checked. One deputy recalled that Ted had shown a particular fascination for Smuggler's Mountain, east of Aspen. Dogs and deputies were loaded into trucks and began scouring the foothills for a trail.

While the police went east, however, their suspect had gone south and headed up the mountains that separate Aspen from Crested Butte. The first rush of freedom had fired Ted's determination to get away successfully. Shedding one of the turtlenecks to reveal a blue-striped dress shirt and popping up on the highway from under the bridge, he strolled down a side street, West End Avenue. Who would have given a second look at just another handsome young man walking the sunny streets that June day?

When Ted Bundy stepped off the blacktop and into the cover of trees, an exultant burst of energy sent him sprinting up the hillside. He'd never feared being killed or hurt in the escape; rather he had dreaded the thought of not succeeding, of being trapped for the rest of his life on a course charted by idiotic police and lawyers he did not respect. The escape meant taking his destiny into his own hands again, meant that his life would begin again in a direction of his own making.

But for now, he would carry out the plan nurtured for over a month in the claustrophobic hothouse of his Glenwood Springs cell. He pulled the aerial photograph from his jeans. First there were the Elk Mountains to cross; then he'd have to hide for a while, probably in one of the many secluded cabins in the mountains. In Crested Butte, after the roadblocks were dismantled and the police were about their regular duties, he'd find a car and get as far away as he could. Not to the west, of course. He was too well known for that. Maybe back east, in the crowded cities, he could slip anonymously into a job, an apartment, friends.

It was four miles to the top of Aspen Mountain south of town. Four miles, and Ted never broke stride. Ten miles beyond lay the peaks of the Elk Range and the Continental Divide. Streams rutted the foothills as they ran down toward Aspen and the Roaring Fork River, like a huge comb with the teeth pointing down the valley. Ted skirted the mountaintop and started along one of the ridges that ran to the distant peaks. He headed for a Forest Service trail, then ran along Conundrum Creek toward Conundrum Pass.

Near the point where Castle Creek joins Conundrum he spotted a cabin. It appeared to be unoccupied, and he quickly filed its location away in his mind.

By dark, a light rain had begun to fall. Ted Bundy had anticipated the cold and could probably have survived a night in the wilderness, but the rain quickly soaked him through. In the early morning hours of Wednesday, he started back for the cabin.

Its owner had anticipated a break-in during the months he usually spent wintering in Arizona. Fritz Kaeser had fashioned his own log home in 1940, but later had it redesigned by an architect. It was an obvious target for vandals, so he took every precaution. The front bedroom window that Ted Bundy smashed had been nailed shut, and Ted could not slip through. Around back were two glass doors leading from the patio to a living room. Cold, wet, and frustrated, he ripped the heavy wire screen from the entrance and pounded through the glass and plywood covering the entrance.

There was little inside of use, but the shelter was enough. Kaeser had left behind some brown sugar and canned tomato sauce, which Ted ate hungrily. He searched each room thoroughly, and in an upstairs closet discovered an old .22 caliber rifle and some ammunition. The weight of the rifle felt good in his hands, and he decided to take it with him when he left. Perhaps he could kill a rabbit or something else to eat later.

The broken bedroom window, clearly visible from the dirt road, began bothering him. What could he do to give himself a little more time if someone happened by? He yanked the broken pieces from the frame, nailed plywood over the hole, and tacked a note to the outside: "Tom—Sorry I broke the window when I was putting in the plywood—Amos." That would have to do.

While Ted rested until Thursday night at the cabin, Aspen and Pitkin County police were getting little sleep. The Mr.

and Mrs. T. F. Bundy registered at a local motel turned out to be an innocent couple from upstate New York. The dogs and helicopter had found nothing on Smuggler's Mountain, while the roadblocks only served to harass tourists (including two Michigan travelers who were carrying 500 pounds of marijuana—so the roadblocks did yield some results).

Local businessmen were worried that a year of bad publicity—first Claudine Longet and now Ted Bundy—would hurt business. The Chamber of Commerce conducted an informal poll in Denver's bars and discovered that only 60 percent said they wouldn't change their Aspen travel plans. Chamber summer conferences director Susan McMichaels issued a "reassuring statement" late Thursday afternoon.

Pitkin County D.A. Frank Tucker got as much mileage out of the escape as possible. Tucker castigated Judge Lohr's "interference" in police security. "Only a damned fool would have allowed this to happen," Tucker opined. "If I'd been there I would have jumped out of the window myself. I would have been on him."

Whitney Wulff, Sheriff Dick Kienast's secretary, suggested on Thursday night that a psychic friend of hers might be able to help. When Pitkin County's cops heard the suggestion, they roared. "Why don't we cut up a piece of the sweater for her," one deadpanned. But Wulff persisted and was soon on the phone to her friend.

"Who is Ted Bundy?" the psychic responded, but agreed to help. They sat the clairvoyant in Ted's chair in the courtroom, and she began to utter bits and pieces.

Pitkin County police had assumed Bundy was wearing his loafers, not the Utah State Prison boots with their distinctive tread mark designed for easy tracking—a misimpression the psychic corrected. Ultimately, however, the medium's tenuous promptings proved too insubstantial for minds geared to "facts," and her further suggestions about a bandana, a "big light-colored car," and a cabin were ignored.

When Ted Bundy left the Kaeser cabin late Thursday night, he took a jacket and some first-aid supplies along with the rifle and food. Thoroughly rested, he was ready for the final push over the mountains and down into Crested Butte.

With helicopters thundering back and forth across the mountains all day, it seemed best to travel at night. Just after midnight Thursday, Ted started up Conundrum Creek Trail. A piece of aluminum foil with a small hole in it reduced and directed the beam of Fritz Kaeser's flashlight. The rocky trail forced a slow pace; he had only gone seven miles by dawn. A nearby grove of aspen trees would do for cover until dark.

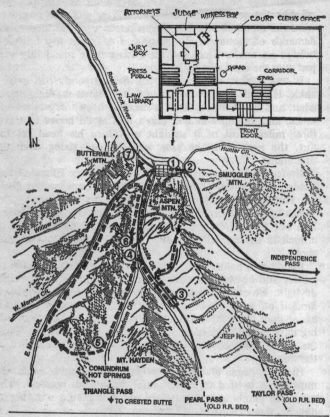

Bundy's escape route from Pitkin County courthouse in Aspen, Colo.

Perhaps Ted Bundy was simply disoriented, or maybe he couldn't quite make his aerial photograph correspond to the land around him, but the sheriff's star prisoner made his first and most important mistake Friday afternoon, June 10. The helicopters had been quiet during the morning, so, around two he decided to scale the peak directly in front of him. But it was Keefe Peak to the west, not Conundrum Pass to the south.

There was no trail ahead, which should have tipped him off. For the next seven hours Ted Bundy picked his way toward the mountaintop. His prison boots were unsuited to the demands of mountain climbing, and near the top he badly twisted an ankle. That and the fading light made him stop just over the crest that night.

It was a risk, but a small fire helped soothe his aching ankle. He built it in an overhang that shielded the light somewhat, and laid back to savor a meal of brown sugar, tomato sauce, and vitamins. It had taken him seven hours to travel three miles, most of it straight up. Once his head hit the dirt, the next thing he saw was the sun rising over the mountains.

Under the impression that he had crossed the Elks and was headed down toward Crested Butte, Ted Bundy hurried down the East Maroon Creek Trail straight toward Aspen. The voices of a family out for a Saturday morning picnic scared him not long afterward, and he scrambled off the trail to crouch in the underbrush until they were safely out of earshot.

Bundy was bolder now, feeling safely out of the reach of police, and he walked along a Forest Service path in broad daylight. He even encountered an armed stranger and passed himself off as a dentist from Philadelphia. It was so much easier than tromping through the underbrush. Four demanding days in the wilderness had begun to wear him out. Even the old .22 seemed like extra weight, and he heaved it into the woods.

His knee began giving him trouble as well as his ankle. He must have twisted it in his jump from the window. The mountain climbing hadn't helped either. By 3:00 p.m. Saturday he was exhausted. Just above the intersection of East Maroon and Maroon creeks, he pushed off the trail again and immediately dozed off.

The chill night air revived him and set his bones to throbbing. He checked his watch. Nearly nine o'clock. A little bit of walking loosened him up, and the going soon got much easier. The trail ran onto a blacktop road just over a little wooden bridge with a brand on it, something with a "T" and a tilted "7." It was nearing midnight when Ted clicked on the flashlight, continuing doggedly at the road's edge toward a little knoll. In the distance the dark mass of another mountain range cut the starry sky.

As the road rose up over the knoll, the lights of a town came into view. Odd, he thought, those lights look familiar. If someone had been watching Ted that night he would have seen Bundy's shoulders sag there on that lonely mountain road. The lights below were Aspen, he realized. Somehow he'd made a mistake, gotten turned around, crossed the wrong ridge. Well, it wasn't over yet, he thought, and began striding purposefully down toward the town below.

Not much farther on, he came upon a crossroads and discovered a sign marked "Castle Creek Road" that pointed back in the other direction. He'd crossed Castle Creek Road two days ago. The Kaeser cabin was on Castle Creek Road. He made a right turn and started back.

Ted Bundy approached the familiar shelter carefully. The note was gone from the bedroom window, and there were footprints under the front porch that he didn't recognize. Staggering, Ted hastily retreated from the cabin and climbed back up Conundrum Creek Trail. He traveled as far as he could before settling about a hundred yards from a campground parking lot.

The dull pounding of helicopter blades in the distance startled him from his sleep. As he watched, police landed in the parking lot. He could hear their voices distinctly in the early Sunday morning stillness as the dogs bounded eagerly from the chopper and began sniffing and straining at their leashes.

A sharp crack behind him, and Ted Bundy froze. Had they circled him already? Another dog team? For a long moment he lay perfectly still, fearing that the next sound he would hear—or the last sound—would be that of a gun. An instant later a deer leaped from cover and bounded off into the woods behind. Ted Bundy drew a long, deep breath.

When the searchers had gone, their quarry slunk quickly off into the trees, heading for the ridge he'd climbed on Tuesday, back in the direction of Aspen. But that had been five days before, when he felt better, stronger than now. He didn't set nearly the pace of the first climb, and when he reached the top of Aspen Mountain it was nearly sundown.

Exhaustion, lack of food, and the cold nights were beginning to take their toll. Ted Bundy fell into a fitful sleep until dark woke him. By now the dull throbbing in his knee had become a stabbing pain whenever he moved. He'd covered nearly 40 miles of rough terrain with little rest. "There's no way I'm going to walk out of this valley," he thought. "I better go back down to Aspen, find a car, and go for it. Maybe the roadblocks are gone by now."

Hugging the creek bed to avoid detection, he made it down the mountain and around the west end of Aspen. Near midnight Sunday he hauled himself up into some bushes at the edge of a golf course. But the strain was too much for his weakened knee, which locked up completely, and he tumbled to the ground and lay there an hour, unable to get up, not really knowing where he was.

When he came to he saw he was among a number of small homes in a subdivision. Most of the cars were open, but it was several tries before his hand hit some keys thrown under the driver's seat of a blue Cadillac. "At least that's solved," he thought, "some transportation."

The best route out of town, he knew, was east, toward Independence Pass, then Leadville, and ultimately Denver. But a winter avalanche still blocked the road, and he was forced back for a run down the highway toward Glenwood Springs and the hated jail. The gas gauge showed about half full, but these Cadillacs could go through a tank fairly quickly. In the back seat lay an expensive 35-mm camera. "I'll trade that for some gas," he thought, "if I make it out of the canyon."

It was almost 2:00 a.m. when the Cadillac rounded a bend at the eastern edge of Aspen.

Pitkin County Deputies Gene Flatt and Maureen Higgins sped through the darkened streets in answer to a call for help. A teenage girl had been grabbed, knocked down, and dragged by the hair on the town's east end. A city patrol car had radioed for assistance. Aspen was quiet this late Sunday night, and Flatt and Higgins did not see any cars until they'd almost reached their destination.

As they rounded the last corner, a baby blue Cadillac nearly veered off the road in front of them. "Another DWI" (driving while intoxicated), Flatt thought, and pulled a quick U-turn on the highway. His flashing lights soon brought the other vehicle to a halt. The driver slouched in the front seat, a Band-Aid covering his nose and his jacket collar turned up over his chin.

"License, please," Flatt asked methodically, before doing a

quick double take. But the driver had turned his back to begin rummaging through a leather case on the front seat. When he turned back with a license, the deputy was sure.

"Hi, Ted." Flatt smiled, and pulled his gun.

22

It was nearly 3:00 a.m. by the time Flatt and Higgins (and a horde of other police officers) hauled Ted Bundy back to his old home in the basement of the Pitkin County courthouse. Word went out on the radios to the roadblocks around town: Teddy was back. Come on in.

What with the 20 pounds he had lost, the fugitive looked even more beaten than he must have felt after six days in the mountains. His eyes were wide and weak, and he walked with a limp. Waving off the curious, Sergeant Don Davis locked himself in an empty office with Ted for a talk. A secretary went for some coffee (lots of sugar), a sandwich, and an orange for Bundy. (The food was from a supply collected in town for the search teams.) Ted thanked her, then eased out of his boots. A wide, raw blister had opened up on each heel. All right, Ted said, he was ready.

"I'm investigating a case of escape. Before I ask you any questions, you must understand your rights." Davis read from a small card: "You have the right to remain silent. Anything you say may be used against you in court. You have a right to talk to a lawyer for advice before I ask you any questions." Ted was nodding; he knew all this.

Revived by the food, Ted launched into an hour-long account of his adventures of the past week. He had been planning an escape for several months, he said, resolving sometime in late May that he would never return again to the Garfield County jail in Glenwood Springs. Calmly, almost proudly, Bundy told Davis how carefully he had watched the habits and behaviors of the men guarding him in the Aspen courthouse—right down to timing the six seconds it took Dave Westerlund to extract a match, strike it, and touch it to the end of his cigarette. It was all planned for June 7: the extra clothing, the boots, everything. He'd have

198

fled earlier if Judge Lohr himself had not suddenly emerged from his chambers. Finally, waiting for a newspaper reporter to clear out from the spot he was aiming for, he had made his leap.

"If it had been six stories," Bundy told Davis without a smile, "I still would have jumped."

Several hours later Ted was back in the courtroom, secured in leg irons and guarded by no less than seven deputies, one with her gun drawn at all times. Judge Lohr told Bundy sternly that his telephone privileges had been revoked and advised him of his rights regarding a new raft of charges, including felonious escape, burglary, and auto theft. Finally Ted was excused and permitted one phone call—to his mother in Tacoma—before he collapsed on the floor of his old cell in the Aspen jail. No sooner had Sheriff Kienast and his crew breathed a collective sigh of relief than the "housecleaning" began: five deputies and staff members were fired or resigned.

Ted's Seattle lawyer showed up and nudged Ted awake in the morning, discovering that the night's rest had done wonders for restoring Bundy's spirit.

"Ted, how's it going?"

"All right. But John, have you figured out yet which guy it was that pushed me out that window?"

In a letter to a friend in Seattle Ted's tone was more passionately righteous: "I have no regrets except perhaps that I was foolish enough to allow myself to be caught. I understood the risk I was taking, but had resolved that two things must happen: first, that I must be free because I deserved to be free as any innocent man deserves to be free. I had concluded that the law had consumed enough of my precious life with its deliberations. I decided that if I knew the truth it would have to be enough.

"Second, I had resolved that no one would be hurt in the course of my gaining my freedom. I wanted to slip away quietly and unnoticed. . . . Ah, but alas, here I am."

If Ted Bundy had taken the law and his life into his own hands, as he told another friend, the court was more than ready to resume command. The escape and four related charges could mean up to 90 years in prison; unlike the cases of kidnapping Carol DaRonch or murdering Caryn Campbell, there could be no doubt that Ted was guilty as charged this time. His hope, expressed just before his June 7 leap to freedom—that he might extricate himself from all his difficulties in time to be home for the July 1978 opening of the

199

Treasures of Tutankhamen exhibit in Seattle—was gone now. Back home and in Salt Lake City the confidence of some of his friends and supporters was eroding. If he was innocent, then why did he have to escape?

Ted countered: "An innocent man has a stronger desire to be free than a guilty one."

The escape had several other immediate consequences. Ted's bail, set at $25,000 before, was raised to an unreachable $200,000. More important, legal advisers Chuck Leidner and Jim Dumas—helpful in damaging the prosecution's case in the upcoming Campbell murder trial and in arguing to strike the death penalty—were forced to withdraw from the case. As potential witnesses in an escape trial they could not continue the attorney-client relationships with Ted.

It was slow going for Bundy as he resumed the routine of reading and study in his cell. The capture, especially its fumbling, luck-of-the-game circumstances, had apparently sapped his energy for work. "It's back to preparing my defense," he told a friend, "but I would rather be free." Brooding alone, he concentrated on his health, jumping rope and supplementing the prison diet with nuts, yeast, and vitamins.

On July 7, in a cheery letter to his lawyer in Seattle, he claimed he had shaken his bad mood. "Today I emerged from both my 'slump' and my Fourth-of-July holiday depression, and decided to entertain myself with the criminal law again." The work, he went on, turning serious, "is challenging, though frightening at times."

Bundy had help again: the expert advice and counsel of Stephen "Buzzy" Ware and Kenneth Dresner, two highly respected attorneys appointed by the court in place of Leidner and Dumas. Ware especially, bright, stylish, known throughout the state for his uncanny instincts as a defense lawyer, impressed Ted with his intelligence and knack for getting at the crucial point of an issue. By midsummer Ted was beaming about "my own very, very first-rate attorneys."

In August Ted went public with news that had fired his confidence all the more. During routine discovery proceedings in the preparation of his Colorado murder defense, Bundy had made a heartening strike: a potentially exculpatory police report by Salt Lake City Detective Jerry Thompson in the Carol DaRonch kidnapping case. This previously undisclosed report, Bundy and his Utah lawyers pointed out in a motion for retrial, presented a substantially different version of the way Carol DaRonch had come to identify Ted.

Initially, the newly discovered report suggested, DaRonch had been far less certain of her ability to identify her assailant than Thompson had testified at the trial. Also, Thompson might have led DaRonch to identify Ted, asking as she held a photo of Bundy in her hand, "if that was the guy." Finally, Thompson had called DaRonch "a very poor witness" in this "suppressed report," but not in any others. "The suppressed report," read the retrial motion, "reflects the frustration of a detective who attempted and failed to get the victim to make an identification of a person he regarded as guilty and dangerous and indicates that those attitudes were conveyed to the victim." The result was "a fraud upon the court and the defense."

Jerry Thompson swore he would never give another thing to Colorado when he heard the news. It wasn't Mike Fisher's fault, but that "lenient judge" in Aspen.

Though Bundy had uncovered the report in May, two weeks before his escape, he waited until August to file his motion, hoping the Colorado prosecutors might yield more damaging information along the way. Two days after filing the motion, Bundy wrote with a kind of breathless excitement to Nancy Hobson in Seattle: "The young woman didn't, couldn't, and wouldn't identify me in the beginning. It was only after she was pushed that she made an 'identification.' I've been asking myself why she would identify someone who wasn't involved. Why me? The answer is coming up. New trial."

But even as Bundy's Salt Lake City lawyers were crowing about the significance of the police "laundering" their reports, there was more heartache in Colorado. Buzzy Ware, whom Bundy liked and trusted as he had almost no attorney before, crashed his motorcycle on August 11 in Denver. Ware's wife was killed instantly; Ware himself was left badly injured and virtually incapacitated for legal work. For weeks, whenever Ware's name came up, Bundy would turn away and dab at his eyes. "I begin to wonder if there is anything life has left in store for me that can shock me," Ted told a friend. "This hardening process worries me. Life goes on, but there are times when it seems a sacrilege for it to do so."

The wheels of Bundy's legal fortunes rolled on imperviously. Ted was back in Aspen often, offering and arguing a variety of motions leading up to his trial. By late summer, as the Colorado sunlight turned thin and cool, the sight and sound of the celebrated defendant clanking up the stairs in his leg irons was routine again. Even so, the Aspen police, burned once, watched him closely. Mike Fisher nodded to Ted one afternoon, let him pass, then leaned to a deputy and whispered, "You know that Bundy's an amazing bastard. Look at him race up those steps, shackles and all."

Upstairs, in Lohr's courtroom, Bundy appealed for and was granted several delays before the beginning of the trial. Finally, on September 16, Lohr set a firm date of January 4, 1978, at 9:00 a.m. The more important date he set, however, was November 14, 1977, when the all-important suppression hearing would commence and Ted would learn what evidence from what other crimes would be permitted in the trial. More and more, in the case of *People* v. *Bundy*, it was clear that the hard evidence wasn't enough for a conviction. But if the prosecution could string out a chain of abductions and homicides and connect them to Theodore Bundy, then the murder of Caryn Campbell might fall neatly in place as the last, inevitable link.

The Colorado law sounds straightforward enough: "The prosecution may . . . introduce evidence of other, similar acts or transactions of the defendant for the purpose of showing a common plan, scheme, design, identity, modus operandi, motive, guilty knowledge, or intent." It's up to the prosecution to demonstrate to the court the purpose and relevancy of such evidence, and the court, in turn, must carefully instruct the jury on the "limited purpose" of such evidence.

But it's the interpretation and application of the doctrine of similar transactions that sends prosecutors and defense lawyers scurrying for precedents so they can try to exercise the law to their advantage. This subtle legal principle looked tailor-made for a case like Theodore Bundy's, where the hard physical evidence was slight and the suggestion of his involvement in other crimes was almost staggering. And that's just what troubled Ted and his legal advisers in September when they learned that prosecutors Milton Blakey and Bob Russell were going to ask Judge Lohr to hear evidence on four separate Utah transactions. If they couldn't prove he had killed Caryn Campbell, Ted said to himself, they were going to make him look like such a monster that a jury would believe he had to have killed her.

The prosecution must demonstrate, in "clear and convincing fashion," two things about an alleged similar transaction:

first, that the defendant committed the act, and second, that its detailed similarity to the offense at hand ("so unusual and distinctive as to be like a signature," as one writer on the rules of evidence puts it) establishes its value in the courtroom. Although admission of such evidence is not subjected to the most rigorous burden of proof (Blakey and Russell were within their rights in trying to introduce crimes for which Ted had not even been charged), the prosecution is not permitted to heap on separate cases in order to paint a generalized picture of the depraved and criminal character of the defendant.

It is up to the judge to determine how such evidence will operate in court. He must balance the degree of certainty and relevancy of the similar transaction against the inevitable (and sometimes sensational) prejudice against the defendant that such testimony tends to provoke.

Judge George E. Lohr had read the section from his text on evidence countless times, but he pulled the heavy volume from the shelf again. The judge has the power to exclude such evidence, Charles Tilford McCormick had written in his commanding style, "if in his judgment its probative value for this purpose is outweighed by the danger that it will stir such a passion in the jury as to sweep them beyond a rational consideration of guilt or innocence of the crime on trial. Discretion implies not only leeway but responsibility." The book fell shut in Lohr's hands. Some difficult decisions lay ahead.

Ted Bundy made no secret of what he thought of the prosecution strategy. It was "appalling," he was righteously indignant, and he accused Bob Russell, who was contemplating a campaign for state attorney general on the Republican ticket, of turning the courtroom into a political arena. After all, he pointed out, irresponsible application of the similar transactions principle was the best way to deny a defendant's basic rights. More and more, Ted Bundy was beginning to wonder about this system he had believed in so much at one time.

But through the early fall of 1977 he was busily absorbed, like any good criminal attorney, in the case at hand. He asked Lohr for still another legal adviser, petitioned the court for a chance to visit the Wildwood Inn and the spot on Owl Creek Road where Caryn Campbell had been found, and ironed out the details of having his own expert in hair analysis examine the various matched specimens. In his cell, Ted hammered out letters to his friends and supporters in the

Northwest, expressing unyielding confidence in the eventual outcome of his trials.

Bundy seemed full of energy, whether discussing the prospects of writing a book ("Could a book be written before the end? I don't see any satisfactory conclusion in the near future") or complaining encyclopedically about the food; yet he was troubled by unaccountable emotional highs and lows, yearning for the outside world. One day, overhearing a farewell party for a jail employee in a nearby garage, he wrote: "It is so totally incongruous to hear the relaxed conversation of men and women having fun together. Incongruous, that is, to be heard in a jail. It seems a lifetime since I heard that mix of happy sounds. Once so familiar, now the voices and laughter of street people take on a dreamy quality, and it has turned this day into a different color. It is so easy to start me living in the past on a sunny, late autumn day."

But Ted couldn't afford to indulge himself too lavishly in reminiscence: his first important hearing, on the admissibility of the Laura Aime and Debbie Kent transactions, was less than a month away.

The prosecution had worked hard to connect Bundy to the two Utah crimes. When the infighting Utah County detectives admitted they had lost samples of Aime's hair, Blakey and Russell moved to have the body exhumed to obtain new ones. And they'd gone for other evidence, offering a tire-track cast taken in the vicinity of the spot where Aime was found; such a track, they said, was consistent with a 1968 Volkswagen Bug—Ted's car.

But Bundy was prepared. His motion to exclude these transactions was elegantly, aggressively argued. He pointed out the substantial differences in age and appearance between Aime and Campbell and the differences in their injuries, and emphasized the important (though disputed) fact that Aime had been held perhaps as long as three weeks before her death. There was no evidence at all, he pointed out, to connect him to the Utah teenager's death. Bundy's discussion of the Debbie Kent case was even more concise: with no body found, there wasn't even any proof she was dead. How could *that* be considered similar to the case of Caryn Campbell?

Judge Lohr met with Bundy and the prosecutors in his chambers. He listened closely to the arguments and stated he would consider the question carefully. Ted was confident

204

as his escorts led him down to the car for the trip back to Glenwood Springs. Another lawyer had told him his brief was the best of its kind he had ever seen.

His confidence was well placed. Lohr ruled there was no compelling connection between the Aime and Kent transactions and the murder of Caryn Campbell. Such evidence, he said, was inadmissible at the trial. It was a victory, if only a small one, for Ted. A more important challenge would come to a head in two weeks, with a hearing on the admissibility of the Melissa Smith and Carol DaRonch transactions. The connections to those cases were stronger: a match of hairs in each instance, to say nothing of Bundy's conviction for the DaRonch kidnapping.

There was work to be done, plenty of it, but sometimes the pressure was just too much. The sharp slapping sound in Ted's cell was like a fist on a wall. It was his handball, flying against the door in the stale air.

When Ted Bundy showed up at the Pitkin County courthouse with his escort of legal advisers and photographers just before 9:00 a.m. on November 14, he wore a thin, serious smile. It was prudent to appear confident and relaxed, but it was difficult to manage. The results of these suppression hearings, he knew, could determine whether he'd hear his own death sentence in a Colorado court one day.

With one purported similar transaction the prosecution was attempting to introduce—the mysterious disappearance and death of Melissa Smith—Ted and his lawyers felt they were on reasonably secure ground. True, the prosecution had a pubic hair found in Ted's car that matched those of the murdered Midvale, Utah, police chief's daughter. But Bundy had an arsenal to disassociate the crime from himself and to prove it dissimilar to the death of Caryn Campbell. First, he was ready to argue, the victims weren't so much alike, six years apart in age to say nothing of their different heights, weights, and backgrounds. Melissa Smith was a teenager who liked to hitchhike, while Caryn Campbell was a conventional, responsible nurse. Their deaths, too, showed important distinctive marks: Smith abducted, hauled off and possibly held for a week, and dumped in a faraway canyon; and Campbell killed immediately and dropped in the snow not three miles from the Wildwood Inn.

As for the hair in his car, Bundy could once again dispute

the reliability of the matching technique. And if that wasn't enough, he had a final, provocative irony to add: the 17-year-old who had bought his car had himself known Melissa Smith. Who was to say he hadn't picked up the hair somehow and left it in the VW Bug?

"We can't expect to find a total identity of crimes," countered Milton Blakey. "The tiny details are insignificant when the overall factors show a common plan."

Several days into the hearings the prosecutors darkened Lohr's courtroom to display comparative closeup slides of the injuries to the two women. Three coroners testified about the injuries. There were "striking similarities," said Dr. Serge Moore, a judgment echoed by Dr. Donald Clark when he mentioned the skull fractures in an "uncommon area" in both cases. Cuts around the left ear of each woman also looked alike.

Ted's new legal adviser Kevin O'Reilly handled the cross-examination, concentrating on the differences in the conditions of the two corpses: hemorrhaging with Smith and injuries to her genitals, and no such findings in Clark's autopsy of the Michigan nurse. Dr. John M. Wood, Arapaho County coroner, announced from the witness box that Smith appeared to have been struck with a blunt object and Campbell with something with sharp edges. He backed off moments later, and admitted the possibility that the same weapon could have killed both victims.

It was complicated, coolly graphic testimony, and sometimes difficult to follow. But the mood of the observers in the courtroom was clear: Ted Bundy and his lawyers had met the test. Sure, Ted might have killed Melissa Smith, but a poorly founded hunch didn't have any place in his trial for another murder.

The prosecution had already lost the chance to read most of their grim mass murder catalog into the court record. The energetic optimism of the Aspen police conference, two years ago to the day, wasn't going to sweep away the careful logic of Judge Lohr's Aspen courtroom. But the fight wasn't over for Ted Bundy. There was still Carol DaRonch and the summer night when a Highway Patrol car had roared up behind him on an empty street. Like a bad dream rewound and spun out again, the men from Utah took the stand, explaining how the snare had caught.

Ted was ready to demonstrate how different the assault on Carol DaRonch was from the murder of Caryn Campbell, how little evidence there was to connect the two, how dangerous and prejudicial the implication was. The victims were not similar in age or background. DaRonch's assailant had used handcuffs and a gun, while there was no evidence of either in the Campbell murder. And so on. His line of argument was familiar by now.

But there was something more troubling for Ted as he sat and listened to Bob Hayward and Daryl Ondrak tell the story of the late night arrest and search of the VW back in August 1975. It was no easier for him to hear again Jerry Thompson's and Ben Forbes's seamless, practiced accounts of the search of his apartment five days after the arrest. Nor could Ted keep from squirming and jerking in his chair when Salt Lake City Assistant County Attorney Gerald Kinghorn offered his view from the stand that the handling of Carol DaRonch as a witness was acceptable and nonprejudicial to the defendant. "We made it a matter of conscience to discover if the procedure with the photos had been all right," Kinghorn said. Ted scowled and turned away.

Bundy knew only too well what this old story meant for him now. Unless he could seriously damage and discredit the word of the Utah cops, proving their searches of his car and apartment were illegal, the DaRonch conviction could be introduced against him at the trial.

By Wednesday morning, it didn't look promising for him. More than likely his jury would hear about the crowbar, ski mask, and assorted junk found in the VW and the map of Colorado and the ski country brochure (with the x beside the Wildwood Inn) found in his room. It was bad, but it wasn't an outright defeat. Ted still had a last best hope: to discredit the source of his troubles, Carol DaRonch. And he wanted to do it himself.

"I've had to listen to that woman four times and keep my mouth shut. I've been waiting two years for this. I want to do DaRonch." An Aspen reporter overheard Bundy quarreling with his legal advisers about who should cross-examine the witness.

"If you hassle her for two hours here, it could adversely affect your appeal in Utah," warned Kevin O'Reilly.

"You don't have enough experience in cross-examination," said Ken Dresner. "It's just a personal thing with you."

"You're damn right it's personal," Ted snapped. "This may be the last time I see Carol DaRonch."

Bundy's frustration boiled over at the midmorning recess

when the deputies insisted he wear his handcuffs during the break. It was during a similar recess, they recalled, that Ted had made his leap to freedom. But Ted resisted and threw an arm out in each direction. Finally, with the help of three men, he was contained and dragged down to his old basement cell. Ted positioned his feet so that the slamming cell door snapped the metal chain between his ankles.

Several minutes later, when he was led back upstairs, Bundy was still walking with short hobbled steps, as if the chain were in place. "He's testing us," Don Davis said when he noticed, "always testing us."

It was a haunting, strangely reverberant sight when Ted Bundy stood up in the courtroom that afternoon. Dressed in a white sweater, her fingers nervously toying, fuller and prettier now at 21, Carol DaRonch watched the man she had sent to prison approach. Accuser to accused, she had to tell her story face to face.

Pacing the floor, wheeling to the crowded, silent gallery, Ted Bundy launched himself on a three-hour exercise of the lawyer's art. Suddenly it all struck a strange balance. Were it not for this woman, Ted Bundy might still have been a student, working nights to put himself through school. Now he was here, with the attention of everyone in court fixed on him. The lives of Ted Bundy and Carol DaRonch were powerfully crossed.

Bundy marched DaRonch through every aspect of her night at the Fashion Place Mall, through the countless police interviews and photo packets, and then through the lineup itself. Again and again DaRonch's voice shook, and all the skips and lags in her memory were visible again. Finally, toward the end of the third hour of testimony, Ted faced her head on.

"Is it possible at the lineup that the pictures you had been shown previously had some effect?"

"No," DaRonch said.

"Are you positive that I was your abductor? You're not really sure that my car is the same car. They told you it was the car in the pictures. You're not really sure I'm the same man, are you?"

For a second before she lifted her head and called her answer out into the room, Carol DaRonch looked straight at Ted.

"Yes," she said clearly, "I'm sure. You can't change your face."

It would be a week or more before Judge Lohr ruled on the suppression questions, but the results would come as no surprise. As in the Aime and Kent transactions, the prosecution had not established convincing connections between the Campbell murder and the murder of Melissa Smith. The "similar transaction" was ruled out. The conduct of the Utah investigation, on the other hand, was adjudged legal and the evidence obtained in the two searches was admissible.

Lohr was of divided mind about the DaRonch assault as a similar transaction. Yes, there was substantial proof to connect Bundy to the DaRonch crime, but its similarlity to Campbell's murder was less than overwhelming. On balance, he deferred ruling on the question until the trial, when the prosecution would have to demonstrate the purpose of such testimony more clearly.

Thursday, November 24 was a quiet day in the Garfield County jail. A few dry slices of turkey at mealtime reminded the prisoners it was Thanksgiving.

Holidays were bad enough for Ted Bundy, depressing and full of memories. This year he had a few extra burdens on his mind. Just that week, he had learned, Appeals Court Judge Roy Banks had rejected his appeal for a new trial in Salt Lake City. Even though it wasn't entirely surprising, it was discouraging. "It could take weeks, months, or even years," he had written to Nancy Hobson. In the meantime, with most of the important pretrial questions settled in Colorado, his murder trial was fast approaching.

Holidays are a bad time for reporters too. Little of any importance happens, and a free-lancer like Nick Isenberg has his best shot for a few extra bucks with a humorous filler. Thanksgiving that year happened to be Theodore Bundy's 31st birthday, and KGLS's Isenberg ("Nicky News," as he's known in Glenwood Springs) had hit upon a great idea. He marched into Sheriff Ed Hogue's office early that morning, girlfriend Dawne Gundel and a Baskin-Robbins ice-cream cake in tow. Would Hogue bring Ted his birthday cake?

Nicky geared up his camera while Dawne lit the candles. Then Hogue shuffled proudly down to the cellblock, trailing clouds of candle smoke. Ted grinned, grabbed the bars, and blew out the candles. When the camera failed he obliged again, and the Ted Bundy birthday party lightened the evening news in a half-dozen western cities.

23

As winter deepened, Nick Isenberg fed the ravenous appetites of several western television stations for film footage of Ted Bundy. Not that there was all that much money in freelancing, but Isenberg could always count on Garfield County's most famous prisoner for an interesting quote or a bit of footage on a slow news day. More and more, Bundy was looking like a modest gold mine.

A cheap police scanner hung from Nicky News's belt wherever he went, squawking incoherently like the sound effects from a Grade B science fiction film. He was a strange sight to citizens of Glenwood Springs: an elfin figure in a tasseled ski cap and heavy boots trudging the snow-covered streets with 50 pounds of TV equipment perched on his shoulder.

His girlfriend Dawne had met Ted one day at the Garfield County courthouse while covering a city commission meeting. Dawne noticed that the "Clark Gable" at the hall telephone was staring at her. "So this is the guy who escaped from Aspen," Dawne thought as she dawdled near the deputies lounging around Ted.

"Hi," she said brightly, "I'm Dawne Gundel from KGLS radio," then hunted for something else to say. "It must be nice being able to spend all day on the phone."

"Yeah, but it isn't nice being in jail," Ted replied, and watched as Dawne smiled weakly and excused herself.

Nicky had known Ted for some months, having covered the first escape. Dawne, newly arrived after a South Dakota divorce, took an instant liking to Ted. She was determined to ignore all the rumors and judge him by what she saw—a nice, personable guy who liked to read. As their acquaintance-ship warmed, Ted and Dawne discussed books and local events. He was rapidly becoming a fan of KGLS—so much

210

so, in fact, that Nicky ran a "batteries for Bundy" campaign that fall.

On any day Nicky and Dawne could be seen leaning on the bars separating the prison common room (where Ted was usually on the phone) from the outside world. The jailhouse lawyer advised Dawne on divorce law—with the caution "Divorce is not my specialty. I'm more into criminal law"—while Nicky would listen closely for the day's story. A fascinating character, Dawne mused, like Mr. Spock on "Star Trek." You don't know too much about him, but he's fascinating anyway.

In a move that surprised many that December, Ted Bundy filed for a change of venue, claiming that publicity about his escape had tainted Aspen's pool of tolerant and sympathetic jurors. It's a standard defense tactic to ask for a change of venue at the last minute to force a delay, and with Judge Lohr's record of ruling mostly in Ted's favor, Bundy felt confident.

Ted's advisers argued with his client about the decision in his jail cell one day, but Bundy stood firm.

"I need more time," he thought after the lawyers had left. "I need more time."

After nearly nine months in Glenwood Springs, Ted Bundy had become a regular, and for the most part, welcome figure. His jailers were used to his pranks and the steady stream of letters, visitors, and phone calls.

Despite Ted's June escape, Sheriff Hogue didn't seem overly concerned about another one. After an initial protest, he fell easily in step with Lohr's sympathetic rulings, even allowing Ted to keep a flashlight a friend had sent to help with his reading. Nancy Hobson visited occasionally from Seattle, chatting with Bundy through the bars and bringing care packages of health foods and vitamins.

"I look horrible. Don't be shocked," he told her one December afternoon. She smiled—a little sadly when she noticed he had trouble meeting her eyes at first—and handed him a root beer.

Bundy never ceased adding bits and pieces to his knowledge of the jail and its activities, but the deputies, tired of continual fencing, paid little attention to his inquisitiveness. He always jested with them about what they did during the day or their plans for the evening. He made quick friends with a new jailer hired that fall, an older man pulled from crossing-guard duty

211

at a nearby school. "It must be tough for them to get jailers on the salary they pay," Ted thought.

Bundy and Isenberg traded stories about the jail too. It was always fun to relive Ted's leap to freedom in Aspen, and "Nicky News," a born raconteur, fleshed the conversation out with stories of other local escapes. As Christmas 1977 approached, Ted began looking tired, Nick noticed. Maybe there was something to his continual complaining about jail meals. He seemed to be losing weight, even with his supplementary cache of health foods.

Ted emphasized his discontent one day by flushing his noon meal down the toilet, but he did seem happier in his new cell. It was farther away from the clanging of kitchen pots and pans. Sheriff Hogue had approved the move to cell number five without a second thought. Only later would he remember it had been a storeroom back in 1970, when inmates had pushed a ceiling light from its spot and slipped through the foot-square hole to freedom. The town welder had been called in afterward to secure steel plates over the openings.

When Ted stopped eating breakfast, stopped even answering the food calls at 7:00 a.m., the jailer chalked it up to nervousness over the upcoming hearing. His prisoner seemed to be working later and later over his lawbooks. Lohr had scheduled a ruling on the change-of-venue motion for December 23, and Ted fully expected to be tried in Denver, where it would be easier to find jurors who'd never heard of him.

But Judge Lohr announced to a startled courtroom and a bitterly disappointed defendant that he was moving the trial to Colorado Springs, prosecutor Milton Blakey's hometown, where the conservative citizenry consisted mainly of military people from Fort Carson, the Air Force Academy, and NORAD headquarters. With only 7 percent of Colorado's population, Colorado Springs juries had accounted for half the men on death row.

"You're sentencing me to death," Ted told Lohr tearfully, pleading with him to change the ruling. But the judge stood firm.

It was a quintessential Nick Isenberg touch, the gift he handed a despondent Ted through the bars on Christmas day: a copy of Eric Berne's *I'm OK, You're OK*. Ted smiled, but his heart wasn't really in it. Even the phone calls that day to family and friends couldn't cheer him up.

Two days after Christmas Lohr handed Ted another surprise on what was quickly becoming an emotional roller coaster. Lohr became the first judge to rule the new death penalty statute unconstitutional, earning himself a place in Colorado history by accepting Jim Dumas's arguments. Ted Bundy might face a conservative jury in Colorado Springs, but the Caryn Campbell case was no longer a fight for his life. A jubilant Ted told Isenberg that evening that the verdict was "terrific—not for me, of course, because I know myself to be innocent—but for all the other defendants in the state." Ted looked straight into the camera. "I am very happy to have been a part of this decision."

"Ted's really rolling again," Nicky thought, smiling to himself. New Year's was coming up, another holiday, and there would surely be some demand for a Ted Bundy New Year's story. Maybe a bottle of cheap champagne with Ed Hogue blowing a party horn. But much to his astonishment, Ted refused for the first time to be photographed or interviewed. His appearance had changed again too. "I bet he's planning something," Nicky thought.

Deputies also noticed a change in Ted's behavior during the holidays. He no longer wanted to stroll along the railroad tracks north of town for his exercise, but instead marched brazenly on Main Street in leg chains. With New Year's Eve only a day away, however, no one was thinking too hard about Ted Bundy. That evening, jailer Bob Morrison and wife talked lazily at their kitchen table. Morrison lived in the jail complex, only a few feet away through a wall from the cellblock.

"Why don't we see a movie tonight?" Mrs. Morrison said.
"Sure. Why not? What's playing?"

Morrison and his wife would not have been so relaxed if they'd known that crouched on a cinderblock wall over their hallway, Ted Bundy was listening to their dinnertime conversation.

For eight weeks he'd sawed at the skimpy welds that held the plate over his ceiling light fixture. Steel cells act as effective echo chambers which limited his cutting time to less than a few minutes a day while the trustees showered before getting loose and rowdy around the TV and the kitchen crew cleaned the pots and pans.

He returned after each trip to Aspen fearing that a sharp-eyed deputy had spotted the faint lines inching their way

213

across the welds. The hacksaw blade ("the finest money can buy," he said later) so carefully smuggled into the jail always went with him to court. Nothing, nothing would blow this second chance.

At last one night the light plate moved easily aside and he hoisted himself into the crawl space. A small sack of clothes was packed and ready to go. The jail was built with heavy roof trusses so that a second floor could be added someday. Lines of cinder blocks traced the room and hallway layouts for him. Plasterboard ceilings hung between the blocks and limited his explorations to careful balancing acts.

It was slow going, and the old crawl space was thick with dust. Ted stifled one sneeze after another. "Shoot, Ted, you're better than this," he said to himself, amused and embarrassed at his own ineptness. After an hour's search, he realized there was no way out—at least there was nothing in the beam of his flashlight that he could get through without taking another light out or tearing a hole in the sheetrock.

So he returned to his cell and his daily routine until he could get back up for another look. Tension added a sharp edge now. Every time deputies escorted him to the law library that December, he dreaded that the loose plate would become the loose end in his plans. "They must know," he thought. "They're just waiting for a full-fledged escape. No," a second's calm reflection reassured him, "couldn't be. Certainly cutting the steel plate is enough of an attempt."

On Friday, December 30, the night Bob Morrison and his wife were quietly planning their evening, Ted had decided he had to go. The old jailer informed him that Captain McNeel, who usually checked the prisoners on Saturdays, would be on stakeout all night and in no shape for an inspection the next day. Immediately after dinner, Bundy began building his alter ego in the bunk—some lawbooks and clothes for the body, then he stuffed the arm of a shirt full of newspapers and laid it over the blanket in clear view of the door window. Not a bad job, he smiled to himself, not bad at all.

By 6:00 p.m., an hour after his dinner plate came rattling through the door, Ted was ready to go. This time, after he'd carefully replaced the steel plate, a shaft of light coming from the direction of the jailer's apartment ceiling startled him. "That's odd," he thought, "I've never seen that before," and he bellied slowly along the wall to discover a six-by-eight-inch opening in the plasterboard.

Jutting through the opening was a muzzle-loading rifle

and below lay a linen closet. The reason he'd never seen it before was that the door had always been closed. But tonight luck was with him, and the hallway light shone brightly.

Indecision stopped Ted in his tracks. If he broke the sheetrock, he had to go. Was he really ready? Ted sat on the wall a full half hour before reaching a decision. Perhaps this was part of their plan? They would be waiting outside, guns drawn to shoot him as he fled. Could it be that the rifle was there to tempt him? Shooting an armed escapee would look better.

Finally his doubts resolved. He hunched over the opening, carefully pulling the rifle up and laying it aside. Then, quietly, slowly, he tightened his grip until the sheetrock cracked. He stacked the pieces neatly behind him, lifted the top shelf out, and dropped down in a cascade of sheets and towels. A little quick dusting, refolding, and straightening—and everything looked normal from eye level. Ted pulled some shirts and a jacket from Morrison's closet, changed into his street clothes, and stepped outside into a starry, snowy Colorado night. Half expecting to be blown away as soon as he set foot on the little front porch, he heard only the soft, snow-muffled sounds of a clear Friday night in a tiny Rocky Mountain town.

Ted sought safety behind the jail's garbage bin nearby and listened for the clamor of pursuit. A second later he hurried toward Main Street and up over the Colorado River bridge. A wispy cloud of steam from the largest outdoor hot-springs pool in the world rose up and covered him like a veil. A moment later he had dropped onto the Hot Springs Resort parking lot, where he could not be seen from the street.

The heavy snow covered his tracks in a matter of minutes while he began searching for a car with keys. Finally he spotted a dull gleam in the ignition of an MG Midget with studded radial snow tires (necessary to cross the treacherous passes outside Vail). He must be out of the Rockies before seven the next morning, when his breakfast would arrive at his cell.

By midnight the Midget was swaying and sliding along the highway nearly 40 miles from Glenwood Springs. The reason the keys are in this thing, Ted thought, is because it's burned to the dickens. A temperature gauge creeping toward the red warning mark kept him on edge the entire time. After a particularly steep climb, the car just quit, right in the middle of the road. A helpful passing motorist pushed it off the highway, then gave Ted a lift to Vail. This ride, too, ended sooner than he'd hoped: the blizzard had closed the passes and his friend's car didn't have snow tires. As the clock struck one in the morning, Ted Bundy bundled along the blustery streets of Vail.

Hoping that his recent haircut and street clothes would be disguise enough, Ted trotted to the bus station. From his pocket he pulled off the top layer from a wad of $20 bills. The next bus left at 4:15 a.m., and—yes, sir, it did have snow tires. By 7:00 a.m. Ted Bundy was barreling down out of the Rockies in a Trailways bus, headed for downtown Denver and the airport.

Back in Glenwood Springs his careful planning was about to pay off. The cook pushed her cart through the usual morning rounds in the cellblock. She tapped lightly on Ted's door, then slid the tray in. When the prisoner didn't stir, she shrugged and thought, "He's sleeping again. It's Saturday morning anyway; let him sleep." Through the small window she could see his darkened form on the bunk.

By 8:55 Saturday morning Ted Bundy was stepping onto a TWA flight for Chicago. By 11:00 he was in the downtown business district. By noon he was tipping his third victory gin and tonic.

As Ted rejoiced to the clink of ice cubes in the Windy City, jailer Frank Perry had just finished knocking twice on the cell door. Moments later the lawbooks and stuffed sleeve lay revealed on the bunk. "Christ," Perry hissed, "we've fallen for the oldest trick in the book."

For residents of Glenwood Springs it was a replay of the previous June, with all the paraphernalia of a manhunt: the dogs, the roadblocks, the noisy helicopters. But no one could even guess which way Ted had gone—they were only sure he was long gone. After 12 hours the roadblocks were called off, and preparations for a wanted poster were under way.

As "sightings" of Ted from Tacoma to New York began pouring in, the FBI entered the case, anticipating a charge of interstate flight to avoid prosecution. Nick Isenberg and Dawne Gundel were questioned at the radio station; Nancy Hobson got the shakedown from an agent at a pancake house in Seattle; and preparations began almost immediately to place Theodore Robert Bundy on the Ten Most Wanted list.

Recriminations darkened the air in Colorado. The sheriff

blamed lack of funds from the county commissioners, and the commissioners blamed the sheriff for lax security. Frank Tucker blamed Judge Lohr for his leniency, promising to empanel a grand jury.

Inside the jail everyone claimed Ted must have had help. As far as Undersheriff Hart knew, Bundy only had seven dollars to his name. How could he get away on that? As for the logistics of the escape a "builder's error" was blamed for the crawl-space exit from the cell. And the light fixture? It was the former sheriff who reminded his successors that cell number five, a storeroom then, might have only been spot-welded after the 1970 escape. An oversight, one of those things.

As he had planned before the escape, Sheriff Hogue retired to work as a security agent for Midcontinent Coal, moving far up to a tiny mountain town to live. The two jailers were fired on the spot.

Up in Aspen, the news turned Ted Bundy from a folk hero to a legend overnight. First there were the T-shirts: "Ted Bundy Is a One-Night Stand." And then the posters, celebrating "Aspen's foremost jumper and cross-country expert." Finally a local folksinger enshrined the story as legend:

> So let's salute the mighty Bundy,
> Here on Friday, gone on Monday;
> All his roads lead out of town,
> It's hard to keep a good man down.

Theodore Bundy had wanted to ride a train ever since he was a child. Saturday afternoon found him gawking happily at Chicago's Central Station. The star prisoner from Colorado had originally planned to head for Columbus, Ohio, but at the last minute decided the campus of the University of Michigan in Ann Arbor was more promising. There, at a large university, he would feel like himself again. In the lyrical strains of a later letter, Ted Bundy would describe the rush of exhilaration:

> I remember my first hours of freedom, walking through the night-darkened snow and ice-covered streets of Glenwood Springs. I recall a bus ride, my first conversations with people, a plane flight. The recollections are intoxicating.

I can see clearly New Year's Eve, my first day of freedom. There was this chaotic city crowd scene, a flash of lights as if seen for the first time, the rush of faces and monotonous calls of the train stations. I can hear the train sounds, feel the sway of the coach, and see my face reflected in the window as I looked through the night scene that moved in shadows across the pane. I drank a couple of beers in the club car, listened to conversations, and felt that I had tasted the security and calm of knowing I had really made it.

I arrived in Ann Arbor amid a crowd of New Year's partygoers. It was nearly ten thirty. No one knew the celebration I was having privately. It was a strange place, but I left the train station walking and and expecting I would find a place there. It is a college town, and I knew how to survive in such places.

Freedom—full strides I walked without chains, and I walked and walked. Everyone has someone on New Year's Eve, but I was content to watch. Near the campus there was activity, although the holidays had drained the district of many of its residents. Though cold and overcast, the area reminded me briefly of the University District in Seattle, and I felt safe. . . .

I found a YMCA open; a room cost $12 and I could sleep on a real bed—a dream come true, and I really did pinch myself that night as I lay in a warm bed and gazed out a barless window into the snow.

Those few days . . . were pleasant. The snow fell, the sun shone, and students returned. I got stinking drunk cheering the University of Washington Huskies while watching the Rose Bowl in a tavern packed to the gills with Michigan fans. God, did I take my life in my hands. I might well have been arrested for inciting to riot.

1978. Bells and horns and firecrackers. I just stood there on the sidewalk and listened. 1978. What was my family doing, my friends? Were they worried? If only I knew. If only they knew. 1978 had started out beautifully, a truly new beginning.

But I had to get off the streets. It was late. Take no chances. Rest and sleep. Take no chances.

Part IV

CAPTURE

24

When Chris Hagen stepped off the Trailways bus in Tallahassee, Florida, on a warm January morning, he stepped into a new life. Born and raised a Northerner, blasted one time too many by months of wind and snow and sleet, he had migrated south in hopes of a less demanding climate, half imagining Florida as a single unbroken stretch of summer sand giving way to bright vistas of ocean at the horizon.

His first glimpse of the Florida Panhandle, just an hour before, had abolished his illusions. He had watched the sun rise through the stands of slender pine and grow bright over the slump-roofed barns of small dairy farms, realizing there was more to the state than the travel brochures pretended. Like the miles of poor, often dreary and desolate Georgia countryside he'd ridden through from Atlanta—silent, unpopulated, draped with Spanish moss—north Florida seemed stagnant and isolated from the window of the bus, the picture of the old South Hagen imagined was long gone.

But he was not discouraged as he nodded to the driver and stepped down. Tallahassee, the state capital, home of two universities, a city of 100,000 just 50 miles from the Gulf of Mexico, was sure to be different: a comfortable and stimulating oasis. Yes, an oasis was the way he liked to think of it, a faraway green and growing place where he could nurture and restore himself. Like many men and women in their early thirties, Chris Hagen had absorbed his share, perhaps more than his share, of disappointment, disillusionment, and pain. Somehow the abundant possibilities of six, four, even two years before had narrowed. His career, his friends, the women he had once loved had all eluded his grasp, and he was left only with himself, wondering what his real resources were.

But now, forced to start again, he had embraced the chance. Chris Hagen sniffed the air and smiled. By seven in the morning he could tell that the sun would shine steadily all day.

221

Inside the terminal Hagen began the first tasks of orienting himself to his new home, searching for a map and the classified section of the morning paper. With only $160 to his name, he needed to locate an inexpensive room in a hurry. The areas around college campuses were usually the best bets; students without much money were constantly in and out, and there was always *something* available. Hagen had been a student himself, off and on, and he knew his way around.

But there was one stomach-dropping shock for him before he began. Rounding the corner from the restroom, Hagen suddenly felt a pair of eyes fixed on him. A man on a plastic seat in the waiting area was staring hard, staring as if he knew him, and for a moment Hagen, improbably, felt he recognized the stranger. His heart began to pound noisily in his chest. If his whole life seemed confused and tenuous at that moment, Chris Hagen knew this much for sure: the last thing he wanted was to meet someone from the past. He turned and pushed open the door into the Florida sunshine.

Hagen walked first to the Florida State University campus, several blocks away on Tennessee Street. There, he expected he would find crowds of students cradling their books on their way to classes, a student cafeteria with its clattering dishes and trays, bulletin boards crammed with offers of dirt-cheap housing. But the campus, with its widely spaced brick class buildings and neat rows of palm trees, looked almost empty. Hagen knew immediately that FSU was not the kind of thriving university complex he'd known up north. Stashing his heavy sweater in a locker at the bookstore, he set out on foot to see what he was up against.

Things looked up at the far edge of campus, where a gym and several acres of athletic fields stretched out in the distance. Hagen liked sports—running, bicycling, and racquet games especially—and resolved to keep in good shape. First, he reminded himself, a place to stay.

The streets around the perimeter of campus are lined with fraternities and sororities—proud, well-kept buildings that suggest a strong "Greek" tradition at the school. Underfoot, the sidewalks wear a colorfully painted tradition of past classes, rivalries, and romances. It wasn't until Hagen reached College Avenue, a shady street that runs from the wrought-iron campus gate to the business district near the

222

Capitol downtown, that he found what he was looking for.

Almost hidden by the sprawling, snaky limbs of a thousand-year-old oak tree in the front yard was the sign on the front porch: ROOM FOR RENT. Ken Ellison, a 20-year old physics student, was smoking a cigarette on the front walk.

"Hi," said Chris. "Know what they're asking for that?"

"Nope. There's the manager's apartment. Right in there."

Room 12 of the Oak was available for $80 a month, but the manager wanted a $100 deposit on top of the first month's rent. $180 was $20 more than Hagen had, and it took some wheedling to get the place for the deposit and a promise of two months' rent at the end of the month. Even at that, Hagen said to himself as he clomped downstairs to finalize the deal late that afternoon, it was no bargain: the room was small and cramped, with a truncated view of the backyard over a fire escape and a poorly equipped communal bathroom down the cheaply paneled hall.

What the Oak lacked in amenities it made up for in a fluid, tolerant social life. Chris's neighbors upstairs were members of an out-of-work rock band; a Korean graduate student lived down the hall, and an ex-air force man in another apartment. Like Hagen, they were ten or more years older than the FSU undergraduates and Tallahassee Community College students who dominated the Oak and other rooming houses nearby. But as long as the newcomer was reasonably affable and willing to endure an occasional long-winded predawn discussion in the hall, he would get along fine. And best of all, as far as Chris Hagen was concerned, he was never asked who he was, where he came from, or what he did. It was all, as the saying at the Oak went, "Be here now."

Hagen spent the first several days at the Oak alone, rolling up his sleeping bag and padding out early in the morning to explore Tallahassee on foot and returning to his room late at night. He had resolved to live frugally, almost monastically, and he struck some of his housemates as aloof, unfriendly, diffident. But Hagen was more attached to his old comforts than he thought, and it wasn't long before he was making nightly trips to the Majik Mart for a bottle of wine or a quart of beer and supplementing his diet of sardines with hamburgers and French fries from Wendy's. He opened up a little more with his new neighbors, smoking dope one night and joining in the game of taunting the police when they stormed up the steps of the Oak to silence the rock band's jam session. Hagen had almost forgotten: college students are beautiful, exuberant people.

Even Ken Ellison, a little wary of Hagen at first, felt drawn to him now. He wasn't sure how Hagen spent his time (a graduate student perhaps?), but he liked the new tenant's sense of humor and his intelligence. His intelligence especially, his apparent capacity for intense concentration: Ellison, bright and thoughtful himself, valued such qualities. What did it matter if Chris owned more than one kind of eyeglasses, parted his hair on the opposite side each day, or trimmed off his mustache only to begin growing it again?

Hagen might have told Ellison, if he'd asked, that it was essential to look your best at a job interview. Chris's money was nearly gone, and he'd been scouting the papers every day to scare up some temporary work. One man at a construction site told Hagen he could go to work the next day if he could produce a driver's license for identification; Chris had to turn the job down.

That was enough to discourage him. He skipped the want ads now and browsed through the sports section instead. After breakfast at the FSU cafeteria he wandered down to the gym and looked for a racquetball partner. Now, when he was hungry, he loaded his backpack with sardines and hurried out the supermarket door without paying. He lifted a bicycle next, "dipped" pocketbooks in the library, and then, according to police, on January 10, 1978, Chris Hagen broke into a 1971 Toyota parked on Pensacola Street and made off with a Panasonic television, a Sony table model radio, and a Smith-Corona portable typewriter.

None of it was according to plan. "Don't do anything illegal," Hagen had told himself. "Don't drive without a license. Don't shoplift. Don't *jaywalk*, for Christ's sake. If you're going to start over, start right." But he was more attached to the little pleasures than he thought, more indolent, less hard on himself.

Hagen's housemates would never have guessed what he was up to. More and more he was a part of the scene at the Oak, looking people straight in the eye and stopping to talk on the street. When a young woman cosmetology student moved into the house in the middle of the month, Hagen—a perfect stranger—was quick to befriend her.

"Need some help?" he said, following her out to the

224

street and stooping to pick up a box. A Doberman bounded out from behind a car.

"That's Sarah," the woman laughed. "She's a harmless. My name's Jeanelle."

Hagen glanced at his shoes, then at her. "I'm Chris."

"Oh, that's a nice name."

Their friendship was cemented minutes later when Chris offered Sarah a mustard-soaked sardine from the stash in his room. Jeanelle and Chris felt comfortable together immediately, she put at ease by his charming, self-confident stream of talk and he glad for the company of someone pretty and unspoiled. But with a past he chose to obscure and an uncertain future, Chris Hagen wasn't ready to spin a web of attachments in Tallahassee. It was enough that Jeanelle should serve him coffee in a rice bowl one morning and open up about her mother's death. Chris nodded sympathetically and listened.

"I'm lucky," he said. "I've never had to go through that."

But there were others in Tallahassee, Florida, those last weeks of January who were not so lucky. Something had shattered the polite civility of this small southern city, something that made a trusting young woman like Jeanelle cling to the safe, reassuring friendship of a man like Chris.

For Kelly Powers, a Tallahassee psychic and astrological counselor, the new year was off to a sour start. Since last summer he hadn't been able to shake a sense of foreboding. It had begun when he'd read of the beating of FSU student Linda Sue Thompson in the *Democrat* in May 1977. Someone had grabbed the fair-skinned Chi Omega pledge outside Dorman Hall and hauled her off to a lonely wooded lot where he beat her with a board and disappeared. She'd survived, to most everyone's surprise, after two boys found her in the woods and went for help. But it left the women of FSU— especially Thompson's roommate Nita Jane Neary—badly shaken.

The summer passed without another coed attack (although a 30-year-old mother of three was found dead in south Tallahassee with her skull battered in). Still, Kelly Powers couldn't fight his feeling: a serious and violent crime connected with the university was coming. In December, Powers later recalled, while driving near the campus, he felt a wave of depression. "Something's trying to come through," he thought

225

to himself—a "leakage," as the people of his profession sometimes call it. Powers went home that night, concentrated hard for ten minutes and jotted down a few disjointed notes: he "heard" a dog barking, "saw" a man raking leaves, and then there was something like an x inside a horseshoe.

A month later, just after midnight on the morning of Sunday, January 15, 1978, Powers was out with friends and again passed by the FSU campus. His feeling was now so strong it was almost like a panic. "I don't feel so well," he said, leaning over the front seat. "Do you mind dropping me off?" Powers lay wide-eyed in his bed two hours later, still trying to calm himself.

Across town, Nita Neary awoke on the second floor of the Theta Chi fraternity house. I must really be coming down with something, the FSU art education major sniffed; two beers put me out. Nita sleepily descended the stairs to find the last hangers-on of the evening's keg party chatting in corners or having one last dance. It was time to go, she told her date.

The cool night air cleared her head. It rarely got really cold in Tallahassee in the winter. Even in January you could often get by with a light windbreaker. "Lucky it isn't too cold tonight," she thought. Her boyfriend's car ran out of gas a block from the sorority house. He walked her dutifully to the door, and they kissed good night.

Chi Omega's back door had a combination code lock, which opened easily as Nita pressed the proper sequence. She gave the door a firm shove, turned into the rec room and frowned. "Someone has left the lights on again," she thought, "and it's after three." She bounced down the single step into the living room and her hand had just found the switch when a loud thump stopped her. "Good old Steve," she thought —"I'll bet he's tripped on the stairs." A half-smile gathered her delicate features as she peered through the window; but the parking lot was empty. She could only see the woodpile below, dimly illuminated by the small light above the back door.

Nita Neary crossed back through the rec room, heading for the living-room lamp and then the front stairway to the second-floor bedrooms. Overhead, muffled footsteps hurried along the carpeted hallway—someone else up late, no doubt. As Nita stepped into the foyer she saw a man crouched at the front door, one hand on the knob and the other holding a two-foot log. In an instant he was gone, and Neary stood frozen until a click from the closing door brought her back.

The Chi Omega sister marched upstairs and woke her roommate, Nancy Dowdy. The sorority's strict rules forbade men upstairs. Only Chi Omega "sweethearts" (as the specially chosen young men who do maintenance work for the girls are called) ever see the inner sanctum on the second floor. Perhaps it was a burglar. Maybe she should call the police. What would sweetheart Ricky Ramoya be doing changing a light bulb this time of night?

Nancy Dowdy donned a robe and grabbed her umbrella. "Can you imagine," Nita whispered on the stairs, "one of the girls getting up the nerve to have a man in her room at this time of night?"

Nancy wanted a description of the man, and Nita carefully recalled what she'd seen. He'd had on a knit ski (or toboggan) cap, a dark blue windbreaker, light-colored pants, a dark complexion, and that log. "I only saw him in profile," she told her friend. "He had a prominent nose, long and straight, and thin lips. He seemed about Ricky Ramoya's build, but a little taller."

"But what would Ricky be doing in the house this time of night?" she repeated to her friend as they climbed back toward President Jackie McGill's room. The sorority president didn't mind being yanked out of bed at three in the morning: it was her duty to deal with all the little concerns and complaints. As they stood in the hallway outside the president's room, debating whether to call the police, a movement caught Nancy Dowdy's eye.

Karen Chandler stumbled from her room, bent almost double, and turned in the opposite direction, holding her head in her arms. Figuring that her friend was suffering from the effects of too much to drink, Dowdy ran to her and placed a comforting hand on Chandler's arm. Her fingers came away covered with blood.

"Oh my God," she screamed, "Karen's hurt!" McGill and Neary dashed to help, and the three of them ushered their sorority sister to the nearest room. By now, women were waking up all along the second floor. Back in Chandler's room Dowdy beheld an even more gruesome scene. Kathy Kleiner, Chandler's roommate, sat cross-legged in her bed, rocking and moaning while blood dripped freely from her head. Nancy Dowdy ran for the housemother and the nearest telephone, while one of the other women placed a plastic pail in Kleiner's lap to catch the blood.

"3:22 a.m.," as Oscar Brannon would later say in his toneless "Dragnet" manner, "I was summoned to the scene of a crime at the Chi Omega sorority house." Nancy Dowdy and Nita Neary met Brannon and Officer Ray Crew of the FSU police department at the door. Both men, having been walking their nearby beats when the call came, ran up the sidewalk together. While Brannon took a description from Nita for a BOLO ("Be on the Lookout"), Ray Crew ran upstairs to survey the damage.

In room eight Kathy Kleiner still sat upright on her bed. Her jaw was swollen, obviously broken, and a stream of blood soaked the bedclothes. But she had a sorority sister with her, and Crew could do nothing until the medics arrived. Karen Chandler was in a similar state—badly hurt but in no immediate danger.

The housemother trailed him closely as he began checking each room. At number four he eased the door open and flipped on the lights. "That's Lisa Levy," the housemother whispered and withdrew. Lisa lay face down on her bed, the covers pulled up to her ears. But clothes, strewn all over the room, told him something was wrong.

"Lisa, wake up," Crew said firmly and then pulled the covers back to reveal a huge, dull red stain. He grasped her shoulder, started to roll her nude body over, but it was already getting cool to the touch.

"Get an EMT," he told the housemother, easing Lisa back onto the bed. His fingers gently probed her neck for a pulse. It was faint, irregular, but if they hurried . . . Eight minutes after Brannon and Crew had come up the walk, the emergency medical technicians arrived. EMT Don Allen helped Crew roll Levy over and place her on the floor. There was what appeared to be a bullet hole in her right breast, but the technician looked in vain for an exit wound. While Allen massaged Lisa Levy's fluttering heart, Crew dashed back to the top of the stairs.

"You better get up here, Brannon. We got a signal seven."

A signal seven was the code for a "deceased person." Brannon radioed the news as he took the stairs two at a time.

Ray Crew left to check the remaining rooms. "There's obviously nothing I can do here," Brannon said to himself as a second EMT arrived, and he too left, this time to comfort

Kathy Kleiner, who was calling over and over for her parents.

But the flood of Leon County, Tallahassee, and FSU police needed information, and Brannon was called downstairs to talk with investigator Don Patchen of the crimes-against-persons unit. Over his shoulder, as he ran down the hall, he heard Karen Chandler hysterically begging technicians to search under the bed to see if someone was there.

Ray Crew, continuing his room-to-room search, burst through the next door.

"Oh my God, we've got another one!" he called back to officers herding the terrorized women into a room down the hall. But Melanie Nelson was unhurt, merely a sound sleeper. When Crew had roused her and related what had happened, Melanie's first thought was for her friend Margaret Bowman. They had been chatting on the stairs only an hour earlier. "Check Margaret. She's home, but she hasn't come out yet."

Another Tallahassee cop was already at her door. Bill Newkirk slipped through and closed it behind him. He switched on the light, and for a long moment he didn't move. Margaret Bowman lay in a limp, awkward pose on the bed. Tied tightly around her neck was a pair of panty hose, knotted at the windpipe. Her mouth gaped open rigidly, and her eyes stared blankly at the wall. He could see her cranium through a large puncture on the left side of her head. There was blood everywhere, but particularly around her shoulders and head. "She's been decapitated," he muttered to himself. On the wall, a bloody palm print was already drying.

Outside, medics were carrying the three other injured women to waiting ambulances below. There was no hurry with Margaret Bowman: she was already dead. With the Chi Omega sisters safely locked away, there was nothing to do until the sheriff and the crime scene technicians arrived. A crowd had begun to gather in the streets, drawn by the flashing police and ambulance lights. A plastic surgeon waited at the hospital. Kathy Kleiner and Karen Chandler would make it through, without even external scars to recall their horror.

Lisa Levy was dead on arrival.

Four blocks from the Chi Omega house, Debbie Cicarelli and Nancy Young had just returned home. They and their friend next door, Cheryl Thomas, had gone dancing at Big Daddy's as they did most Saturdays. The old tin-roofed duplex with the sagging front porch might as well have been one apartment. When Cheryl Thomas returned after driving her date home she turned on her TV. Even at low volume, the sounds of a late movie clearly echoed through the walls.

Both apartments (called "railroad flats" because the back door is visible from the front) have the same layout of living room, bedroom, and kitchen. As Debbie Cicarelli lay falling asleep on her mattress on the floor, a few feet through the wall Cheryl Thomas was doing the same. Just as Cheryl drifted off she heard something knocked off a table. "That cat," she thought wearily, "he isn't used to his new home yet."

Thump. With her ear only inches from the floor, Debbie awoke instantly. Thump. Thump. "Someone's under the house," she thought. "Why are they hitting the floor with a hammer?" Through the wall she could hear whimpering in Cheryl Thomas's bedroom. "Something's definitely wrong." She shook Nancy awake. "What shall we do?" Debbie called her boyfriend, who told her to go back to sleep.

The three girls had worked out a "security system." Each would answer the phone, no matter what time of the day or night—if she was home. Debbie dialed Cheryl's number. The phone rang twice, and an incredible banging and smashing came from the other apartment's kitchen—"like the kitchen table was slammed into the cabinets," she would later say.

Debbie called the police and was stunned when a minute later not one car but 12 showed up. Nancy Young showed the cops the hidden key, but they had trouble opening Thomas's front door. Someone had placed a chair under the knob. One officer ran around to the north side. A window screen, as if just removed, leaned against the wall below. The bottom sash was stuck, but the top was already cracked an inch or two. The officer went through the window and opened the front door.

Nancy and Debbie retreated to their apartment after the police had entered. They hadn't wanted to know the rest— "Oh, my God, she's still alive" had already come through the walls.

Two EMTs had just gotten Kathy Kleiner to the Tallahassee Memorial Hospital when the call to 431A Dunwoody Street came at 4:57. But the law enforcement officers re-

230

fused to let them enter for a minute until the "crime scene" had "been secured." Tangled in the covers of Cheryl Thomas's bed was a panty hose mask. Before anyone contaminated the "scene" the officers wanted to make sure that such evidence was safely out of the way.

Cheryl Thomas was sitting upright in her bed, mumbling and groaning, when police had first arrived. Now the medical techs found her prone and covered, but still alive.

Cheryl Thomas, too, would survive.

Sunday dawn broke in Tallahassee with searchers fanning out through the city in hopes of finding a bloody oak limb. On campus, university officials unlocked their offices, drew in their breaths, and reached for the telephone. Better that the parents of Margaret Bowman and Lisa Levy should learn of the deaths of their daughters from them than on the radio or TV that morning.

Most of Tallahassee did learn of the predawn murders from the news that Sunday. Planning a trip, anticipating the Super Bowl, they had passed a typical Saturday night while police detectives and medical technicians worked frantically to save lives and catch a man with a club.

At the Oak, four blocks from the Chi Omega house, that Saturday night had seemed just about like any other weekend night to Henry, an Oak resident, and Rusty, the sound man for Henry's rock band. It was somewhere around 5:00 a.m. Sunday when the two friends returned to the big white rooming house on College Avenue and found one of Henry's housemates at the front door.

Nothing strange in that. Chris Hagen kept late hours just like lots of other people.

25

Ken Katsaris fitted his heel into the bottom of a cowboy boot, ran a dot of hair cream through his thin black hair, and hurried out the front door. The call had come right at 3:30 a.m. "You'd better get over here, sheriff. Two of 'em are dead already."

Elected Leon County sheriff 14 months before, Katsaris was rushing headfirst, in the middle of this cool January night, toward the sternest, most publicized test of his administration. He had handled murder cases before, but nothing like this—and both his supporters and detractors (not to mention the political pros around the capital, always on the watch for a rising star) would follow the investigation closely.

Katsaris's reputation had grown more complex since his election in November 1976. At the time many voters had seen him as a shining emblem of the new South. Thirty-five years old, articulate, an ex-junior college criminology professor and the author of a textbook on evidence, Katsaris could not have presented voters a clearer alternative to the gruff, cigar-chomping incumbent. "Sheriff Hamlin may not have been an old-style, backroom, bigoted cop after all," one observer put it, "but he *seemed* that way enough to get Ken elected."

Once in office, the new sheriff began a program of high-minded reform, increasing the retrieval rate on stolen property and markedly improving antiquated jail conditions; yet, to the distress of many who had helped elect him, another side began to emerge: an instinct for incautious grandstanding, opportunism, and an obsession with public image that made some people wonder what Katsaris was trying to hide. One courthouse regular noted that even his style of dress had changed subtly after the election: "He never wore them cowboy boots before."

"Maybe it's just accepting the realities of compromise," said one member of Tallahassee's legal community, "but Katsaris is looking more like Hamlin every day."

By the time the sheriff arrived at Chi Omega, most of his investigative staff were already on the scene. Jack Poitinger, captain of the detectives' division and a coolly unshakable recent law-school graduate, had taken command. Howard Winkler, chief crime scene technician, had already brought the sorority sisters downstairs and closed all the doors to prevent contamination of the crime scenes.

Every patrol car in Leon County already carried Ray Crew's BOLO: Be on the lookout for a dark-skinned white male or light-skinned black male 5'8" to 5'10", 150 pounds, early twenties, with a navy blue jacket, light-colored pants, and a knit ski cap. Should have blood-splattered clothing.

Patrolman Oscar Brannon was scanning the downstairs

rooms for clues. By the back door, leading into the rec room, he discovered a trail of bark and moss. He carefully measured the distances between the pieces and plotted each location on a sheet of graph paper. "This must be the killer's point of entry," he thought.

He and Winkler "processed" Lisa Levy's room, taking photographs from every angle, gathering up the sheets, pillowcases, and bedspread, and retrieving torn underwear from the floor. Later a more thorough search would be made: fingerprint specialists would dust the entire floor, pulling away hundreds of latent prints to be compared with an elimination list of 250 people having a "legitimate reason" to be in the sorority house. But for now, Winkler worked methodically up the hallway, sealing each door with a piece of tape and dusting the door and doorjamb with fingerprint powder.

Downstairs in the dining room, each Chi O sister was interviewed by two women officers who elicited anything they might have heard or seen. For the third time that night, Nita Neary described the man she had seen at the door. "I might possibly be able to recognize the man again," Neary spoke hesitantly, "if I saw a profile." "She looks remarkably calm," one woman officer thought, "considering what she's been through."

EMTs carried Margaret Bowman out of the sorority house last, as Winkler extracted a gold chain from around her neck. He searched her room and collected a yellow nightgown, the bedclothes, numerous pieces of bark, and a pair of Hanes panty hose obviously designed as a weapon. The elastic waistband had been neatly clipped in two spots above each leg and the left leg cut away entirely. When the remaining leg was slipped back through the panties and knotted, it would make a very effective garrote. There was no way of telling if the one on Bowman's neck resembled the pair in his hand. The coroner removed it later.

As Winkler closed the door to seal it, a single bloody fingerprint on the door's edge caught his eye. He would let the fingerprint technicians handle that. Right now he was needed over on Dunwoody Street.

431A Dunwoody Street was swarming with cops when Winkler arrived. Cheryl Thomas had already been lifted into the ambulance with wounds strikingly similar to those over in Chi Omega. His suspicions were confirmed when an officer pointed out a bloody board and a panty hose mask—a Sears brand with eye, nose, and mouth holes. Winkler lifted it from the tangled bedsheet and placed it on the floor for photographing.

Later the whole room would be vacuumed for hairs, dusted for prints, sealed. But now Winkler was due at Tallahassee Memorial to assist at the unpleasant task of autopsy. He left orders to turn the plastic bags with Thomas's sheets and coverlet over to the Florida Department of Criminal Law Enforcement crime lab.

Assistant Medical Examiner Thomas Wood arrived at the hospital morgue soon after Margaret Bowman did that Sunday morning. By noon he'd completed a thorough examination of both women, combing their heads and pubic hair for "foreign material," scraping the fingernails, and detailing the numerous bruises and wounds. Combings from both contained bits of bark, and in Lisa Levy's hair he found a wad of chewing gum.

Levy's head and jaw were caved in on the left side, probably by a "blunt instrument," with plenty of hemorrhaging. The apparent puncture wound on her left breast showed ragged edges, and when Wood spied a double bite mark on her left buttock, he realized what had happened. The assailant had bitten Lisa Levy's nipple off.

Thomas Wood knew a little about bite-mark analysis, despite its status as one of the newer areas of forensic medicine, and the four deep bruises in Levy's buttock seemed distinct enough to be of some use for later analysis. Winkler, meanwhile, had been carefully photographing the bodies from different angles. While the medical examiner held a little plastic lab ruler next to the bite marks, Winkler pulled in close and snapped a last shot. It would be the most important photograph he had ever taken.

Then Wood carefully cut away a chunk of tissue under the marks and placed it in a saline solution for preservation.

On Levy's thigh there was a deep abrasion—a "rope burn," he would later call it—indicating that her underwear had been torn off. There was indication of "blunt trauma" to the vaginal and anal cavities and some odd little pinpoint bruises on the uterus. Wood was puzzled.

The examiner also took blood, saliva, and tissue samples and swabs from the vagina for later analysis. He followed the same pattern with Bowman, first cutting away the panty hose in a way that left the knot intact. Despite the massive wound in Bowman's head, Wood concluded that both young women had died of strangulation.

Shortly after dawn that Sunday, Katsaris and his men began a systematic round of visits to the other sororities around campus, urging the women to stay calm and to keep their windows and doors securely locked. Back in his roomy second-floor office at the Leon County courthouse, Katsaris rearranged assignments, shuffling every possible man-hour to the case.

An obvious first step was Nita Neary's sighting of the man at the door. They would need every bit of information she could supply from her brief encounter. On Sunday evening, the same woman officer who'd interviewed Neary that morning fetched her from Nancy Dowdy's parents' house. Waiting in the Chi Omega house foyer was Francis Kenniston, chairman of the FSU art department and a former television storyboard illustrator from Chicago. On a couch facing the front door at almost the same angle as she had stood the night before, the artist and the art ed major were left alone to bring Nita's memory to life.

Kenniston's series of drawings began with the stranger's posture as he crouched at the front door, in a squarish, almost abstract image of a human being. But the two spent most of their time getting the profile right, Nita struggling to describe the angle and shape of the nose and the size and slant of the lips.

On Monday a special command post was established in an office building donated by a local developer, and the FBI and the Florida Department of Criminal Law Enforcement were called in. "In effect," Katsaris told a reporter, "we've created a new agency for the sole purpose of solving this one crime."

What the new agency had to work with, however, was slim. Aside from the panty hose and board from Dunwoody and a piece of chewing gum and a bloody fingerprint from Chi Omega, virtually no physical evidence had turned up yet. But investigators' hopes were buoyed later that week when a fingerprint technician stumbled across a bloody Clairol bottle in Lisa Levy's room. The "pinpoint bruises" Wood had found were easily explained as telltale markings from the bottle's pump top.

As for eyewitnesses, Nita Neary's "might possibly" statement offered the only hope. None of the three surviving victims remembered a thing, nor did any of the other women who'd been in the house that night. Providing, of course, that a suspect was found, it was a real question how Neary's identification would hold up under the grueling cross-examination of some tough defense lawyer in a trial.

When her name made the papers Nita Neary dropped out of school and went into hiding back home in Indiana, terrified the attacker would be out to silence her. First, in May, her roommate Linda Sue Thompson had been beaten nearly to death. And now this.

Phones rang steadily at the command post and detectives taped every conversation, no matter how remote the tip seemed. There was a strange maintenance man on campus, someone advised. Or what about that escaped mental patient, or the stranger who'd been combing College Avenue for a man named Mike, or that brown-haired man who was bad-mouthing sorority girls in a bookstore the week before? Within a week more than 500 names and descriptions had poured in, even from out West. "Ted Bundy," said the Washington State cop. "Check him out."

A few leads seemed more promising than most. Like the call from a student who'd been outside his house on College Avenue about 4:30 a.m. on Sunday. A man had appeared from behind some bushes, the informant said, then slunk toward the 400 block of College Avenue. He was a white male, in his late teens or early twenties, wearing an orange scarf, a light jacket, and—here the investigator's interest peaked—a dark knit cap.

Nita Neary's mention of Ricky Ramoya seemed promising too. Even though Ramoya, a gentle FSU music student and former steady of one of the Chi O girls, was well spoken of, no one could be automatically eliminated as a suspect. Ramoya, the police learned from his roommate, had come home at the usual time and been there for breakfast Sunday morning. Still, no one had actually seen him asleep in his bed at 3:00 a.m. Ramoya easily passed a polygraph test and was shifted to the bottom of the suspect list.

As the days wore on, Ken Katsaris had less and less for the band of reporters who trailed him, and he began, occasionally, to indulge in speculation. It was certainly possible, he admitted, that the recent killings were connected to last spring's Linda Sue Thompson attack; maybe it was more than a coincidence that she was a Chi Omega pledge. And

236

then there was the theory (later discounted) that all the victims had been at the same disco, Big Daddy's, the night of the murders. (Lisa Levy, however, had been next door at Sherrod's.)

Dr. Julian Arroyo, a retired policeman with 20 years' experience as a hypnotist, flew to Tallahassee to practice his art on the three survivors and Nita Neary. Kathy Kleiner remembered a flash of light and the rustle of leaves, but the other two remembered nothing at all. "The next thing I remember after going to sleep," Karen Chandler said, "was being lifted into the ambulance."

Neary might be more helpful. Even though she'd caught but a brief look at the man with the club, perhaps under hypnosis they could draw out a few more details.

Ken Katsaris, Arroyo, and Neary trooped into the polygraph room in the state attorney's office at the Lewis State Bank. A tape recorder would provide insurance against any later charges that the hypnotic session had tainted their witness's memory and also give a thorough opportunity to review any new evidence uncovered.

"The biggest problem I have with hypnosis," Arroyo began, "is convincing my subjects that they have really been hypnotized. Hypnosis won't make you do anything against your will, only help you pinpoint your recall." With Captain Poitinger watching through a one-way mirror, Arroyo stood behind Nita, coaxing her to relax. "Put your toes and heels together," he instructed. "Roll back and forth, rock. Fall right into my arms. I'll catch you."

As Neary gradually relaxed, Arroyo began, almost chanting: "Heavier. Deeper. Heavier. Deeper. Let yourself go. Let yourself sink down. Heavier. Heavier. Heavier. Deeper."

Then the hypnotist walked her through the early morning hours of January 15, just until the moment when the pretty, long-haired blonde came through the foyer door. In a small, oddly deliberate voice, Nita Neary repeated almost exactly the description she'd given so many times before. But now, to a chorus of "deeper" and "heavier," Arroyo got her to fix the image in her mind, and she was able to discern some straight, dark brown hair circling the back of the ski hat. She was almost positive that the man hadn't seen her. He'd been in such a hurry to leave the sorority house.

One thing kept bothering her, however. The profile in her mind kept flashing back and forth with Ricky Ramoya's. "Well, I want you to look at the guy that's going through the door with the club in his hand," the hypnotist urged. "I want you to compare this Ricky Ramoya with this guy that goes to the door. Look at the two faces. You got them separated like a split screen. Are they the same person?"

"They could be."

"Just relax now. Go deeper and deeper. Let's go really deep now, come on honey. The further your mind is, the clearer your memory is. I want you to picture Ramoya and picture this guy with a club. Are they the same? Is there a similarity?"

"Yes."

"Strong or weak?"

"Strong."

With Ricky Ramoya basically eliminated, the hypnotic session was a disappointment. True, they now had a hair color, but they'd hoped that Nita Neary would recognize the man at the door. Later, when the tape of the hypnosis became public, reporters would hear Sheriff Katsaris gleefully planning to lie to the press about Arroyo's work. "Just protecting a witness," he would offer in his own defense.

It was the rainy slump of winter, and Tallahassee mourned. "I was going to talk about the death of Hubert Humphrey and the birthday of Martin Luther King, Jr.," a Methodist minister began at a memorial service for the women, "but my heart is somewhere else." "Fate," offered Florida State University President Bernie Sliger the next day, "is no respecter of fortunes; and certainly no finer young women could have been the focal point of a madman's rage." Lisa Levy's father bravely told the press: "I believe in reincarnation." And, quietly, from her hospital bed, Cheryl Thomas murmured, "Pray for me."

NBC canceled a local broadcast of *Stranger in the House,* a television film about a psychopathic killer of sorority sisters. The papers ran profiles on what sort of twisted soul the murderer might be, while two professors cautioned the media against serving as a catalyst for more crimes of the sort. Security guards joined the staff at each dorm. Calls to the campus escort service jumped dramatically (many escorts brought along an escort of their own now). And for a while, it seemed, no one made a new friend. Finally, a spokeswoman from the Tallahassee Feminist Project declared, "Sometimes we must emerge from our fortresses to carry on our daily lives." The police and university officials, she went on, had turned the incident into "a morality play for women" with the suggestion that women "got what they were asking for."

Fear hardened with determination, and Katsaris said he was only meeting public demand when the Leon County sheriff's office offered Saturday clinics in the use of handguns. A familiar theme began to run through the letters in the *Tallahassee Democrat:* readers thought it was time to enforce the death penalty.

Despite all the clamor, the Chi Omega investigation seemed to be running in circles. By the end of January there were 13 full-time investigators on the case, down from 40 several days before. (The figure does not include the countless amateur detectives spurred on by the $16,000 reward for information leading to a conviction.) The professionals who remained on the case ranged more widely in their search for clues. After several attempts, the psychic, Kelly Powers, finally interested one detective in his story. It was the *x* in the horseshoe, Powers told the detective, that made him think he might be in touch with something. The strange symbol that Powers had imagined a month before the crime was strikingly similar to the Greek letters for Chi Omega: XΩ.

After police had eliminated Powers himself as a suspect (why, they wondered at first, was he so interested in the murders?), one investigator sat with him for several long, fascinating sessions. Powers has a faint, gentle manner, and the detective had to lean forward to catch everything he said. They should look for someone who was over the age of 22, Powers began, and living in a seven-block area around the sorority house. He wears track shoes or tennis shoes a lot, sometimes has a mustache and beard, and may be a well-educated literature or drama student. Powers put his head back and shut his eyes.

"There's a mental drive in him," the psychic continued, "an intensity. He's the most observant person in the world. Not a single detail gets by him. Technically, I think he's an introvert, more concerned about what the world out there does to him than what he does to it."

"What about women?" the detective asked.

"It's very complex. His mother, I'm picking up some strong, fervent beliefs in her, maybe religious beliefs. She pushed him to be what she couldn't, pushed her feelings about what life had done to her. But I think he respected her, in a formal sort of way."

239

The detective dropped his pen on a yellow pad. This was all well and good, but he needed something specific, something he could work with. Did Powers know, for example, how the killer might have chosen his victims?

"He definitely had contact with them in advance, though they probably weren't aware of it. There's something about a lounge or a bar or a clothing store, like maybe he's watching them and feeling this attraction-rejection thing."

The detective thanked Powers for his time, showed him to the door, suggested he drive around campus a little more, and told him to call if he came up with anything. His skepticism was unmistakable. But two weeks later the detective phoned Powers at his office and asked him if he would come visit an apartment with him. They drove to a rooming house near campus and knocked on the door. Inside, a man was spraying for bugs and a woman stood quietly in the corner.

"No," said Powers, "I'm not getting anything." He never heard from the detective again.

Just as police ran aground with their psychic, they were about to venture out on other new and unfamiliar waters in their investigation. It began on January 21, six days after the murders, when a dentist from Coral Gables, Florida, came to Tallahassee. Dr. Richard R. Souviron, youthful-looking, crisply businesslike, made the 500-mile trip from south Florida for a good reason. As one of the country's only 41 forensic odontologists (experts in dental evidence as it applies to the law) and the state's only authority on bite-mark identifications, Souviron was the man to consult about the marks on Lisa Levy's breast and buttock. Was there any way, police wanted to know, that Souviron could match up the impressions and bruises in Levy's skin with the teeth of a suspect?

The first and crucial question for any expert in physical evidence is the condition of the evidence. Souviron was in for a disappointment when he showed up at the state crime lab to inspect the tissue that had been excised from Levy's corpse. Preserved in a saline solution rather than frozen, the tissue had lost the original size and shape of the bite: mistake number one. Number two, no one had thought to take a saliva smear; saliva, like blood, can often be matched with a known sample.

At Katsaris's command post Souviron was introduced to Captain Jack Poitinger and several other detectives. What about photographs taken at the scene? Souviron asked. Levy

240

was still alive in the house, he was told, and they rushed her to the hospital. And after she was dead? Mistake number three could have happened to anyone: the medical examiner's film jammed in his camera. Number four Souviron didn't even know about: a piece of chewing gum, found in Levy's hair, had been turned over to a serologist. If it had the tooth marks of the assailant, he'd never know: the serologist would eventually cut the chewing gum in half.

But it was not a total loss. Poitinger produced a set of autopsy photographs, including a close-up of the bite on Levy's left buttock. There was no scale in the photograph by which to measure the dimensions of the bite, but Souviron thought the evidence was salvageable. They might measure the autopsy table and extrapolate a scale from that, or perhaps exhume the body and restore the picture to an exact one-to-one relationship. There was one other possibility, Poitinger told him: Sergeant Winkler might have gotten some usable shots.

It was difficult for Souviron not to hide his feelings as he said goodbye. Spotty evidence is as frustrating to a forensic specialist as a dirty canvas and frayed brushes are to an artist. Without his tools in top condition, his craft of precision can be worthless. Nonetheless, the dentist from Coral Gables had made a few immediate observations that encouraged him. The bite itself, as captured in the autopsy photographs, was clear and strongly marked in the flesh, and it made one thing obvious to his trained eye: whoever made that bite had awfully crooked teeth.

So crooked, in fact, that you could pick teeth like that out of a crowd.

Four weeks after the murders there was no more absorbing subject around the FSU campus than the events of January 15 at the Chi Omega sorority house and Cheryl Thomas's Dunwoody Street apartment. Students and staff may have given reporters and other outsiders some coldly noncommittal answers to the incessant questions, but they were buzzing away to each other when their guard was down. Rumors and theories ran unchecked through the classrooms, residence halls, and rooming houses. The Oak was no exception. There the talk went on and on in the hall until a kind of contemporary myth, complete with Osceola Indian tales and black humor, had grown up. It wasn't long before the residents were kidding each other about membership in "the

Oak Club"—a double reference to the name of their building and the supposed Chi Omega murder weapon.

Ken Ellison sat on the steps one night, listening to just such an exchange. Chris Hagen, he noticed, wasn't joining in. Ellison's initial uneasiness about the new tenant had never entirely vanished; the two had not become friendly. There was no hostility, however, and Ken had been meaning to tell Chris it was probably unwise to wear a dark knit cap around Tallahassee, given what the papers had been so full of recently. The murderer, Ellison felt certain, would be wild-eyed and incoherent—a far cry from Hagen. Even so, there was no sense drawing attention to yourself.

Chris Hagen couldn't have agreed more. Above all, his own activities required scrupulously inconspicuous behavior. On January 21, according to later police reports, Hagen embarked on a new means of supporting himself when the wallet of a criminology student was lifted at the Northwood Mall. Hagen used the stolen VISA card for ten days, dining regularly at the Holiday Inn and shopping for clothes, athletic shoes and socks, bicycle supplies, and books on sailing at Tallahassee's better shops. He was always polite, one merchant recalled; Hagen made it a point to commend the service at Uncle John's Pancake House.

By early February, say police, Hagen was using a handful of credit cards that had been stolen all over town. (On February 3, several women reported cards disappearing from their purses left under the tables at Sherrod's, a disco next door to the Chi Omega house.) Hagen had grown practiced in the use of the stolen cards. At Smoker's World he worked the owner for a deal on a pipe, a lighter, and some Rumcake tobacco; the $49.35 tab was just shy of the $50 call-for-clearance figure.

At home, as much as possible, Hagen kept the signs of his new affluence to himself. He was content, head propped up on his hands as he began each morning with the "Today" show, to quietly contemplate his future. Overall, he admitted to himself now, Tallahassee just wasn't what he was looking for. He was going to start over one more time, start fresh as a new man. Right around February 1 a letter arrived from Vital Records in Raleigh, North Carolina, containing the birth certificate of Kenneth R. Misner, an FSU grad student and onetime track star whose student ID card Hagen had found on the desk at the registrar's office. Hagen and Misner, with their handsome, angular faces and

242

brown hair, were striking look-alikes. Hagen had his identity well planned.

In spite of himself Chris Hagen began to let his new look show. It was Jeanelle, the cosmetology student, who first noticed the sport jacket and the trousers with their crisp crease.

"Looks nice, Chris. Where you going?"

"Nowhere," said Hagen. "Out."

On February 6, according to the police, Chris Hagen left town, grabbing a 1976 white Dodge van from space 343 of the Seminole Building lot on campus. Stealing a license plate from another car to cover his tracks, Hagen headed east in the FSU media center van. The highway was empty and the tires sang, but for Chris Hagen time was running out.

The next day in Jacksonville, a thriving city on the St. John's River estuary of the Atlantic Ocean, 160 miles east of Tallahassee, Hagen pulled into a Gulf service station and filled the white van's tank on a stolen credit card. On February 8, charges would later read, he bought gas in Lake City, a tiny provincial town 60 miles back toward Tallahassee. That afternoon he was in Jacksonville again.

School had just let out at Nathan B. Forrest High when a white van turned across the parking lot and stopped where Leslie Parmenter, age 14, was waiting for her brother to pick her up.

A man stepped out of the van and said hello. Leslie held her schoolbooks tightly to her chest; she'd been taught not to talk to strangers. Moments later Leslie's brother pulled up, just in time to see the white van drive off.

"What was that all about?" Danny asked.

"He tried to pick me up."

"Come on. We'll get the license."

Twenty-year-old Danny and his sister had paid attention to their father, a Jacksonville policeman. They recorded the white van's number in a legible hand: 13D-11300. Leslie would later identify the driver.

That night around 8:30, a man signed the guest register at the Lake City Holiday Inn. "Ralph Miller" charged his $16 room, a draft beer, and a buffet dinner on his credit card. After dinner, "Miller" returned to the Board Room—the motel's bar decorated with overstuffed chairs and worn book spines along the wall—and ordered the first of four gins. He fell into conversation with a fellow traveler, and the two passed a quiet evening.

It wasn't until morning that a maid discovered that "Ralph Miller" had skipped out on his bill, and it would be several weeks before the man in the bar would come forward and identify the thief. But a petty credit card forgery was the last thing Lake City police had to worry about on the afternoon of February 9. It was hard to believe, in this prim family town: Tom Leach's girl, a twinkly-eyed seventh grader, was gone.

With its freshly painted door arches and window frames, the main two-story brick building of Lake City Junior High wears a proud face. But the eye travels quickly to a tilting, ill-repaired fence; the dry sandy-soil playing fields; a slack, sea-green classroom building out back. Like the core of the old town it is named for, where weedy vacant lots alternate with sleepy small businesses, Lake City Junior High seems an admirable anomaly, if only because it has survived at all. The commercial and residential life of the town has spread outward like a fan, to fast-food restaurants and sprinkled lawns that duplicate those of any town in America.

By the second week of February 1978 the results of the Valentine Queen election were out. Kimmy Leach's friends were still stewing over it on the morning of Thursday, February 9: Kim was the runner-up, and she and her mom were going shopping that afternoon for a dress for Saturday night's dance. It was difficult for Kimberly, a buoyant, popular honor student, to concentrate on anything else. Sure enough, just before nine o'clock, in the middle of her first-period class, she raised her hand and asked to be excused. Her purse, she explained, she'd left it in her homeroom.

Kim turned into an empty hallway and headed for the green building out back. Behind the classroom doors, as she passed them, there was murmuring, laughter, the familiar, ringing voices of her teachers. Outside, a warm winter sunlight lay on the wet grass. Kimberly Diane Leach banged open the old school door, never to be seen alive again.

One after the other her teachers reported her absent through the morning and afternoon, but it wasn't until after two o'clock that anyone thought to call her home. Her mother glanced at her daughter's room on the way to the phone; the Shaun Cassidy poster sent back a vacant grin. The pieces fell together in a hurry. Her parents, her friends, her teachers all agreed: "She was just a good, sweet, average seventh-grade student," as one teacher put it, no runaway. By dusk police were looking for a girl wearing jeans, a football jersey with the number 83, and a long brown coat with a fur collar. She had brown hair, and she was 12 years old.

"I can't think of anything more important that I could be doing than to locate this little girl," Florida Highway Patrol Colonel J. E. Eldridge Beach told a reporter. The largest and most agonizing body hunt in north Florida history was under way.

No one at the Oak even knew Chris Hagen had been gone. He was back in Tallahassee the night of February 9, charging dinner at Chez Pierre, a comfortable stucco-and-wood-beam restaurant that features crepes and a strolling guitarist. The next night, Friday, he invited Jeanelle to come along. Unaccustomed to fancy restaurants, she hesitated at the door.

"Don't you need a reservation?"

Chris held open the door. "Let me take care of it."

Inside Jeanelle began to relax (the two bottles of Great Western champagne didn't hurt) and enjoyed her meal, even if it was the most expensive one on the menu. Chris, too, chose the pepper steak, insisting he didn't mind the expense. By dessert she had opened up about her problems with her boyfriend.

"It's a maturity thing, Jeanelle," Chris advised. "Everybody has to go through it. I did."

By the time the check came, Chris and Jeanelle were giggling and joking. After a daiquiri and Bloody Mary at Clyde's across the street, they watched the end of "The Rockford Files" back at the Oak. Chris saw her to the door and said good night. Jeanelle couldn't remember a more pleasant and mannerly date.

On Saturday, February 11, five weeks after he had moved in, Chris Hagen went by to see the assistant manager. He was trying, he said, to pull together the rent money, and borrowed the phone to call his mother. He hoped they would be patient. That afternoon he set a box of cookies in front of Jeanelle's door. After clearning up—wiping the windows, doors, walls, and furniture with a cloth—Hagen locked room 12 from the inside and left by the fire escape.

It would take his housemate down the hall a week to realize the coincidence: Chris Hagen split the same day an article on a possible profile of the Chi Omega killer appeared in the paper. That's right, he remembered, it was Hagen who had borrowed his copy of the *Democrat* that day.

Late that night, Leon County Deputy Keith Daws rounded a corner just off College Avenue and saw the shadowy figure of Chris Hagen fiddling with the lock of a 1975 Toyota. Daws, suspicious, angled his unmarked patrol car so that the headlights focused squarely on Hagen. He stepped out and good-naturedly inquired what was going on.

"I've just come out to get a book and the lock's stuck," Hagen responded and stepped to the passenger side.

In a pile of books and papers on the floor, Deputy Daws spied the corner of a license plate which Hagen readily handed over, claiming he'd found it and didn't know what to do with it. There was nothing in Hagen's manner to make the deputy overly cautious, and he returned to his patrol car to check the number: 13D-11300.

But he'd no sooner plucked his radio from the seat than Hagen sprinted across the street and into an alleyway behind the Oak. Daws took a few halfhearted steps in pursuit, but quickly gave up the chase. Chris Hagen had just given him the tag Leslie and Danny Parmeter spotted on the white van in Jacksonville.

This was Hagen's last night in Tallahassee. His hand had practiced a whole range of signatures over the past three weeks, and the cards would provide the wherewithal to move on. Tallahassee was getting too hot for him, and he was leaving for sure.

On Sunday morning the 12th he nabbed a white Mazda from the Mormon Church parking lot but drove it only as far as another parking lot across town. The decrepit brakes and transmission made him fear for his life. Minutes later he spotted a 1968 VW Bug with the keys in the ignition. The car touched a fond spot in Hagen's heart: he'd owned a '68 Bug himself once.

From the looks of things—the schoolbooks on the passenger seat and the bouncy trinkets hung from the rearview mirror—it was some girl's first car. Chris had been every bit as attached to the clunky old VW that served him so well. Hagen left the stolen car on East Carolina Street, trusting it would shortly be reunited with its owner.

It was after 10:00 p.m. before he found an acceptable means of transportation out of town: an orange '72 VW that showed no signs of the owner's emotional attachment. By morning he was on the highway heading west across the Panhandle toward Pensacola. The Alabama border was an easy drive away.

26

Hunger had made Chris Hagen edgy Monday morning, and the Crestview Holiday Inn was the first thing that caught his eye. A waitress seated him near the window and lazily held a menu in his direction. Hagen paid little attention to the food, however, while his mind raced ahead, busily planning for the future.

With Kenneth Misner's birth certificate he could pick up a fake driver's license and some work that paid a little better than washing dishes. He'd done enough research in Tallahassee on Misner's background to fend off casual questions.

Hagen knew he had to settle down soon. Many of the credit cards would surely be on the lost or stolen lists. So far he'd been lucky, but now he was determined—no more stolen cards, cars, or anything.

Without really thinking, Hagen slipped a credit card from his wallet and tossed it on top of the check. When the slip came back, he realized with dismay that it was one of the cards with a woman's name. He scrawled his name brusquely and rose to leave, the cash register stuttering behind him. Moments later the waitress called her manager and dashed into the parking lot, where Hagen was rearranging some of the things in his car.

"This card is stolen," she snapped.

"That could create danger for a person," Hagen replied evenly, as he slid into the front seat, "coming out and confronting somebody like that." The door slammed.

"Listen, I'll give you the card back," Hagen sneered, throwing it in her face as the engine roared to life. Rocks shot from under the VW's squealing tires as the restaurant manager charged up, pistol drawn. But he never fired, and the two of them managed only to get a fix on the license plate number.

Chris Hagen swore at himself as he veered up the highway ramp. In a deserted, sandy area a few miles down the road, part of the huge Elgin Air Force Base reserve lands, he bolted on a new set of license plates. But when he shoved the stick into first, the back wheels dug quickly into the soft sand. A few minutes of frantic work and everything not bolted in the rear of the car lay outside—backseat, floor mats, and all his possessions. It was no use, however: every time he hit the gas the wheels dug deeper.

Chris leaned back in the shade of a nearby tree. The car was out of sight, and this was as good a place as any to wait out the inevitable BOLO. When darkness settled he hitchhiked to a gas station for a tow. Less than an hour later he cruised into Pensacola.

By Tuesday morning this new city felt a little more secure. But now, more than ever, he resolved to be careful. Rather than risk driving a hot VW he stayed under cover most of the day, walking the sandy beaches along the Gulf of Mexico. After a long, leisurely dinner, Hagen pointed the VW down the highway toward Mobile, Alabama.

But something made him decide to turn around.

Pensacola Patrolman David Lee cruised the darkened streets of his hometown on early Wednesday morning patrol. About 1:30 a.m. his usual circuit took him by a favorite local restaurant, where he checked the locks and squinted through the window for signs of prowlers. As the patrol car bounced back onto the road, he noticed an orange Volkswagen he did not recognize in the alley behind. It wasn't long past closing time, but he knew it wasn't the chef's car.

On Lee's second trip around the block, the Volkswagen had already pulled into the street ahead. He radioed the tag number, and learned it was stolen. When Lee hit his lights, the suspect speeded up momentarily, then quickly pulled over.

Experience made David Lee wary. Was that someone hiding in the front passenger seat, he wondered.

"Out of the car and face down on the sidewalk," Lee growled, yanking the handcuffs from their case.

"Is there anyone else in that car?" he demanded, but got no reply.

"Is there anyone else in that car?" Still no response.

Lee leaned over and clicked the first handcuff into place, still watching the car for any movement. The next thing he knew, he was lying on the ground, his feet sprawled out in front. As he struggled to sit up and pull his gun, his suspect shoved him to the ground again.

The blue-black barrel of Lee's .38 gleamed darkly in the

patrol car's headlights, but his assailant had hold of his wrist and the bullet shot straight for the stars.

With one final shove, Chris Hagen was free of Lee and dashing down the street.

"Halt," Lee shouted and leveled his revolver at the fleeing figure. "Halt!"

In the violent struggle he'd forgotten the handcuffs. When Hagen hit a pool of light, the patrolman saw a bright flash of metal. For a split second the man turned. Lee thought he was going to shoot and fired his own gun.

Hagen dropped to the ground, face down, barely breathing. The police officer stopped for a moment, already beginning to regret the shooting. He dunked the gun into its holster.

David Lee entered the streetlight's circle and kneeled beside the still figure on the pavement. "I better see where he's hit, how bad he's hurt," the cop thought. Gently, he rolled the slim figure over . . . and was hit squarely in the jaw.

Although the patrolman was a well-built, solid man, the fight continued fiercely for several minutes, Lee struggling for his gun and Hagen shoving his arm wildly back and forth.

"Help," Hagen screamed, "help!" A neighbor came to his doorstep. "What are you doing to that man?" he said, but saw the uniform and backed off.

Finally, the other handcuff snapped firmly on Hagen's wrist. The patrolman whipped the gun barrel across Hagen's cheek before dragging him, bloodied and beaten, to the patrol car.

After a methodical reading of his Miranda card, Lee shoved his prisoner into the backseat. He wasn't waiting for assistance on this one, and the patrol car screeched away from the curb in a sharp U-turn toward headquarters. On the way, in a calmer frame of mind, Lee began examining his despondent prisoner in the rearview mirror.

The life Hagen had wanted to leave behind had caught up with him—not by chance, but because of his own lack of discipline, his own failure to avoid calling attention to himself.

"I wish you had just killed me there on the street." Hagen looked deadened, all alone in the back seat.

"I don't kill people unless I have to," the officer replied.

"I wish you had just killed me."

"Oh, Christ no," Detective Norman Chapman thought as he rolled over and reached for the phone. Chapman, a burly, genial veteran of the Pensacola police department's crimes-against-persons unit, knew that the insistent ringing was probably the dispatcher. He wasn't due at work until 7:00 a.m., but it looked like he'd be going in earlier today.

By 4:00 a.m. he was dressed and on his way. Officer David Lee had been assaulted, and the suspect was in custody. His job was to run the story down for trial. Chapman heard the heavy steel door ram shut behind him. The suspect was sound asleep on the holding-tank floor, with a nasty abrasion, the detective noticed, on his cheek.

In the detective's office Lee waited, guarding a pile of stolen credit cards, IDs, and wallet photographs. Hagen had given his name as Kenneth Misner, explaining that he had a B.S. in education from Florida State University. Chapman was more interested, however, in the other items salvaged from the VW—including a notebook with details of Misner's parentage, education, and background. Hagen had also admitted to lifting pocketbooks from some taverns in the Tallahassee area and a TV from the backseat of another car.

Looking to back up a charge for "assaulting an officer," the detective returned to Hagen and inquired about the scuffle with Lee.

"I just want to make it clear," the prisoner explained. "I guess technically under the law it's assaulting a police officer, but the intent was not to hurt the police officer."

"Your intent was just to get him . . ." Chapman pressed for a clarification while Lee gingerly felt his jaw.

"I didn't hurt the police officer, I hope." Hagen looked sincerely concerned. "All I wanted to do was run away."

"If these cards were stolen from Tallahassee," Norman Chapman mused to himself, "it's really their evidence and their case. No point in getting involved in chain-of-custody problems," he thought, and dialed the Tallahassee PD. The Chi Omega murders still topped everybody's list for first assumptions in Tallahassee, so the dispatcher's response to news of the FSU coed's IDs found in Hagen's possession was to give Chapman the home number of Don Patchen of Tallahassee's crimes-against-persons unit. Patchen was a key investigator in the Chi O murders. Using the credit card numbers and the vehicle identification number for the Volkswagen, Patchen, and later Steve Bodiford of Leon County, chased leads that morning for any connection to the murders.

North Florida papers carried news of Kenneth Misner's arrest that morning, and Misner, a well-known college track star, learned of his arrest in Pensacola over breakfast in Tallahassee. He phoned Chapman to inform him that his wallet had been stolen but that he was still going about his business 200 miles away. When checked with minor questions about Misner's life, Chris Hagen couldn't answer. Chapman now had a "John Doe" on his hands. And the newspapers had their most provocative story in weeks: who was this guy and what did he know about the Chi Omega killings?

When Hagen struggled awake around noon Wednesday and saw the familiar steel walls, he realized his dream had died on a Pensacola street the night before. But the bloody lacerations across his face and the painful knot on the back of his head didn't allow for much reflection. Chapman granted his request for a doctor and commissioned a patrolman for the trip.

Perched gingerly on the edge of a hospital examination bench, Hagen waited for a physician to attend to his wounds. He was no longer handcuffed, and it wouldn't have been very difficult to dart out the door and down the corridor.

But time had run out for Chris Hagen. He was physically and emotionally exhausted from the last few days. He toyed for a few minutes with the idea of escape. "I just can't seem to get up on my own two feet," he thought, "and go for it."

Another surprise awaited him back at the police station—Chapman's conversation with the real Ken Misner. But Hagen staunchly refused to give his real name. At 4:30 p.m. Patchen and Bodiford arrived with a "John Doe" warrant for Hagen, and along with Chapman wheedled and pleaded, but their prisoner wouldn't budge.

The argument flared all afternoon and into the evening, when Chapman left to teach his class at Pensacola Junior College. Every time detectives stormed out of the room for another strategy session, Chris Hagen would glance longingly at the open window. He had jumped out of windows before, but he simply had no will to get out of the chair.

"This is the end of the road," he admitted bitterly to himself. "I might as well face it. They will find out who I am sooner or later. Then the newspapers and television crews will descend." Tallahassee could have been a fresh start. He could have conquered his past and lived anonymously if he had just been more careful, if he had just been able to con-

251

trol things a little better. The bright hope of freedom, a new beginning, had burned out in a string of blunders and petty thievery.

"If you don't tell us your name," his interrogators finally threatened, "we've got an NBC camera crew outside and we'll plaster your face all over the country."

"Look," Hagen began, "I want to call my attorney in Atlanta so he can advise me whether I should tell you my real name or not. OK?" Chapman allowed him to use the police WATS line, but his counselor was busy with another client and asked him to call again the next morning.

Early Thursday morning, February 16, Patchen, Bodiford, and Chapman seated their prisoner in Chapman's office again. He was scheduled for a first appearance that morning before First Circuit Court Judge Jack Greenhut on charges of grand larceny, possession of stolen property, and assaulting an officer. The detectives discovered a much more pliant inmate that morning, willing to tell everything about the credit cards and car, but adamant about his name. Then, out of the blue, Don Patchen, asked:

"Somewhere around the twelfth, do you recall in Tallahassee you stooping behind a car and trying to obtain a tag and a deputy sheriff telling you to halt?"

"No, nothing, l-l-l-let's not talk about it," Hagen stuttered anxiously.

"You don't want to discuss it. You're not denying it, is that right?"

"I don't want to discuss it."

"How about a white van that belongs to Florida State University?" Bodiford burst in. "Do you know anything about that?"

"No, sir. I have stolen a Volkswagen, but you are not going to pin every missing vehicle on me either."

"What is the reasoning behind your use of Misner's ID, his birth certificate, in essence taking over his name as yours?" Patchen switched gears again.

"To establish another identity."

"Would you like to tell us at this time why you want to establish another identity?"

"Because I don't want to use my old identity."

"Why don't you want to use your old identity?"

"Because I wanted to shake loose of my past and I didn't want some people to know where I was."

252

"Is it for criminal or noncriminal reasons you did this?"
"Noncriminal reasons."

An hour later, Isaac Koran of the Pensacola public defender's office worked his way through a crowd of defendants packed into an old storage closet turned holding room in the courthouse. Usually he didn't do this kind of leg work, being primarily an administrator, but his office had an astronomical case load that week and everyone was thrown into the breach. When he reached a tired and listless "Chris Hagen," who refused to tell him his name, Koran learned only the bare outlines of the grand larceny and other charges and that his client had substantially confessed to police. "Odd," Koran thought, passing on to the next client, his pudgy face intent as he copied down the particulars for the various defendants' first appearances.

It was even odder when the state attorney himself, Curtis Golden, marched into the room followed by a string of police officers. "That's *never* happened before," Koran said to himself, as Golden rose to handle the Hagen appearance. "Whoever this guy is, he doesn't look like he's feeling too well." Koran watched as a disheveled Chris Hagen stood before the judge and refused to give his name. Greenhut denied bail until "such time as the defendant sees fit to reveal his true identity."

When Chapman plumped back down in his desk chair after court that morning, a Millard Farmer in Atlanta was waiting on the line. Evidently the mystery prisoner had connected with his counsel.

"Has my client admitted to any crimes?" Farmer began bluntly.

"Yes, to a number of counts of credit card thefts and grand larceny."

"I've told him not to talk to you. And I hope you won't interrogate him until my associate Alan Holbrook arrives this afternoon."

Keeping Hagen's mouth closed occupied the attention of the public defender's office as well. Koran prepared a motion for a protective order that afternoon asking that "John Doe" not be questioned, placed in a lineup, or moved to another jail without notification of his attorneys. By 4:30 Greenhut had initialed a somewhat watered-down version of this request. Terry Turrell and Liz Nicholas, having assumed the

253

case from Koran, also penned an affidavit for their recalcitrant client to sign, stating that he did not wish to be questioned.

Alan Holbrook came dashing in from the airport around 5:00 p.m., and the four lawyers began negotiations to hammer out a deal where Hagen would reveal his true identity to police for certain considerations—a chance to call his family and friends beforehand and no release of his name to the press until the following morning.

Chapman OK'd this solution, then waited patiently for two-and-a-half hours while his prisoner huddled over the phone in the corner. Terry Turrell became increasingly concerned as he watched the haggard figure in the corner light one cigarette after another. "He's deteriorated since this morning," Turrell thought as the young man began crying into the phone, bent almost double in the chair, a thin hand supporting both head and phone. "This guy's going to break," Turrell realized. "I've got to do something."

When Hagen had whispered his last goodbye into the receiver, everyone filed into a captain's office for the big event —public defenders, Holbrook, several detectives. "I could probably hold out for another couple of weeks," their prisoner thought to himself as he eased into a chair in the center of the room, "but I might as well get on with it." Turrell reiterated the deal, and got a firm promise in return. Finally, after a few expectant pauses, the man in the chair spoke:

"My name's Theodore Bundy. That's all I'm going to tell you. I think you'll find out pretty quickly what's happening."

Ted Bundy later described the feeling at that moment: "They made their solemn commitment to me. We all sat around the room, and the tension mounted. I thought it was really quite dramatic. Maybe I overstate the event, but to me it was the end of the road, you know, right there."

When it happened, however, Ted was startled by Chapman's response. He snatched a note pad from his desk and said eagerly, "Bundy? How do you spell that?"

"They all ran out of the room," Ted would remember, "and one of my attorneys from the public defender's office went with them. He saw them patching through to the FBI. They were also making all sorts of phone calls to the National Crime Information Center, and believe it or not, they couldn't come up with anything. Finally, I guess they made me, and that night the local FBI agent walked in with my as-yet-undistributed Ten Most Wanted poster, saying, 'We know who he is.'

"What I think really happened, and I'm sure this is how the local FBI knew what was coming down, was that after I started making phone calls to Seattle, guess-who was listening on the lines of certain people I called."

If authorities were listening to Ted Bundy, all they caught were several rambling, emotional calls to his family, friends, an attorney, and former fiancée Melanie Pattisen. Attorney John Browne urged Ted not to talk, alarmed at the incoherence of their conversation. It had taken Browne four or five minutes just to learn what the purpose of the call was, and when his client had wanted to chat about local events in Seattle, Browne waxed even more perplexed and worried.

Ted's Pensacola public defenders worked desperately to get their client to clam up with police. But Ted slouched in his chair, exhausted and withdrawn, and their concerns met a silent rebuff.

After an hour of almost pointless persuasion, Ted asked to see a priest. Koran darted for the phone book and plucked out the name of Father Michael Moody. "At least if he's got to talk," the lawyer thought, "this is as good a way as any." What Ted Bundy "confessed" to Father Moody that night remains shrouded in a privileged relationship. But as the atmosphere around the capture of a Ten Most Wanted criminal heightened the pressure of Tallahassee's Chi O murder investigation, more than one cop thought longingly of a Pensacola priest who probably had all the answers. Moody's last counsel to Ted was to refuse police questions and leave his defense to the lawyers.

Almost as soon as Ted Bundy had revealed his name, "the phones began ringing off the hook," as Steve Bodiford recalls. Somehow a television station in Seattle heard the news even before authorities in other states, and Chapman intercepted a breathless call from a reporter, but refused to comment until the following morning at the scheduled nine o'clock press conference.

Pitkin County, Colorado, DA Frank Tucker was next, and he provided the detectives with a partial account of the trials and suspicions surrounding Ted Bundy in the West. While Bundy spoke to his lawyers and the priest, Bodiford, Patchen, and Chapman hunched over their desks, listening to one account after another of brutal crimes. Police and prosecutors in Washington, Utah, and Colorado all sketched in their gruesome beliefs, but press calls were turned away in accordance with the agreement. As the hour got later, Patchen finally pinned down a vague memory that had nagged him all evening. "You know, right after the Chi Omega killings, we had a cop from Olympia, Washington, call and tell us to check out Ted Bundy."

When Father Moody left, Chapman visited Ted's cell, and his famous prisoner indicated he wanted to talk later, that he had "some things I want to get straightened out." The detective's first response was to get some food and coffee. "If I'm going to be up tonight with Ted Bundy," he thought, "I better be in shape for it."

Just after midnight, he and Ted shared a bag of hamburgers and several cups of coffee. Then, at 1:30, they shuffled into Captain Harper's office, where Don Patchen and Steve Bodiford were waiting. With all the discussion aimed at guaranteeing Ted's silence that evening, Chapman was understandably nervous about the interview. He launched into an exhaustive review of his prisoner's understanding of his Miranda rights, his emotional and mental state, and anything else he could think of to show for the record that Ted was there of his own free will.

"You mind if I crack this window open?" Norman Chapman asked. "It's a little stuffy here."

With that gesture, a long, aimless account of the adventures and misfortunes of Theodore Bundy began, from his early days in Seattle, through the law-school years in Utah, and the ensuing trials and escapes in Colorado. Occasionally, one of the two Tallahassee detectives would try to gently nudge the conversation toward his activities around Florida State University or the string of stolen cards and vehicles, but Ted repeated mostly what he'd already told them and refused edgily to delve deeper into his memory. Yes, Ted admitted, he had stolen some credit cards from Sherrod's, the disco next door to the Chi Omega house. But that hadn't been until the first week in February, just before he'd left town.

Ted began crying during his description of those first days when he had returned to the world outside a prison.

"There's something I've noticed since I've been talking to you here this morning," Bodiford gently inserted. "When you start thinking about certain things, certain places, you start crying. What is it that disturbs you so much when you start talking about watching people play racquetball?"

"It wasn't racquetball or anything in particular about racquetball, I don't know . . . well . . . hold the phone. . . . It may be tearful, but not sobbing or crying or anything. It was just so good to be around people, just so good to be a part of people, not to be looked at differently."

Ted had held himself to that one date with Jeanelle, he explained, because he couldn't really reveal his past, and without a past it was impossible to have a "meaningful relationship."

Somehow Steve Bodiford had secured a copy of Ted's rental agreement at the Oak, dated January 7, 1978, which placed Ted three blocks from the Chi O house a week before the killings. But Bundy hesitated and began to regress, so the detective pressed on and tried to discover how Ted had gotten the license plate he'd handed to Daws—again to no avail. The white van, too, didn't "spark my memory," Ted said. He thought he might have taken the 13D-11300 tag off of a "pickup truck."

Ted didn't like weekend frat parties, he claimed, nor was he ever out late at night unless it was to ride his bike. There weren't any fingerprints in those stolen cars, he said: "I wore gloves."

"I asked you earlier about a white van," Bodiford persisted, watching Ted light another cigarette. "You said at the time you didn't want to talk about it."

"Yeah."

"You want to talk about it now?"

"There's really nothing I can say about it."

"Did you take it? It was stolen off campus with the keys in it."

• "I really can't talk about it. I don't know anything about it, so, we-we-we better not talk about it."

"Are you telling me you didn't take it, or are you telling me you just don't want to talk about it at all?"

"It's just one of those situations where we just better pass on."

As the conversation gradually assumed its own rhythm, ambling on toward 5:00 a.m., Chapman realized with dismay that he had only brought three hours of tape and it was nearly gone. They'd all been impressed with their prisoner's apparent determination to be honest with them—up to a point.

Later Chapman would castigate himself a hundred times for not bringing enough tape that night. Their conversation

257

continued clear to ten the following morning—"until the telephones started ringing and the traffic began below."

But Ted Bundy had wanted the tape recorder turned off anyway. What he was about to circumspectly tell these three detectives a lot of people desperately wanted to know. It was an odd conversation, in a stilted, circuitous language, almost a code created for the occasion. The only record that remains is that pieced together later from the memories of the three detectives—memories that would matter very much to Ted Bundy one day.

Liz Nicholas of the public defender's office appeared at Pensacola police headquarters at 7:30 a.m. Friday, demanding to see Ted.

"Under no circumstances are you to see Mr. Bundy," Captain Joseph announced. "I am only concerned with Mr. Bundy's welfare."

Nicholas repeated her demand, threatening to call Judge Greenhut. But Joseph was adamant, and quickly left to fetch Assistant State Attorney Ron Johnson. Nicholas waited 45 minutes before a perturbed Johnson returned with Joseph. Now Johnson refused permission for Nicholas to see her client, claiming that Ted was asleep.

"I want to see for myself," she said.

Ted Bundy was certainly not asleep. Chapman, tired and antsy, wanted badly to appear on national television to talk about Bundy, but the 9:00 a.m. press conference had begun ten minutes ago and Ted still didn't seem ready to halt their session. After a night of chain smoking, coffee, and arduous interrogation, Ted looked awful when Ron Johnson—now under strict instructions from Greenhut—told detectives that Turrell and Nicholas were outside wanting to see their client. Johnson agreed to stall them a few more minutes. Finally Isaac Koran arrived, and the three lawyers were more than he could handle.

"Ted, we have to know," Chapman said firmly. "Did you kill those girls in Tallahassee?"

"Guys," Ted said slowly, eyes brimming as he bent down, "the evidence is there. Keep looking for it. Don't quit digging. Keep looking for the evidence. It's there."

Ted looks bad, Terry Turrell thought when the public defenders finally got in. I bet they kept him up all night. Koran had an affidavit prepared, saying Bundy didn't want to talk to investigators, and all three lawyers began working on him to sign it. But Ron Johnson wasn't ready to throw in the towel.

"I'm looking out for your best interests, Ted," Johnson raged. "And your best interest is not to sign that." Then, turning to Koran: "You don't know what you're doing, Koran. You're not competent. I knew more about the law when I got out of law school than you do now."

Koran backed off a step. "You just want to fry him," he snarled.

27

The reporters who converged on Pensacola from across the country knew nothing of Norman Chapman's efforts or the confrontation that had just taken place outside the interrogation room. Pensacola police and representatives of the FBI were on the station's front lawn at that moment, about to begin a full-scale press conference. All the doors to the police station, they told reporters, had been locked. By now everyone had heard of Ted's Glenwood Springs escape, and his new captors wanted to show the world that they were taking no chances.

The FBI claimed to have discovered Bundy's identity through fingerprints, even though their prisoner had revealed his name voluntarily the evening before. While Ted slept into the afternoon, the story of his capture hit newspapers all over the country. The western papers had an obvious interest in the case, but news of a Ten Most Wanted criminal made the papers in other cities too. Ted Bundy was an instant suspect in the Chi Omega murders. The pictures of Lisa Levy and Margaret Bowman stood next to Ted's on many front pages.

Photographers got their first chance at Theodore Bundy that afternoon when he appeared in court for arraignment on charges of stolen credit cards and grand larceny. Ted Bundy had gained a lot of weight since his last days before slipping through the ceiling at Glenwood Springs. His face was rounder, but more noticeable than his new girth was his haggard appearance. Rumors spread quickly that Ted was talking to police. A sense of expectancy hovered over the Pensacola station.

Repeated pleas by Ted's public defenders for his silence met with a stoic response. "I know I can waive this affidavit," he told them, "any time I want."

Early Saturday morning Ted and the three detectives sat through another bleary-eyed interrogation. But now Bundy was looking for a deal, had a proposal for an ultimate solution. Sheriff Katsaris was under burgeoning pressure. Why was Bundy still in Pensacola, people wanted to know? What was going on? The sheriff's answer sounded lame even to him, and he was getting impatient with the verbal cat-and-mouse in Pensacola. "Bundy is talking to investigators," he told the press, "although he avoids the FSU murders. But it still looks real good."

Late Saturday afternoon two unmarked patrol cars pulled up behind the Pensacola jail for the 200-mile journey back to Tallahassee. Security for their infamous prisoner was on everyone's mind. All during the day rumors had circulated about the move to Tallahassee: they would fly Ted on Sunday, or drive him Monday morning. Chapman was especially worried that someone would try to "hit" Ted Bundy during the move.

"It's 200 miles over there," he told Bundy. "That's a rural southern town. It's not a metropolis. Those people over there are rednecks, and you can bet your ass they've got guns and knives and use 'em."

Bodiford and Patchen left Pensacola in a two-car caravan with Ted soundly asleep in the backseat; Norman Chapman rode in the rear car. Their negotiations would continue in Tallahassee, but Chapman was losing hope of success.

Ken Katsaris greeted Ted Bundy at the door and escorted him to his new high-security, armor-plated cell. "Up to now, we've probably been playing by his rules," the sheriff said, "but a change in jails might make a difference. The feeling here is that we're going to let Bundy sit in jail for a while." The order went down to the jailers—no visitors, no exercise, and 25-watt lighting for the windowless cell.

Bundy's arrest had an instant, energizing effect on the Chi Omega murder investigation. Days before, Ken Katsaris had been floundering with a stack of flimsy leads (a man who'd vomited constantly the week of the murders, dream visions from psychics around the country) and dodging complaints that his investigation team had grown divisive.

Now he would always have news of Ted Bundy with which to tantalize the crowd of reporters: "It looks real good," he said. "The chance of having two people with the same M.O. in the same community at the same time is pretty remote."

Katsaris wasn't the only one making good brave news copy out of Ted Bundy. On February 23 Pitkin County, Colorado, District Attorney Frank Tucker flew to Florida to make preliminary arrangements for Ted's extradition to Colorado Springs. Officials in Tallahassee were unimpressed. Bundy had a string of auto thefts and credit card offenses (to say nothing of a possible murder charge) to answer for in Florida before they would turn him over to prosecutors in the Caryn Campbell case.

Tucker might have learned as much over the telephone, but he was glad to get away from his own troubles back home: 13 grand jury indictments for theft and misuse of public funds, including the financing of a high-school girl's abortion.

Despite the dramatic news stories, all was not smooth sailing for Katsaris. Bundy might have "looked real good" as the number one Chi Omega suspect, but the clues that ought to have secured the case were falling apart. The student who'd reported a man hiding in the bushes on College Avenue shortly after the January 15 murders could not pick Bundy out of a photo lineup. Nor could the two friends who had seen "Chris Hagen" in the Oak about that time agree on what he was wearing. Their testimony might look shaky in court. All the same, the scattered investigation now had a prime suspect to focus on. It was the first real break in a month.

"This is the hardest thing we've been through in our lives. In my heart I don't believe the child is close to home. It's my feeling someone just grabbed her and left Lake City. I hope I'm wrong." Freda Leach, Kimberly's mother, sat talking with a reporter from the *St. Petersburg Times* on February 20, less than a week after Ted Bundy had been arrested. Even as Freda Leach quietly explained her fears, newspapers around the state were going to press with another headline: POLICE TRY TO LINK BUNDY, MISSING GIRL.

An anonymous phone call to a Tallahassee television station sparked the news. The caller had seen Bundy's picture on the air and recognized him immediately; he was "Ralph Miller," the fellow he'd visited with in the Lake City Holiday

261

Inn on February 8. The caller refused to give his name or contact police.

Reporters quickly seized on the other puzzle pieces and jiggled them into place: Leslie Parmenter's conversation with the man (she now identified him as Bundy) in the white van; the scrap of schoolbook paper with the van's license number; and Bundy's fingerprints found on that same plate—13D-11300—which he'd handed to Keith Daws in Tallahassee on February 11 before running toward the Oak. It was soon no secret what police had in mind. They were checking the credit card records of every motel in the area and buzzing low over the nearby woods in search planes.

But two weeks had passed since Kim Leach's disappearance from Lake City Junior High, and some searchers had already despaired of finding a body in Columbia County's 900 square miles of scrubby pine and oak forestland—assuming the body was even in Columbia County and not Suwannee or Hamilton or elsewhere. As one official put it, explaining the logic of moving the search to a new area: "We ain't looked there yet."

Still, the possible link to Bundy restored hopes. By the end of February police were sifting through a garbage dump in nearby Live Oak on the strength of a tip that a white van had been spotted near a trash bin. Two days later a Florida highway patrol spokesman said there had been an "extraordinary" discovery somewhere else and refused to give details. The next day assistant state attorney Bob Dekle announced unhappily, "The find is most likely unrelated to the Leach case." New discoveries of cigarette butts, old shoes, bits of clothing, and other debris poured into the Florida Department of Criminal Law Enforcement crime lab for analysis every day. Coins from pay telephone boxes were dusted for prints. Psychics were called in; a machine to detect methane gas—from buried bodies—was employed. Columbia County Sheriff Glenn Bailey squinted out at the sunlight late one afternoon. "We've got nothing," he said, "absolutely nothing."

But authorities were keeping quiet about one last place they were looking—the FSU media center van. Recovered by campus police on February 13, the van contained possibly critical, possibly disorienting evidence. The officer who discovered the stolen van parked on West Tennessee Street sensed that it might be critical and had it towed to the crime lab. Police waited expectantly while technicians vacuumed the rear floor and separated out the debris. Was there any hope that the animal, Negro, and Caucasian head hairs could be connected to the death of Kimberly Leach? What about the price tags from a place called Green Acres? Or the soil and weeds littering the back? Underneath, on the exposed floor, technicians found one more thing to analyze —bloodstains. Unknown hair and blood samples are virtually useless without known samples to compare them to. By early March the search would move to the courtroom.

Problems with physical evidence troubled Ken Katsaris too. More and more, as if it were some mysterious inscription waiting to be deciphered, the bite mark left on Lisa Levy's buttock seemed to hold the key to the Chi Omega murders. Without a known dental impression to compare it to, however, it was only a bite, anonymous and worthless as evidence. And unless the investigators could demonstrate "probable cause" to believe Bundy had inflicted the bite, they could not take an impression of his teeth without violating his constitutional right barring unreasonable search and seizure. Evidence gained in such an illegal search is inadmissible in court. Somehow, some way, they'd have to substantiate their hunch before they could hope to provide the dental experts with a known sample for comparison.

Like professional specialists in any field, forensic odontologists often do some of their best work in the hallways and elevators of hotels. There, in breaks between seminars and meetings, they can exchange information and experiences with their colleagues—the informal, knowledgeable discourse worth its weight in newsletters and scholarly articles.

Richard Souviron greeted his Maryland colleague Duane DeVore at just such a moment in February 1978 and mentioned a Florida murder case on which he'd just been called in to consult. The victim was bitten on the breast and the buttock, Souviron explained, but the tissue had been badly preserved. The two doctors discussed various methods of reconstituting tissue, then parted, with DeVore offering his assistance if needed. Typically, neither had gone into names, suspects, or other details: forensic odontologists like to think of themselves as scientists, operating as much as possible in a realm of pure objectivity.

DeVore, in fact, had become a spokesman in the field. Just the month before, in a wire service story that appeared in major papers around the country, he'd been cited as a leading authority in the new and fascinating technique of bite-mark identification. Forensic dentistry itself, DeVore claimed, dated back to antiquity, when Nero's body was identified from a black tooth. But it was only since 1973, he continued, that U.S. courts had admitted bite marks as evidence. It was even possible to determine if a flesh bite resulted from an attack or sexual activity. And elsewhere, in an article in the *Maryland Law Forum*, DeVore had pointed out the possible match value of bites in food or other hard substances.

But DeVore also noted problems with the method. While each set of teeth may not be exactly like any other set, a bite mark won't necessarily record its uniqueness. There's the dynamic of the bite as it's inflicted to consider, as well as the curvature, the pliability, the overall "distortion" inherent in the skin. DeVore was aware of a 1975 British study of human bites in pig flesh. Even then, under supposedly optimal conditions, known teeth and their bites could only be matched three times out of four. The courts, too, were a problem: DeVore had testified at the landmark Milone trial in Illinois in 1973, absolutely certain that the defendant could not have inflicted the bite in question. (It's generally easier to rule someone out than to rule him in.) The defendant was convicted in spite of the testimony of several forensic odontologists.

Overall, Duane DeVore believes in the use of bite-mark identifications, believes in it enough that he doesn't want to see the practice misused or misunderstood. The slightly stooped, somber-looking dentist's cautiousness is evident as he speaks. The technique is a useful tool—not as good as fingerprints, he told the wire service reporter—but a tool that must be handled with care.

Later that month, after Richard Souviron had returned from the odontologists' convention, he received a package from Captain Poitinger in Tallahassee. Enclosed were the complete dental records and X rays of Theodore Bundy's teeth (obtained from Utah authorities) along with several recent photographs of Bundy in a courtroom. The photographs were unremarkable newspaper shots, except for one detail: Bundy was smiling as he faced the camera. Souviron peered closely at the tiny image of the exposed teeth, then examined the X rays. Obviously, Souviron told Poitinger, this wasn't enough to make a positive match between the bite mark and the suspect's teeth, but he could say this much: it was certainly possible, from what he could see, that those crooked lower teeth had made the mark on Lisa Levy's buttock.

Katsaris and his detectives kept their trail well hidden through March and early April, determined not to let anything slip in their quest for probable cause and a warrant for an impression of Bundy's teeth. Their efforts sometimes had a strange, fanciful twist. In hopes of getting a good, usable impression of Ted's bite, the jailers were on constant watch for a gnawed-off hunk of cheese or a half-eaten piece of fruit on his dinner tray. At one point, an apple core was rushed off to Dr. Souviron before it dried out, only to have the expert call back and say it was of no help.

With all that had been publicized about bite marks, Katsaris grumbled to himself, Ted himself was probably an expert on this way of gathering evidence. Several detectives had already expressed the fear that Bundy might break or file down his teeth if something didn't happen quickly.

Convinced they were on the right track, but frustrated every time they tried to build up the investigation's momentum, police finally decided in mid-March to give their first hope a last try. Leon County Deputy Sheriff Steve Bodiford placed a call to Muncie, Indiana, where Nita Neary was now enrolled at Ball State University. The first thing Bodiford wanted to know was if Neary had seen any pictures of "the man we have in custody down here"; he carefully avoided mentioning Bundy's name.

Yes, she said, she remembered a composite of six full-face shots and "a sort of profile" her mother had pointed out in an Indianapolis newspaper. Bodiford asked if she thought she might be able to identify the man she'd seen at the door of the Chi Omega house from a photo lineup of profiles.

She hesitated. "Well, I hate to promise anything I can't do."

The deputy sheriff asked Neary to refrain from looking at any more newspaper photos and hung up.

Three weeks later, on April 6, Jack Poitinger flew to Muncie with a packet of ten profile photos in his briefcase. At Neary's apartment on North Martin Street the next afternoon, he chatted a minute about her new school, then got down to business. Snapping a cassette into his portable tape recorder, Poitinger began the session in a flat, practiced, undemonstrative voice. He was handing Ms. Neary the

265

photographs, he noted. She went through them one at a time.

Hesitating over one, Nita Neary finally selected photograph number four. Did that resemble the man she remembered? Poitinger asked.

I don't know," she replied, "a pretty definite resemblance."

The last thing the captain did was place his hand over the upper portion of the man's head, as if to simulate a stocking cap pulled down over the ears. "You've selected number four, is that right?" Poitinger announced for the tape.

"Right," said Neary.

The investigator was back in Tallahassee that night, without a word to anyone. The results of the trip, destined to become a pivot of the case, were under wraps.

Had Nita Neary identified Ted? Would such an identification complete the state's ground of probable cause and convince a judge to sign a warrant for the seizure of Bundy's dental impressions?

And why had the police waited so long—weeks after the hypnosis session and more than enough time for Bundy's face to become common currency in the press—to have Neary attempt an ID? Dark questions had a way of attaching themselves to Theodore Bundy wherever he went.

From his steel-plated cell at the Leon County jail, Ted Bundy wasted no time getting his message to the outside world. First it was through Millard Farmer, a crusading Atlanta attorney who had vowed to defend Bundy if he were charged with a capital offense. Referring to the FBI figure of 36 murders that might involve Bundy, Farmer said, "If they really thought that, there would have been tighter security when he was in prison." Ted himself, in a letter smuggled out of his cell to Denver reporter Tony Polk, put it simply: "I feel calm because outside of a few minor thefts I have done nothing wrong. I have killed no one. I am innocent of the charges in the press."

Murder may have been on everyone's mind, but in the meantime Bundy had another legal battle to face. "Yes, sir, I understand the charges as read," he told Circuit Judge John Rudd on February 20, when the list of credit card offenses committed in Tallahassee had been run down. "No, sir, I do not have the money to hire an attorney."

266

Requesting the right to defend himself, Bundy pleaded innocent to auto theft and burglary counts as well as all the credit card forgeries. Authorities soon amassed more than 60 separate charges, good for about 200 years in prison if Ted was convicted.

Bundy's first important fight in a Florida courtroom came in March, when the state attorney's office requested samples of his blood, hair, saliva, and handwriting in an effort to tie him to the notorious white van, the Lake City Holiday Inn, and possibly to evidence from the Chi Omega and Dunwoody assaults. A striking, square-jawed young attorney from the public defender's office, Joe Nursey, protested on Ted's behalf, calling the request a "fishing expedition."

"What makes them think the Caucasian hair was left there in the van by the defendant?" Nursey demanded. "I ask how many people in Jacksonville, Tallahassee, and Lake City appear to be Caucasian and do have hair." Nursey offered a similar argument about the type-B bloodstain and maintained that someone from the media center—instead of his client—might have driven the van to Jacksonville. But his efforts were in vain. On March 17 five cubic centimeters of Bundy's blood were drawn from his arm and hairs plucked from his head, legs, and arms.

Ted was philosophical. In a letter to a friend he deadpanned, "Now they want my blood. Blood? Next comes the motion for a pound of flesh."

His mood those first weeks back in captivity was not always so blithe. "I'm like a bottled-up cyclone," he wrote to Nancy Hobson in March, "mind spinning with memories, regrets, and fears. To anchor me and calm me I conjure up fond memories of the past, but these excursions shortly turn pleasant reverie into deep sadness. I constantly attempt to avoid the reality that I failed miserably in my attempt to become a free man. . . .

"I am tired of outmaneuvering the prosecutors and courts. I am tired of playing the news media, of staying calm and smiling for the cameras, of being stared at, of being whispered about, of being suspected and hated. I am tired of knowing what people must think, of being vilified and dehumanized. Life has always had surprises in store for me. Many of them have been pleasant. Will there be more, and will I be free again?

"How can I be sure, what can I do to satisfy myself I've had my ration of happiness and the rest is all pain?"

Months later in Seattle Hobson would recall the letter. "There were times when we were really worried about Ted," she said. "It's just incredibly hard on him down there."

But along with his now customary jail routine of legal work, Ted also found diversion in his double-padlocked cell. He was reading a great deal (*The Seven Per Cent Solution, Coma, Meeting at Potsdam, Nothing by Chance*, whose freedom-affirming final pages he admired), keeping up on Republican party politics back in Washington State, and doing battle with the ants and spiders who shared his cell. Through it all, Bundy's sense of humor remained intact. A letter from HEW demanding repayment of his student loan amused him, and so, at first, did the sheriff's policy of opening and photocopying all his mail.

But more and more Ken Katsaris had become the foe, a symbol of all the injustice and oppression of his imprisonment. Bundy complained about the heavy leg shackles and chains he was forced to wear to court, about his lack of outdoor exercise and the poor lighting in his cell. He objected to Katsaris's practice of calling press conferences and issuing press releases while he, Bundy, was denied access to the media. "It pisses me off. Only the sheriff can have facts," Bundy observed sarcastically to a friend. "I, on the other hand, have only assertions."

Katsaris was righteous about his position. "I don't want to try this case in the newspapers," he said. "If Mr. Bundy begins talking, he can say the kinds of things that would taint the prosecution, and he knows well what they are from his study."

But even the sheriff's allies winced at his irrepressible habit of mentioning the case, as if he were delighted by the subject, on almost any occasion. "I will have more time for charitable things and other things I would like to do when my favorite criminal is out of my hair," Katsaris told a crowd at a March of Dimes football banquet. Nobody had to ask if he was referring to Bundy.

Millard Farmer looked on unhappily from Atlanta. "It's just like shooting at ducks on the ground," he sighed.

Ted was back in court in early April, asking Judge Rudd for three days a week in a law library and then for access to the news media. Both motions would eventually be denied, despite Bundy's admonition that his right to a fair trial was being jeopardized. Observers in the courtroom had already

268

perceived the mutual and unmistakable distrust between Bundy and Judge Rudd, a plainspoken and often indelicate former prosecutor. These first skirmishes, however, would seem mild in the months to come.

On April 13, two Tallahassee store clerks identified Bundy as a credit card customer they remembered serving. A handwriting expert, testifying at the same preliminary hearing, asserted that all the receipts in question had been signed by the same person. Tallahassee Police Detective Don Patchen claimed Bundy had confessed in Pensacola to using the 21 cards found in his possession at the time of his capture.

Hitting on all cylinders, the prosecution machine was moving forward on the theft and forgery charges. But by now, in the fragrant, mid-April spring of north Florida, Ted Bundy had deeper worries on his mind. It began when the detectives from Lake City pulled up in front of the Leon County jail. They had news, and wanted to see how Ted would respond.

Florida Highway Patrolman K. W. Robinson had only been back on the search team a day when he tramped down toward a sinkhole near the Suwannee River State Park. Thin, high-topped pine trees stood like so many fence posts, but Robinson didn't see them: he was watching at his feet for snakes. Up ahead, the rumpled tin roof of an old hog shed sent off a faint shine. The patrolman had to duck to peer through a hole in the wall, and it took a moment for his eyes to adjust to the loamy darkness. He didn't believe it at first; he half expected the sneaker toe to move. "It's one of those deals," he later tried to explain, "like you think you are dreaming." But the sneaker didn't budge, and Robinson spied bare bone.

Just after five, that Friday, April 7, afternoon, a two-toned hearse bearing the remains of Kimberly Leach bounced down a nearby dirt road and disappeared. The runner-up to the Valentine Queen had been found, 35 miles from home.

The papers were full of the news that weekend. In Tallahassee, the *Democrat* ran a copyrighted story quoting sources as saying it was the dirt and oak leaves—not the hair or blood—found in the stolen white van that had led police to the spot near the Suwannee and Withlacoochee rivers. Another report mentioned a man's bloodstained jacket that was under analysis. But Bob Dekle, who was heading the

269

investigation, held a tight rein on the clues, calling it a "miracle" that certain items were picked up, "a tribute to thorough law enforcement."

Decomposition, said Duval County Medical Examiner Peter Lipkovic, made it difficult to determine if Kim Leach had been raped or even to ascertain much about her injuries. There did appear to be pelvic injuries, and the cause of death appeared to be "homicidal violence to the neck region." Lipkovic, a gregarious, outspoken sort, raised a familiar theme: "There has been a lot said about this individual, Mr. Bundy, but you wonder sometimes if it isn't just a tendency on the part of law enforcement to clear some of their cases."

Ted agreed. When the Lake City policemen showed up at his cell, he refused to talk. Kimberly Leach was buried on Sunday, April 12, at a service attended by her classmates, who had been excused from school. There were still some "loose ends," Bob Dekle said later that day; a murder charge was not expected right away.

There was still more to occupy Ted Bundy's thoughts by the end of the month. Without warning and, uncharacteristically, without notifying the press, Katsaris, Poitinger, and other Leon County officials showed up at Ted's cell late on the afternoon of April 27. Richard Souviron had just flown in from Miami, and a dental assistant, a doctor, and an identification photographer were waiting in a dental operating room. The probable cause it contained was strictly secret, but Katsaris had his warrant for an impression of Ted Bundy's teeth. And, he believed, he had his case as well.

Bundy shouted and struggled as they pushed him down in the chair. But the work went on, his lips stretched back by plastic cheek retractors while the photographer closed in for a close-up shot of his teeth. Warm wax was pressed into his gums. And finally, Ted sank his teeth into a fresh sheet of Alluwax and made a perfect impression of his bite.

Attention shifted from Ted Bundy in May when a confessed killer was picked up hitchhiking in Jackson County by a sheriff's deputy in an unmarked car. After admitting to the murders of a mother and daughter near Marianna, Florida, and another murder, multiple rapes, and attempted strangulations, in Texas, the suspect submitted to a polygraph examination regarding Chi Omega and Kimberly Leach. The 24-year-old passed the test and the work continued on Bundy.

On May 30 Richard Souviron received a photograph at his office in Coral Gables. His spirits lifted as soon as he tore open the envelope. It was the shot of Lisa Levy's buttock—the one with a yellow ruler just beneath the bite mark—that Sergeant Winkler had taken the night of the murders in Tallahassee. More than four months after the crimes, the forensic specialist finally had a measurable photograph to compare with a known dental impression.

Souviron went to work immediately, instructing a photographer to enlarge Winkler's photograph to life size. (Bundy's wax impression, of course, was already life size. Now the two items to be compared would be on the same scale.) Several days later Souviron contacted a bite-mark specialist in New York, Lowell Levine, and asked for a preliminary opinion.

After examining the photographs and a set of models of Bundy's teeth, Levine, known among his peers for an almost artistic, instinctive grasp of a situation, offered his opinion that there appeared to be considerable areas of consistency between the bite mark and the models. Levine suggested that a computer in New Mexico might be helpful in "enhancing" the photograph for more detailed analysis.

Souviron also conducted an independent evaluation, painstakingly comparing the configuration, relative heights, and irregularities of Bundy's teeth with the bruising and hemorrhaging patterns in Levy's skin. It wasn't long before he had made up his mind. By July Souviron was double-checking himself, trying to fit models of other teeth to the bite. The process only convinced him all the more. Bundy's teeth, he said to himself, and the phrase came easily to mind, "fit that bite like a key in a lock."

While results of the dental comparisons remained under wraps, Bundy concentrated his legal efforts on postponing his credit card forgery and auto theft trials. Bundy and public defender Joe Nursey complained they hadn't had access to the state's evidence. The prosecution reminded Judge Rudd that Bundy had still not complied with the order for a handwriting sample.

At one point, a plainly exasperated Rudd peered over the bench and asked, "Mr. Bundy, do you ever anticipate being ready to go to trial in this case?" Warning Bundy about the dangers of trying to defend himself, Rudd grudgingly granted the delays.

The terms of Bundy's confinement in the Leon County jail, meanwhile, continued to be a source of dispute. Ted's motion for a contempt citation against Katsaris was denied, although the sheriff did admit to interfering with the defendant's mail. Even in the minds of many north Floridians, inflamed as they were by the monstrousness of the Chi Omega and Kimberly Leach murders, the behavior of the police was beginning to add up much as Millard Farmer saw it: "They're playing to get public acceptance," he said, "and to charge somebody in those crimes."

In a decision denying Ted access to the press, Circuit Judge Charles Miner wrote that "fundamental fairness" required him to stave off reporters and "protect Bundy from Bundy."

Ted began to feel the heat as the summer wore on. He could still smile and sniff the honeysuckle on the way into the courthouse or joke about his nicotine-stained cell walls (he was trying to cut down on the Winstons), but his mood sunk so badly at one point that Nancy Hobson made a quick trip to Tallahassee to bolster him. Ted responded gamely, kidding about the Tacoma man who had written and offered to explain Ted's "crafty" second personality to him, and promised Hobson to keep up the fight.

But Bundy could read the papers just like anyone else, and by mid-July, as grand juries convened in both Lake City and Tallahassee, the ominous theme grew still more pronounced. "It's not news anymore that someone somewhere is planning on charging me with something," Ted wrote to an old political friend. "Nor, for that matter, is it news if by some luck they manage to procure a charge of some kind. The real test is conviction, and I can say with absolute certainty that I will never be convicted of a serious offense in Florida or anywhere else."

He was calm, he said, because he'd "had time to perfect the technique, living for over two years in a hybrid existence." But the Florida hothouse summer, the longest, most agonizing season in Ted Bundy's life, had reached its terrible peak.

It was headline news for several days: Ted Bundy was sure to be indicted for the murders of the Chi Omega sorority sisters and Kimberly Leach. But Ken Katsaris was not to be denied his own, startling way of handling the news.

"Step out, Mr. Bundy." Sheriff Ken Katsaris wore a dark, neatly pressed suit as he spoke. The elevator door in the holding room at the Leon County jail had just opened on July 27, 1978, and his captive stood dressed in green overalls and flat, terrycloth prison issue slippers. Ted Bundy looked slight, pale, shadowy across the cheeks and bleak around the eyes. The television camermen Katsaris had summoned to the jail couldn't help but pick up the contrast. The law, right now, seemed mighty indeed. Katsaris held a sheaf of papers in his hand.

But Theodore Bundy wasn't going to crumple. Before Katsaris could begin to read, Bundy started in. "What do we have here, Ken? An indictment? Let's read it! Let's go!" The sarcasm, one reporter couldn't help feeling, was Ted's only possible defense.

Katsaris read on, quickly, while Bundy paced back and forth, leaned over his shoulder, then pulled back a step and glared. There were two counts of murder, three of attempted murder; Katsaris turned the page.

"He said he was going to get me," Ted snarled, then darted toward the cameras nearby and raised his right hand. "Well, that's all you're going to get, Ken, an indictment. I'll plead not guilty right now. My chance to talk to the press." Bundy smiled and turned back to hear Katsaris to the end.

Finally, as detectives led Ted back into the elevator, he called out his last words: "It's my turn now. I will be heard from." The doors closed to the sound of his tearing the indictment to pieces. Three detectives—Norm Chapman, Don Patchen, and Steve Bodiford—waited in a holding room of the jail. Katsaris was hoping his prisoner would confess to the familiar faces. Instead they heard an hour of indignant raging.

Moments later, at a crowded press conference elsewhere in the jail, Katsaris explained why he'd handled the reading of the indictment the way he had. "It's the public's right to be informed of the steps of justice along the way," he said.

A member of Tallahassee's legal community fairly shuddered at the sheriff's logic the next day. "This case is going to turn into a trial of the accusers instead of the accused."

Bundy appeared in Judge Rudd's courtroom on Monday, July 31. His plea—not guilty—was no surprise. Nor was his request to be represented by Millard Farmer and his refusal to accept the counsel of the public defender.

Nor was the news that broke several hours later in Lake

273

City, 100 miles away. At the top of the indictment for the "premeditated design to effect the death of Kimberly Diane Leach" was the name of Florida's now most notorious defendant: Theodore Robert Bundy.

28

It was clear to everyone in Judge John A. Rudd's Tallahassee courtroom that August morning. The presence of Atlanta attorney Millard Farmer, seeking to represent Ted Bundy on the Chi Omega murder charge, meant more than a routine session. With Rudd and Farmer the lines were boldly drawn: this was nothing less than a symbolic conflict of the opposing forces in southern courts.

Fifty-five years old, rich in Florida and Georgia land, John Rudd had risen through the old-style criminal justice system: first a city judge, then a member of the city commission, next a county prosecutor, and finally in 1973, running unopposed on the ticket, election to the circuit post. Like any political figure, he learned the trade along the way, making allies and enemies and establishing an unmistakable style. He was, above all, a knowledgeable, almost classic jurist—a steely, unflinching respecter of the law as it stood, hardly inclined to break new ground with his decisions. By age 50 his views seemed immovably set.

Lawyers responded differently to the Rudd court over the years. He was "stern but fair" to some, to others a black mark on the system, "a hanging judge," "a disaster all too typical of the South." But for both those who respected him and those who feared him, several things about Judge Rudd were indisputable: first, he tolerated not the slightest variance from orderly courtroom procedure; everything ran by the book. Second, he exhibited, as if by reflex, little sympathy for the indigent defendant—even less if he suspected the defendant was actually a well-qualified person out to bilk the system by requesting a public defender.

Millard Farmer, too, had developed his own style. In 1976, after six successful years in private practice, the views of this thin, frizzy-haired attorney, then just turning 40, suddenly crystallized. It was the poor and the helpless, particularly those charged with capital offenses, who occupied the lowest rung of the ladder—a ladder, he realized, that he had climbed without a thought to his own lofty perch. With public sentiment for the death penalty on the rise again in the South, Farmer grasped his own purpose and pursued it with missionary zeal. In conjunction with a North Carolina psychologist Farmer founded Team Defense, a nonprofit Atlanta-based corporation dedicated to defending indigent defendants in death penalty cases.

"Make no mistake about it," as one colleague says, "Millard Farmer is a preacher with a law degree. It's all fire and brimstone, and he means every word of it."

Indeed, with his shock of gray hair, his dramatic brow, and an undying gift for oratory, Farmer has the effect of an Old Testament prophet. But in court, his philosophy takes shape in a series of calculated procedures and techniques, all designed to avert a sentence of death. First, stacks of preliminary motions are filed, fast and furiously, "to capture the atmosphere of the trial." Then experienced social scientists are used to select and tailor a jury that will be unlikely to recommend a death sentence. Next, by wheedling, persuasion, and repetition, Farmer and his associates concentrate on prolonging the trial; over time, a jury comes to view the defendant as a person rather than a frightening and nameless evil. And through it all, Millard Farmer takes his antideath-penalty crusade to the public through the press.

His tactics quickly became notorious—so frustrating to Georgia prosecutors on one occasion that they burned a lawbook on the courthouse lawn in protest; so infuriating to judges that Farmer was frequently cited for contempt.

Judge Rudd peered down at Farmer and Bundy seated together at the defense table. Here was a problem, his gaze seemed to be saying, that he just didn't need.

According to Florida law Farmer, a Georgia lawyer, could be admitted as Bundy's counsel only with the approval of the judge. The argument heated up immediately. It was true, was it not, Rudd wanted to know, that Farmer made it a habit of speaking extensively with the press during a trial. And wasn't it also true that he had been cited for contempt in a recent Georgia case? Yes, said Farmer, offering to explain his side of it: the judge had repeatedly overruled his objections to a prosecutor referring to a black

275

defendant by his first name while calling everyone else in court by his last name.

Farmer had soon worked his way under Rudd's skin, chiding the judge when he asked Farmer to repeat something: "Well, Your Honor, if you don't pay attention, I can see why you get confused."

"Mr. Farmer, I don't like to play games."

Rudd's ruling the next day came as no surprise. "With no small sense of gravity," the judge began, he was denying the request in the interest of "an atmosphere of fairness, calm, and reason." Millard Farmer employs "maximized obfuscation"; there would be no "bizarre circus" in his court.

Farmer immediately filed a federal suit in response, but Rudd's ruling was a painful defeat for him and for Ted. After Bundy's escape from Glenwood Springs and his subsequent difficulties in Florida, Farmer was especially eager to defend him. (Ted had first contacted Farmer in relation to the Caryn Campbell murder charge.) In a way, he said, he felt responsible. "If he'd had us in Colorado, he'd have been through that case by now." As far as Ted was concerned, there was no other lawyer who understood the scope and the issues of his case, no one so closely attuned to his own thinking. Sometimes, Ted said, he and Millard Farmer could communicate in court without exchanging a word.

But Ted forged ahead to fight the preliminary battles on his own, moving to disqualify Judge Rudd and firing off an angry letter as a follow-up: "It is characteristic of you, although it never ceases to amaze me, that you exercise the power of your office with a haughty disregard for the law and the facts." To some observers his parting shot had more than a little validity: "This goal-oriented justice . . . will not be lost on an appellate court."

Simultaneously, with Farmer's assistance, Bundy had filed a $300,000 civil suit against Leon County to improve his living and working conditions in jail. His "constitutional, statutory, and human rights" were being deprived, he said, by poor lighting, lack of outdoor exercise, a filthy toilet, interference with his mail, denial of access to the press, and inappropriate conversations between prosecutors and the judge. In five months, Bundy had been allowed on the jailhouse roof five times for exercise, heavily shackled each time. A psychologist said the lighting in his cell was the worst

276

he had ever seen; "apathy and hostility" were bound to result.

Meanwhile the legal pressure was building. Ted was in Pensacola one day, pleading for a delay in his trial for resisting arrest, then in Lake City, 300 miles to the east, the next. A crowd gathered on the town square in front of the courthouse that August 14, children clamoring onto the gazebo roof for a glimpse of the trim, composed man in blue jeans who, police said, had killed Kimberly Leach. Millard Farmer was at Ted's side when he stood up to enter his plea: "Because I am innocent I will plead not guilty." Tom Leach, the murdered girl's father, sat quietly at the back of the courtroom.

The following week, the Florida Supreme Court upheld Judge Rudd's ruling denying Millard Farmer's request to serve as Ted's counsel in the Chi Omega case. Judge Wallace Jopling's decision in Lake City was the predictable follow-up: for his "frivolous motions" and "insulting, disrespectful, contemptuous, and contumacious assaults on prosecutors and judges," Farmer was denied once again. Ted would have to find another lawyer, or work on his own defense, in the Kimberly Leach case.

Farmer saw it all in the bleakest terms: "We're just failing, failing, failing to explain to society by what standards we kill."

If Ted felt he was losing his best legal advocate, back home in Seattle his strongest supporter was growing even stronger. Over the years, since Ted's first arrest in Salt Lake City, Nancy Hobson had educated herself about the intricate web of police work and suspicions that made her friend out to be the most prolific mass murderer in American history. Like many, she hadn't believed it at first. But like few others, she stuck by him, studying the police reports Ted shared with her, talking to lawyers and detectives across the country, first convincing herself of the injustice Ted was suffering, and then carrying the word to reporters, friends, anyone who would listen.

By the summer of 1978, when the Ted Bundy story was beginning to break into national attention, Hobson was often spending upward of 12 hours a day on the case—a half hour each Tuesday on the phone with Ted (his weekly allotment of phone time was an hour), countless nights over autopsy reports, and perhaps most importantly, long sessions with members of the press. She was always knowledgeable and precise. It was the so-called chain of circumstance that bothered her most; she went at it like a surgeon with a knife.

"You start to look hard," she would say, "look hard at the *evidence* instead of what police want you to believe, and this spectacular chain begins to fall apart." As far back as the Washington cases of 1974, she could tick off the inconsistencies from memory.

Susan Rancourt in Ellensburg: a woman approached by a suspicious character around that time reported a *yellow* VW, not a tan or brown one like Ted drove. Roberta Parks in Corvallis: receipts showed that Ted had charged gas in Seattle—235 miles from Corvallis—twice the day that Parks disappeared. A round trip, without buying gas along the way, is impossible in a VW; the infamous credit card links didn't always hold up.

Then on to Utah. "Here the chain breaks down right away," Hobson said. "The very first case, Sandra Weaver, took place on July 1, when Ted was still living in Seattle. And then they use *that* to link him up to Laura Aime." Hobson held up a page from the Aime case file to prove her point: "This is concerning the progress that Salt Lake County is having with the case concerning the Grand Junction, Colorado, murder. [Weaver disappeared in Utah, and her body was found across the state line in Grand Junction.] This murder, in all aspects, is probably committed by the same person." Hobson stabbed at the report and added, "No one ever pays attention to little details like this. They're too interested in a sensational story." She went on.

If Melissa Smith was abducted and held for several days before she was killed (as the controversial autopsy report suggested), how could Ted, off hunting with Melanie Pattisen's father the two days after Smith disappeared, be involved? The Carol DaRonch case, Hobson said, with the victim's waffling identification and a suppressed police report, spoke for itself.

It was the same story in Colorado, where a promising suspect like the ex-Seattle flasher Jake Teppler—promising in both the Caryn Campbell and the Washington cases—was dropped after a polygraph test in Oregon. Upcoming trials prevented her from discussing them, she said, but there were other strong suspects in the Florida cases. She was up on the circumstantial nature of microscopic hair identifications and quick to dispute the theory that the victims all looked alike and that the M.O. in the murders was always the same. "Half the time," she pointed out, "there isn't even conclusive scientific proof of sexual assault." And even that pornographic book with the chapter about a man named Ted (found near the site where Janice Ott and Denise Naslund were dumped) was left there in October, a month after Ted Bundy had moved to Salt Lake City.

Late one afternoon, outside her apartment on Seattle's Queen Anne Hill, Hobson turned to a reporter after a marathon session. The facts were there, she said; anyone could see if he'd only look. Suddenly her eyes brightened with tears. She used Ted's nickname when she finally spoke. "Basically Bunny," she began, "he's still just the good Republican boy he always was."

In Tallahassee, denied direct access to the press, Ted nonetheless kept up a correspondence with reporters from Seattle to New York. The letters were instruction as much as anything else, as he lectured newsmen on the lack of hard evidence and the dissimilarities between the crimes, and scolded them for their unwillingness to look beneath the surface of what police were telling them. " 'We're considering Bundy mainly because it's a college-type case,' " he quoted one investigator, and then demanded: "Why, why, why Bundy? Why is Bundy a suspect in college-type cases? . . . As long as they persist in tailoring their investigation to me as a suspect, they will fail because they have the wrong man but can't admit it to themselves."

He parried inquiries about alibis ("Where were *you* on the evening of January 31, 1974, for example? Can you prove it conclusively with documentary and/or eyewitness testimony?") and sneered at a suggestion that he ought to have cleared out of town right after the Chi Omega murders: "I am discouraged by human nature, yours included, as it applies to my case," he told the reporter, pointing out the guilty inference police could have drawn from such a flight, "because no matter what I say or do, I am damned if I do and damned if I don't. Sincerely yours, Theodore Robert Bundy."

He was unshakable, finally, on one point: his past, his personal life—everything from illegitimate birth to the color of his socks—were simply no concern of the press. There was nothing abnormal about him, he said, nothing to "explain" the insinuations of the police. Yes, he had

279

wondered from time to time about his biological father, and no, he was not a loner. Beyond that, he reserved his privacy. "I am still too young to look upon my life as History," he wrote to a weekly magazine in Seattle. "I am at a stage in life, an egocentric stage, where it matters only that I understand what I am and not what others may think of me." Several weeks later he phoned the reporter and added this sentiment, in a soft, measured voice: "I would rather live a lifetime in anonymity than have a dishonest fame." The quotation, he said, was from ex-Attorney General John Mitchell.

Ted persisted in his patient, uphill campaign against the image of a clean-cut monster etched in many minds. Ever since his first arrest, in fact, the bitterness had reached him by return mail. The mother of one of the murdered girls had written to him at every stop along the way— Utah, Colorado, now Florida—plastering the envelope with now faded wallet photos of her daughter. He didn't need to read the letter inside.

Despite Judge Rudd's continued warnings, Ted Bundy proceeded as his own lawyer in the Chi Omega case, scheduled to come to trial on October 3. A court order improved the lighting in his cell, and he was busy familiarizing himself with the state's case. (Discovery rights had been granted to him just three weeks before.) On Tuesday morning, October 3, 1978, Ted sat by himself in the courtroom, a Michelob beer packing case stuffed with legal files on the defense table in front of him. Spectators, reporters, witnesses waiting to be instructed and sequestered filled most of the wooden benches in the room.

Not surprisingly, Bundy's first request was for a delay. "I get a little cocky," he told a visibly unsympathetic Judge Rudd. The last thing Rudd wanted was an appeal based on the defendant's claim of inadequate time or resources to prepare his own case. Grumbling about the "misguided incompetence of the defense," he rescheduled the trial for December 4. The judge's displeasure didn't apparently faze Ted. "I'm staying with the man I know best," he said on his way back to the Leon County jail, "and that's me."

Confident or not, Bundy had his work cut out for him. Along with a lengthy list of tangible items (blood, hair, photos, dental evidence, and more) the state intended to introduce, the discovery motion provided him with the names of 119 possible witnesses. One by one, with a court reporter and prosecutor Larry Simpson present, Bundy summoned the witnesses to a holding room at the jail for depositions—a tool for discovering what their testimony might be at the trial.

Depositions, normally the routine legwork of a case, turned to irony, tension, and high drama with an accused murderer conducting the interviews. "I understand it's very difficult for you," he began one session. "I'm going to ask you some questions about Theodore Bundy, and I *am* Theodore Bundy." Across the table was a Chi Omega sorority sister, spared from attack on January 15. Did she think there was much speculation around Tallahassee about Bundy, he asked another Chi O woman. "Some people wonder what makes him tick," she replied.

Karen Chandler, still nursing her broken jaw when she showed up at the jail, excused her short answers: it was sometimes painful to talk. No, she said, she didn't know who her assailant was.

"You still feel like you have an open mind?" Ted asked.

"Pretty much so."

At other times Ted was pressing hard for the facts, questioning the patrolmen, investigators, detectives, and crime lab experts who had handled the state's evidence. He pieced together the way the various elements of the case had been assembled and picked up some technical data on hair and fingerprint analysis. He was especially eager to sift the sketchy information about other suspects investigated by police. Several fraternity men remembered a man running along Jefferson Street the night of the murders. Someone else had reported a suspicious person asking for directions to the Holiday Inn.

In late October he summoned Ricky Ramoya, the Chi O "sweetheart" Nita Neary had mentioned under hypnosis a week after the killings. Ramoya provided little more than a rare light moment in the days of testimony in the jail. Working around the sorority house after Ted's arrest, Ramoya had found a tennis ball inscribed with a message. Even Larry Simpson, the sober, earnestly boyish prosecutor, smiled when Ramoya told them what the tennis ball said: "Ted Bundy didn't do it."

"A message from heaven," Ted put in.

Some days he might have felt he needed divine intervention. In their separate depositions, Don Patchen, Norm

Chapman, and Steve Bodiford told the story of Ted's veiled, late night conversations with them in Pensacola and Tallahassee eight months before. Patchen was aggressively familiar with Ted now, but both Chapman and Bodiford were scrupulously, professionally distant, referring to Bundy in the third person. Ted knew perfectly well the fight he was facing with the three detectives: if they were permitted to testify before a jury, the inflammatory implications they could raise might prove overwhelming. Ted had said a great deal just after his arrest, a great deal.

While Bundy scrambled to build his defense, the state was busy reinforcing its case. By the fall, bite-mark specialists Lowell Levine in New York and Norman Sperber in San Diego had added their conclusions to Richard Souviron's: the teeth of Theodore Bundy had, "within a reasonable dental certainty," left the distinctive bruise pattern on Lisa Levy's left buttock. On October 21, however, the ship suddenly sprang an unexpected leak.

Richard Souviron had eagerly accepted an invitation to address a meeting of the American Society of Clinical Pathologists and the Florida Medical Examiners Commission. For several years he had lectured to various groups of crime lab specialists, prosecutors, and police throughout the country about the techniques and evidentiary value of bite marks. The science was relatively new, and Souviron saw himself as a kind of teacher and crusader for the cause.

Among the examples that Souviron chose for his October speech in Orlando was the bite mark in the Chi Omega case. "That bruise on that rear end," he said in the darkened room, as more than 100 people viewed a blowup slide, "contains a tremendous amount of information." The odontologist went on to explain the identification process and the importance of well-handled evidence, citing the errors made in this instance and revealing how the one crucial photograph of the mark with a ruler had saved the bite as evidence. "If you do everything else wrong, you can still come out smelling like a rose."

Throughout the speech Souviron was careful not to identify the case or the suspect by name, but if the facts alone weren't enough for a knowledgeable observer, the presence of Leon County Sheriff Ken Katsaris in the front row made the context plain. The state's star witness had just linked Theodore Bundy to the Chi Omega murders.

There was, as it turned out, just such a knowledgeable observer in the room: *Miami Herald* reporter Gene Miller. His story detailing the particulars of Souviron's lecture hit papers across Florida and across the country the next week. Outraged, Bundy responded immediately as he moved the court to drop the murder charges against him. Calling Souviron the state's "hired gun," Bundy claimed the "prejudicial impact cannot be cured by a change of venue." Katsaris's presence didn't go unnoticed by Ted either.

"There was no conspiracy," Larry Simpson said edgily, wondering to himself if the upheavals in this case would ever end.

Judge Rudd denied the motion to drop the Chi O charges, but Ted was still steaming when Dr. Souviron showed up at the jail a month later for deposition. Souviron's role was now clear—he was the accuser—and Bundy was determined to march him through his paces if it took all day. It did. Souviron would later say he'd never forget those seven hours in the interview room.

They began with a general discussion of bite-mark study, Ted poking and prodding to see if the doctor had made any slipups in his work. It wasn't long, however, before Souviron's pedagogical mode had taken over. Pointing first to the photograph of Ted's mouth and singling out a chipped filling on an upper tooth, Souviron then circled a spot on the bite-mark photograph and asked rhetorically, "It's really amazing, isn't it, how that fits in?"

"I guess," said Ted blankly.

The dentist had an answer for every criticism of the evidence—skin distortion, the effect of body position, the shortcomings of photography as a tool in comparison. Finally Ted fell into step, adopting a smart-aleck student pose.

"This is fun," he said. "Let's do this some more."

"This may be fun to Mr. Bundy," Souviron shot back, then stared right at Ted, "but you are talking about something really serious here, and this really isn't a joke."

"Oh, I understand that."

"If I were in your shoes it wouldn't be any joke to me. It would be very, very serious business."

"You don't need to lecture me," Ted said finally.

The discussion of teeth and skin went on for hours. Finally, near the end of the session, Bundy asked about the publicized Orlando lecture. "I think that article did a great disservice to both of us," Souviron said. Bundy frowned.

Souviron's regrets were brief. One more time, before he left the jail, he repeated what he'd said all along: "And that's the way I see it, that your teeth made that bite. That's it."

As Ted Bundy's trial approached, more eyes across the West turned to watch. Since 1975, more than three years before, this single name had been wound around a chain of murders, tightening suspicion into fascinated certainty in many minds. How easy it seemed, in Seattle, to fix that hazily remembered "Ted" at Lake Sammamish on a sunny afternoon with the second name of Bundy. How certain the connection, in Salt Lake City, between the handcuffs swinging on Carol DaRonch's wrist, the key at Viewmont High, the cuffs on the floor of a tan VW Bug. How obvious the reason for the Colorado escapes.

Years later, ongoing events still sounded like echoes of Theodore Bundy to Westerners. In October a skeleton was found in rural Juab County, Utah. From bone structure and a wisp of hair police could reconstruct this much: a young woman, with long brown hair parted in the middle, dead about three to four years—no name. On November 24, Ted Bundy's birthday, five prisoners pushed out a plaster-board ceiling panel in the Garfield County jail in Glenwood Springs, Colorado. They were up in the crawl space—Ted's route to freedom—when the panicked jailer's wife finally heard the noise and notified the dispatcher.

It was all so clear in so many minds. The story was too suggestive not to believe. Ted Bundy was bad news wherever he went. A conviction in the Chi Omega case was the only logical result. Presumption of innocence was the farthest thing from so many minds.

No matter what his image, Ted was not about to give up the fight. Millard Farmer may not have been calling the shots, but Bundy had learned the Farmer method well, showering down a host of motions on Judge Rudd, including several motions for the judge to disqualify himself, and still more seeking to suppress virtually every piece of evidence in the state's case.

A major victory for Bundy was just around the bend. In early December, pointing to improper conversations Rudd had had with prosecutors without the presence of the defendant or the defendant's attorney, the Florida Supreme Court instructed the judge to demonstrate why he should not be disqualified from the case. Ted had been making his complaints known for weeks, and now, just before the trial was to begin, his plea was heard. The final decision took three weeks, but it was a triumph: because of this "intolerable adversary atmosphere" between the defendant and the judge, the court ruled, Rudd was out.

After the immediate elation had worn off, Ted's first thought was of Millard Farmer. A new judge might well permit the Atlanta lawyer to act as Ted's attorney. 1978 was ending well for Ted.

There were some dark moments, to be sure—like the Utah Supreme Court's rejection of his appeal in the DaRonch kidnapping case. And December 30 was tough, too: that was the day, a year ago, that he'd dropped down from the ceiling and walked into the swirling hush of a snowy Colorado night.

But that was all behind him now. There was nothing to gain from anguishing over the past. The best he could do was look ahead with confidence.

29

"Fat, dumb, and happy." It was Edward D. Cowart's description of himself, and reporters realized instantly that the Miami judge appointed to assume control of the Chi Omega trial would breathe a warm, welcome personality into the case.

But Cowart brought more to the Chi Omega case than comic relief. As the chief circuit judge of Dade County, he was well acquainted with the complexities and demands of first-degree murder cases. He'd tried many himself over the years, and as the administrator of the largest circuit in the state, the 53-year-old judge was as knowledgeable as anyone on the bench. While his mannerly southern charm and humor leave an engaging first impression, lawyers who know his record respect him almost uniformly for his judicial consistency, intelligence, fairness, and solid understanding of the law. Rarely overturned on appeal, Judge Cowart could draw undiluted praise from a source as unlikely as a big-city public defender: "He's the best trial judge I've ever seen."

Convinced at last that he had neither the time nor the resources to prepare his own defense adequately, Theodore Bundy accepted the counsel of the Tallahassee public defender's office, a modest but respected team of young lawyers headed by Michael Minerva. By the end of January, Minerva and his staff had filed a raft of motions seeking time and more information about the state's case. Two maneuvers in February were already familiar: a request to have Millard Farmer appointed as defense attorney and a motion for the judge to disqualify himself. Cowart denied Bundy on both counts, citing the same grounds that Rudd had for rejecting Farmer.

Ted did win some minor battles, the most satisfying of which was an out-of-court settlement with Katsaris and Leon County over his jail conditions. In addition to the improved lighting and exercise he won, Ted gained a psychological lift: Millard Farmer had represented him in that civil suit. Shortly thereafter, following an unorthodox conference attended by both Judge Cowart and Judge Jopling (presiding over the Kimberly Leach case), a more reasonable schedule was set—the Chi Omega trial in June and the Leach trial in September.

Scheduling was by no means the only unorthodox thing about the upcoming Ted Bundy trials in Florida. Public attention and interest had grown almost obsessive over the months, precipitating a strange and virtually unprecedented confrontation between the press and the courts. A reporter showed up at the Leon County jail to cover some of Ted's deposition proceedings in preparation for the Kimberly Leach trial. Depositions, the reporter maintained, were an important part of the judicial process and thus open to the press.

Prosecutor Bob Dekle, tight-lipped about his case all along, quoted Shakespeare in his brief opposing the press access: "But men may construe things after their own fashion, clean from the purpose of the things themselves" (*Julius Caesar*). Judge Jopling said he'd never had to make such a decision when he ruled against the reporter and a string of newspaper publishers who had joined in the suit. He'd never seen a case where the media interest was so intense that depositions were considered newsworthy. It was an especially difficult ruling to make in Florida, where print and broadcast journalists enjoy as free an access to the judicial system as they do anywhere in the country. Even as Jopling ruled, the Florida Supreme Court was allowing television cameras in the courtrooms.

Ted barely noticed he was making headlines again. He was concentrating on his defense, specifically on the crucial pretrial hearings set to begin in Tallahassee on May 14. He hoped that Judge Cowart would suppress some of the state's testimony. The defense now had its own bite-mark expert working with the evidence in hopes of casting doubt on the conclusions of Dr. Souviron and Dr. Levine. Ironically, that expert was Duane DeVore, the Maryland forensic odontologist who had discussed the case informally with Souviron at a professional meeting almost a year before.

Ted's teeth were on everyone's mind as the trial approached. In late March he complained that a toothache was preventing him from chewing his food. The alert went up. Was this some sort of tactic to invalidate the bite-mark evidence? After a consultation with the prosecutor, Sheriff Katsaris agreed that Ted could visit the dentist. The toothache was in a lower rear tooth, a tooth that Dr. Souviron hadn't even considered in his analysis.

In April the long, tangled tale of Theodore Bundy reached the United States Supreme Court in two separate appeals: first, Millard Farmer's request to serve as Ted's lawyer in the Chi Omega trial; and second, the appeal of the Utah Carol DaRonch kidnapping conviction. Both lower-court rulings were upheld. Judge Cowart tried not to notice the perpetual stream of Bundy news in the papers. With some 27 years of cases behind him as both lawyer and judge, he had seen his share of highly publicized trials. But the speculation and innuendo swirling thickly around the Bundy case were precedent-making.

"We women want to see this sex murder evil monster die in the electric chair," one letter to the judge read, blue ink handwriting fairly bristling across the wide-lined page. It was signed "50 church women in Greeley, Col. 80631."

Judge Cowart had one thing set in his mind before the proceedings began. He was going to do everything in his power to ensure a fair trial for Theodore Bundy, a trial founded on the evidence that related to the charge. There'd been enough hinted at and whispered about the Chi Omega murders already, and none of it had a place in a court of law.

Sixteen months had passed since the killings had shaken the peaceful, shady north Florida city of Tallahassee. By May 1979 people had tried to put the Chi Omega killings out of their minds. Clerks, waitresses, even FSU students seemed only faintly, abstractly stirred by questions about their feelings, as if they'd been asked about the death of a distant ancestor. "Sure, people have kinda eased off," an accounting major said. "You can't live like that forever."

But the recollection, the presence of the crimes in this community hadn't died. "Sexual Assault," the ads on the city's buses read; "Every Female is a Potential Victim!" The public service campaign had been running with good response for about a year. On campus the escort service for women students was still functioning at a higher volume than it had before January 15, 1978. At the *Tallahassee Democrat* the calls came in as regularly as ever—sometimes weekly, sometimes daily—from as far away as Norway and Laos: Send us anything you've got on Mr. Ted Bundy. By early May almost 200 reporters, photographers, and cameramen had applied for credentials to cover the pretrial hearings and the trial itself.

The significance of the extraordinary press interest was not lost on Bundy or his lawyers. In a stack of motions filed just before the hearings began, they were seeking to close out reporters from the crucial suppression motion arguments. If the results were widely reported, they claimed, any potential juror would be prejudiced by advance knowledge of the state's evidence. Finally, with the help of a public opinion expert who was polling a sample of the registered voters in Tallahassee to test their awareness of the case, Mike Minerva and his assistant public defenders asked that the trial be moved. The defense attorneys' apprehension was well placed: in addition to eyewitness, hair, and bite-mark testimony, the prosecution had indicated its intention to introduce evidence from Ted's arrest and interrogation in Pensacola, the Colorado charges and escapes, the Utah kidnapping case, and the "junk" found in his car—even a statement from Ted's former fiancée, Melanie Pattisen.

Bundy took the lead for the defense when hearings began at 9:00 a.m. on Monday, May 14. Dressed in a gray leisure suit and a striped tie, Ted flipped a file folder shut and rose from his place at the defense table to argue a motion to prohibit a television camera in the courtroom. He glanced at Sheriff Katsaris, seated alone at the front of the courtroom, one foot tapping the rug.

Judge Cowart exhibited his cordial, even hand right away.

"I might say you look nice," the judge remarked to Ted. Tanned and relaxed, free to move without a leg brace, he did seem to be benefiting from the less stringent conditions at the jail. Ted smiled back.

"Thank you, Your Honor. I'm disguised as an attorney today."

His argument was a little unpracticed at first, but he soon geared up. "It's a novelty," he said, gesturing to the small blue camera perched inconspicuously in the balcony, "like a curtain drawn back, and the public has a chance to view something for the first time." Millions would see the former law student at work in the courtroom on their sets that night. Despite his plea for the court to "take giant strides toward desensitizing the trial," Cowart permitted the camera to stay. He saw no reason why the print media should have any advantage over the broadcasters.

Ted's lawyers followed with a string of motions seeking to close the suppression hearings. Cowart, calling himself an advocate of public dissemination, resisted. "We're conducting the public's business," he said, "and we're going to conduct it in the sunshine." Moments later he repeated a sentiment he'd put in the record many times before: "The public has an interest in how the system works. It's a matter of confidence in the judicial system."

Cowart issued his ruling that afternoon. A jury would be chosen and sequestered before potentially prejudicial pretrial arguments about the evidence would be heard. An untainted jury and the public's right to know would both be preserved. "It satisfied everyone," one lawyer said. In this most sensational and volatile of trials, Judge Cowart had taken control with firmness and discretion.

For the next several days Minerva and his assistants Lynn Thompson and Ed Harvey picked and prodded the state's case, hoping for inconsistencies or improprieties that would force some of the evidence to be thrown out. Two witnesses who had seen Bundy at the Oak the night of the murder remembered him in different clothing. The student who'd seen a man in a dark knit cap on College Avenue the night of the killings couldn't pick Bundy out of a photo lineup. Ted's hair samples had been seized without an oath. The dental search warrant also came under attack. Minerva claimed there was information about other suspects that the defense had not seen. There was a motion to quash the grand-jury indictment because of an unethical conversation Judge Rudd had had and another attempt to disqualify Judge Cowart on similar grounds.

Prosecutor Larry Simpson's rebuttals were often swift and quick. At times he seemed indignant, even offended by the defense efforts. "The fact is, Your Honor," he snapped, "they were a day late and a dollar short." For the most part Cowart ruled in his favor.

It was apparent after a day in court that the proceedings weren't sitting well with Ted. A frown had set on his face, and his foot bobbed nervously as witnesses followed one another to the stand. Frustrated, he finally rose to advise Judge Cowart he was not convinced he had "adequate counsel for this extremely important motion." There was a long weekend to cool off and regroup, but Ted knew he was facing a more critical battle the next week: testimony on the notorious bite mark and a decision whether such evidence would be permitted at the trial.

The defense planned to attack the bite-mark evidence in three ways. First was the possibility that they could discredit bite-mark analysis itself—unlikely, since appellate courts had regularly upheld such evidence. Second was an attempt to undercut the probable cause foundation the state had laid for the warrant to take the impressions of Ted's teeth. Part of this approach hinged on Nita Neary: if they could discredit her as an eyewitness, then the justification for the warrant to get the dental impressions would be weakened. The last, best hope was an all-out attack on the methodology of the man who'd made the match, Dr. Richard Souviron.

Souviron, who had testified in court over 20 times, was not about to be an easy mark. Trim, smartly groomed, and stern, he exuded a disarming confidence in the witness box —a clearheaded, professorial style that seemed to come naturally. Defense attorney Lynn Thompson was keen on one point: that the search warrant was served on Ted *before* Souviron had the scale-accurate photo of the bite mark necessary for accurate comparison. "'Ain't no way,'" Thompson reminded the dentist of his statements in deposition, that the ruined tissue from Lisa Levy could have been used for comparison.

Souviron broke into a short, sympathetic smile. What he had *meant* in the deposition, he carefully explained, was that he *could* have made an identification before he got the photo with the ruler, but it would have involved some costly and impractical procedures. Bundy smiled grimly in his chair. This Dr. Souviron had rankled him before. He wasn't about to let him squirm off the hook now, when it really counted. After a recess, Ted himself called the dentist back to the stand.

Directing Souviron's attention back to early April 1978, Ted asked, "Were you aware they were seeking a search warrant for impressions of my teeth?" Bundy faced the witness, squared off, and unclasped his hands. "What evidence did you have then to arrive at your conclusion?" That "conclusion," also part of the probable cause foundation was that from photographs of Ted, Souviron could not rule him out as a suspect.

The odontologist repeated his story once again, from the first time he'd seen the bite mark to the smiling photos of Ted he'd received, to his opinion, offered before the warrant was served, that Bundy's teeth might have made the mark on the victim's buttock.

"Then why, doctor," Ted finally put in, "didn't you tell me the truth in deposition?"

Cowart had to break in as referee between Bundy's aggressiveness and Souviron's knife-sharp if slightly calculated responses. "The court's aware there's an inconsistency."

The remainder of Souviron's testimony—three hours of it—was calm: a well-organized lecture, complete with photographs, enlargements, models, and acetate overlays, detailing the relationship of Ted's teeth to the bite. The technical language was entrancing after a while—lower central incisors forward, lateral incisors back, canines lower in the arch. As Souviron pointed from the enlarged photo of Bundy's teeth to the shot of deep bruises in the flesh, the evidence took on a strange, abstract quality. "It's just phenomenal," the doctor said, "this beautiful mosaic pattern. It's like a key in a lock."

Mike Minerva's cross-examination was game and intelligent. No, Souviron admitted, there were no established, mutually agreed-upon standards for points of identification in bite-mark analysis. And yes, the movement of the suspect and the action of the bite itself could cause "distortion" in the mark. But he was not to be shaken from his crucial conclusion—that Ted Bundy had bitten Lisa Levy twice on the rear end.

The next witness, New York bite-mark expert Lowell Levine, was barely into his testimony when the defendant got to his feet. "I won't hesitate to stand up and ask for a recess if I don't know what's happening. I'm not sure if my counsel is prepared." Ted wanted time to confer with his lawyers, but it was growing clear that the cracks in the defense team ran deep. So deep, in fact, that Minerva had called in a Detroit psychiatrist to examine his client. "Just for my own information," he had explained to Ted.

Levine resumed. With his black, barblike beard and wide, dark eyes, Levine projected a slower, more studious style than Souviron. He spoke of beveling and wear patterns on the teeth and mentioned a technique of computer enhancement he used on the bite-mark photographs. In the end, he was every bit as sure as his Florida colleague.

"Were you able to reach a conclusion?" asked Larry Simpson.

"Yes, sir." No one had to ask what it was.

Minerva had done his homework on this witness, too, citing an article Levine had written in which he'd warned about the reliability of skin as a recording medium.

"That was the state of the art at the time," the doctor said. "We've seen more bite-mark cases in the last five years than we had in the 50 years before that. We've learned a great deal."

Finally Dr. Norman Sperber, a San Diego forensic odontologist, took the stand for the prosecution. The terminology and the conclusion were familiar by now: everything lined up between the defendant's teeth and the bite mark. Minerva reiterated his points but reserved most of his energy for the next day, when the defense would have their shot at the bite mark.

It was a two-part strategy. First an orthodontist would testify that the crooked pattern of Ted's lower teeth was not so uncommon as the prosecution made it out to be; the general configuration occurred, in fact, in perhaps 20 percent of the population. And second, the defense's big gun—Duane DeVore—would take the stand.

Like the prosecution experts in bite-mark analysis, DeVore was a leader in the field—experienced, knowledgeable, reputable beyond a doubt. He expressed several reservations about the evidence in this case immediately: the poor preservation of the tissue and the absence of a color bar in the bite-mark photograph. And there were other curiosities in his view, most notably the odd misalignment of the marks apparently made by the lower and upper teeth.

From the start, DeVore admitted he could not eliminate Bundy's teeth as possibly having inflicted the bite, but issued a carefully worded caution: "At the present time the evaluation of bite-mark evidence is subjective. Without objevice methods we've got to be extremely careful that the methods are not impermissibly suggestive."

The defense reserved its best shot for last. Producing three sets of dental models from a Maryland orthodontic clinic, DeVore claimed they also matched up with the bite mark in question. He wasn't suggesting he'd found new suspects, he explained, but only that it was clearly possible that someone else—with teeth similar to Ted Bundy's —had made the bite. "When we make an identification," he concluded, "we must be positive in our minds."

Simpson looked concerned when he began his cross-examination, and was unable to shake DeVore. The prosecutor asked for a 15-minute recess, grabbed up the sets of models and disappeared.

Fifteen minutes stretched to an hour before court resumed, and Simpson was still nervously pressing his hair back into place as the judge climbed to the bench. The prosecution recalled its last witness, Lowell Levine, to the stand. Simpson came right to the point with his questions. Levine had examined DeVore's models during the recess, noting first that they represented the teeth of patients around 12 years old. That much was obvious from the eruption patterns in the lower jaws. Then Levine had made wax impressions of each set to compare them to the bite mark.

"And what was your finding?" Simpson asked.

"That none of them are consistent with the bite mark."

"Can each of these three sets of teeth be excluded as the perpetrator of the bite mark?"

"Yes, sir."

"No further questons, Your Honor."

Those last moments in court Wednesday afternoon had the feel of a dramatic victory for the accusers of Ted Bundy, the last shred of "reasonable doubt" snatched away from the defense. Ken Katsaris leaned back behind his wide desk after court was adjourned. "It would only be appropriate," he mused, "if the Ted Bundy story came to a close in his own mouth. To think that his most credible tool, that silver tongue, has been darting over those very teeth all this time."

But there was a second interpretation to Levine's dramatic rebuttal. By impeaching one expert with another, the prosecution was taking a calculated risk. If these scientists could disagree with each other about an identification, a judge or jury might see it, then maybe bite-mark analysis itself wasn't so reliable and definitive after all. That's all it would take in the end: for one juror to have a reasonable doubt.

The sky over Tallahassee darkened that afternoon, and the rain beat down so hard on the pavement that it bounced and jumped like so many electric sparks. Ted Bundy rode across town in silence to the Leon County jail, hardly noticing the wind and the rain. His own summer storm was still ahead.

After hearing final arguments and commending both lawyers the next morning, Judge Edward Cowart ruled the bite-mark evidence admissible at the trial. This would be the first time a Florida jury would hear bite-mark testimony, but Cowart noted 11 precedent cases in other states. The judge delayed ruling on a change of venue until after an attempt was made to empanel a jury in Tallahassee.

Ted himself brought the pretrial hearings to a close with a last statement for the record about the preparedness of his lawyers. Buttoning his sport coat as he rose, Ted spoke in a slow, twanging voice: "I do not believe they are ready to go to trial on June 11." Bundy had made his point three times now. There weren't just cracks in the defense, as far as he was concerned; the very seams were giving out.

There was another story unfolding in Florida's capital that week. It had begun on Friday morning, May 18, 1979, when Governor Bob Graham signed death warrants for convicted murders Willie Darden and John Spenkelink, and it continued, agonizingly, as their final maneuvers for stays ran out and the day of death approached.

A wail of protest went up. Chanting, hands linked, protesters gathered outside Graham's office. Letters and telegrams poured in from capital punishment opponents around the world. Millard Farmer descended, like an angel of mercy, and pleaded with Graham for time. It looked briefly like the protesters had a chance. Darden won his stay, and Farmer engineered a temporary one for Spenkelink on Tuesday afternoon. But then on Friday morning, the U.S. Supreme Court voted 6–2 not to intercede in the case of the man convicted of killing a companion at a Tallahassee motel in 1973. Just after 10:00 a.m., May 25, John Spenkelink was strapped into the solid oak electric chair at the Florida State Prison. The flesh on his left leg singed; his fist curled up. He was dead within five minutes—the first man executed against his will in the United States in 12 years.

Across the country, the news confirmed a classic picture of the South, where justice was vengeful and quick. The networks pounced on a story out of Jacksonville, Florida: "1 Down, 133 to Go," the legend across a drawing of the electric chair read. The police department softball team was doing a steady business in new T-shirts bearing that phrase! Spenkelink, criminal lawyers agreed, had paved the way for Florida to execute again.

It was quiet in the Tallahassee public defender's office that day. Ted Bundy's pretrial hearings had ended with a crucial defeat the day before. And now this. Unavoidably, the two stories were linked.

It was ominous, one lawyer in the office thought to himself, the way the death penalty haunted the story of Ted Bundy. Gary Gilmore, the last man executed in the United States, was Ted's fellow inmate at the Utah State Prison. In Colorado it was the Bundy case, among others that helped overturn the capital punishment statute. And now, in Florida, it didn't take much imagination: Ted was facing a sensational double first-degree murder trial with the door to the death penalty open again.

Steadily, over the next week, the pressure on Ted Bundy built. Mike Minerva and his other lawyers were in and out of the jail and then off, mysteriously, to Lake City. Millard Farmer called, called again, then contacted Ted's family in the Northwest. Sheriff Katsaris, meanwhile, was quietly getting the word out to law enforcement officials around the state: Be in the courtroom Thursday the 31st.

It was to be a routine hearing, but the crowd that gathered expected much more. Police who had directed the Chi Omega and Kimberly Leach investigations sat together in one row. Farther back, Ted's mother, his Seattle lawyer, Millard Farmer, and Nancy Hobson waited for Judges Cowart and Jopling to file in. The reporters were buzzing with speculation: Bundy was going to plead guilty to three counts of second-degree murder and escape the electric chair. It had all been worked out.

Worked out or not, it was not to be. Instead Ted stood to argue a motion to fire his lawyers and delay both trials. That afternoon he telephoned his hometown newspaper, the *Tacoma News Tribune*. "There's only one hang-up with pleading guilty," he said, "and that is that you have to plead guilty." His friends, Millard Farmer, everyone had pressured him to go along with the bargain as far as he had. "I know that I face death if I am convicted . . . but there are some principles that are more important than the fear of death.

"I simply am not guilty."

Determined again to fight, Ted had calmly argued his reasons for wanting to scuttle Minerva and his staff. Minerva was incompetent, convinced of Ted's guilt, unable or unwilling to come up with a solid defense, Ted claimed. Furthermore Minerva had stated his opinion, according to Bundy's motion, that Judge Cowart was out to "engineer a conviction while glossing over and prettying up the record to prevent reversible error." Basically, Bundy claimed, quoting a friend, " 'They've just fizzled out.' " On Monday Minerva himself joined forces with Ted—their first agreement, perhaps, in weeks. It was an "irreconcilable conflict," he told the judge. He wanted out.

It was dangerous last-minute brinksmanship, and lawyers on both sides were concerned about how Ted, who seemed at times his own worst enemy, might affect his own trial. They had petitioned the court privately for a hearing on Bundy's legal competence to stand trial.

Two psychiatrists were summoned to Tallahassee to testify: Emmanuel Tanay, the Detroit psychiatrist Minerva had asked to examine Ted in May, and Hervey M. Cleckley, a leading authority on psychopathic and sociopathic personality disorders.

Tanay's analysis was straightforward: he thought Bundy had an antisocial personality, was characterized by bad judgment, "thrilled" at the chance of defying authority, and could be dangerous. There was no cure or treatment, the doctor went on, but under the legal definition, he was certainly competent to stand trial. Cleckley's testimony was much the same: Ted was legally fit to proceed. With the television cameras poised to take it all in, the last piece of

296

scenery had been moved into place for the most vivid real-life drama in recent north Florida history.

But the curtain didn't remain up for long. Judge Cowart heard just five prospective jurors before he was convinced that a fair and impartial jury would be impossible to find in Tallahassee. In two weeks, Judge Cowart said, the trial would begin in Miami.

Cowart turned down Ted's request to fire his attorneys that day, but the defendant smiled broadly as he left the Tallahassee courtroom for the last time. The move to Miami was the important piece of news. "Excellent," he said to reporters, "it's just excellent."

Besides, he thought to himself later on, he hadn't had the last word yet about his own defense. Ted Bundy wasn't about to take a supporting role—not now.

30

The move to Miami by prosecutors, public defenders, and the press was a logistical marvel. Files, evidence, and equipment needed office space. Lawyers and witnesses needed housing. On the ninth floor of the Dade County metropolitan hall of justice, ABC Television organized a closed-circuit video system for what was to become one of the largest gatherings of electronic media reporters in history.

Florida's cameras-in-the-courtroom ruling laid the groundwork and recent technological advances in videotape-editing equipment encouraged television stations from Seattle, Salt Lake, and Denver to ferry complete crews to Miami. Inserts for nightly newscasts could be made on the spot and transmitted home via satellite. Live satellite links allowed western viewers to watch courtroom action as it happened.

Ken Katsaris had the biggest transportation headache of all—Ted Bundy. It was a 500-mile trip to Miami, and the sheriff would have to make substantial security arrangements. Provisions in the Dade County jail would have to be checked as well. Katsaris wanted to make sure the Miami cops knew they had a skilled "rabbit" on their hands. Determined that

Bundy was going to be tried in Florida, he was not going to blow it at this late stage.

The sheriff's "favorite criminal" (the press hadn't let him forget that off-hand remark) stepped off the single-engine plane on Sunday, June 24, into the intense south Florida sunshine. Now, instead of the Panhandle's oak and pine forests Ted saw rows of palm trees and mangroves under the big city's gritty haze. Miami's urban sprawl dwarfed Tallahassee. The city is a melting pot of Latin-American immigrants, blacks, and retirees from the cold northern states. With its hurried, bustling, abrasive energy, Miami feels more like New York in the tropics than a southern city.

One member of Bundy's defense team did not follow his client south. After the blowup with Ted following the plea-bargaining debacle Mike Minerva stayed in Tallahassee, destined to play only a small part in the upcoming proceedings. In his place was Robert Haggard, a 34-year-old Miami criminal lawyer who'd previously tried murder cases before Judge Cowart. Haggard, a former intern in the Tallahassee public defender's office, had that special something Ted needed in a private attorney—he volunteered his services for free. Known for his skill in the art of cross-examination, Haggard was just tough enough, the defense team hoped, to crack some of the prosecution's witnessses on the stand.

"Everybody rise!" The bailiff's booming voice echoed in the wood-paneled courtroom Monday morning, and Judge Cowart took the bench. It seemed oddly inevitable that courtroom 4-1 should be the scene for the Ted Bundy TV spectacle. Two years before, when 15-year-old Ronny Zamora stood trial for the murder of an older woman during a burglary, courtroom 4-1 had become the focus of a fascinated national audience. Zamora's defense lawyers claimed the boy was not responsible for his crime because he was a victim of "television intoxication." Florida had just begun to permit TV cameras in the courtroom, on a trial basis. Television watched in 4-1 while television went on trial. Zamora was found guilty. Television, it seemed, got off.

Before jury selection began in the Bundy trial, the defense offered a slew of motions. Ted complained about conditions in the maximum security section of the jail. Reaching his hands out to demonstrate, Bundy declared that the only way he could read in his dimly lit cell was to hold the book through the bars and under the hallway light. Judge Cowart visited the cell during lunch and ordered Chief Jailer Jack Sandstrom to allow Ted and his lawyers to use the well-lighted jail conference room until eleven every night.

"I'd hate to read in there myself," Cowart quipped.

The camera in the courtroom came under attack by defense lawyers next, in a motion to have it barred. It was clear that the trial's silent partner in the first row of the press section bothered Ted. This was only the first in a series of halfhearted attempts to have it removed.

The next order of business was to authorize payment for the services of the man sitting beside Ted at the defense table. Emil Spillman, a pathologist turned hypnotist turned jury selection expert, was there to ensure a favorable jury for the defense. Spillman, crew-cut and heavyset, bragged to reporters that he "lost the first one, but I haven't lost one since." His clients didn't always get acquitted, but they rarely got the death penalty.

Spillman stared intently at each potential juror throughout the long week of choosing 12 from the 80 questioned, watching their "body language," listening for voice inflections and Freudian slips which might reveal something about their attitudes toward the defendant. Spillman may have been the expert, whispering in Ted's ear, but it was clearly Bundy who would have the final say on the jury.

After eliciting a short personal history from each prospective juror, Bob Haggard or Prosecutor Larry Simpson would ask several key questions, hinting at later arguments. "Who is your dentist?" Haggard inquired. (Richard Souviron practiced in nearby Coral Gables.) Simpson wanted to gauge feelings about the death penalty. Juror after juror heard the same questions: Have you ever been the victim of a crime? Did you ever belong to a sorority? Would extended sequestration present an undue hardship? Occasionally a prospective juror would say he'd read about Ted in the newspapers.

"Have you formed an opinion about the defendant's guilt or innocence?"

"Guilty," most would respond and be excused immediately "for cause."

Bob Haggard's style began to emerge in this first week of trial. Slow, methodical to the point of laboriousness, the newest member of the defense had already irritated Cowart by Monday night.

"It's going to take six months just to get a jury, unless you get along with your business," Cowart said angrily. "Now get along with it."

Occasionally, during the arduous process, Haggard overstepped the limits of courtroom procedure, once earning a sharp rebuke from the judge and the threat of a contempt citation for asking a prospective juror if he'd read a book called *Convicting the Innocent.* "Mr. Haggard, if that happens one more time, I'll see you in chambers. Seek and ye shall find."

By Monday night four people had passed the initial hurdle; by Tuesday night, nine. Cowart was not about to let the defense drag the trial on for months, and when the peremptory challenges and the slow pace began pushing the opening arguments farther and farther off, he ordered night sessions. In a contest of endurance, the judge would clearly be the winner.

Not that jury selection was an entirely colorless process. The parade of the unwilling and uninformed was like a quick cross section of Miami. Some said forthrightly that Ted Bundy was guilty and left the courtroom, while others scrambled for an excuse. "I get hot flashes in a crowd," one woman said as the spectators tried to muffle their laughter.

Haggard rose to the occasion and deadpanned, "Do these hot flashes affect your ability to think rationally?"

"Oh yes," the woman replied hurriedly. "I always keep a glass of ice water near me at my desk at work." Cowart excused her from duty.

Another man said he couldn't possibly serve because his wife had just had a "very serious operation." When asked what kind of operation, he looked toward the ceiling for a few seconds and said hopefully, "Gall bladder?" He was excused too.

By late Friday night the jury had been chosen: seven men, five women, a majority of them black, middle-aged, and middle-class. Court Clerk Shirley Lewis swore in this assortment of Ted Bundy's peers, and off they went to the posh hotel where they would spend the next five weeks. Bundy and his lawyers were pleased with the results, especially the juror they saw as a potential leader, Rudolph Treml. A Texaco senior project engineer from south Florida who had once worked for NASA as a laboratory test director for Apollo heat shield research, Treml had read nothing of Ted Bundy in the newspapers. He paid more attention to *Platt's Oilgram* than to murders and trials.

The rest represented a broad selection of occupations and life-styles: a maid from Homestead Air Force Base, a Cuban émigrée working as a bookkeeper for an exterminating company, a grocery store checker, a retired assistant principal, a clothing designer, an automotive vocational teacher, an awning installer, a janitor, a truck driver, and a mailroom employee for the *Miami Herald* who claimed he hadn't read about Bundy because "We don't have time to read the paper."

Reporters following the Bundy trial had been waiting for this moment for weeks. Judge Cowart had earlier ruled that when the jury was safely sequestered, dozens of depositions would become public. Some had been taken and sealed more than a year ago, and three in particular were the source of intense interest.

Newspaper and television people gathered in the clerk's office on the seventh floor to dig into the cardboard boxes. "Anybody finds Chapman, Bodiford, or Patchen, shout." By the end of the day, three recollections of Ted Bundy's conversations following his arrest in Pensacola—by three detectives who had sat up until dawn with him—would become headline news.

Norman Chapman's memory proved startlingly specific. "Fantasies are controlling part of my life," the detective claimed Ted had told them that night almost a year and a half before. It was the tip of Chapman's iceberg of recollections. At points in his deposition he recalled only the general drift of Bundy's conversation, at other points phrases and sentences Ted had spoken. In the Northwest, Chapman continued, Ted said he "made mental concessions to keep himself going because he was working with patients who had mental problems at Harborview in Seattle. But in order to control his fantasies, he had to do things which were very much 'against society' although the act itself was always a 'downer.'

"Guys, remember this," the detective quoted Ted. "It might be important later." Bundy, Chapman said, began an account of how his "problem" first surfaced in Seattle while he was walking along a street one night on the way to Melanie Pattisen's house. "There was a girl on the street ahead that aroused a feeling he'd never had before. He wanted to possess her by whatever means necessary and followed her home until she entered the house and he never saw her again.

"During his year at the University of Puget Sound Law School," as the detective summarized Bundy's words, "his grades suffered because he became a voyeur. While the other people in his car pool sat in class, he would walk the darkened streets of Tacoma peeping in windows." But, said Chapman, Ted had insisted he had mixed feelings about his voyeurism. "One night he was back in Seattle, walking the streets, when he saw someone else with their eyes glued to a window. Ted became so enraged, he chased the man several blocks." The detective recalled his own remark: "It's OK, as long as it's not your neighborhood."

Don Patchen's deposition added more detail. Bundy claimed an affinity for Volkswagens, Patchen testified, because they were economical and he could drive a long way on a little money. He seemed to be able to get along on very little sleep, Bundy told the detective, sometimes only three hours a night on a regular basis, using the early morning hours to drive for miles and miles.

"Sometimes I feel like a vampire," Patchen recalled him saying, "just driving all night long." Ted also said he preferred VWs because the seats would come out, and Bodiford's deposition contained the following word-for-word conversation:

"Well, why?" Bodiford inquired.
"Well, I can carry things easier that way."
"You mean you can carry bodies easier that way?"
"Well, let's just say I can carry cargo better that way."
"That cargo you carried, was it sometimes damaged?"
"Sometimes it was damaged, sometimes it wasn't."

That eerie February conversation eventually turned to his conviction for the Carol DaRonch kidnapping. Investigators hoped to bring the rambling, vague discussion down to specifics, they claimed, and asked him to confess to the crime. But Ted refused, saying he'd worked hard on the appeal and didn't want to ruin it. All he would say, the detective remembered, was that Carol DaRonch was "lucky she got away."

Ted believed in Colorado that he had learned to control

302

his problem during the two years in Utah and Colorado jails. While he was free for those five days after the first Aspen escape, Ted never reexperienced his problem. He told detectives that he'd run "some experiments" on himself during that period, which he refused to discuss in detail because of the "consequences," but he would say that he had done "certain things and no one came up missing," the detective recalled. Bundy's belief that he had conditioned himself to control his problem gave him hope that the next time he escaped, he could get along in the outside world.

But after the second dash for freedom, he told Chapman, his problem had recurred and "it wasn't controllable. I guess I have a fool for a doctor," he reportedly said. Reporters hustled for the telephones that afternoon, when Clerk Shirley Lewis closed the office, carrying more than enough quotes for an explosive story.

Margaret Good rose to her feet Monday morning, July 2, to argue a pretrial motion. There were some major battles to be fought for suppression of prosecution evidence that week, and Good, an appellate specialist, would figure prominently in them. The young lawyer wore her long blond hair brushed back off her face and fixed with barrettes behind her ears. Her manner with witnesses was not as polished and persuasive as that of the other lawyers, but her knowledge of legal precedents might have to save Ted Bundy from the electric chair.

The defense offered 15 minor motions before the main task got under way—the suppression of Nita Neary's eyewitness identification of Bundy. Even at this late stage of the trial, most of the motions pursued "discovery" of various police reports and evidence logbooks. The defense charged the prosecutors had not submitted a comprehensive list of suspects and confessions. Good went after every detail, down to the text of a confession written on the restroom wall of the Rose Printing Company in Tallahassee.

It would take three days to hear all the testimony and argument on the motion to supress Neary's testimony. Nancy Dowdy, Nita's Chi Omega roommate, topped the witness list Monday, and the prosecution traced her memory of events that night in the sorority house, from the moment Neary woke her to the horror of discovering a battered Karen Chandler in the hall. Again and again, Defense Attorney Robert Haggard explored exactly what Neary had said to Dowdy in describing the man she saw, particularly her comparisons of the intruder to Ricky Ramoya. "She told me," Dowdy testified, "that the man was about the same build as Ricky, but taller. That he was bigger and taller than Ricky Ramoya."

A string of police officers followed Nancy Dowdy to the stand. Neary, the court heard, had vacillated on the weight of the man (from 150 to 165 pounds), and on his age (from early twenties to mid to late twenties). One officer had interpreted her "dark complexion" remark to mean that the intruder could have been a "light-skinned black male."

But the highlight of the afternoon's testimony was Captain Poitinger. He'd brought along cassette tapes of Nita Neary's hypnotic session and the crucial photo lineup identification. Bob Haggard concentrated on the lack of certainty in Neary's final statement in April to the captain—"I don't know, a pretty definite resemblance"—and on her fixation on Ricky Ramoya under hypnosis. If the prosecution was going to base "half their case" on Neary's testimony, her degree of certainty would have to be more substantial, the defense charged.

The jury, resting in luxurious seclusion, heard none of the pretrial testimony and paid little attention to the news from Washington D.C., that day. The United States Supreme Court, in ruling on another case, had just found itself in substantial agreement with Ted Bundy. The Bundy defense had demanded all along that the potentially damaging pretrial hearings be closed to the public and press to prevent further prejudice to the defendant. Cowart had refused. In a 5-4 decision the Supreme Court declared it was impossible to measure with any degree of certainty the effect of such publicity on the fairness of a trial. Trial judges now had the discretionary power to close pretrial hearings to the public. Cowart had already sequestered the jury to prevent the taint of publicity. The Supreme Court decision would not directly affect Bundy in this trial.

Nita Neary ran a nervous hand through her hair and leaned back in the witness stand Tuesday morning. She fully expected an onslaught from the defense.

Prosecutor Larry Simpson set a calm pace as he led her through her various encounters with police. Yes, Neary admitted, she had seen a series of six newspaper photographs of Ted. "But they all looked different and none of them were profiles." Neither had the hypnosis tainted her memory, only "made things more clear." Finally, Simpson reached the crucial moment.

"Do you see that man in the courtroom today?"

"Yes, I believe I do."

"Your Honor," Simpson continued, "we ask the defendant to stand." But Haggard objected.

Having only Bundy stand, he said, was prejudicial and guaranteed an identification. Cowart ordered the spectators and press to stand as well. But the defense attorney objected again, arguing that her "I believe I do" testimony did not meet the test of certainty. The judge agreed. Neary was not allowed until later that afternoon on redirect examination to point a long, elegant finger at Ted Bundy. "I feel more certain at this moment," she testified, "than I have ever been before."

As the afternoon's cross-examination crept on, the logic of the defense's argument became more and more evident. Neary had had a couple of beers before returning home. The lighting in the Chi O foyer had been somewhat dim. The patterned wallpaper was not a good background for discerning a profile. Three to four seconds was not an adequate amount of time to ensure an accurate memory.

By midafternoon Nita Neary's fine features looked worn, and she rested her head in one hand while Haggard dissected every word, every response, often repeating a question several times from a slightly different perspective. Finally, Neary broke into tears.

"Your Honor, he keeps repeating and repeating the same questions." Tightly controlled frustration sharpened her voice. "How many times do I have to answer the same questions?"

Cowart spoke harshly about badgering a witness, but Haggard's only response seemed to be a newly developed tic in his cheek. Moments later he handed her the photo lineup Poitinger had shown her the previous April. But Haggard, undetected, had removed Ted's picture from the stack. Neary's brow furrowed when he asked her to pick out the proper photo.

"Mr. Haggard," Cowart roared, "I will see you in chambers if this type of questioning continues."

Before adjourning for the Fourth of July holiday, the court heard the testimony of a defense psychological expert. "Depending on conditions," said Dr. Robert Buckhout, "there is a lower limit of about three seconds below which it is highly unlikely that an accurate memory of an event can be formed. Buckhout, the defense elicited, once contracted with the army to study "weapon focus" and discovered that an observer tends to concentrate longer on a weapon than on the person carrying it. If Neary had seen the log, focusing primarily on it as a weapon, then the likelihood of her remembering a profile was very small.

Cowart planned to hear arguments about introducing as evidence the panty hose mask which Utah Highway Patrolman Bob Hayward had plucked from Ted's VW almost four years before, and more arguments on the motion to suppress Nita Neary's ID when court resumed two days later.

Theodore Bundy finally appeared as his own attorney Thursday—and his own witness. The double role was curious, like a pitcher who can throw with either arm. Under his jacket Ted wore a Seattle Mariners T-shirt like a vest. First he cross-examined Bob Hayward about his "traffic stop of the century" and then took the stand to contradict the trooper's testimony.

"Before I forget the $64,000 question," Ted said, "did you have a search warrant for my car?" Hayward replied that Bundy had told him to "go ahead" when he asked to search.

Jerry Thompson had flown from Utah to testify that Ted Bundy was a law student at the time and well aware of his rights, despite the fact that none of the policemen had bothered to read their Miranda cards to him before searching the vehicle.

Cowart wouldn't rule on the legality of the search, stating that the Utah Supreme Court had already declared it legal in their decision on the DaRonch kidnapping conviction appeal. He delayed ruling on whether the mask could be introduced later in the trial.

It was an apprehensive defense team that rose for Judge Cowart Friday morning. All week they'd chipped away at Nita Neary, and now they hoped that their tenaciously argued criticism of the investigation would end the trial before it had even begun.

But Cowart, in a long, carefully worded decision studded with legal citations, ruled that Nita Neary's identification had been obtained lawfully and was admissible. He believed that her description had remained essentially the same throughout its many repetitions, and seemed impressed with her testimony, at one point calling it "deliberative and careful."

The day had begun poorly for Ted Bundy's defense. But the schedule for that afternoon posed an even greater threat. Detectives Norman Chapman and Don Patchen would take the stand and relate their versions of Ted's Pensacola statements. With the jury out of the room, spectators and press would hear a long tape recording of a despondent Ted Bundy talking to police. Many had been waiting expectantly for this moment since the depositions were unsealed.

The crucial moment for the lawyers—and for Ted—would come when Cowart ruled if the jury could also hear the tapes. This trial could be over before it had even begun, all right, over with a conviction virtually assured.

31

The courtroom was hushed that afternoon, spectators and the press—but no jury during this suppression hearing—straining to hear through the static and crackle of the tape. At the defense table, a model of self-control, Bundy sat erect. Only his incessant straightening of a stack of papers on the table betrayed him.

It seemed odd that here, 660 miles and a year and a half away, the mood of these long sessions in a Pensacola office should be so effectively evoked. There was Chapman's voice, sincere and amiable through a haze of background noise. And Ted, cautious but persistent, testing the detectives. Again and again he worked around to discussing a deal.

Gradually a complete picture of those early morning conversations emerged from the testimony and the tapes, a picture of iron-willed detectives and the oblique, evasive answers of a man they thought was so close, so close to ending the long, transcontinental trail of murders and missing women.

Norman Chapman followed his colleague Don Patchen to the stand and repeated much of the testimony contained in the depositions unsealed a week before. He concentrated on two conversations, electronically bugged and taped by Captain Poitinger—one in Pensacola in the early hours of Saturday, February 18, and the other in Tallahassee, also early in the morning of Monday, February 20, 1978.

Chapman testified only in outline to the content of these later tapes. The transcripts themselves reveal a Ted Bundy drawing back from the emotional crisis of the first night after his capture. Bundy had a deal he wanted to propose, slouching into the familiar chair in the Pensacola police captain's office, and the three detectives could tell that something big was in the wind. That night, however, when Ted asked for the tape recorder to be turned off, they would be ready. Headphones in place, Jack Poitinger would catch every word in another room.

It was 12:30 before the exhaustive reading of the Miranda rights was completed and the four men settled down to talk.

"We'll let you go ahead," Patchen began, "and take it from there, like we did last night. How about it?"

"One of the reasons I asked to speak to Norm, since I heard you guys from Tallahassee are going to make it your case soon, was that he would be able to respond to anything I wanted. I wanted to make some phone calls because I felt it would be able to shake me loose on a lot of questions I feel inside."

"Do you still feel like you have a desire to do something you've never done before as far as getting things straight?" Chapman asked, gingerly testing Ted's mood.

"Yeah. I'm in a different place than I've ever been before," Ted replied. "I knew that talking to my attorneys tonight was going to change things. I sat down and said some things that I've never said to an attorney before." Chapman must have wished he'd been a Pensacola public defender at that moment. "Not that they know anything in particular," Ted went on, "but I mean I made some pretty strong statements." He stopped for a second and uttered a quick, astonished laugh.

"I've never done that before with an attorney. It's always been straight down the road. I've laid around today when I had the chance to develop some way that I could do this easily. Ah, well, not easily—there's no way to do this easily. But in a way that would be most satisfactory.

"And I came up with something I thought was very

comfortable. Laying in bed, I said to myself, 'Shoot, it's going to be easier than the dickens and it would all come out.' Again, I know what you want, but I'm interested in the whole thing, in everything. It's the whole ball of wax, and it's got to be dealt with."

"In other words," Chapman pressed him, "you're interested in everything from Seattle all the way down to Florida."

"Well, I'm interested in clearing up everything." Ted wasn't about to step in any snare. "And in giving answers to questions that would be helpful."

"You have admitted to yourself, Ted," Chapman prodded, "that this is a different situation than has ever happened before. You relate to us three. If you give us this statement to everything you've done, anywhere you're going to stand trial, we're going to be there."

"Well, it requires starting with somebody in Seattle to make some inquiries." Ted went on in broad, general terms about attorneys and police investigations in Washington and Utah. "I want them to know that I might be in a position to answer questions."

"You know the pressure was on us last night," Chapman put in. "Now there's no pressure at all. If there's any way we can comply with you, we'll do it, within reason." "Anything," the detective thought, "to keep Ted Bundy talking." "You told us last night, for example, that 'I've never told this to anyone else before.' So, we're starting off eight hours ahead of where we did last night."

"So where do you want to go from here?" Patchen picked up. "Do you want to start talking about this stuff and go through it? Or do you want to contact them first? Tell us what you want to do."

"Well, let's see. What is it I wanted to do? It's not as clear to me now as it was before."

"Did we confuse you?"

"No. It's just bringing it out and speaking it in so many words, as opposed to laying back and thinking about it. I'll give you some background and let's see if this makes sense." Ted mentioned a meeting with his public defenders earlier that evening and came to the point.

"My attorney's position is that all the state and you all want to do, besides solve these cases, is to execute me. And that would be the logical result of anything you were attempting to get from me, if indeed that's what you wanted. There's no doubt in their minds, given the laws of the state of Florida, that's what would happen if the guilty party were captured.

"They advocate a different point of view: going right down the line and eventually securing my freedom. I like these kinds of situations because it allows me to take—well, it doesn't allow me really anything.

"Now if I had my choice—and I don't necessarily—but if I sit back and think about how I would like the thing to resolve itself, everybody satisfied by getting all the answers to all the questions they want to ask, then after that was all over, I would like to be back in Washington State, because that's where my mother is, that's where my family is, and that's where I'm from."

"In other words," said Chapman, pouncing on the first concrete suggestion of the night, "you don't mind answering questions about anything you've done as long as the end result is you're back in Washington State so that you'll be in an institution close enough where your mother can visit you."

"That's what I'm saying. It's just being home, back where I was raised, being close to my family. Let's turn off the tape."

Jack Poitinger pressed the earphone closer to his ear. The transmitter mike wasn't working as well as it should. As the conversation became tense at certain points, voices fading in the background interference, the Leon County captain of detectives strained to catch every word. Later, an audio expert in Gainesville would enhance the tape, but it would never attain the quality police hoped for.

The three detectives facing Ted in the other room were dismayed also. What Bundy wanted was an extremely complex deal, perhaps impossible. Almost as soon as it was mentioned, they began to back off. Chapman spoke forcefully:

"If I had the authority right this minute to say, Ted, you give us a recorded, detailed statement of everything you've ever been involved in, and in return we will assure you that what incarceration takes place will take place in Washington State, I'd do it. Could you then bring yourself to give us the information that we need, could you at that point sit down and say, 'Yes, I agree to those terms,' and sit down and tell us?"

"Yes."

Norman Chapman hadn't expected such a quick answer.

310

Now he had to backpedal again. The political realities of making a deal like that with Ted Bundy were just too overwhelming. The detective would have to find some other way.

"Ted, let me tell you right now. You're asking for the world and you know it."

"I'm asking for a complex situation . . ."

"Is there any other way that it can be worked out? Because I can tell you the truth—what little bit I know about laws, and we're dealing with God knows how many states—the chances are it ain't ever going to happen."

"There may be, but I haven't thought of it yet."

"Washington was the first place you started," Chapman said, trying another tack. "Is this correct? These are the people who ultimately want you back the most in your mind, and this is where you want to go back?"

"Well, Washington has a lot of questions to ask me."

"Right."

"And I've got a lot of answers, too."

"OK. If we could work something out where we would extradite you back to Washington and have you stand trial for those charges and then come from there back to here . . ."

"I'm not talking about trials. What I'm talking about there would be no need for trials."

"In other words, you would plead nolo contendere to these charges?"

"It would be very satisfying to all parties concerned," Ted replied as Chapman laughed weakly. Ted seemed so direct, but what did he really mean? What was he saying? "I know it sounds rather complex," Bundy went on, "but it just seems to work for me now. OK, Ted Bundy wants something out of this and maybe that's not right and maybe he doesn't deserve it—and in a way that's true. But still I've got to take care of my own survival. Ted Bundy wants to survive, too. I have many responsibilities, as I've told you before, to my parents—and that's part of it. The second part is getting out of the limelight as quickly as possible without all these horrendous trials."

"Right."

"And getting close, back close to my parents, and giving the knowledge and peace of mind that can be returned to people who don't know what happened."

"To their loved ones . . .?"

311

"Who don't know what happened," Ted persisted.

The conversation turned for several minutes to the danger Ted faced if he were ever released; someone was sure to be out for him on the streets. But Norman Chapman kept returning to the hopelessness of a multistate deal.

"You know you're asking for more than we can give." Chapman stopped to collect his thoughts. "There's a lot of people who are heartbroken because of missing people they don't know what happened to. You could ease a lot of people's minds. They're going to be heartbroken anyway, but at least their minds would get eased. They'll be able to make decent burials and so forth, and set things right."

"Yeah, but I want to be in a position to make contributions beyond that. And this requires being in Washington."

"There are lives that are gone and lives that are destroyed that could be refilled, and Ted Bundy is the only person in this world that can begin the reconstruction of the lives—those mothers, fathers, sisters, and brothers," Chapman ran on.

"It's up to me to release the information I have and I want to do that in a way that's satisfactory to me. I'm not asking to be back on the streets, but I don't have a death wish either."

Chapman took a long breath. "Ted, how many people have been executed in the United States in the last ten years?"

"Gary Gilmore."

"The only reason he got it was because he begged for it. A guy from Leon County had his death warrant signed, hell, a year ago, and he's still sitting down in Raiford." Chapman suddenly switched gears again. "There must be some other way," he thought. "Are you familiar with Florida's mentally disordered sex offenders statute, whereby people who commit sexual-type crimes are treated in a special light? They're prosecuted with the intention in mind to rehabilitate, if possible. And if not, to confine them in mental institutions where they can live and exist and won't hurt others or themselves." Don Patchen and Steve Bodiford hunted for a copy of the statute in a bookcase. Ted watched them a moment, then turned back to Chapman.

"It's not the same as last night, Norm. I'm not emotional the way I was last night. Obviously, I'm coming at you differently tonight."

"Right."

"I wanted to get it all off my chest last night, and out of the way. I wasn't getting down to specifics or details. But decisions were made, and I recognize my responsibilities."

"You perceive the goal," Patchen interjected, "and you just have to pick the route to get to that goal."

"Exactly. Now I'm trying to avoid infuriating you, believe me. I don't mean to be saying this is the way it's going to be, because I can't do that. There's one thing I know for sure: that I've got the answers here and they're mine and they're for me to give. I want to get to the point where it would be the best all around, not excluding me. I still place a value on myself."

"Let me ask you this, if you can answer, of course." Don Patchen picked up the thread of the conversation. "Can you answer how many states we're going to be concerned with, so we know how wide a range we are looking at?"

"Well, I think you'd be talking about investigations in six states. I'm not sure about that, all right? I'm going to have somebody check it."

"Whew!" Patchen exhaled. "Six."

"Some of them don't even know they're involved, so I suppose they would be left out initially."

Chapman felt they were onto something specific again, something specific at last. "If a person was to estimate . . ." he led in.

"Let's not get into that part right now."

Sensing a rhythm, Chapman obliged, turning to the book of Florida statutes and pointing out the section he wanted Ted to read. There was a pause while Ted scanned the page. Chapman kidded Patchen about his smelly feet. Finally Bundy looked up and said he needed the case law in order to interpret the statute.

"Which section is it that you feel doesn't apply to you?" Chapman asked.

"You will get the answers to your questions when I'm satisfied. I'm not going to say what the answers will be." Ted continued a moment, but he'd shut the door in Chapman's face again. This time the detective pushed back.

"Tell us where the little girl is," he whispered. They all knew he meant Kimberly Leach. "At least let the parents have the satisfaction of burying their daughter and going on with their lives. Tell us, Ted!"

Bundy leaned back in his chair and began playing with an empty pack of Winstons on the desk. Suddenly he crumpled it and threw it hard on the floor. "But I'm the most cold-hearted son of a bitch you'll ever meet."

"Ted, if you will tell me where the body is, I will go get it and let the parents know that the child is dead."

"I can't do that to you, because the sight is too horrible to look at."

"Is there a little girl dead?"

"Well, you gentlemen knew that you were getting involved with a pretty strange creature. And you have known it for days."

It was nearly dawn. The three detectives had worked hard, worked Ted Bundy right up to the edge, they thought. But he wasn't about to jump.

"You people are just anxious for a confession," he said.

"Don't, don't do that. You're covering now. I'm still of the opinion you have made a start," Chapman pleaded.

"This story is one that I have always intended to give to you, and a psychologist or psychiatrist. I'm a psychologist," Bundy said, "and it really gives me insight."

"You have made a start, Ted. Why wait? This is the first chapter, so don't stop now. The book's on the mount, so go ahead. You apparently have come to the point now where you can at least talk about the first chapter, and that's a great stride forward."

"I do think it would be an important thing to have it for psychologists, psychiatrists, but I don't see the pertinence right now. The understanding that you may achieve through this knowledge of my behavior is not directly related to criminal behavior. In the future you may read it in a book."

"Ted, I don't want to read it out of a book. Don't shut us out now."

"I'm not shutting you out. I'm quite prepared to talk to investigators. I'm in the same place I was yesterday."

It was time, Chapman sensed again, to reset the pace. Ted had requested to be allowed to phone Melanie Pattisen in Seattle. Chapman acceded, and sat back to wait.

"Ted, you talked to Melanie," Chapman began when Ted hung up. "Apparently, she is in agreement that you should go ahead and clear the air of some of these things. So why don't you go ahead and do it and quit stalling? What you're asking for can't be done."

"Well, that's why I want to talk to my friends, and find out who's investigating these cases."

"Last night I really felt it, but tonight you haven't been as open with us as you were last night." Chapman's voice was warm and coaxing.

"I know."

"It scares the living shit out of me, to be quite honest with you."

"You heard the conversation I just had with Melanie?"

"Yeah, but I didn't hear what she said. She could have told you to lead those guys on as long as you can and then escape the first chance you get."

"I told you straight."

The detectives exchanged looks, and Steve Bodiford jumped in. "All right. The goddamn politicians ain't gonna deal. You were a politician of sorts—you understand politics— and when it comes right down to a politician getting a vote, he's gonna get the vote. And that's one of the problems I'm having right now. The sheriff is on my captain's ass, and my captain is beginning to put pressure on me to put pressure on you. I've been telling him that that's not the way to talk to you and I'm not going to do it. But you're asking for a deal that can't be made."

"Well, why won't it work? It won't work in Florida—is that what you're telling me?"

"How is the state attorney in Salt Lake City going to justify never prosecuting Ted Bundy and allowing him to be incarcerated in another state?"

" 'Cause he gets a lot of answers."

"He gets a lot of answers, but those answers are just going to make the problem worse. It would be political suicide for a district attorney or prosecuting attorney or state attorney to even consider dealing with Ted Bundy."

"I've got the answers," Ted said firmly, "and the answers are mine to give. That's a hard-ass position, I know, but I just want to save the horse. If it doesn't work, Steve, it doesn't work." Bodiford blew out his breath, and Chapman once again tried to put the interrogation on track.

"Ted, I think you have talked to Melanie the way you're talking to us now, and I think Melanie and you have agreed that you need to get it all cleared up."

"That's correct."

"She realizes the magnitude of what we're talking about, maybe not all of it, but she realizes that you're involved in it."

"And she knows no details."

"There's no more you can do for her."

But he had other friends, Ted said. "I've got a plan."

"Ted, I ain't trying to antagonize you, or make you mad, but where along the line do you figure you have deserved a break? Or have earned one? There's a supply of a lot of people in this world that you could give a break to."

"I know where you're coming from. And I knew that taking the position of mine would arouse a response. I told you that I'm not asking to be cut loose."

"You have been around long enough to know that no matter what you do, whether you tell us or not, Ted Bundy is gonna look bad."

"Well, I know there are no guarantees, but they think I don't care. I want to guarantee myself the chance to talk with psychologists."

"You ain't gonna have to worry about that. Every doctor in this country would give his left nut to talk to you."

"Are you personally going to tell us about your things?" Patchen demanded quietly.

"Slowly and truthfully," Chapman chimed in.

"True, person to person," Patchen persisted.

"On tape?" Bundy sneered. "I haven't confessed and I'm not going to. And I'm not going to answer any questions about your situation in Tallahassee."

"Sooner or later," Patchen warned, "you're gonna be charged and put back in jail. And then you're gonna revert and say to hell with y'all, and everybody loses that way."

"Yep."

Perhaps it was the realization that Ted had withdrawn totally, that there was no future to the night's ramblings, but Norman Chapman burst out in a torrent. For 15 minutes he talked, pressuring, pounding, almost arguing, it seemed at times, with himself.

"Tallahassee's case hasn't even got started. All we're doing is just talking. I don't know what they've done. OK, this is hypothetical. If you go back to Utah, they can put you back in a cell, and you sit there, and nobody's ever gonna know what you know because you're already hurting. Nobody'll ever know the peculiarities or the particulars about your type of personality so that we can stop this again. No, not from you, but say another individual comes up out of the billions of people here on this earth. Out of the 200 million people here in the United States, we will never be able to spot them.

"Your purpose in life is to go back to Washington, have these psychologists pick you apart and be able to take a profile of you. But if you go back to Utah, they're not gonna do this. You said before that they know you from day one, but they don't really because you were psychoanalyzing them as they were psychoanalyzing you. You let them know exactly what you wanted them to know, and they said you were normal. But they don't know what you've done. Nobody knows but you. And they're gonna stick you in a cell, and your purpose in life will be defeated.

"There are people that would crawl on their hands and knees to get a crack at you. I think that's the reason you don't want to go back to Utah, because you know Utah is gonna get you before you can give yourself a chance."

"I'm not afraid to die," Ted said.

"But we're not talking about you being afraid to die. You're afraid you're gonna go before your story gets told."

"Sure."

"That's right. And Ted Bundy will have lived for nothing. See, the only out you have right now, Ted, the only out you have as far as believing in a supreme being or anything like that is to tell your story so that nobody else will get in the same situation you're in."

But Ted remained unconvinced. The more they pressured, the farther he withdrew, insisting that he wanted to give his "deal" a try.

"It ain't gonna work, Ted. They ain't gonna meet those deals," Patchen said. "Our case in Tallahassee is just beginning. We may develop a case and then we ain't gonna turn you loose. But if we don't, then Utah will, or Colorado. We don't have time to fuck around and try to make deals that we know from the beginning we can't make."

"I don't believe it is so impossible."

Norman Chapman raised his voice in frustration. "It would be the greatest loss we have ever had if you don't come up with this information so these people can talk to you. As far as criminal psychology is concerned, you are the man. You know that? You have known it for how long? How long have you known that, Ted?"

"Known what?"

"We sat over here the other day and you started telling me about how easy it was to escape from places. You told me you'd be out of here in no time at all. And it has bothered me for two days. Why would a man who is facing what

317

you're facing want to tell a police officer that he can get out of this place in no time at all?"

"I sat alone in that examination room without handcuffs on," Ted said wearily, but the detective wasn't really paying attention.

"I've got two of the prettiest little blondheaded daughters that you'll ever see. And they're gonna grow up, and I don't want nothing to happen to them. 'Cause I couldn't live with it. And now I'm in a position to say Ted could do something that would help me and my daughters. The chances are slim, but the chances are there.

"I don't want to see my daughters hurt. 'Cause they mean more to me than my life. I'd gladly give mine in exchange for theirs. I can relate to how some of these parents feel, 'cause it's a really special feeling between a father and a little girl. So, I want to help all the little girls in the world.

"I want you to tell me right now. I want you to start with Chi Omega. Tell me how it felt when you walked in there. When you knew you were going to kill. Come on, Ted, open up! Talk! You talked to us before. Tell me what it was that caused you to go in there?"

"I can't talk about it. I'd be a fool."

"You'd be a fool, yeah, you'd be a fool."

"I can't talk about it."

"You'd be a fool that was helping more people than he could ever imagine. So tell me about it."

"I can't talk about this situation."

"Yes you can, Ted! I believe you can. I believe at this point you have made up your mind that you are going to, and I believe you can. So go ahead, Ted. Tell us why, tell us what urged you to want to go into the Chi Omega house."

"I tried to help you understand me," Ted said softly. "I tried to help you understand me a little bit more."

"We can understand your position. You don't have to explain. Everybody can understand Ted Bundy—a man who does things he regrets, but can't stop himself. Start with the Chi O house. Don't stop when you're so close. Tell me which door you went in. Start some place, Ted!"

"I don't know anything about the Chi Omega house. I don't know anything about your investigation in Tallahassee. I want you to understand me, but that's not going to happen right now." His voice was strong again. "I have resigned myself to answer questions when the time is right, but I haven't allowed myself to choke. I want to survive, and it's still very strong, and it's normal."

"Ted, if you didn't want to tell us your story, you wouldn't even be fucking with us."

"I know it, goddamnit."

Jack Poitinger had heard enough. Flipping off the earphones, he charged into the interrogation room just as Bundy picked up the phone, once again, to call another friend out west to arrange his "deal."

"Go ahead," snapped Poitinger, grabbing the receiver from Ted's hand, "take him back. I think we've reached the point now where Mr. Bundy is no longer going to be in the driver's seat."

It was a discouraged Detective Chapman who ushered Ted back to his cell early that morning. He had come so close, without the prize. Ted, too, seemed to sense that a fork in the road had been passed, an opportunity lost.

"Norman," Ted began as the door clanged shut behind him, "I realize I will never function in society again. I don't want to escape, but if I get the chance, I will. I want you to be professional enough to see that I never get the chance."

Ted Bundy had been transported to Tallahassee that weekend, and it didn't take him long to sense what he was up against. The Leon County jail, a boxy, well-kept facility on the outskirts of town, looked escape-proof. Sheriff Katsaris was filling the local papers with tough talk about this hot new suspect in the Chi Omega case. Even the room they'd reserved for interrogation, a tiny nurse's office, looked grim. It was an equally tough-talking Ted Bundy who asked to speak with Chapman and Bodiford early Monday morning, February 20.

The first thing he told detectives was that he was strongly considering acting as his own attorney. "When I'm confined like this," he said, "the best way for me to stay together is to become involved."

Chapman nodded and began easing Ted around to the subject of Saturday's conversation. But it was not the same as Pensacola. With the move east, it seemed, everything had changed.

"As I was laying in that cell last night," he explained, "I started to get that old spirit back—to just fight it. I saw

319

the front page of the newspaper today, a little box about Katsaris. It said, 'We're no longer gonna play by his rules.' What does this man mean by these things?"

"I read it too," Bodiford said ruefully, "and I did some real enough begging this afternoon."

But Ted had made up his mind about Sheriff Katsaris in a hurry. "I don't want to see him. There are people that become bad guys to me real quick." The discussion returned to the tense situation in Tallahassee and the storm of publicity already in the newspapers.

"You see, now I'm really in the public eye. I'm going to court for appearances and this whole thing. You all know that it's important how people perceive me. Now they've got Theodore Bundy out there, master of disguise, Ten Most Wanted List, involved in x number of things.

"I've got to show them that I can stand up in a court of law and run these people ragged. That I'm not a fiend, necessarily. That's not all there is to me. I've got to show them that I'm more. That's really important to me, that I'm more."

"We know that," Bodiford said.

Ted reflected on the nights in Pensacola and commended the detectives. But it was clear Ted Bundy felt in control again.

"Hey, there have been a lot of investigators trying to get me for a long time, and I wouldn't even sit in the same room with them. There was a certain couple of days there—that first night it was a matter of walking right up to the edge and looking over. Not that the prospect of really getting down is gonna be particularly thrilling, but there was a thrill in that—maybe just the thrill of getting it off my chest. I got right up to the edge each time, and nobody could've pushed me over. It was a matter of me pushing myself over. Falling over."

The detectives knew there wasn't much hope now. "Do you have less remorse, feel less responsibility now?" Chapman ventured.

"It's not that I believe I'm gonna get out of everything, and be back on the streets someday," Ted replied.

Steve Bodiford agreed, and ran through a long accounting of the credit card and auto theft charges. Surely, he said, Ted knew they were going to stack as much time on him as possible.

"I understand that feeling to fight back," Bodiford added. "Everybody's got it."

"One of the reasons is that I screwed my life over. I did it and nobody else," Bundy declared. "But still, I've always wanted to be an attorney. And now, I've got this particular satisfaction of getting up there and doing it, and I know I've been doing it fairly well. Maybe it's a Walter Mitty kind of thing. It's not the publicity. I'd rather do it if there wasn't a reporter for a hundred miles. It's just that with a man like the state prosecutor, with all his skill and training, that a guy with a year and a half of law school can let the air out of his tires. We're not talking about right or wrong. We're not talking about conscience or duties anymore."

The session in the nurse's office was over shortly, but Norm Chapman, an ordinary detective from a southern city who'd stumbled on the most astonishing suspect of his career, just couldn't let go, and followed Ted back to his armor-plated cell.

"Ted, I'm fixin' to leave, and the likelihood of this thing ever being worked out is pretty small. I just want to know, you know, how big a case I've been working on. I just want to know how many problems you have, or how many times you have been involved in this problem?"

"I can't tell you."

"Ted, are we talking about two-digit figures or three-digit figures?"

"We're talking about three-digit figures."

"Are we talking about more than a hundred or less than two hundred?"

"I'm not answering any more questions."

Spectators in Judge Cowart's court that day heard only a portion of the conversations between Bundy and the detectives back in February 1978. Even with the transcripts and Poitinger's bug, there was only a partial document of the interrogations.

And that was precisely the problem the judge faced. If these highly suggestive, sometimes explosive conversations were going to qualify as evidence to be heard by the jury, he had to be certain the record of them was a fair and accurate one. And he had to be sure the defendant's rights had not been violated in the course of obtaining that record.

Clearly it was a difficult decision—a decision that could very well tip the balance of the trial.

32

"Disaster with a capital D," Prosecutor Dan McKeever told reporters in the hallway Saturday morning. McKeever was fond of overstatment, but this time his face looked pale and blank. Judge Cowart had just handed down his most important ruling so far in the case.

After a string of lawyers from the Pensacola public defender's office described Assistant State Attorney Ron Johnson's refusal to admit Ted's lawyers during the interrogation, the judge granted the defense's motion to suppress the tapes.

"The court is concerned about two things in this matter," Cowart began. "I can't understand an assistant state attorney saying 'I'm not going to let you in' to the defendant's counsel. Second, I can't discern when this tape recorder was turned on and off. A lot went on that's not on this tape, and the possibility of picking and choosing exists. If your tape had been on the entire time, I would have admitted it. But I cannot discern when the statements were given."

A broad grin spread across Ted Bundy's face at the defense table. It was a major victory, the defense's first that week, but there was more to worry about just ahead. After a lengthy debate on whether to separate prosecution of the Chi Omega killings from the Dunwoody Street assault, which Cowart denied, opening arguments were scheduled for that afternoon.

Late Friday night, defense lawyers moved to delay opening arguments until Monday, to allow them more time to prepare. The judge refused: "There's not been a case in the second circuit that has been so protracted," Cowart declared. "The defendant does not control the flow of the proceeding. Motion denied. I see no reason to wait."

"I do, Your Honor." Ted Bundy jumped to his feet. "Because my attorneys are not ready. They're totally unprepared. They haven't even begun work on an opening statement."

"Opening arguments will be heard Saturday at 1:00 p.m.," Cowart replied calmly.

"Then start it without me, Your Honor," Ted shot back.

"That's fine, Mr. Bundy," Cowart said as he stepped lightly down off the bench.

Bob Haggard shook his head to a crowd of reporters later. Cowart will have him chained to the chair, he said, if Bundy doesn't show for opening arguments.

The 12 men and women who Ted Bundy hoped would save his life looked rested from a week in their Sonesta Beach resort hotel. Cowart leaned over toward the lawyers as the jury took their assigned seats and whispered happily, "They always lend color to the courtroom."

"Poll the jury, Mr. Watson," and with those words the long-awaited, long-delayed trial of Theodore Robert Bundy began.

"Good afternoon, ladies and gentleman." Larry Simpson smiled as he wheeled the court's blackboard over in front of the jury box. He would be brief and direct in his opening argument, priming the jury to focus on and interpret the evidence the prosecution would present. First, Simpson listed seven charges the state was seeking: two counts of first-degree murder for Lisa Levy and Margaret Bowman; three of attempted murder for Kathy Kleiner, Karen Chandler, and Cheryl Thomas; and two of burglary with assault for entering Chi Omega and the Dunwoody Street apartment. Burglary with assault is one of the more serious crimes in Florida, carrying a sentence of up to 30 years.

Carefully, slowly, Larry Simpson traced the state's version of the events on January 15, 1978, following each girl home from her date, then describing Nita Neary's experience and the physical evidence discovered at the two crime scenes. For the first time Simpson revealed that two hairs from the panty hose mask found on Cheryl Thomas's bed were "microscopically similar to those of the defendant, Theodore Bundy." The jury would also hear, he said, two forensic odontologists state that Ted Bundy made the bite marks on the buttocks of Lisa Levy.

When Simpson finished, the blackboard was a maze of chalk marks and key words. Three times he had dramatically pointed to an impassive Ted Bundy. The faces of the jurors were equally inscrutable.

"Good to see you back again, ladies and gentlemen," Bob Haggard began. "The prosecution has spent a good deal of time telling you how this crime was committed," Haggard said forcefully. "The true question, ladies and gentleman, is not that a crime was committed, but who committed it." Haggard's voice rose as he leaned farther over the podium directly in front of the jury. "The true issue is: did Ted Bundy commit these crimes—and no other man," the defense attorney shouted at the jurors, "beyond a reasonable doubt."

"Objection."

"Sustained."

It set the tone for Haggard's opening argument. Chosen at the last minute, the Miami lawyer delivered a 45-minute tirade, drawing 34 separate objections from the prosecution. How, courtroom observers wondered, could a jury pick up the thread of the defense arguments between the cries of "Objection," "Sustained"?

Calling Nita Neary's identification "manufactured" (and earning another rebuke from Cowart), Haggard sketched the history of her eyewitness identification, from that first frightened statement to police on January 15 to the day in October that she saw Ted for 20 minutes in a Tallahassee courtroom. As for the physical evidence—bite marks and the newly revealed hair samples—the defense stressed that such evidence was not like fingerprints and could not be used for identification "beyond a reasonable doubt."

"You've got to ring their bell," said Haggard later as an explanation for his overbearing opening argument. But the other members of Ted's defense team were increasingly dissatisfied with his courtroom manner. It's possible, they believed, to "ring their bell" without antagonizing the jury, without making enemies of the very people who would sit in judgment later.

The testimony opened on Monday, July 9, with the prosecution parading 14 witnesses before the jury in seven hours. Each added a little block of evidence to the edifice Larry Simpson was constructing. Neary's roommate Nancy Dowdy and police officers Oscar Brannon, Ray Crew, and William Newkirk painted a lurid picture of discovering the sorority house crime.

For the first time, too, the jury saw Ted Bundy, the would-be lawyer, in action. "Did you say anything to Kathy Kleiner?" a composed, professional-looking defendant cross-examined Ray Crew. "Or Karen Chandler?" Ted probed Crew's memory for the bloody scene in Margaret Bowman's room. Although Bob Haggard objected bitterly to the prosecution's graphic description of the murdered women, Ted Bundy pursued the details with equal vigor. "How did you open the door to Miss Bowman's room," he asked, "with your right hand?" "Describe the scene." "Was her mouth open? Her eyes?"

Ted continued, unflustered, demanding to know why Crew's BOLO had included a "light-skinned black male."

After more horrifying detail added by the Tallahassee medical technicians who testified that afternoon, Simpson called Kathy Kleiner DeShields and Karen Chandler to the stand. It was the women's presence, more than their testimony, that was intended to make an impact on the jury. Kathy, attractive, vivacious, married just the month before, explained to the jury that she still carried a steel pin in her jaw and several loose teeth. There were no visible scars. Neither woman had any memory of that night.

"The next thing I remember after going to sleep," Karen Chandler said, "was being lifted into an ambulance." The defense did little cross-examination during the afternoon. Better to have these women out of the courtroom as fast as possible.

Out in the hall, during a recess, the two victims joked and traded stories with their Chi Omega sisters. "Hey, you look like you need a medic," Kleiner teased one of her friends, obviously in the last stages of a pregnancy, "and I know a good one."

Prosecutor Dan McKeever had not yet conceded defeat on the suppression of the Pensacola transcripts. Seeing a loophole in the judge's suppression ruling, he had prepared another motion. By limiting themselves to the earlier tape-recorded statements, he argued—before the Pensacola public defenders were turned away at the door—Ted's rights would not be violated. Cowart was still not convinced.

The judge followed that with another decision damaging the prosecution the next day. The panty hose mask confiscated from Ted's Volkswagen four years before could not be used to connect Bundy to a similar mask found at the Dunwoody apartment.

"There is every similarity," Dan McKeever argued, "between not only the murder weapons we found at Chi Omega, but also the panty hose found at Dunwoody. There's a similarity in the knots and a similarity in the eyeholes. And we can explain the remoteness in time. Mr. Bundy has not been out on the streets since then, except when he escaped fifteen days before this crime."

"I have reviewed the panty hose evidence," Cowart said evenly, "and the court is not satisfied that it has attained the credibility that would be necessary upon which its use could be made."

The defense was jubilant. The prosecution's case had now been whittled away to only two pieces of evidence connecting Ted Bundy to Chi Omega—Neary's identification and the bite-mark comparisons. Any juror would have to be somewhat skeptical of a three-second sighting. And the bite-mark analysis, the defense would say repeatedly, had no "objective standards."

After spending the morning studying Sergeant Winkler's gruesome crime scene and autopsy photographs, the jury must have found Medical Examiner Thomas Wood's courtroom testimony almost mild. In the stilted, abstract jargon of a coroner, Wood told jurors that both women had probably died of strangulation, holding up the bloodstained panty hose "ligature" removed from Margaret Bowman's neck. But if Wood's technical language puzzled the jury, forensic serologist Richard L. Stephens's account of his blood tests on 58 exhibits must have been stupefying. Using blood samples from the four women at Chi Omega, Stephens proved that Lisa Levy and Margaret Bowman were bludgeoned before Kleiner and Chandler.

But Defense Attorney Lynn Thompson picked up on a remark the serologist made about a large semen stain found on Cheryl Thomas's bedsheet. Stephens explained his tests of the stain for the presence of antigens which indicate blood types (A, B, AB, and O). They had proved negative— no antigens present. The serologist had also looked for a blood enzyme (called PGM) in the stain and had not found it. Based on the two tests, he declared his attempt to determine the assailant's blood characteristics "inconclusive." Either something was wrong with his testing, which was unlikely, or these blood chemicals had deteriorated during the three months Thomas's bedsheet lay in a paper bag in his evidence locker.

But Thompson challenged the finding. Wasn't it true, he demanded, that 20 percent of the population does not secrete the A-B-O antigens into other bodily fluids? Wasn't it possible that the man who attacked Cheryl Thomas was one of those nonsecreters?

Everyone secretes the PGM enzyme, the serologist responded. With the enzyme missing, he said, the A-B-O antigen had in all likelihood been destroyed with it.

With all the lengthy and persistent questioning of Richard Stephens that day, the scientific testimony was clearly losing some of the jurors. It had been a long week for everyone. Friday morning's announcement came both as a surprise and a relief: Ted Bundy was ill. A jail physician had examined him early that morning, and Cowart told the court the defendant had a "communicable viral infection" and would need at least 48 hours to recover.

Monday, July 16. The jury, having finished a crash course in forensic serology, was about to learn the mysteries of microscopic hair examination. Patricia Lasko, a hair microscopist from the Florida Department of Criminal Law Enforcement crime lab, took the stand. By now, Larry Simpson's trial tactics with scientific experts had become clear: question them exhaustively about professional qualifications to establish their expertise, then elicit a strong conclusion.

Lasko had examined several bagfuls of hair vacuumed from the two crime scenes, but Simpson was particulary interested in three hairs—the three plucked from the panty hose mask. One was an animal hair, but the other two, Lasko concluded, were "microscopically similar to the standards of Mr. Bundy." Cautioning that hair comparisons were not like fingerprints—"I have not examined all the hairs of everyone in the whole world"—Lasko went on to state a forceful conclusion: "Either those hairs came from Mr. Bundy, or from someone else whose hair is exactly like his who happened to have been at the Dunwoody apartment."

While Ted flipped testily through an FBI publication, *Don't Miss a Hair*, Bob Haggard attacked Pat Lasko's qualifications. Only admitted in a trial court as an expert three times before, Lasko was a relative newcomer to the field of hair analysis. She'd had a year of on-the-job training and a seminar at FBI headquarters in Quantico. Haggard dissected her procedures, repeatedly criticizing her for not examining a cross section of the hairs, and nearly earning a contempt citation in the process. Finally he

327

requested a detailed description of the specific "morphological characteristics" of Ted's hairs, peering at Lasko's notes and finally grabbing them away from her.

Larry Simpson was on his feet in an instant, wrestling the notes back from the defense attorney. The two faced off and glared at each other in front of the witness stand.

"Take the jury out, Mr. Watson," Cowart bellowed. "I approve of good strong advocacy from counsel," the judge began in an unruffled voice after the jury were safely ensconced in their soundproof chamber, "but if I get any more problems like this one, I'll see you both after court today." Cowart had mastered the minor explosion in a line. He smiled impishly at the prosecutor: "Let me congratulate you, Mr. Simpson. This is the first time I've seen you with your dander up."

Still more scientific testimony awaited the jury after returning from their brief exile. But when a fingerprint technician who had checked Bundy's room at the Oak announced he had not discovered a single "latent print" inside, several jurors leaned forward in their seats. From telltale marks on the desk, the technician concluded that "somebody had wiped the room clean." But in the meticulous cleaning, only the outside door jamb was overlooked, and there, on the top, was a single index fingerprint—Ted Bundy's.

Coupled with the testimony of Leon County Deputy Keith Daws and Pensacola Patrolman David Lee, the state had now effectively painted the image of a man "in flight from prosecution." They had conjured a Ted Bundy who wiped his room of every fingerprint—a room, not far from the Chi Omega house, that he had occupied in January 1978. Now they were ready to place him on the night of the murders, awake and away from his room at the Oak.

Carla Black, a red-haired FSU sociology student, was out dancing at Sherrod's, a disco located next door to the Chi Omega sorority house, on the night of January 14, 1978. Suddenly she noticed a man staring intently at her.

"It made me very uncomfortable," Black testified, "like he didn't really want to talk to me. Like he was looking right through me."

"Have you ever had men look at you before in a bar, Miss Black?" Margaret Good inquired. Earlier in the trial, Good had referred to "the scared young girl from Tallahassee syndrome."

328

"I can usually handle that." Carla Black smiled politely. "But I couldn't handle this."

Moments later, Carla Black identified Ted Bundy as the man who had stared at her.

Connie Hastings and Mary Ann Picano were also at Sherrod's that night. Chatting near a table, Hastings noticed a man with "greased-back hair, his arms folded, scanning girls on the dance floor." She remembered that he looked older than a college student and was wearing a dark, waist-length jacket. He approached Picano, a stylish, beautiful brunette, for a dance, but she initially refused.

"I'm about to dance with an ex-con," Picano whispered to her friend when the man persisted.

Hastings also pointed out Ted Bundy in the courtroom.

Mary Ann Picano was the last of the "scared young girls from Tallahassee" to testify. "I had a really scared feeling. And I regretted the whole thing." She couldn't identify the man, she explained, having stared at her feet till the dance was over.

Margaret Good was openly skeptical. Why had police waited five months (in one instance, *nine*) to obtain the identifications? Each girl had seen photographs of Bundy in the newspapers by then. Furthermore, she asked, hadn't they told police the man had had a rough face, like "acne scars or someone who was unshaven"?

Monday was the first day in which testimony before the jury had actually connected Ted Bundy with the crime. But even at that, the connection consisted of no more than the statement of a hair examiner and testimony that Bundy had been next door three hours before the murders. During the next two days, Larry Simpson, who'd saved his best for last, would go to the heart of his case—Nita Neary and the bitemark evidence. It promised to be a strong finish.

But when court came to order on Tuesday morning, Ted Bundy was not behind the defense table. Instead, on the stand, was a jailer. At one o'clock that morning, he explained to a scowling Judge Cowart, the defendant had flung an orange at a hallway light, scattering glass across two cells. When guards arrived to escort him to court, Bundy was sprawled out on his cot, toilet paper stuffed in the cell door lock. Coward dispatched the court reporter and bailiff to bring Ted to the courtroom, and Ted sent back his response: "Tell the judge to hold his robes. I'm coming."

"The court has already found you in contempt," Cowart

told Bundy when he finally appeared in a gray pin-striped suit, "and I want to tell you something, young man. This court is not going to follow your schedule."

"I apologize to the court," Bundy said in an unapologetic voice, and shortly worked himself up about his jail conditions, consultation time, and some files he claimed Katsaris had never sent from Tallahassee. He slapped a pad on the defense table and gestured toward the judge.

"Don't shake your finger at me!" Cowart's jowls trembled. "Don't shake your finger at me, young man." Ted continued shaking, but turned his hand to the side. "That's fine," the judge said, regaining his composure, "you can shake your finger at Mr. Haggard."

"He probably deserves it better than you do," Ted replied.

The odd exchange grew even more sarcastic. "Now, this railroad train is running," Ted started angrily, "but I'm going to get off if I need to demonstrate to the court that there are things happening outside this courtroom that are influencing and affecting me. I have a great deal of potential to deal with the situation, and I've only exerted that part of my potential which is nonviolent."

"You're indicating to the court your potential for violence?" Cowart asked, lifting an eyebrow. "Seek and ye shall find. Knock and it shall be opened unto you. Remember that, always remember that."

"Hallelujah, Your Honor.

"I'm getting special treatment, a special brand of coercion," Bundy continued, "and I'm enough of a man not to take it. I'm not going to stand in front of a jury and watch my chances for acquittal go down the drain. I have to come into this courtroom every day with everyone assuming that I'm here fresh as a daisy after coming back from my condominium. I leave here and go back to that hellhole of a jail." Cowart had allowed Ted Bundy to vent himself for almost 20 minutes.

"So today was an extraordinary situation and I apologize to the court, but I don't apologize in one respect because I think it's warranted. There comes a time when you have to say 'Whoa.' "

"If you say 'Whoa' to these proceedings anymore," Cowart closed him off, "I'm going to be using the spurs."

"Giddiyap, Your Honor."

"You bet!"

After days of scientific testimony, the lineup of witnesses for Monday afternoon was like a breath of fresh air for the jury. Into the three-piece-suit formality and tense atmosphere of the courtroom lumbered Henry Polumbo, bandleader of the Smoke Screen and former resident of the Oak. With his long hair combed energetically back from his forehead, Polumbo dropped into the witness box, a red toothbrush sticking from his rumpled suit pocket. He and his friend Russell Gage, who would testify next, had come home early on the morning of January 15 and encountered "Chris Hagen" in the Oak's front doorway.

The defense wanted to know what Polumbo and his friend had been smoking that night, but the two budding rock stars claimed only to have chugged a couple of beers.

Perhaps as important to the prosecution's case was a conversation the band members remembered taking place after the murders. Polumbo and friends were of the opinion that whoever murdered the sorority girls was a "lunatic" and was "probably still hiding out in Tallahassee." But Chris Hagen, Polumbo testified, "thought it was a professional job by somebody who'd done it before and would be gone by now." Finally, Gage remembered Hagen bragging that he'd been a law student and "knew his way around the law." He told me he was "a lot smarter than the police," the young man claimed, and "could get away with anything he wanted."

Nita Jane Neary walked into court dressed in a long, light blue dress. She had been in the witness box so many times before—so many long hours of the same questions. Now she seemed at ease, as if nothing could unnerve her this one last time. For the rest of the day Neary retold her story—the thump overhead, the man crouched at the doorway, the discovery of Chandler upstairs, the hypnosis, and the photo lineup with Captain Poitinger in Indiana.

The jury seemed especially curious about the artist's drawings, spending several minutes passing the sketches from hand to hand, occasionally looking over surreptitiously at Bundy. It was a moment that had lost its power for everyone but the jurors when Nita Neary pointed one last time at Ted Bundy.

"He's the one with a dark, pin-striped suit and a red tie," Neary said, and was quickly seconded by Simpson: "Let the record reflect that the witness has identified the defendant, Theodore Bundy."

Bob Haggard stood at one end of the defense table reviewing his notes. But instead of the pretrial fireworks, the jury witnessed a tedious, methodical review of each aspect of Nita Neary's involvement with the police investigation. Haggard worked and reworked every detail. With repeated objections from Simpson, the cross-examination seemed, at times, to have virtually brought the trial to a standstill. Margaret Good asked for a sidebar at the bench.

"Your Honor, juror number five is dead asleep," Good whispered after the lawyers had gathered around.

"No, she's just concentrating, believe it or not," Cowart replied to general disbelief.

"It's my fault she's asleep," Haggard deadpanned. Even the defense lawyers nodded energetically.

Captain Poitinger followed Neary to testify about the photo lineup. By now Bob Haggard's precarious balance between a proper question and a prosecution objection was faltering. Time after time Simpson leaped to his feet with objections, finally not even bothering to rise, but merely leaning forward to shout his complaints toward the bench. Haggard's version of "good hard advocacy" was beginning to sound like an ill-tempered badgering of the witness. At the defense table Ted Bundy looked dismayed, then angered. As Haggard wrestled with a recalcitrant Poitinger, Ted's jaw muscles flexed furiously.

"There's a stranger in our midst." Cowart smiled happily Thursday morning at Mike Minerva organizing his notes at the far end of the defense table. Minerva had flown in to argue a single motion—to limit the testimony of Dr. Souviron and Dr. Levine "to the circumstantial mode."

"The science of forensic odontology is not sufficiently advanced," Minerva claimed, "to admit advanced conclusions." But the public defender could not persuade Cowart to tone down Souviron's adamant opinion about the bite mark: the odontologist would be permitted to enter his conclusion "with a reasonable degree of dental certainty."

Twelve jurors attended a lengthy lecture that afternoon from a professorial Souviron on the science of bite-mark comparisions, complete with illustrations and charts. The Coral Gables dentist clipped a display with four photographs on an easel in front of the jury box: a blowup of Lisa Levy's buttocks showing the bite and a ruler for scale, a life-size photograph showing the position of the bite, another of the impressions of Ted's teeth in Alluwax, and a startling close-up of Bundy's mouth with his cheeks stretched so tightly that the pink gums under his rear molars were plainly visible. So were Bundy's irregular front teeth.

For three hours Richard Souviron carefully mapped his comparison of Ted's teeth to the bite mark on Lisa Levy, pointing to each tooth, rattling off its technical name, then pointing to a tiny bruise mark on the blow-up. At times cocky, Souviron was almost overbearing in his certainty. But somehow the climax of his testimony seemed diffused, less dramatic than this crucial evidence seemed to deserve. Perhaps Larry Simpson wanted it that way.

"Dr. Souviron, can you say with a reasonable degree of dental certainty," Simpson phrased his question cautiously, "whether or not the teeth in the photo and those in exhibits 85 and 86 on your exhibit, if those teeth made the mark?"

"Yes, sir."

"What is that opinion?"

"They made the marks."

The jurors shifted in their seats when Ed Harvey stepped to the podium for cross-examination. The task before the defense might well decide the case. Souviron's brash, unbending conclusions had to be successfully challenged. By this third time as a witness, however, Souviron was well prepared for the attempt to undercut him.

He'd conducted experiments on cadavers at a local morgue to see if he could reproduce bruise marks similar to Lisa Levy's, he said, and succeeded. Although admitting that bite-mark comparisons were "part art, part science," Souviron refused to be shaken from his opinion. "They made those marks," he said repeatedly, and finally, under pressure, added, "The odds of finding another set of teeth that could make the same bruise marks would . . . the odds of finding this would be like a needle in the haystack."

Lowell Levine had approached the bite-mark comparisons somewhat differently, but his testimony only corroborated Souviron's. With photo enhancements produced in New Mexico, Levine explained how to interpret the bite. The enhanced photos gave the illusion of depth to the bruise marks. Again and again, Defense Attorney Ed Harvey reiterated that the photos were really only a "topographical map" of the color intensities in the negative. Several jurors studied the exhibits closely.

Levine's manner was somewhat less definite than Souviron's, but his findings were not. "It would be a practical impossibility," he said, "to find another set of teeth like Mr. Bundy's which could make a double bruise mark like that."

It had been a strong finish for the prosecution, a strong finish indeed. Everyone in the courtroom, including Ted Bundy, seemed aware that the two odontologists had offered compelling testimony.

"The prosecution rests, Your Honor," Simpson announced late Thursday afternoon. The ball was clearly in Bundy's court, and it would take some deft and powerful rebuttal to save the match.

33

It was only fitting that Ted Bundy should rise first to address the court when the defense opened its case on Friday morning, July 20. His concern, he said, was his own counsel, "or lack thereof in this case. None representing me are of my choice. I've chosen no members of the team." He paused, glanced back to the rows of reporters, and continued.

"It's not a defense I agree with, but there's more than a disagreement. There's an attempt basically to avoid me and avoid my input. What we see going on is something I have no responsibility for, but will bear the complete consequences of."

Eyes narrowed, Cowart waited until Bundy was through. "I don't know of any case I've seen where an individual who is an indigent has received the quality and quantity of counsel that you have. There have been five separate counsel here. It's unheard of. Who's defending the other indigents?" Cowart's voice was even but strong. Citing the barrage of memoranda from Ted's lawyers and their practice of consulting with him frequently during the questioning of witnesses, the judge said it was a defense unprecedented in his 27 years of experience—one of the best he'd seen. He softened a little and asked if Bundy wished to defend himself. "The lawyer who represents himself has a fool for a client," he cautioned.

Smiling, shifting his weight as he stood before the bench, Ted returned to an old theme: since the Supreme Court had turned him down, perhaps the church would admit Millard Farmer as his counsel. But Cowart was in no mood for the bantering, even with the jury out of the room. "This dancin' around and puttin' innuendos in the record is not satisfactory," he said sharply. The judge was not about to let the defendant lay groundwork for an appeal right under his nose. "This issue of competency of counsel is going to be settled on the *first* appeal," he said, "not five or ten years down the road." His opinion, unmistakably, was that it would never be an issue at all.

Millard Farmer commented by phone from Atlanta, calling Cowart's praise for the defense hypocritical. "He said it to protect the record."

None of this was exactly new to the Bundy story. His problems with defense lawyers went back a long way. Back to Utah, where he grumbled about the way his attorney John O'Connell handled the Carol DaRonch case. Back to Colorado, where he mistrusted and eventually fired the public defenders assigned to his defense in the Caryn Campbell case. And in Florida, from the first days after his capture, Bundy had conducted an incessant campaign about who would represent him. Denied Millard Farmer by the courts over and over again, he had accepted the services of the public defender in name only—never in spirit.

With the state's damaging dental evidence fresh in the jury's minds, the defense moved quickly to throw a shadow of doubt across it. John M. Grewe, a Maryland orthodontist who had studied dental patterns for the World Health Organization, testified that the configuration of Bundy's lower teeth was not uncommon. There were many adults in the population, the orthodontist said, with crooked teeth like Bundy's, and he added with a smile, "The defendant might be a typical patient."

Duane DeVore looked determined as he raised his hand and took the witness oath. He'd put in a good deal of work on the bite-mark evidence since the pretrial hearings in

Tallahassee in May. DeVore began as he had then: "A unique set of teeth might not leave a unique mark—because of the material of skin itself." He repeated his contention that the upper and lower tooth marks in the bite-mark photograph could not be lined up and went on to say the upper marks were too indistinct to be of use for a comparison. Finally, reaching for a shoebox at his feet, DeVore produced what was perhaps the most potent weapon for the defense: five white plaster models of teeth DeVore claimed could be matched to the bite. Leaning into the jury box, he held a photographic transparency of the bite mark over each set of lower teeth to demonstrate his point.

Defense lawyer Ed Harvey carefully phrased his next question: "Can you exclude any of the models based strictly on the configurations?"

"No, based strictly on configuration, I can exclude no one."

Larry Simpson began his cross-examination even before he'd stood up. Quicker and more aggressive than he'd been so far during the trial, the prosecutor wanted to know how old the people were whose dental models DeVore had lined up in front of him.

"Eleven years, nine months; thirty-two years; twelve years; thirteen years, five months; fourteen years, three months."

Simpson nodded and directed DeVore's attention back to the pretrial hearings, reminding the witness that Dr. Levine had eliminated one of these sets of models at that time. DeVore agreed, and Simpson stepped forward and removed that set from view. What followed was more surprising: DeVore admitted that he himself could now eliminate another set, based on the individual characteristics of the teeth. Simpson grabbed that set away, leaving only three—including the plaster models of Bundy's teeth. The prosecutor drew in his breath.

"Are not the individual characteristics of Mr. Bundy's teeth consistent with the bite mark in this case?"

"Some of them."

"Are there any that are inconsistent?"

"Inconsistent to the point of exclusion? No, sir, because I said I cannot exclude them."

DeVore winced and looked down at his bright red tie. He wasn't saying anything new, of course, but Simpson was drawing it out dramatically for the jury. Several jurors sat forward in their seats.

"So your testimony would have to be, doctor," the

prosecutor said at last, "that the defendant in this case could have made the bite marks on the buttocks of Lisa Levy. Is that not correct?"

"I believe so. Yes."

Simpson's final questions were pure theater. Did Dr. DeVore happen to know if any of the *children* whose models he'd brought along from Maryland were living in Tallahassee in January 1978? "Were any in a nightclub named Sherrod's on the night of January 14?" DeVore smiled weakly. "I have nothing further," said Simpson.

Ed Harvey tried to rescue his prize witness on redirect examination. Wasn't it true, he asked DeVore, that one of the other models was a more likely match for the bite marks? Yes, his witness replied, Ted's teeth were not the "most probable" of the models he'd examined. Furthermore, the dentist claimed, it was awfully suggestive to compare a bite to a single set of models. "You shouldn't attempt to explain the unknown by the known," he said. Finally he explained the use of children's teeth for comparison: kids' models were just easier to find in an orthodontic clinic. That didn't mean there weren't adults with teeth similar to Ted's.

But Larry Simpson couldn't have been more pleased. Not only had he made the defense look like it was hedging on the distinction between "configuration" and "individual characteristics" of teeth, but he'd accomplished it in a way that was immediately accessible to the jury. "It went down just like we wanted it to," he whispered during a recess.

Moments later, when court resumed with the jury still out of the room, Bundy stood for the second time that day. He'd sat stone-faced through the testimony of Dr. DeVore, and now he'd made up his mind. The courtroom was still as he walked out to the center of the floor. "Your Honor," he began, "I would like to take you up on your offer and proceed as my own counsel." Ted Bundy had just fired his entire defense team.

Cowart intoned an official acceptance of the move, and assigned Ed Harvey, Lynn Thompson, Margaret Good, and Bob Haggard as standby counsel. For the time being, Ted said, the standbys would continue questioning the witnesses. The packed ranks of spectators and reporters were still buzzing when the jury returned.

For about an hour it looked as if Bundy's dire opinion of his defense team had some merit. Two witnesses called to discredit Russell Gage's and Henry Polumbo's recollection of Bundy's remark about the "professional job" at Chi Omega didn't make a dent. Then a minor witness was not permitted to read a police report to the jury because the defense lawyers couldn't phrase the question properly according to the law. Ted sat back, smiling distantly and shaking his head as they paged frantically through their lawbooks. *This* was the great defense Cowart was talking about? *This* was his idea of a defendant's right to counsel?

Fifteen minutes later the lawyers took a "hint" from the judge and the witness read his report—complete with an incorrect date that invalidated it as evidence. Now Ted couldn't contain his smirk.

But before Bundy left court that day, Cowart summoned the lawyers to a bench conference. The judge listened as Ted explained his reasons for assuming command of the case. Mainly, the defendant said, he wanted to choose who would give the closing argument. Bundy was "unalterably opposed" to the person his lawyers thought best—Bob Haggard.

Cowart rolled his tall leather chair closer to the knot of lawyers and looked straight at Ted. "I say this to you in the deepest sincerity," he began. "The situation is not nearly as acute as you might feel. It's best to get you all together." One by one Cowart picked out the tight, drawn faces of the defense lawyers with his eyes. "The only thing I say to you is," and here he paused and turned to Ted, "is hang loose."

Judge Cowart had shown Ted three faces in response to his desire to handle his own defense. First, a firm warning about the risks. Second, a coolly professional acceptance of the defendant's decision. Finally, from behind the legal mask, a direct, uncomplicated appeal to Bundy to guard carefully against acting in anger against his own best interests.

By morning Ted's young lawyers had sorted out their feelings about the case. Ed Harvey, sturdy and expressionless throughout the trial, was unusually forceful when he spoke. With the "total breakdown of the lawyer-client relationship," he said, he wanted off the defense team. Harvey described the team's infighting, especially the disagreement about who would deliver the closing argument, and concluded that it was Ted who stood squarely in the way of a good defense. Harvey suggested another competency hearing. Bundy's behavior, he said, "can only be described as self-defeating and detrimental. It goes beyond bad judgment."

Prosecutor Dan McKeever opposed the last-minute delay, calling Bundy "almost cunning in his ability to work against his lawyers, almost unbearable." Ted listened closely and scribbled notes on a yellow pad while Cowart, agreeing with McKeever, issued his ruling. "He might be a miserable client, but there's no question he meets the legal standards to stand trial," the judge said.

Harvey renewed his plea: "This man's life is on the line. He should not be forced to take counsel of lawyers he doesn't have confidence in."

Ted opposed Harvey's withdrawal, claiming he had only gone pro se in order to decide who should give the closing argument. He spoke for several minutes in general terms about how "insecure" lawyers were, how they guarded "the power exercised in the courtroom."

In the end, Harvey's motion to withdraw was denied, while Bob Haggard, the persistent, sometimes abrasive Miami lawyer who brought more direct experience of murder trials to the case than any of the others, was permitted to resign. Haggard shortly became a regular in the ninth-floor pressroom, shedding his tie and standing patiently in front of the hot television lights. "In eleven years I've never seen a defense fall apart like this. With Mr. Bundy, it's a new game every day." Soon he wasn't so oblique about his relationship with Ted: "We hated each other."

It fell to Margaret Good, a 29-year-old appeals specialist in her first felony trial, to prepare a closing argument for the most highly publicized case in America. Bundy's choice of her was an astonishing, perhaps inspired risk. Inexperienced as she was, Good held one potentially winning card: she was a woman, attractive, educated, not much older than or different from the women murdered in their beds. It would only take one juror to feel the subconscious message: how could a bright girl like that stand up and defend Ted Bundy unless he was innocent?

But through all the upheavals in court that morning it was the seemingly innocent opening exchange between Bundy and Cowart that would stick in people's minds. Ted had grinned and waved cheerily to Nancy Hobson as he was escorted into the courtroom by his guards. Leaning back, hooking one ankle over the other, he chatted with the lawyers he had fired the night before. Moments later, when Cowart was on the bench asking what had been resolved about the defense, Bundy began brightly:

"We had a meeting last night. I don't particularly care to air our clean linen in open court—"

The judge leaned forward to interrupt. "Well, Mr. Bundy, there's a time in life when whatever you do behind closed doors must come out in public."

"Really?" Even Bundy seemed astonished.

"Yes, really," Cowart said. "Sooner or later the evidence of it will crop up." The judge rocked back in his chair.

With their internal difficulties resolved, at least for the moment, the defense called their final witnesses to the stand. The prosecution, with its 49 witnesses stretched out over two weeks, had looked powerful. Now, after Duane DeVore, the defense knew they had precious little else to present. But they didn't want to rest their case too quickly and leave the prosecution's side of things fresh and overpowering in the jurors' minds. Slow, painstaking, and dramatic as possible: such was the defense strategy for the last witnesses.

A week before Nita Neary had testified that a familiar face flashed through her mind just after she'd seen the man with the club. Now the jurors, having heard Ricky Ramoya's name, would get to judge for themselves. Handsome with his dark eyes and long, straight nose and visibly uncomfortable in front of the television camera and the crowd, Ramoya briefly explained his duties as a maintenance man and sorority "sweetheart." After a short conference with the judge about the legality of her next move, Good asked Ramoya to stand side by side with Bundy in the middle of the courtroom. On a signal, both would turn their right profiles to the jury box for a comparison.

The jurors looked impassive. No one seemed to notice that Ted wore a pair of heeled boots that added an inch or so to his height.

Good dismissed the witness without suggesting he was a serious suspect in the case. Instead she'd left the implication that other people fitted the description Neary had given. How could the jury be sure if Nita Neary wasn't?

A nervous and unhappy Francis Kenniston, the FSU art professor who had made the suspect sketches, was called to buttress that view; but he could recall little of what

Neary had told him at the time. Months ago he had testified she remembered the lighting in the sorority foyer that night as dim; now he couldn't remember that statement.

Jack Poitinger played the tape of Neary's hypnosis session, when she'd called Ramoya's resemblance to the man with the club "strong." Steve Bodiford played his tape of a March 1978 phone call with Neary; on it Bodiford warned her not to look at any more photographs of Bundy. The strategy was clear. Recapitulate the doubts about Nita Neary's ID. Remind the jury of the pressure she'd been under.

Finally the defense went after the remaining physical evidence in the case. A deposition from an FSU botanist suggested that two kinds of bark—from water oak and laurel oak—were found at the crime scene; the prosecution hadn't even mentioned that. Hair examiner Pat Lasko returned with several bagfuls of debris from the Dunwoody Street apartment of Cheryl Thomas. Reminding the jury that the panty hose mask had been untangled from the bedsheets and laid on the floor to be photographed, Lynn Thompson asked if any of the hairs found in the sheets or on the floor were similar to Ted's. None were, said Lasko, and furthermore, some of the samples didn't match Cheryl Thomas's hair either. There were *lots* of hairs in that apartment, Thompson was suggesting. Who knew what could have gotten on that panty hose mask when it was on the floor?

The testimony of a fingerprint expert ran along similar lines. Numerous prints at Chi Omega—on the doors, doorjambs, even the television set—and Dunwoody had never been identified. Not one was matched with Bundy. Whose were they, then?

Simpson sneered at the reasoning on cross-examination, asking the witness, "Can you tell me what a club-totin' murderer's doin' with a TV set?"

The last, crucial piece of physical evidence for the defense was the semen stain found on the bedsheets of Cheryl Thomas. Here, at last, it seemed there might be hard evidence showing that it was *not* Ted Bundy in the apartment that night.

Earlier in the trial, prosecution witness Richard Stephens had offered some highly technical testimony about the various identifying factors present in bodily fluids. These factors could often be detected in a dried stain, he had said, but in

341

the case of the semen stain in question, the results were "inconclusive."

But Lynn Thompson had pressed Stephens on cross-examination for a further subtlety. Those tests *might* indicate that the person who made the stain was a nonsecreter of the A-B-O antigens that identify blood type. How did he know that the more fragile PGM enzyme had not quickly decayed? Wasn't it possible that the more stable A-B-O antigens had never been there in the first place, indicating a nonsecreter? How could he prove *both* blood factors had, in fact, been destroyed? It was a narrow crack in the evidence, but the defense saw light. Now they hoped to widen the crack even more.

Stephens again took the stand, this time to recite the results of his examination of Bundy's saliva: the defendant was a secreter.

Then came Michael Grubb, a tall, bearded criminalist from a forensic lab in Oakland, California. Grubb had arrived in Miami the night before, he said, and performed 24 separate tests on a semen sample from the defendant, Theodore Bundy. His conclusion? Bundy was a secreter.

"If a person is a secreter," Grubb added, "he can never be a nonsecreter."

Grubb went on to say that dried, aged stains were often preferable for testing to fresh ones and that a sample two or three years old could be perfectly useful for analysis. The defense was at the point of an astonishing breakthrough. All they had to do now was produce testimony that the dried semen stain on Cheryl Thomas's sheet was in fact conclusive, that it had been made by a nonsecreter— someone other than Ted Bundy.

"Nothing further," said Thompson softly.

It took Larry Simpson one question to seal up this crack of "reasonable doubt." "Mr. Grubb," the prosecutor said, his voice heavily cadenced with cynicism, "you came all the way from California and didn't examine the exhibits in this case?"

If the defense hadn't managed to poke any significant holes in the physical evidence of the state's case, they had succeeded, at least, in carrying the trial over to the next week. A charge conference (for determining precisely what instructions would go to the jury) was set for Monday morning, with closing arguments expected on Tuesday. Back home in Tacoma, Louise Bundy was packing her bags. Once again, as she had in Utah, Ted's mother would be present for the final days of the trial.

Ted would have a surprise for her, for everyone, when court resumed on Monday afternoon. Scanning the courtroom, he stood to inform Judge Cowart there was "new evidence, material in favor of the defendant" that he wanted to offer. With the jury absent, his first witness on the motion was Joe Aloi.

Aloi, a veteran investigator for the Tallahassee public defender's office, is stout, black-haired, and wears a perpetually skeptical expression. Fond of wheedling reporters for their day-to-day assessment of the trial, he now had a substantial bone to pick with the press. After weeks of trying, he said, he had been unable to obtain from the media negatives of certain photographs, taken of the defendant around the time of his arrest. The photographs, perhaps, would show that Bundy's upper front tooth did not, in fact, have a chip at the time.

The story fell in place when Ted took the stand and claimed he'd chipped the tooth around the middle of March 1978, while eating dinner in his cell—after the Chi Omega murders but before his dental impressions were taken. If his upper teeth had looked one way at the time of the murders, he asked, and another when Dr. Souviron made his impressions and models, how could they be matched to the abrasions on Lisa Levy's buttock?

"Your Honor, they've twisted my teeth every which way but loose to make them fit." Bundy asked for time to subpoena the newspapers for the photographic negative that would prove his point.

Cowart refused, declaring that the chipped tooth, more than a year old, could not be considered newly discovered evidence. Moments later in the hallway, one of Bundy's lawyers did not seem overly disappointed. "There were reasons, good reasons, why we didn't pursue that," he said. Once again, for perhaps the last time, Bundy was operating on his own.

The jury returned for one last witness, on prosecution rebuttal. It was Lowell Levine, called as he had been in Tallahassee, to flatten the dental testimony of Dr. DeVore. Yes, he told Simpson, he had examined the models DeVore had shown to the jury. After making Alluwax bites of each, he had concluded that all the models but one could be eliminated.

343

"And which model was that?" Simpson asked.

"Model number two. Mr. Bundy's teeth."

The jury filed out past the defense table as they had each day for more than three weeks. As usual, about half of them shot a quick glance at Ted as they left—these laborers and retirees, these women in brightly colored pants suits whom Ted had chosen to decide his fate. Tomorrow they would hear the closing arguments and retire to the jury room, finally at liberty to discuss the intricately detailed evidence that had brought them all together. They'd been told by the judge not to consider it as a factor, but some of them couldn't help wondering: Why hadn't Ted Bundy gotten up on that witness stand to tell his side of the story?

He was 30 when he wheeled a podium around and faced the jury for the summation of his case, but Larry Simpson seemed even younger. It wasn't just his looks—a fair complexion, a flap of sandy-colored hair—but also the quiet, almost studied determination he had exhibited since taking over the case more than a year before. While his associate Dan McKeever would tease and jaw with the press like an old political pro, Simpson would offer little more than a simple, noncommittal response and hurry away self-consciously. Up until now, Simpson's low-pitched, conformist style had given the impression of a newcomer showing he knew the ropes.

"Good morning, ladies and gentlemen," he began, and his voice took on an easy rhythm as he recalled the scene at the Chi Omega sorority house. His case, he explained, stood on three legs: a positive eyewitness identification, circumstantial evidence, and scientific evidence. Larry Simpson had had this framework in his mind for months. The real challenge, he had always said, was to boil it down and clarify the evidence for a jury. Now he would ask them to see it as he did, to fit the pieces together in a portrait of guilt. Simpson warmed to his task, conjuring Nita Neary as she turned into the foyer that night.

"She heard a thump. She heard a thump, folks. Do you know what that was? Right at that moment upstairs at the Chi Omega house an assault and a murder was taking place!" The description she gave, he said, was solid, with "a very unusual feature that stuck in that girl's mind." Reminding the jurors that Neary was an art student, Simpson

344

raised his voice: "Look at her intelligence. She was fixin' to graduate. She was one of the few people in the Chi Omega sorority house—in the whole world—who could have grasped what she'd seen. It was a stroke of luck," he said at the height of his hyperbole, "it was almost fate."

Finally Simpson grabbed one of Francis Kenniston's sketches from the clerk's desk and held it up. "It might be the most important piece of evidence in this case," he said of the drawing the defense had paid so much attention to earlier in the trial. "Look and see. Look at that sketch. That sketch is an identification of Theodore Robert Bundy going into the Chi Omega sorority house on the morning of January 15, 1978. Look at it yourself." A long pause followed the demand, just as it would in a hell-raising sermon.

Bundy sat stock-still at the defense table, one hand supporting his chin, the index finger poised on his cheek, as Simpson shifted to the circumstantial evidence of the case. Four years ago, as Ted had said so many times, police across the West had begun to spin their web. Not until now had a jury been asked to test such a web, to consider possibility, probability, how the strands were joined.

"Why did he sign the name of Chris M. Hagen to his lease?" Simpson began. "What was he doing in Tallahassee trying to hide his existence? It's a circumstance that's consistent with guilt and inconsistent with innocence." Choosing this phrase from the jury instructions, the prosecutor set up a litany as he ticked off the various coincidences in the case. There was "that intense, unnerving stare" the women at Sherrod's had seen the night of the murders, then Bundy back at the Oak later that night. "Isn't it strange, that within minutes of the attack at the Dunwoody Street apartment, the defendant was seen standing at the front door of the Oak? Ah wonder why?" Simpson's voice turned to a husky whisper. "Ah wonder why?"

As to Bundy's flights from Deputy Daws in Tallahassee and Officer Lee in Pensacola, Simpson was succinct: "He was gittin' outta Dodge. That's what it amounted to—consistent with guilt and inconsistent with innocence." And his statement to Lee that he wished he'd been killed? "Here's a man who's committed the most horrible murders known to the Tallahassee area. He can't live with himself."

Simpson touched only briefly on the scientific evidence, calling it the "extra mile" in the case, and sped toward a climax. "How many people in the world have hairs *exactly*

345

like Theodore Bundy's?" he asked, crouching forward over the podium. "Huh?" Finding teeth that were exactly like Bundy's was "like finding a needle in the haystack," he said, quoting Dr. Souviron's phrase, "a practical impossibility," as Dr. Levine had put it. Dr. DeVore, according to Simpson, was "a desperate move, a gamble that might have worked. But they just couldn't do it. They just couldn't put a dent in the evidence."

Larry Simpson rolled back the podium and stood up straight. "There's only one conclusion that you can reach. Ladies and gentlemen, it is your duty to return a verdict of guilty as charged in this case." Simpson took his seat and began chewing the end of a pen. He'd saved a little for his rebuttal. He hoped he'd saved enough.

It was no accident that Margaret Good ended up in a public defender's office. From her girlhood in Ohio through her work with juveniles in Dade County, Florida, after her graduation from law school, she'd always championed causes, sometimes desperate ones, to make a point. Her choice for president in 1972—Shirley Chisholm—didn't have a chance, but Margaret Good worked every bit as hard in the campaign as others did for the front-runners.

As a legal appeals specialist, Good articulates her views in a technical, sometimes abstract language that is tedious if not impossible for jurors to follow. Again and again, in the course of the trial, she had parried with the judge on questions of law. Gesturing stiffly, speaking slowly, she had made no sustained impression so far. But clearly, beneath an unrehearsed courtroom manner, the 29-year-old assistant public defender's zeal was no less real, no less deeply felt than any other lawyer's in the room. The call to give Ted Bundy's closing argument was a call to convey that zeal to the jury. It wasn't enough for Margaret Good to *believe* the evidence was not sufficient to convict Ted Bundy. She had to *show* it.

"The defense does not deny," she began, "there was a terrible and unfortunate tragedy in Tallahassee. But I ask you not to compound that tragedy by convicting the wrong man." Referring to notes, quoting from the Constitution and Lord Eldon, Good launched her argument like a thoughtfully prepared lecture. But gradually, as she turned to the case itself, she spoke more and more from the heart.

"The first problem is the quality of the evidence. The

346

police can—and do—make mistakes. They can find the suspect and decide to make the evidence fit that suspect." Good ran off a long string of examples of possible evidence missed or botched: the Clairol bottle kicked around on Lisa Levy's floor for five days after it was apparently used to rape her; the panty hose mask on the floor at Dunwoody; the many unidentified fingerprints; 102 other suspects in the crime.

She zeroed in on the state's eyewitness identifications, pointing out the long delays—up to nine months—between the time the women in Sherrod's saw the man and the time they were shown photo lineups. "It's too bad the police waited," she added. Good drew in her breath and rattled off the objections to Nita Neary's ID, heightening her argument by exaggeration. "The state would have you believe that the protruding nose is remarkable. It's the nature of a nose to protrude from your face. If it didn't, your glasses would slide off." Several jurors smiled. Good recalled the hypnosis session, the photographs Neary had seen in the newspapers, Poitinger's photo lineup in Indiana. "Nita Neary has been caught up in a terrible situation," the lawyer said. "She wants to help if she can."

Good hurried over the circumstantial evidence that Simpson had painted so vividly—Ted standing outside the Oak at 5:00 a.m., the flights from Daws and Lee—and opened the door on the scientific evidence. Here, the defense had known all along, was the crux of the case. If the prosecution could get away with the swift certainty of indisputable-sounding judgments by experts, all was lost. It was the job of the defense to expose the imprecision, the complicated, imperfect methods and conclusions of the forensic specialists.

First she took up the dental evidence, pointing out the different techniques used by the various odontologists and the lack of quantifiable data on the uniqueness of marks made by teeth in skin. Invoking Dr. Grewe's testimony, she expressed herself elegantly: "Anyone with crooked lower dentition would be in trouble if he was unfortunate enough to be a suspect. It's a sad day for our system of justice if a man can be convicted because they say he has crooked teeth. All citizens suffer." Black jurors, Good knew perfectly well, are traditionally sympathetic to the idea of a man wrongly accused. She was, as Bob Haggard had put it, "ringing their bell."

Good felt on firmer ground with the hair comparisons. Not

only was the examiner relatively inexperienced, she said, but "you can't make an identification with hair. It's not like fingerprints. 'Trust me,' these experts are saying, but does 'trust me' amount to proof beyond a reasonable doubt?"

Margaret Good was at her best—organized, confident, compelling. Then a curious thing happened: she dropped a paper clip and paused a long moment, staring down where it lay. Her decision—to pick it up or leave it—was trifling, but her hesitation, her ordinary, mundane uncertainty, was like a great weight shifting.

She went on to finish with the serological evidence. Even though the lab had found the semen stain inconclusive, she said, such results were also consistent with its donor being a nonsecreter. "The inescapable conclusion is that the stain was made by the assailant, and the assailant was a nonsecreter."

Margaret Good had spoken for an hour. Her conclusion was a textbook appeal to the jury: "All of you *individually* must find that the state has proved its case beyond a reasonable doubt. Each of you has a soul-searching decision to make. Don't vote with the majority. I would ask that you consider carefully."

Simpson sprang from his seat for rebuttal. "Page one, chapter one of any defense attorney's manual: when all else fails, you try to put the police on trial. It just doesn't work, ladies and gentlemen, it just doesn't work." Simpson's voice was deep and ringing, and his appeals to the jury were more like commands. "*You've* got the ability to evaluate *all* the evidence." If one piece of the case didn't convince them, he demanded, what about the next? "You have *all* the evidence." It was captivating, risky reasoning the prosecutor was stringing through his argument: circumstance added to circumstance where no one piece of the evidence would necessarily convince 12 jurors. He'd saved one last ominous image to tie it all up.

Simpson shot back at Good's argument where he needed to, reminding the jurors that the test on the semen stain was "inconclusive," belittling the inconsistencies in the clothing descriptions of the man at Sherrod's, then turned his back on the jury for a moment. He returned from the clerk's desk with the panty hose mask found at the Dunwoody apartment, stretching it open with his fingers. "This man premeditated that murder," he said softly. "Anybody who took the time to prepare this mask," and Simpson shook it in his hands, "isn't going to leave fingerprints." He paused to remind the jurors of the testimony from the crime lab technician who had found Chris Hagen's room at the Oak wiped clean.

"The man who committed this crime was smart enough to use false names." Now Simpson produced the notebook filled with facts on Kenneth Misner found in the stolen car in Pensacola and marched it up and down in front of the jury. His voice was nearly at a shout. "This man is a professional. He is the kind of man smart enough to cross-examine witnesses in this case, because he thinks he's smart enough to get away with *any* crime. It is your *duty* to return a verdict of guilty."

Usually, when the jurors filed out of the courtroom, Ted Bundy sat studying a page of notes or huddled with his lawyers. This time he sought each face—12 jurors and 3 alternates—with his eyes. At three o'clock that afternoon, after Judge Cowart read them their instructions on the law, they filed out the other door, into the jury room for deliberation. "Disregard the consequences of your verdict," the judge had read. "Lay aside personal feelings."

Lawyers, spectators, Ted's mother, Kathy Kleiner's parents took up the wait on the fourth floor of the Dade County metropolitan hall of justice. Five o'clock, then six passed. Margaret Good, smiling thinly, hurried off to dinner with her mother. She'd lost 15 pounds since the start of the trial. The longer the better for the defense: that meant the jury wasn't sure. At 7:30 she was back in the building, talking nervously about her houseplants. Again and again she asked for the time.

At 9:30 p.m. bailiff Dave Watson answered the knock at the jury-room door.

Verdict forms folded lengthwise in his hand, Foreman Rudolph Treml, the oil company project engineer, had his jacket back on and his tie knotted tightly again. Some of his fellow male jurors also wore coats today. None looked straight at Ted Bundy. Treml, from his seat in the second row, handed the forms to the clerk.

"Publish the verdicts, madam clerk," Cowart told Shirley Lewis after he'd read through the seven forms without expression.

"In the Circuit Court of the Second Judicial Circuit, in and for Leon County, Florida . . ." It was a long, familiar paragraph to her. The news itself came near the end. Breaths were shallow in the courtroom. Louise Bundy sat forward in her seat on the back row.

". . . find the defendant, Theodore Robert Bundy, as to count one of the indictment, burglary of a dwelling and committing an assault upon the persons therein, to wit Karen Chandler and Kathy Kleiner, guilty as charged."

Louise Bundy fell back, holding a hand to her forehead. The next count was for murder, then murder again, then attempted murder. Six more times Louise Bundy heard the phrase. Her son was guilty as charged.

34

Five guards walked Ted Bundy back to his jail cell. It was a standard precaution for a man just convicted of murder, whether he was an ex-law student in a business suit or not.

But it was not a standard precaution to suddenly alter the route—down a back stairway, out from an underground garage, and across the street. Ted looked straight ahead and took his long, stiff strides. The night air was heavy, and a breeze rattled the palm trees. One guard trailed behind, hand at his hip, fingers closed tightly on the handle of his gun.

While a swarm of 50 reporters and cameramen jostled one another near the fourth-floor elevator, two cops, snickering about how they'd outsmarted the press, bounded down the jail steps and headed for their cars and home.

Upstairs in the courthouse the reporters surged forward when Louise Bundy appeared in the hall, TV spotlights bearing down like the headlights on a truck. Her eyes narrowed in the glare, and she turned her head away a moment. Then she walked straight for them with the promise she'd make a statement but answer no questions.

"The jury is wrong." There was silence as she began to speak. "There'll be appeal upon appeal. This is not the final answer." The tiny woman in a sleeveless Dacron dress, her gray hair fixed in a puffy little crown on her head, drew a breath. "The family is devastated by this, of course, but we know he's not guilty." Louise Bundy offered a faint, brave smile for the cameras: she was his mother; she'd stand by her eldest son. Nancy Hobson stepped forward and steered her through the crowd and down the escalator.

With Larry Simpson the reporters were less delicate. "Will you ask for the death penalty?" they asked, circling him in a tight knot.

"Certainly, certainly." Simpson didn't smile.

The defense team waited in their office for 20 minutes, then hurried grim-faced down the hall to the elevator. Margaret Good set her jaw and shouldered past a TV man who waved a microphone in her face. Only Ed Harvey spoke on the ride down. "We lost it on the first day. As soon as they showed that jury those gruesome photos it was all over." The lawyers pushed open the courthouse doors and followed the path Ted had walked to the jail less than a half hour before.

Harvey and Lynn Thompson mulled the possibilities of appeal, the weaknesses in the state's case. Margaret Good, the appellate specialist who never imagined the role she would take in this trial, did not join in. Worked up that afternoon to an elegant and passionate closing argument she hardly knew she possessed, Good was tightening now with exhaustion. "Let's go," she said at the door of the jail. "What we need to do right now is see Ted."

It was a puzzled, analytical client they met in the cell upstairs. Bundy had gripped one knee and listened to the verdict without sign of a response, winked and waved to his mother on the way out of the courtroom, and now he wanted to talk. Within the hour he was on the phone to a reporter from the *Seattle Times*. "They didn't take enough time to deliberate," he told Dick Larsen. "Good heavens, just to read the jury instructions would have taken three hours."

With his lawyers, with reporters, step by step in his own mind, Theodore Bundy would replay the events of the last month that had led to his conviction. He had been so confident of an acquittal at one point—he'd said as much to the judge. And so pleased with the jury—Rudolph Treml, the scientist, to interpret the weaknesses of the technical evidence; Alan Smith, the clothing designer, to see how poor the artist's sketches were; a solid, sympathetic core of blacks. It was Ted Bundy's jury; several times he'd even overruled the advice of jury selection expert Emil Spillman.

There was the evidence to think of, the testimony, Bob Haggard's cross-examination and opening statement, all the other problems with his own defense team. How much had that hurt him? How much had been conveyed, if only subliminally, to the jury?

For Ted Bundy, this was no idle exercise of bitterness and regret. He needed to be organized, clearheaded, direct. That was the only way to look forward to the appeals, to a new trial, to a conviction overturned. Strategies had to be considered and weighed. There was the photographic evidence to prove his upper tooth had not been chipped when the murders took place. There was the dental search warrant to carefully review for challenge. There was still more work to do on the serological evidence. And then, of course, there was the whole question of his right to counsel of his choice.

It was Ted Bundy's biggest challenge yet—but not so different from challenges he had faced before. How different was this from DaRonch, all the preparation and the work on the appeals? How different from Campbell? Hadn't he written that keenly argued brief on similar transactions and convinced Judge Lohr to rule out Aime and Kent and Smith from the Colorado case? And how different from the kind of challenge that had drawn Ted Bundy's energy all along? Psychology, politics, the law: they all demanded a certain kind of mind.

But even back then, in those days of unbounded ambition, he wouldn't have imagined the scope of things he might have to handle six or eight years later, at the age of 32. According to the court calendar in Lake City, Columbia County, Theodore Robert Bundy would stand trial for the murder of Kimberly Diane Leach, the 12-year-old schoolgirl found in an abandoned hog shed. That case was no different from Chi Omega, Ted had said, an invention of circumstance. From their own perspective prosecutors and police agreed: it was no different at all.

Beyond the Chi O appeals and the trial in Lake City, the trail went snaking off in the distance: over 60 credit card and auto theft charges in Tallahassee; resisting arrest in Pensacola; the Caryn Campbell murder charge, two escapes, and various escape-related offenses in Colorado; the remainder of a sentence to serve in Utah. Yes, sir, the cops back home in Washington State told reporters, Ted Bundy is still the prime suspect in our missing and murdered girls cases. We haven't stopped investigating.

But Ted Bundy faced one looming barricade along the way. On Saturday at 10:00 a.m. he would return with his lawyers to face the jury and Judge Cowart for the second phase of the Chi Omega trial. In this "penalty phase," the jury would hear the aggravating circumstances presented by the prosecution and the mitigating circumstances presented by the defense, retire to deliberate again, and return with an advisory sentence of death or life in prison.

"Advisory," Ted knew, was the key word, for under Florida law a judge may ignore the advice of the jury and sentence the defendant as he sees fit. Ted had been saying it to reporters for days: Judge Cowart—who'd overruled a jury before in a capital case—was bound to sentence him to the electric chair, regardless of what the jury said. Almost no one disagreed with the prediction.

Following the conviction—a conviction the prosecutor doubted he'd get at several points during the trial—Larry Simpson was confident the jury and Judge Cowart would concur and the sentence for Ted Bundy would be death. "If this isn't a capital punishment case," he asked, "what is?"

Simpson's confidence inspired a swift, abbreviated strategy for the penalty phase. Three witnesses—Salt Lake City detective Jerry Thompson, Carol DaRonch Swenson, and Aspen investigator Mike Fisher—would testify to the facts of the Utah kidnapping conviction and establish that Bundy was "not on parole" when he arrived in Florida. That was enough, Simpson believed, to convince the jurors that five of the eight statutory aggravating circumstances—and none of the mitigating circumstances—existed in the case.

"We could go in there and dump the *real* blood and gore pictures in the jury's laps," the prosecutor said. "We're not going to do that because we don't need to."

As it turned out, the testimony was even more abbreviated than the prosecution planned. The defense stipulated most of it into the record. Thompson produced a copy of the kidnapping conviction. Neither the victim of that crime nor Mike Fisher spoke a word. Carol DaRonch Swenson, now 22 and recently married, served her purpose just by sitting for three minutes on the stand while the stipulation was worked out. Dressed in a silky blouse and white pants

353

knotted loosely with a rope belt at the hips, she brushed the long, wavy hair from her face, glanced self-consciously at the crowd and smiled, then stared at her hands. Only once did she turn her dark, deep-set eyes toward the defendant.

"We just wanted to parade her by," said one member of the prosecution team. "That was enough."

Court was about to adjourn until Monday morning when Ted stood up, perfectly composed, and asked what had become of his phone privileges. "I am still acting as my own attorney," he argued levelly. "I should have those rights."

Cowart leaned back and teased the defendant a moment, discounting his complaint: "You even managed to call me. I'm sorry I wasn't in." Then, as had happened so often in these exchanges with Bundy, Cowart flashed knife-sharp, observing that Ted on the one hand complained about the press and on the other used his "attorney's" phone privileges to call reporters and conduct interviews. "I consider that probative to all these motions about the press interfering with this trial."

With that Cowart was out of his chair, black robe flying as he swept out of the courtroom. But Ted Bundy had made his point. He'd shown the pressure hadn't gotten to him. He'd shown he was still fighting.

The battles went on behind the scenes as well. Over strenuous objections from some of his lawyers, Ted had vetoed the idea of putting two psychiatrists on the stand to testify. If he was innocent, he argued, why should he let two doctors he'd seen only once show him to a jury in a bad light?

Kathy Kleiner DeShields hesitated when a reporter asked for her view. "Well," she said, "I feel sorry for him—he needs help—but what he did, there's just no way to compensate for that."

Louise Bundy led the attempt to save Ted's life on Monday morning, July 30. Walking quickly to the stand and settling herself in the chair, she looked up, smiled expectantly at Margaret Good, and awaited the first question. She answered in a steady voice about Ted's birth and family history. Good didn't ask about Ted's natural father; Louise Bundy only said that Ted had been adopted by Johnnie Bundy when the boy was four and a half. There were four other children in all, she said. "They had the best we could give them on a middle-class income. The most we

354

could give them was lots of love." It was suddenly obvious, as she sat there in her diamond-patterned summer dress: Ted resembled his mother, especially through the eyes and mouth.

Louise recalled her eldest son's school years: "Many a night we stayed up well past midnight. He'd have a big test coming up the next day, and I'd go through with him and ask the questions." Her testimony captured a placid, un-extraordinary childhood: Ted's after-school jobs, his visits to a grandfather back in Philadelphia, his "interest in the plight of the inner city," the various political activities, and most of all, his desire to attend law school. "He mentioned it many times," she said, "ever since he was a boy." Later there were the jobs with the Crisis Clinic and the Crime Commission in Seattle.

"Can you describe your relationship with Ted?" Good asked.

Louise Bundy searched the ceiling with her eyes a moment. "I've always had a very special relationship with all my children," she said. "But Ted being my oldest, and you might say my pride and joy, our relationship was very special. We talked a great deal together." Ted didn't see his mother glance over at him. He was staring at the edge of the defense table.

At Good's final questions, Mrs. Bundy's voice began to shake. "What effect would it have on you if Ted were executed?"

"I've had to consider the possibility," she said, pausing to look into the jury box, "because of . . . what's happened here." Capital punishment, she continued, was "the most primitive, barbaric thing that one human being can impose on another"—a view, she said, she'd held long before this trial. Louise Bundy looked straight out over the crowd in the courtroom and spoke her final words:

"My Christian upbringing tells me it's wrong to take a life, under *any* circumstances. And I don't believe Florida is above the laws of God."

To follow Ted's mother, the defense team had lined up a series of witnesses with testimony about capital punishment. But the strategy got into trouble right away when a Texas journalist who had witnessed 189 executions tried to testify about the sight of a man dying in the electric chair. "That goes to the character of the punishment, not the character of the accused," Cowart ruled. The jury heard little more than the newsman's general observations about prisoners sentenced to life: "It amazes me to see the talent. It's a wonder they do so well."

"Have you met with Ted Bundy?" Good asked.

"Briefly," the witness replied. "Here's a young fella with a pretty good background and a better-than-average education. Here's a young fella that could do a lot of good."

The remaining defense witnesses—a criminologist, a religion professor, and a Catholic priest—met with the same prosecution objection: the character of capital punishment wasn't at issue.

Closing arguments this time were brief. In contrast to his earlier vivid scene painting, Larry Simpson was understated and methodical as he ran down the list of aggravating circumstances. Bundy was a prisoner without parole and had been previously convicted of a felony involving violence, he said; that much had been stipulated by the defense. There was a great risk of harm to many people; the crime occurred during a burglary; and most important of all, said the prosecutor, the attacks were "heinous, atrocious, and cruel."

"Theodore Robert Bundy took it upon himself to act as jury and judge in the lives of Margaret Bowman and Lisa Levy. Wouldn't it have been nice if the mothers of those two girls could have had a defense team askin' for mercy at the time this man was killin'?" Simpson had reserved his fire for the end. "Ladies and gentlemen, give him the same amount of mercy that he gave Margaret Bowman and Lisa Levy—which was absolutely none!"

Margaret Good could only hope to construct a wall of mercy around her client. "This is a new decision," she began her address to the jury. "This part of the trial is just as important. There are many people in prison Mr. Bundy can help. Don't destroy his potential for good. Death is not mandatory in this case."

There was little Good could say about the five solid aggravating circumstances the prosecution had established. Instead, she had to convince the jury of a strong mitigating circumstance. "Any one mitigating circumstance," she reminded them, "can outweigh all the aggravating circumstances." But without the support of any psychological testimony about the traits or possible disorders of the defendant, she was on shaky ground. "The mental disturbance of the person is indicated by the circumstances of the crime, the frenzy of the biting," she argued. "No normal person could commit these acts."

In the end, Good's appeal was a cry for mercy. Over and over she returned to the theme that "death is admitting failure with a human being": "Society *does* have an interest in keeping Mr. Bundy alive: to find out how and why someone would commit these crimes. It is wrong to kill the problem because we don't understand it. . . . I ask you not to answer murder with murder," she concluded. "The jury is the moral conscience of our country."

Back inside the plain white jury room for the last time, 12 men and women voted: 6 for life in prison, 6 for death. The foreman, Rudolph Treml, called for a ten-minute meditation and then a second vote. This time the tie was broken—9 to 3—but a vow kept: all 12 swore not to reveal which jurors had changed their minds.

Again Rudolph Treml handed over the forms. Again Cowart reviewed them and delivered them to the clerk. "Death" said the first one, and "death" again. Ted Bundy leaned back and flipped over a page of his notes.

"See you in the next trial," he smiled to reporters on his way through the hall after court was adjourned. But in this trial there was still tomorrow, when Judge Cowart would impose his sentence.

Theodore Robert Bundy, hands in the pockets of his blue-gray suit pants, stood facing the bench to await his sentence for first-degree murder. It was July 31, 1979, shortly after 2:00 p.m. in an air-conditioned Miami courtroom. Four years ago, a law student in Salt Lake City, he had been arrested in his dented VW Bug on a suburban street. So much had happened since the kidnapping conviction that followed—Colorado, two escapes, Florida. A year ago, almost to the day, the indictments for murder. And a week ago, exactly, the verdict. It had all happened so quickly, all beyond his control. When had he had the chance to sit down, think it all through, put it all straight?

Ted's lawyers stood beside him as he waited. No, Margaret Good told Judge Edward Cowart, there was no legal reason that sentence should not be imposed. But her client, she believed, had something to say to the court.

He might have been one of his own lawyers, and a disinterested one at that, the way he began. There were some "housecleaning" details, Ted Bundy said—some files he needed delivered from Tallahassee, visitation rights for his family.

And then he paused, turned and picked up a yellow legal pad from the defense table, and his voice went up a tone when he resumed. "It was obvious to some people in this courtroom that I was anxious to get up before the jury. Well, I'll have the second-to-last word. As usual, the court gets the last word.

"I'm innocent of the charges of which I've been convicted. I am not convinced, in any objective sense, of the strength of the state's case. But I'll save my evidence of that for the appellate review." His voice may have trembled once or twice as he spoke, but he held to the thread of his thought.

"Go ahead," Judge Cowart said softly. "This is your time."

Ted wondered aloud about the jury, about what they might have heard about his case before they were chosen, then turned his attention to the press. "I've been waiting a long time for this," he said, a chance to respond to their "vilification, their attempt to make a notorious individual out of me." Yesterday's *Miami Herald,* he said, grabbing a copy from the table behind him, was a prime example, typical of the conniving press that was "bent on making me look like an idiot. The news media are out for blood."

Twenty minutes passed while Ted discussed the camera in the courtroom ("It's always staring at me"), the quality and experience of his lawyers, and the court. He reflected at one point on the nature of important criminal trials. "Guilt and innocence can become almost immaterial," he said. "It's all in how you marshal the evidence." For a moment, as he stood there in a crowded courtroom, that was just what Ted Bundy seemed to achieve—"the tools to become a more effective actor in the social role I have defined for myself," as he had written in his application to law school. But then he lifted his eyes to the judge.

"I'm not asking for mercy," he told Edward Cowart. "I find it somewhat absurd to ask for mercy for something I did not do. In a way this is my opening statement. This is just the first round in a long battle of appeals." He was struggling, fighting down the tears. "The sentence is not a sentence of me. It's a sentence of someone who's not standing here today."

His voice cracked and wavered again. He was near the end. "So I will be tortured for, and suffer for, and receive the pain for that act. But I will not share the burden or the guilt."

Cowart waited just a moment, then spoke quietly. "As the law is written," he said, "there is no other choice."

The judge raised his voice and began reading from the sheaf of papers in his hand. The stiff, legal language came quickly to the point: "This court does hereby impose the death penalty upon the defendant, Theodore Robert Bundy."

Cowart described the aggravating circumstances he found present and the absence of mitigating circumstances established by the defense. Despite Bundy's "distorted perceptions of reality" and his "attempt to conceal and reveal his acts simultaneously," he found "no overall indication of a personality disorder." Theodore Bundy would be transported to Raiford state prison, there to suffer "a current of electricity sufficient to cause your immediate death." Two consecutive sentences of 99 years each for the assaults on Karen Chandler, Kathy Kleiner, and Cheryl Thomas were appended to the two death sentences for the murders of Margaret Bowman and Lisa Levy.

Cowart laid the papers down and turned his gaze on Ted, the judge's face and voice softening at once.

"Take care of yourself, young man. Take care of yourself. I say that to you sincerely. It's a tragedy to this court to see such a total waste of humanity. You're a bright young man. You'd have made a good lawyer. And I'd have loved to have you practice in front of me." Cowart started to rise, then spoke once more:

"I bear you no animosity, believe me. But you went the wrong way, pardner. Take care of yourself."

Ten minutes later the courtroom was dark. And then it was locked.

ABOUT THE AUTHORS

STEVEN WINN is a journalist and fiction writer. He was born in Philadelphia and educated at the University of Pennsylvania and the University of Washington. He has worked as an editor and staff writer for the *Weekly*, a Seattle newsmagazine and is currently a Wallace Stegner Fellow in fiction writing at Stanford University.

DAVID MERRILL was born in Baltimore, Maryland. He graduated with a B.A. from Washington University in St. Louis and an M.A. from SUNY Binghamton in English. He now lives in Salt Lake City and works as a journalist and historian.

137-26